Also by Richard Whelan

Anthony Caro
Double Take: A Comparative Look at Photographs
Robert Capa: Photographs (edited with Cornell Capa)

Robert CAPA

Robert CAPA

a biography

Richard Whelan

Alfred A. Knopf New York 1985

This Is a Borzoi Book
Published by Alfred A. Knopf, Inc.

Grateful acknowledgment is made to *Life* magazine for permission to reprint an excerpt
by John Mecklin from the June 7, 1954, issue of *Life*. Copyright 1954 by Time Inc.

Library of Congress Cataloging in Publication Data
Whelan, Richard.
Robert Capa: a biography
Includes index.
1. Capa, Robert, 1913–1954. 2. Photographers—
United States—Biography. I. Title.
TR140.C28W54 1985   770'.92'4   85-40126
ISBN 0-394-52488-8

Manufactured in the United States of America
First Edition

Acknowledgments

No biographer could hope for a better relationship with his subject's family than I have enjoyed with Cornell Capa and his wife, Edie. Enthusiastic from the outset, they granted me both unlimited access to the files of Robert Capa's estate and complete editorial freedom, and they have remained extraordinarily helpful, supportive, and generous. Without their warmhearted cooperation I could not have written this book. I shall never be able to thank them adequately for the many, many kindnesses, both small and great, that they have shown me.

I wish to thank all of Robert Capa's friends and colleagues who agreed to be interviewed or who responded to my inquiries by letter. A complete list of these people begins on page 303, but I must single out the following, who took exceptional pains to help me or extended special courtesies: Eve Arnold, Eva Besnyö, Rossellina Bischof Burri, John Fernhout, Erich Hartmann, Seiichi Inouye, Geza Korvin, Millard Lampell, Alexander Liberman, Susie Marquis, Hansel Mieth, John Morris, Hans Namuth, and Diana Forbes-Robertson Sheean.

Jozefa Stuart most generously made available to me the manuscript of the biography of Capa that she began in the late 1950s; I have drawn quite heavily on her work for anecdotes of the period from 1913 to 1936, the years covered by her completed chapters. I am extremely grateful to her for allowing me to do so.

I offer special thanks to my agent, Melanie Jackson, not only for her brilliant handling of every detail of the business end of this project but also for her unfailing enthusiasm and encouragement.

Carol Shookhoff not only did a superb job of typing the manuscript but also offered much valuable editorial advice, for which I am very grateful. Phillip Pocock made wonderfully clear copy negatives of a number of the magazine layouts and personal pictures for the book, and Cheung Ching Ming made beautiful prints of those and other negatives.

In addition to thanking collectively the friends and colleagues too numerous to name who have contributed to this book, I wish to acknowledge my debt of gratitude to the New York Public Library, whose staff has been helpful beyond the call of duty and whose incredibly comprehensive collections have provided the key to many a puzzle that I had despaired of solving.

Finally, but most emphatically, I thank my editor, Robert Gottlieb, without whose labors and guidance I could never have transformed my mass of accumulated data into a readable narrative. Chuck Elliott and Martha Kaplan also worked extensively and most helpfully on the manuscript. I would also particularly like to thank, from among the many people at Knopf who have worked on this book in one way or another, Nancy Clements, Stephen Frankel, Jane Becker Friedman, Carin Goldberg, Janice Goldklang, Kathy Hourigan, Andy Hughes, Carol Brown Janeway, Tamar Katz, Karen Latuchie, Ellis Levine, Bill Loverd, Mary Maguire, Edmée Reit, Nina Salter, and Iris Weinstein.

Illustrations

MAGAZINE LAYOUTS

Unless otherwise specified, all original tearsheets are in the collection of the Estate of Robert Capa.

PHOTOGRAPHS follow pages 56 and 216.

Robert
CAPA

1

Endre Ernö Friedmann was born on October 22, 1913, on the Pest side of Budapest. The birth was marked by three exceptional circumstances: when the baby emerged from his mother's womb, his head was still wrapped in his caul; when the caul was removed, the child was found to have so much dark hair that he looked as though he could already be several months old; and he had an extra little finger on one hand. His mother and her friends interpreted these aberrations as signs that the child would grow up to be a famous man. He did indeed—not as Endre Friedmann but as Robert Capa.

In 1913 Budapest was still very much a city with a split personality. The cities of Buda and Pest, situated on opposite banks of the Danube, had united only forty years earlier. Theirs was a marriage of convenience rather than of love.

Buda, built on an outcropping of hills and surmounted by the medieval castle of the Hungarian kings, was the seat of government, of the feudal aristocracy, and of the wealthy German Lutheran bourgeoisie. Pest, located on flat land on the east bank, was the seat of intellectual and artistic life, of commerce and industry, of the liberal Jewish middle class, and of the no longer wealthy Hungarian Calvinist gentry.

Pest had most of the smart hotels, all the best shops, and all the theaters. It was a sophisticated, cosmopolitan, bustling city, expanding rapidly out onto the Hungarian plain. It was also terribly crowded, with a great deal of poverty, genteel and otherwise. But appearances counted in Pest, and its citizens went to great lengths to appear prosperous, glamorous, and debonair. Apartment buildings that were little better than tenements had façades as ornate as Victorian chests of drawers, with cupids gamboling over doorways and caryatids supporting globe lamps. Even the poorest middle-class citizens of Pest spared no expense in assembling a wardrobe in which to promenade along the city's fashionable streets. Behind these traditions there was not only much pride but also an element of shrewdness that was perhaps a legacy from the bazaars of the Turkish occupation that had lasted 250 years, ending in 1686. Traditional Hungarian wisdom has it that to make money one must first give the impression of being rich.

In contrast to Pest, Buda was like the setting for a fairy tale. Its palaces

3

and ministries were old and elegant; the stucco façades of its two- and three-story houses were painted ochre yellow or pastel shades of pink, green, or gray; its spacious parks were drenched in sunlight; and its narrow lanes snaked up the hills that limited the city's growth. Much of the city retained something of the air of a country village.

Together, Buda and Pest formed a microcosm of the dual monarchy of Austria-Hungary. Because of its large German population and its role as the second capital of the Austro-Hungarian monarchy, Buda was until the end of World War I predominantly German-speaking, while Pest spoke Hungarian. Buda was quite content to pay homage to the Hapsburg court at Vienna, for the Emperor had treated the Hungarian upper classes well, but middle-class Pest was the center of Hungarian nationalism and anti-imperialism. Behind its carefully-tended façade of gaiety and contented prosperity lay great bitterness, sadness, and rebelliousness. Robert Capa was very much a man of Pest, even in his aspirations to the aristocratic luxury of Buda.

Robert Capa's parents were as different from each other as were Buda and Pest. His mother, Julia, was a formidable woman, sturdy, extremely strong-willed, hard-working, and determined to provide a comfortable life for her family. As the proprietress of a successful fashion salon, she was an excellent businesswoman, efficient, charming, shrewd, well liked by her clients, and able to command great respect from her employees. With her children she was demanding, adoring, and possessive. She was the boss at work and the matriarch at home.

Her husband Dezsö, co-owner and head tailor of the salon, was, on the other hand, a rather slight and dapper man, irresponsible, light-hearted, and good at coming up with excuses for leaving work early and staying out late to play cards. Julia believed that you had to work for things; but Dezsö believed that charm, cleverness, connections, and *chutzpah* counted more than hard work.

Julia and Dezsö (one instinctively puts Julia first) clashed constantly. Capa later described their relationship as one long, pitched battle. But he loved both of his parents deeply and incorporated, to an unusual extent, many qualities from each one's personality—as different as they were—into his own. These qualities were to war within him for the rest of his life.

Julianna Henrietta Berkovits was born on May 1, 1888,* in the Carpatho-Ruthenian village of Nagy Kapos (now known as Vel'ké Kapušany), which then lay within the borders of Hungary but is now in the extreme eastern part

---

* Some records say April 25.

of Czechoslovakia, only a few miles from the Ukrainian border. Carpatho-Ruthenia, virtually all of its land owned by absentee aristocrats, was at that time one of the most backward areas in Europe, both economically and culturally. The predominantly Roman Catholic peasants of the region, who lived on a bare subsistence level, were hardly better educated or less superstitious than their forebears had been during the Dark Ages. Only the Jewish tradesmen, doctors, and teachers in the towns upheld any standards of nineteenth-century culture or even spoke Hungarian. But for them, too, life was very hard. Although Nagy Kapos was a county seat, it was little more than a quiet country village with rather primitive one-story shops along the unpaved main street and with barns attached to many of the log or clapboard houses.

Until 1920, when the Treaty of Trianon stripped Hungary of two-thirds of its territory, the nation was so diverse, ethnically and linguistically, that the Magyars had to encourage widespread and rapid assimilation of other ethnic groups in order to maintain a Hungarian-speaking majority within their own country. No group was assimilated more completely or more enthusiastically than were the Jews. Julia's father, Herman Berkovits—a shoemaker whom a photograph shows to have been a handsome and intelligent-looking man—spoke Hungarian but did not convert to Christianity. His eldest son, however, became so completely assimilated as a Magyar that he changed his surname to Bartos, a non-Jewish, Magyar name, and, after attending the university in Pest in preparation for a career in law, went on to become an officer in the Imperial Austro-Hungarian Army during World War I.

Julia's mother, Betti (née Klein), bore ten children, of whom Julia was the fourth or fifth. It was not unusual in the region for a woman to have ten children, since several of them would undoubtedly die in infancy, as at least four of Julia's brothers and sisters did. A photograph of Betti Berkovits reveals a peasant-like woman—strong but terribly worn, and aged far beyond her years.

Those young women of Nagy Kapos who did not manage to escape to the city and learn a trade were destined to suffer the same fate as their mothers, but Herman Berkovits endowed his daughters with the family traits of stubbornness and determination and sent them off to Budapest to be apprenticed. In 1900, when she was twelve, Julia was apprenticed to a dressmaker. Through her work, she eventually met the handsome and charming Dezsö David Friedmann, whose neatly trimmed mustache and elegantly cut suits gave him more the look of an English gentleman than of a Budapest tailor.

Dezsö Friedmann, the son of a humble Jewish merchant, had been born on June 7, 1880, in the small village of Csucsa (now known as Ciucea) in western Transylvania, which then belonged to Hungary and is now part of

Rumania. Family memory records very little about his early years, but he probably had little formal education before being sent off to Budapest to be apprenticed to a ladies' tailor. In his late teens, after completing his apprenticeship, he wandered around Europe for a while, spending some time in Paris and ultimately reaching London. Although relatively uneducated, he was a very bright young man who learned to speak French and English on his travels and acquired a good deal of sophistication along the way. He also acquired a taste for such decidedly un-Hungarian foods as onion soup and raw tomatoes. (He loved the former so much that he learned to make it himself, and whenever he became nostalgic for Paris, the Friedmann apartment would be pervaded by its aroma.)

Dezsö loved to tell his children how on his travels he had survived through charm and cleverness. He claimed, for instance, that he had used a small, ornate menu for a passport, simply waving it with an air of authority whenever anyone asked to see his papers. His picaresque stories evidently made a great impression on Capa, who inherited his father's gifts for living by his wits and for making a good story better. Early in his life the son would begin trying to surpass the father, both in the doing and in the telling.

Shortly after Julia and Dezsö were married in May 1910, they opened a custom dressmaking salon on the Városház utca (City Hall Street), a handsome street of elegant shops and apartment buildings a few blocks from the Danube in the fashionable Belváros (Inner Town) district of Pest. The salon, which became known for its nicely designed, very well made, conservative clothes, attracted the wives not only of prosperous Pest business and professional men but also of government officials and aristocrats from Buda, and before long Julia and Dezsö were employing almost twenty fitters, cutters, and seamstresses. Julia dealt directly with the customers in the salon and supervised all aspects of the business, from buying cloth and patterns to handling the accounts. Dezsö, who on official records listed his profession as "master ladies' tailor," was in charge of the workshop. Together they went to Vienna each year to see the new fashions and to buy patterns.

Julia and Dezsö could soon afford to move into an apartment on the third floor of a large new building at Városház utca 10, on the corner of the Pilvax Passage, a very short distance from their salon.* The building was a typical Pest apartment house, with a plan in the form of a squared-off U and open corridors with wrought-iron balustrades on each floor running around the tiny,

---

* The Pilvax Café, where the leaders of the Hungarian revolution of 1848 had gathered, was still open for business just around the corner from the apartment building's entrance.

paved and glass-covered central court. Solid professional people—doctors and lawyers—occupied the large apartments in the front of the building overlooking a lovely square; the Friedmanns occupied one of the less imposing, yet spacious and comfortable, apartments in the rear.

László, the first of Julia and Dezsö's three children, was born in 1911. Two years later, Endre was born—a plump, sturdy, healthy baby who looked a bit like a Gypsy, with his slightly swarthy complexion, his gorgeous head of dark hair, his dark eyebrows and large, dark eyes. Julia adored her second-born and spoke constantly to her friends about how beautiful and precocious he was. The omens of the caul, the premature growth of hair, and the extra finger (which was soon removed by surgery) only confirmed her certainty that Endre was very special.

When World War I broke out less than a year after Endre's birth, Hungary was drawn immediately into the conflict. Although family tradition has it that Dezsö Friedmann served in the army during the war, no one seems to remember where or in what capacity he served. In 1914 Dezsö was thirty-four, rather too old to be sent to the front, and the available evidence suggests that if he was away from Budapest at all, it was not for long. He renewed his identification papers at the Budapest police headquarters in 1915, and there is no indication of military service on those papers. Furthermore, a third son, Kornel, was born to Julia and Dezsö in the spring of 1918.

Both during and after the war, Julia was so occupied with her business that she had little time to spend with her sons. While she was busy in the salon, the boys were cared for by a maid-governess, who taught them to speak German, the second language of all educated Hungarians. On Sundays, however, if the weather was nice enough, Julia would dress her sons up in Eton jackets or in sailor suits with short pants and take them to one or another of the fashionable cafés on the Corso, the street that runs along the Danube embankment on the Pest side of the river, with a magnificent view of Buda.

There can be no doubt that Endre—whom his family and friends always called Bandi, the Hungarian diminutive of Endre—was his mother's favorite child. The arrival of a second child often displaces the first-born from the center of a mother's affections, and Bandi was the baby of the family for almost five years. His favored status was not as threatened as it might otherwise have been by the arrival of a third son, for Julia was at first badly disappointed that her third child was not a girl.

By all accounts Bandi was the great love of Julia's life. She loved him more than she loved her husband, her parents, or her other children. She was immensely proud of him and spoiled him; in her eyes he could do no wrong. She indulged him so much that, far from scolding him for such traits as messiness and clumsiness, she found them adorable. Shortly before her death in 1961, she told one interviewer, "His pants were always torn. He was always walking into a lamppost because he was talking too hard. He was a good-natured child, with no rudeness in him. Always the face smiled. Sometimes he was a little clumsy, and his clumsiness made him shy. And he loved the girls already—even when he was a baby." From Julia's absolute devotion to him—from his Oedipal triumph as her favorite of all the men in the household—Bandi must have derived his extraordinary sense of self-worth and self-confidence.

Following the collapse of the Austro-Hungarian empire in 1918, Hungary was declared an independent republic, and the liberal Count Michael Károlyi was chosen to be premier. As it became known that the victorious Allies were giving two-thirds of Hungary's territory to Czechoslovakia, Rumania, and Yugoslavia, Magyar refugees from the regions to be ceded streamed into Budapest. Economic hardship, political unrest, and severe shortages followed. There was so little coal in the city that most people were without heat throughout the cold winter.

Károlyi, trying to steer a moderate course between the Right and the Left, found himself by the middle of March 1919 unable to hold his government together; he resigned and handed the government over to a coalition of Socialists and Communists. The latter, led by foreign-affairs commissar Béla Kun, quickly gained the upper hand and proceeded to declare Hungary a Communist republic.

During the four months that the Communist government remained in power, Budapest was pervaded by a heady spirit of optimism and festivity, and the streets were often filled with carnival-like marches and demonstrations. They were also often filled with peasants from the surrounding countryside who, not trusting the new regime's paper money, came into the city to barter their chickens, eggs, cheese, sausages, and vegetables for clothes, furniture, and other goods. They did a brisk business, for the government had rationed food so severely that practically everything except cabbages, turnips, and vanilla ice cream had disappeared from the shops.

At the end of July 1919, the Rumanian army routed the units of the Red army that were guarding Hungary's eastern frontier and began to march toward Budapest. The panic-stricken leaders of Hungary's Communist government fled, many of them going to the Soviet Union. The equally panic-stricken peasants stopped bringing their food into Budapest and began hoarding it for the bad times they saw coming. With Budapest suffering from near-famine, Dezsö Friedmann often left home in the morning carrying a knapsack full of bolts of fabric. Returning laden down with food, he demonstrated to his family that his stories of his youthful resourcefulness were not without basis. His example must have impressed Bandi—and Bandi must have learned his father's lessons well—for in later years he would constantly amaze his friends with his ability to come up with the seemingly unobtainable, even in the most devastated, war-torn places.

On August 3 the Rumanian army occupied Budapest and began a campaign of terror against the Reds. Because the reactionary Rumanians—who were joined by reactionary Hungarians—equated being Jewish with being a Leftist, the White Terror, as it was called, had a violently anti-Semitic cast. When it began, the Friedmanns shuttered up their apartment and announced that the children must remain indoors until the storm had passed. At work, the employees of the salon constantly reported fresh atrocities: they had seen Jews dragged from streetcars and later heard that they had been taken out to the woods, beaten, and shot. Gangs of hoodlums roamed the streets in working-class neighborhoods looking for Jews to beat up.

The Friedmanns were fortunate to be living in a middle-class neighborhood, but even there the violence came terrifyingly close. On the ground floor of their building, Jewish philanthropists had set up a *mensa*, a free dining room for Jewish students. Inevitably, the *mensa* became a target for the vengeful mob. One afternoon, when Julia heard a commotion in the building's central court, she cautiously opened the door to her apartment and, peering over the balustrade, watched in horror as a crowd rushed into the *mensa* and dragged the screaming students out, kicking and beating them brutally.

Although the White Terror was to continue unabated in many rural districts of Hungary for almost two years, in Budapest—and especially in middle-class neighborhoods—the violence subsided after a few weeks. By September things were calm enough for the Friedmanns to let Bandi, now nearly six, enter the distinguished Evangelisches School. At this excellent non-denominational boys' school favored by the liberal Calvinist gentry, the students divided up for religious instruction several hours a week. A rabbi from one of the smaller synagogues in Budapest came in to teach the Jewish boys Hebrew and to verse them in the tenets of Judaism, but since the Friedmanns brought him a substantial supply of his favorite cigars from Vienna every year, he was lenient with Bandi, who paid little attention to his Hebrew and Judaic studies.

In September 1923, having completed the four grades of elementary school, Bandi entered the Imre Madách Gymnasium on the Barcsay utca. Named for a nineteenth-century Hungarian playwright, the non-denominational boys' school offered the standard eight-year curriculum that was taught in secondary schools throughout Hungary: Latin was required every year, as were mathematics and Hungarian literature; the study of history and German literature began in the third year, Greek literature in the fifth, physics in the seventh, and philosophy in the last. No living language was then taught, Hungarian and German being studied only as literary, not spoken, languages. Hebrew and Judaism were taught by the same rabbi who had been so easy on Bandi at the Evangelisches School. Bandi's school record, a thin book bound in green and stamped on the cover with the official seal of the Madách Gymnasium, shows that throughout his eight years at the school most of his grades fluctuated between good and passing, although he failed mathematics and geometrical drawing his first year and had to be tutored over the summer by his uncle Adolf.

Throughout the 1920s, Julia and Dezsö were too busy to give their children much direct supervision. The salon had so many orders for dresses that Julia and her employees often had to work until midnight to keep up. Dezsö, however, felt that there was more to life than work, and late every afternoon he made his way to his favorite café.

The Café Moderne, at the foot of the Elizabeth Bridge connecting Buda and Pest, was where, as Capa later wrote, "the tailors of Budapest held their daily meetings, which began with complaints about business and ended with pinochle." Relatively little money changed hands during these games, but Julia, in an effort to keep her husband at work, where she needed him, scolded him mercilessly for his losses. She was determined to gain absolute control over the purse strings so that Dezsö would have no money with which to gamble, and asked her customers always to pay their bills directly to her. She even refused Dezsö money for cloth or thread, for he would lose it at cards. But despite all her efforts, he continued to spend almost every evening playing cards with his friends. Returning home late night after night to Julia's wrath, he became a master of evasion and excuses. Capa later loved to tell how Julia, waiting up for her husband, would be so angry by the time he got home that she would threaten to stab him with a big pair of scissors. Dezsö would say, "But I wasn't playing cards. I went over to see Mr. Hertz, who is ill." In the morning, Julia would say, "So Mr. Hertz is ill," and Dezsö would reply, trying to cover his tracks, "No, no. I said Mr. Kurtz . . ." And so on.

Because his parents supervised him so little, Bandi became increasingly independent, and, from the age of about ten, he spent as little time at home as he could. Although he was a reasonably well-behaved student, after school he and his friends became little devils—like the "Paul Street boys" in Ferenc

Molnár's novel of Budapest childhood—playing jokes on strangers and hitching rides on the back of streetcars, squealing in delight and scattering in all directions when in danger of being caught.

When he was about twelve, Bandi grew so fond of the three teenaged girls who lived in the large apartment on his floor that (as he admitted years later) he used to daydream about saving them from robbers so that their parents would allow him, as his reward, to choose which one he would marry. The fact of the matter, however, was that their mother did not like Bandi. Hungarian society was rigidly stratified, and the gulf between a lawyer's family and that of dressmakers, even if they owned their own very successful salon, was wide and all but unbridgeable. Mme. Besnyö didn't approve of her daughters' spending so much time with Bandi—especially since he seemed to her, with his hair disheveled and his clothes dirty and torn from his after-school play, little better than a boy of the streets.

Bandi was perfectly aware of Mme. Besnyö's dislike, but he didn't let it deter him from visiting her daughters almost every afternoon. The girls, whose father had progressive ideas about women's emancipation, all went to a classical Gymnasium, but Eva, who of the three became Bandi's closest friend, was more interested in taking pictures with her Kodak Brownie than she was in schoolwork, and soon Bandi began to accompany her on her photographic expeditions through the streets of Budapest and the surrounding countryside.

Although Eva was three years older than Bandi, she found him good company. "He was a good fellow," she recalls. "If he liked you, he would do things for you. He was warm, but he also had a nice touch of irony. Very smart and eager to learn, sharp-minded, but not too hard-edged. A little cynical. He was very amusing and could tell things in an interesting way—funny and exaggerated. Life was too dull for him. He made it seem more interesting."

In 1928 Eva Besnyö decided to make a career of photography and began to study with the Budapest photographer József Pécsi, who specialized in studio portraiture and architectural photography. Although Pécsi worked primarily in a Pictorialist style, imitative of nineteenth-century painting, he was becoming interested in more modernistic photography.

Documentary photography—which is to say unsentimental photography of the poor, motivated by socio-economic reform—was very much in the air in Hungary in the late 1920s and early 1930s. By 1929 Eva was spending much of her free time using her new Rolleiflex camera to photograph dockworkers unloading coal barges, destitute men and women sleeping the day away on benches in downtown Budapest, and peasant women working in nearby villages. Such photographs must have made an impression on Bandi, who was by that time himself becoming seriously interested in social and political reform.

In 1930, after Eva had completed her studies with Pécsi, she went to live in Berlin. But her influence on Bandi's life and career did not end; their paths would continue to cross for many years to come.

In his early teens Bandi was a restless, rambunctious boy with a lot of excess energy, some of which he dissipated in sports. He was not especially athletic, but he played soccer with such determination and élan that he was in great demand on the Gymnasium teams. He was well liked, not only for his high spirits but also for his great loyalty and generosity to his friends. When, for instance, another boy was hurt during a soccer game, Bandi took him to the streetcar, put him on, and, not having enough money to pay his own fare, ran alongside until the tram reached his friend's stop, then helped him off and got him home.

During the summer Bandi and his friends swam in the Danube, and in winter they skated around the little island with imitation-medieval buildings in Pest's Városliget Park, while a live band provided music. For several weeks each winter there was enough snow for skiing on the Buda hills, which could be reached by cogwheel railway from the city. Some of these hills were big and steep, and on them the clumsy wooden skis with simple leather footstraps that Bandi's friends used were difficult to control, making the sport relatively dangerous. Although Julia encouraged Bandi to play sports, she drew the line at skiing, for she was afraid that her daring and reckless son would hurt himself. But it was precisely because skiing was such an exciting sport, with an attractive element of danger, that he wanted so desperately to try it. All his friends could go, he complained to Julia; why couldn't he?

One Sunday he rose early and dressed in a brightly colored quilted jacket that he had borrowed from his older brother. Around his waist he tied a crêpe-de-Chine scarf with a pattern of red and green squares, borrowed from his mother. Looking more than ever like a Gypsy, he appeared in the doorway of his parents' bedroom and announced that he was going skiing, and to show that he meant business, he brandished the pair of skis he had borrowed from a friend.

"I am going skiing, Mother."

"No, you are *not* going skiing," Julia replied.

"Please give me some money for the tram fare."

"I will not give you any money, and I forbid you to go. It's too dangerous."

Bandi was furious, but he controlled his anger and softly closed the bedroom door. Julia rolled over to go back to sleep, pleased with her victory, but five minutes later Bandi opened the door again.

"Julika," he said, switching to the familiar form of his mother's name to show just how defiant he was feeling, "will you give me your permission, or do you want me to lie to you?"

Confronted with such a disarming declaration of independence, the formidable Julia was left defenseless. Realizing that she had no choice, she gave Bandi her blessing—and money for the train. But she was so concerned about her son's safety that she followed him out to the hills later that morning, remaining at a discreet distance so that she could watch him without being observed. By the time he was sixteen, Bandi was confidently navigating the steep Svábhegy (Swabian Hill), and skiing would remain a lifelong passion.

Soon after the American stock market crashed in October 1929, repercussions began to disrupt the Hungarian economy. The patrons of the Friedmanns' salon suddenly had less money to spend on beautiful new dresses, prices for cloth and all the necessities of daily life rose sharply, and short-term credit became difficult to obtain. The Friedmanns were forced to economize radically, but rather than lay off employees, they moved their business into the family apartment. The living room was transformed into the showing and fitting salon—with the same brocade-covered chairs, heavy drapes, and full-length, gilt-framed mirrors that had decorated the old salon. The boys had to give up their bedrooms, which were needed for workrooms, and so Dezsö, Julia, László, and Kornel all began sleeping in one room. Bandi, however, rebelled against such overcrowding and insisted on sleeping—in the nude and with the windows wide open, even in the middle of winter—on a chaise longue in the salon.

Since Julia and Dezsö now employed between thirty and forty people, many of whom often worked until midnight, the apartment was almost always full of employees, not to mention customers. Bandi made a point of spending more time than ever away from home, and if he found himself at home during working hours, he would seek privacy in the bathroom, soaking in the tub and reading for hours on end. For the rest of his life, whenever possible he would spend a couple of hours every morning reading in the bathtub.

It must have seemed to Bandi that he had lost not only his home but his family as well. Julia had to work harder than ever to keep the business afloat, and Dezsö was spending more and more of his time at the Café Moderne. Since the family was broke, his gambling losses, however small, enraged Julia all the more.

By this time, Dezsö's role in the workroom had been largely assumed by his eldest son. In 1926, at fifteen, László had contracted rheumatic fever and dropped out of school. As soon as he had recovered sufficiently, he started to work in the family business.

For his part, Bandi was becoming more certain than ever that the boring routines of bourgeois life were not for him. He saw that although his mother was working herself to death, she was hounded constantly by bill collectors. It seemed that Dezsö was right, after all—there was no point in working too hard and failing to enjoy things. Rewards in life went not to those who worked hard but to those who were clever.

Deprived of a sense of home and rebelling against bourgeois values, Bandi strengthened old friendships and made new ones with like-minded teenagers. For these young rebels, who felt few ties except to each other, friendship meant everything. They developed an extraordinarily deep sense of comradeship and took responsibility for helping one another, as they would continue to do as political refugees in Berlin, in Paris, in Spain, and wherever else their paths later crossed.

Among Bandi's closest friends was Kati Deutsch, the beautiful and rebellious daughter of a wealthy banker. One day during the summer of 1930, running into Bandi on the street, she told him that she was so depressed she was going to bicycle out to a resort in the Mátra hills northeast of Budapest and camp there for a week. The next day, Kati was amazed to find him and their mutual friend Zoltán Kellerman waiting for her in the village when she arrived. Bandi had decided that she shouldn't be alone and had enlisted Zoltán to travel with him to the resort. Kati was immediately cheered by this demonstration of friendship.

The three friends pitched a tent beside a little river outside the village, which boasted some very fancy hotels, and after a few days, word of the campers spread; to the local inhabitants, such an arrangement smacked of free love and Communism. One morning, when Bandi went into town to buy supplies, the proprietors of the shops announced, one after another, that they wouldn't sell him anything. Returning to his companions to report the situation, he shrugged his shoulders, cursed the shopkeepers' small-mindedness, and declared that he didn't need them; he'd find some other way to get food. He went directly to the most luxurious hotel in the village, stationed himself in the garden until he spotted a family with a pretty daughter, and then proceeded to charm them. It was lunch time. Was he alone? Yes? Well, then, why didn't he join them? He would love to. The family treated him to a delicious lunch of roast goose with all the trimmings. As a hungry, growing boy, he wondered whether he might take along the substantial leftovers. Yes, of course he could. And so Bandi—undoubtedly pleased with himself for living up to his father's example of resourcefulness—was able to provide for his hungry friends.

In the fall of 1929, when he was beginning his seventh and penultimate year at the Madách Gymnasium, Bandi encountered a man who was to change the course of his life. Lajos Kassák, forty-two at the time, was a poet, a novelist, a painter, a graphic artist, an editor, a Socialist, and the midwife of avant-gardism in Hungary. In 1928 he had founded a magazine called *Munka* (Work) and an artistic and political group called the Munkakör (Work Circle), which attracted many of Budapest's brightest and most radical minds between the ages of fourteen and fifty. The largely self-educated son of a pharmacist's assistant and a washerwoman, Kassák had left school at an early age, apprenticed himself to a blacksmith, and become involved in the Hungarian Socialist and trade-union movements. In 1909 he journeyed on foot to Paris, where he saw and responded instinctively to much that was new in the arts. Back in Hungary during World War I, he became a leader of both pacifistic and artistic movements, but when in 1919 he lobbied to have the Communist-led government adopt his group's brand of Futurism as its official style, he was denounced by Béla Kun as a "decadent bourgeois," a rebuff that made Kassák permanently hostile to the Communist Party and suspicious of political parties in general.

Marginal though Kassák's involvement with Kun's regime was, the fall of the Communists forced him to seek refuge in Vienna, where he edited an activist artistic magazine entitled *Ma* and collaborated with his friend László Moholy-Nagy on an anthology of the most avant-garde art then being created in Europe. In the autumn of 1926 Kassák was allowed to return to Budapest, where he founded *Dokumentum*, a magazine devoted not only to Constructivist art, Bauhaus architecture, Russian films, and Surrealist literature, but also to a wide range of interests—including documentary and journalistic photography, radio broadcasting, the sociology of urban life, sports, and aeronautics—which had until then been thought to lie safely outside the realm of art. *Dokumentum* went bankrupt after only a few issues, but Kassák quickly started up again with *Munka*.

By 1929 Kassák was regularly publishing in *Munka* many of the powerful images of the poor that Hungarian photographers, inspired especially by the American reformer-photographers Jacob Riis and Lewis W. Hine, were then making. Outraged by the horrible inequities of capitalism and rural feudalism, such photographers as Tibor Bass, Károly Escher, Sándor Gönci (Frühof),

Kata Kálmán, Lajos Lengyel, and Lajos Tabák focused their cameras on the worn faces, the dehumanizing work, the squalid homes, the inadequate clothing, and the meager tables of impoverished men, women, and children. The unsentimental directness, the graphic boldness, and the passionate reformism of the work of these "Szociofoto" (Socio-Photo) photographers, all of them affiliated with the Munkakör, were surely among the earliest direct influences on the work of Robert Capa.

The men and women who contributed to *Munka* made up the inner circle of the Munkakör. They lectured and debated in the group's meetings, usually held in one or another of Budapest's trade-union halls, and they organized the group's poetry readings, art exhibitions, choral concerts, social gatherings, excursions into the countryside, and sports events. Outside this core group of perhaps forty or fifty was a devoted faction of precocious teenagers—including Bandi—who avidly read *Munka*, attended as many of the Munkakör's functions as they could, marched—and sometimes fought—in demonstrations, and gathered afternoons and evenings around the table in the Corona Café at which Kassák, in traditional Budapest fashion, sat to write his poems and to edit his magazine.

In a 1930 photomontage self-portrait, Kassák—with his concerned expression, his clean-shaven face, his high forehead, his short hair combed straight back, his black turtleneck shirt, and his dark suit jacket—looks much like a manly Roman Catholic priest who today might be in charge of an inner-city youth group. He was, indeed, a tough man, a genuine revolutionary, and an uncompromising idealist, whose politics, like his aesthetics, were an unorthodox and eclectic mélange of radical ideas. Out of his admiration for such men as Karl Marx, Thomas Jefferson, Voltaire, Lajos Kossuth (the great nineteenth-century Hungarian patriot), and Walt Whitman, compounded with his commitment to Socialism and the trade-union movement, Kassák formulated a political philosophy that was democratic, egalitarian, pacifistic, semi-collectivist, pro-labor, anti-authoritarian, and anti-fascist, with a strong emphasis on the dignity of man and the rights of the individual in society. Bandi was to adopt this liberal, undogmatic philosophy and to maintain it for the rest of his life.

"During my last two years in high school [i.e., Gymnasium]," Capa later wrote, "I became interested in literature and politics and decided to make my career as a journalist." Bandi's growing interest in literature and politics was undoubtedly both a cause and an effect of his involvement with Kassák. His decision to make a career of journalism was surely influenced not only by

Kassák's example as a writer and editor but also by the opportunities that the profession provided for travel and adventure. Resentful of Hungarian dictator Admiral Miklós Horthy's anti-Semitism, impatient with the restrictions of bourgeois life, and pessimistic about their prospects for employment,* Bandi and his friends became eager—desperately eager—to get away from Budapest. As one of Bandi's friends later recalled, their desire to leave was so intense that it was "like a fever." Unwilling to attend a Hungarian university as second-class citizens, these young people planned to study, and to pursue their careers, abroad.

Although Bandi apparently had no intention of being a journalist in Hungary, the great Hungarian tradition of journalism would naturally have influenced him. Budapest, a city of about one million, had at that time twelve morning and seven evening papers. The Hungarian press was very powerful, and censorship laws were remarkably lenient; the great majority of newspapers were critical of the government, more or less leftist, and owned and staffed by Jews, who, barred from direct participation in the government, had settled on journalism as the best alternative.

At this time Bandi's closest friend was Imre Weisz, whom everyone called Csiki (pronounced "cheeky"). A gaunt and ascetic-looking boy who was preparing for a career in music, Csiki, like Bandi, was restless and daring. Together the two boys would go out to the working-class suburb of Angyalföld, where, with the courage and self-righteousness that characterize evangelists of all persuasions, they would talk to workers about the repressive nature of the Horthy government and encourage them to demand their rights and a decent wage.

Such political agitation was a dangerous game. If they had been caught by the state police, the two boys would have been expelled from school immediately, after which no other school in Hungary would have admitted them or allowed them to take their Abitur (university-qualifying) examinations. By inciting the workers in Angyalföld, Bandi was gambling with his future.

A further involvement in politics was even more dangerous. As the economic crisis that began in 1929 led increasing numbers of activists, both of

---

* Although the government permitted Jews to attend Hungarian universities, it discouraged them from doing so, for Horthy feared the resurgence of a large class of unemployed left-wing intellectuals, and there were already far too few jobs available for university graduates. Jews were officially encouraged to go into commerce, banking, and industry, for which a university education was not necessary and where jobs were available. Law, medicine, and journalism were the principal professions open to university-educated Jews, and by 1930 these fields were becoming seriously overcrowded.

the Left and of the Right, to organize demonstrations, the Munkakör took to the streets. Bandi spent a good deal of his seventeenth and eighteenth years marching through the working-class districts of Budapest with crudely lettered banners, shouting inflammatory slogans. The demonstrations naturally brought out not only supporters but adversaries as well, and hardly a week passed without some sort of street battle. Sometimes Bandi would be in the mood for a good fight and would throw himself exuberantly into the melee. At other times he would shinny up a lamppost and shout encouragement to his comrades below. After the fight, before anyone had a chance to accuse him of desertion, he would disarm his critics by announcing matter-of-factly, "Well, today I felt like a coward."

As committed as he was to Kassák and the Munkakör, he was too cynical to be taken in completely by political rhetoric. Moreover, he was something of a wise guy. In the midst of one demonstration, as the crowd shouted its real but futile demands, Bandi began to yell, over and over again, as loudly as he could, the phrase "scrap iron." The cry spread quickly, and soon everyone was shouting "Scrap iron! Scrap iron!"—though they had no idea why they were shouting it. "It was an experiment," Bandi told his friends afterward. "I knew I could get them to shout anything." It was an experiment that provided a devastating critique of political sloganeering and a convincing exposé of the unthinking responsiveness of an excited mass of people.

On Monday, September 1, 1930, the Hungarian Trade Union Council staged a general strike and march in Budapest to protest unemployment, and since Kassák was an enthusiastic supporter of the trade-union movement, the Munkakör took part. Bandi and his friends got up early that morning and rode the streetcar out to one of the industrial suburbs where workers were gathering for the walk to Pest's Városliget Park. Mass marches were illegal, so the demonstrators strung themselves out, walking singly or in pairs and chanting "Give us work. Give us bread." They were grim but peaceful.

Having been informed that the demonstration was to be massive, the government was nervous. Mounted police were ordered to surround the crowd of several thousand once they reached the park, just in case anything began to happen. Soon Communist Party provocateurs, desiring a dramatic confrontation with the police, began to shout revolutionary slogans and managed to incite several pockets of violence. When the police started to charge, brandishing their swords, the crowd panicked and began to riot. The organizers of the demonstration yelled for order and calm, but to no avail. The crowd broke into the Gundel, a fashionable restaurant in the park, and carried tables and chairs outside, using them to construct barricades. Some rioters overturned a coal cart and pelted the police with its contents. Bandi armed himself with a long pole.

Soon the crowd began to run out of the park and down the broad avenue toward the Belváros district, where Bandi's family lived. The starving, poorly clothed mob looted as it went. The mood was vicious, but neither side used firearms, and the police struck only with the flat sides of their swords. They were determined to suppress the riot, but they were not Cossacks.

Bandi soon found himself swinging his pole at a mounted policeman, whose sword then wounded him on the shoulder painfully but not dangerously. He knew that if he went to a hospital or a doctor for treatment, he ran the risk of being reported to the authorities and being expelled from school. Instead, he got a friend to treat the wound, which was deep enough to leave a scar for life. Although Bandi boasted of his wound to his friends in the Munkakör, he kept it secret from his parents, who—especially his mother—would have been horrified by his political activism and its risks. Not until the following spring would Julia learn of her son's activities.

In the 1940s, Capa wrote that when he was seventeen, he had made an appointment to meet a Communist Party recruiter late one night under the old Lánc Bridge. He did so both because he was "deeply interested in the world revolution" and because he wanted an exciting adventure. Other adventures, he said, had proved less exciting: a few months earlier, when he delivered a dress one afternoon to one of his mother's middle-aged clients, the woman had told him that her husband would not return from his office for hours and then proceeded to seduce him. But sex "did not fully justify all the expectations" and now that he was disillusioned with all that "love-stuff nonsense," perhaps the Communist Party could offer him the excitement he was looking for.

The man who fixed my date [wrote Capa] was highly doubtful of its success. The Communist Party, he explained, was an exclusive society of the proletariat. My father's tailor shop not only stamped me as a bourgeois, but my pretensions made me an intellectual. . . .

When the "important man" arrived, he looked rather young and carefree; only his steadily looking over his shoulder showed his importance. By four in the morning we had covered most of Budapest's empty streets and all aspects of the world revolution. He found that I was a fuzzy-headed intellectual with five half-digested books in me and a bourgeois father. I found that his views were far less radical than I had hoped and that his looking over his shoulder was a rather pretentious act. I decided not to join the Communist Party.

It seems highly unlikely that the Hungarian Communist Party would have been unwilling to admit Bandi because of his bourgeois background and intellectual pretensions. Its membership still greatly depleted by the White

Terror and exile, the party had been infiltrated early in 1930 by a police informer who had impersonated a radical firebrand so convincingly that he was soon elected secretary of the Budapest membership. With his help, the police were able to arrest over a hundred of the Communists who had turned the demonstration of September 1, 1930, into a riot, and as a result, the party was so weakened that it was unable to organize a single public demonstration during 1931; its efforts to sway the general elections that took place in June 1931 were futile. In short, the party was in no position to turn away so promising a young radical as Bandi. Nor would his youth have been an obstacle, for the party was then recruiting many new members who were in their late teens or early twenties. And as for his being a pretentious bourgeois intellectual, then, as always, many of the party's most loyal and active supporters were disaffected intellectuals from bourgeois backgrounds.

Shortly after he returned home and went to sleep, Bandi was awakened by his parents and "two rather big gentlemen in bowler hats." Julia demanded that her son tell her what he had done, and when he said he had done nothing, she slapped his face for the first time in his life. Then she tried to persuade the policemen that if they would only leave Bandi with her, she would punish him as harshly as they would, but they insisted that Bandi get dressed and come with them.

Capa later wrote, "In the big square police headquarters Horthy's chief of police, Peter Heim, whistled Beethoven's Fifth while beating up long-haired young men. . . . I was a young man of seventeen with very long hair." Bandi later told Eva Besnyö that as soon as he entered the questioning room a man standing at the door hit him, at which point Bandi laughed—so the man hit him again. Bandi laughed again, loading his forced laugh with all the arrogance and disdain he could muster. The hitting and the laughing alternated until Bandi was badly bruised. Two men then took him and knocked his head against a wall until he fell unconscious.

> When I awoke much later [wrote Capa] I was lying on the floor in a small cell on the ground floor of the police headquarters. The door was open, and two fat, unfriendly-looking Hungarian policemen were sitting by the entrance. Looking around, I saw a lot of names pencilled on the wall. The last two were Sallai and Fürst,* two young Hungarian Communists who, after returning from Moscow six

---

* Capa obviously invented this detail to improve his story. Imre Sallai and Sándor Fürst were not arrested until almost a year after Bandi had left Hungary. They were falsely charged with having blown up a railway bridge, given a summary trial, and executed.

months ago, had been caught and executed. The discovery of my importance made me feel very uneasy.

As Capa told the story, his father went to police headquarters later that morning, bribed some officials and guards for access to his son's cell, and, impersonating a secret policeman (saying "with undisguised disgust, 'You young Jewish punk, follow me' "), led Bandi out of his cell and then out of the building. "He hinted," wrote Capa, "that the information about my cell had cost quite a lot and he'd have to play a lot of card games to get it back."

It appears, however, that Bandi's rescue may not really have been quite that dramatic. Among the best customers of the Friedmanns' salon was Mme. Hetényi, wife of Imre Hetényi, who, as deputy chief of the Royal State Police and chief of its political division, was one of the very few Jews to hold a high position in Horthy's government. Mme. Hetényi had always been very friendly toward the Friedmanns, and through her Dezsö had met her husband. Using this important connection, Dezsö had in the past frequently managed "to get passports for the less fortunate Hungarians against small favors," and Bandi had often accompanied his father when he went to the police headquarters on these errands. It seems, then, that Dezsö got Hetényi to agree to release Bandi on the condition that the boy leave Hungary as soon as possible.

Although Capa always claimed that he had had to leave home within twenty-four hours of his release, Eva Besnyö maintains that he did not. Nor is that the only significant aspect of the story that Capa may have changed for dramatic effect. Although he was indeed arrested by the secret police, beaten, thrown into a cell, released through his father's intervention, and ordered to leave Hungary, it is possible that all this did not actually come about because Bandi had spent a few hours one night wandering the streets of Budapest with a Communist Party recruiter. Besnyö recalls that Bandi told her he was picked up by the police as a result of having participated in a demonstration, and Bandi's friend Csiki told one interviewer that shortly before their graduation an informer reported Bandi and his activist friends to the police; the group disbanded, but the police soon rounded up its members.

Whether Bandi was arrested before or after his graduation in May, it is certain that he finished school and passed his Abitur examinations. It was then decided that he would go to Berlin, where he would enter school in the fall. German was his second language, although he didn't speak it very well. Having studied (and received passing grades in) German literature for six years at the Gymnasium, however, he could presumably read the language with some facility.

Julia and Dezsö could spare little money to send Bandi off to school in

Berlin. At that moment they didn't even have the money to pay for his train fare. The mother of a schoolfriend lent him money for the train to Vienna and gave him letters of introduction to Jewish welfare organizations in cities along the rest of the way. Bandi would have to seek assistance in each city as he went. If he couldn't get money for train fare, he would have to hitchhike—or walk.

Julia took him to buy some new clothes—some shirts, a jacket, a pair of sturdy, double-soled mountain boots (for she knew he would be doing a lot of walking), and a couple of pairs of knickers; he was old enough to become a political refugee, but not yet old enough for long trousers. She also promised that somehow or other she would scrape together enough money for his tuition and living expenses and send it to him every month. Then, since she couldn't bear to watch him leave home, she said goodbye to him in advance, left Budapest for a few days, and didn't return until after his departure.

Setting out on the morning of July 12, 1931, having received gifts of provisions and small amounts of money from all the employees of his parents' salon, Bandi was on his own at last. Having dreamt for years of leaving Hungary he was finally realizing that dream. And yet it would be only natural if his elation over his freedom was mixed with rage at the situation that had driven him away from home—rage at the government's anti-Semitism and repression, rage at the constraints and hypocrisy of bourgeois life, and rage that his mother had been both too attentive and not attentive enough. Bandi must have felt all this and more as he set out from home, the only home he would ever know. For the rest of his life he was to live essentially as a nomad, residing mostly in a succession of hotel rooms and never occupying any one apartment for more than a few months. But he was ready for such a life: he had spent years of precocious independence preparing for it.

2

It took Bandi two or three weeks to travel from Budapest to Berlin, by way of Vienna, Brno, Prague, and Dresden. Although he later told at least one friend that he had walked from Prague to Berlin, he also claimed, to others, that a rabbi in Prague had given him money for the train fare to Berlin. The two stories are not necessarily contradictory—it's quite possible that the rabbi gave Bandi money for his train fare and that he then proceeded to spend it on something else, setting a pattern he would follow over and over again throughout his life. Having gotten his hands on a sum of money, he wouldn't have wanted to waste it on something as prosaic as train fare; he would certainly have preferred to show off by treating a group of friends to dinner—and if Bandi was in Prague for more than a few hours, he undoubtedly had already made friends there. Indeed, in a letter to his mother from Prague, he said that soon after arriving in the city, tired and hungry, he had sat down on a park bench beside a beggar who immediately offered to share his black bread with him.

Whether he arrived in Berlin on foot or by train, one of Capa's favorite stories about his life there began on a platform at the railroad station. He had been told that the best way to find a cheap room was through the agents sent by boarding-house keepers to meet arriving trains, and when he arrived at the station, he was approached by an especially attractive young blonde who said she could offer him a very cheap room. He happily accepted her offer, and they set out together. Arriving at the boarding house, which turned out to be in a very run-down part of the city, they were greeted by the owner, a fat, repellently ugly woman, who showed him a tiny, dark room, which, being right off the kitchen, reeked of many years' worth of stale cabbage aroma. But Bandi thought that no matter how unpleasant the room might be, just being around the blonde would provide some daily consolation, so he took the room. Then, much to his surprise and disappointment, the pretty agent collected her commission and disappeared—though not before giving him a look that clearly said, "So long, sucker."

Soon after reaching Berlin, Bandi wrote his mother promising to stay in his room and study German so that he would be fluent by the time school started. But his room was so disagreeable that he spent as little time as possible in it, and furthermore, as a foreigner alone in an unfamiliar and unfriendly city, whose streets were already swarming with uniformed Nazis, he needed friendship.

For the refugees whom the political upheavals of the 1930s were to toss around Europe—and then around the world—as if they were dice in a cup, friendships took on an extraordinary intensity, the kind of intensity that prevails among comrades in front-line trenches. One's closest friends were one's family. You would do anything for those friends. If a friend needed money and you were broke, you still found a way to give him something. If a friend was in danger, you risked your own neck. If you had food, you shared it. If someone did you a favor, you paid him back—somehow, sometime. And beyond the often quite large circles of close friends were vast networks of acquaintances and friends of friends.

No group was more fanatic about friendship or more committed to compatriotic nepotism than the Hungarians. Oppressed by Horthy's regime and condemned to reach only a small, provincial audience as long as they went on working in their native language, artists and intellectuals became a major Hungarian export to western Europe and America. By the 1930s, so many positions of power and influence in fields such as journalism and cinema were filled by Hungarians—all of them apparently ready to help any needy and worthy Hungarian refugee who came along—that there existed a widespread Hungarian network, with connections in Berlin, Vienna, Paris, London, New York, Hollywood, and other comparable cities. No one was a more loyal or more generous friend than Bandi, and no one knew how to make better use of his Hungarian birthright.

Bandi's entrée into Berlin's colony of young, artistic, leftist Hungarian émigrés was provided by Eva Besnyö. For about a year after her arrival in Berlin in 1930, Eva had worked for Dr. Peter Weller, a photojournalist who sold many of her photographs, under his own name, to such publications as the prestigious *Berliner Illustrirte Zeitung*. At about the time Bandi arrived in Berlin, Eva was able to rent a studio with a darkroom and set herself up as an independent portrait photographer, although she continued to do journalistic reportages which she sold through Neofot, a leftist press bureau.

In Berlin, the heretofore politically conservative Eva had been converted to the leftist view of the world. Her mentor in politics as well as art was György Kepes (pronounced "Juri Kepesh"), who had been a close friend of hers in Budapest and was now one of her closest friends in Berlin. He was also to have a great influence on Bandi. In Budapest, the seven-year difference in age between Bandi and Kepes (who was born in 1906) had been enough to keep them apart, but the shared fate of being Hungarian expatriates in Berlin brought the two young men together.

György Kepes, who has had a distinguished career as a painter, photographer, designer, teacher, and writer on the visual arts, studied painting at the Academy of Fine Arts in Budapest from 1924 to 1928, at which time he became a member of the Munkakör and was first exposed to Constructivism. Post-revolutionary Russian abstract artists, feeling a need to affirm their solidarity with the Soviet proletariat, had rationalized that if they *constructed* their work—especially if they used industrial materials and mechanical techniques—then they, too, would be workers, bona fide members of the proletariat. An artist could justify his existence in a Communist state, they said, only if he or she became a designer or a communicator, working in such fields as architecture, photography, and the designing of textiles, books, posters, and advertisements. The imaginative geometry of their innovations soon began to influence artists all over Europe.

In the late 1920s, when the Soviet government began to condemn abstraction not only in the fine arts but in the graphic and decorative arts as well, many of the Constructivists turned to film and photography. Both had the virtues of being produced with the aid of mechanical devices (i.e., cameras), of seeming to be scientifically objective (and thus free of "dangerous" individualism), and of being easily comprehended by the masses. To maintain their status as "constructors," the Russians, picking up on ideas first developed in Germany and the United States, began to treat the individual images produced by a camera as though they were mechanical parts to be used in the visual "machine" that was the finished work, be it a film, a single image composed from bits and pieces of many different photographs, or a layout of photographs on a printed page. To denote this treatment of images, they adopted the French term *montage*, meaning "the process of assembling," as of a machine.

Shortly after Kepes joined the Munkakör and came under the influence of Constructivism, he gave up painting, which then seemed to him an art form without political or social impact. Having a lively interest in folk art and folk life, he began photographing in the Hungarian countryside and in rural villages. Soon, however, although he continued to photograph and to make politically oriented photomontages, he was drawn to film, which he had come to consider "the most advanced, dynamic, and accordingly potent social form of visual communication." In 1930, with Kassák's encouragement, he wrote to Moholy-Nagy, who invited him to come to Berlin and work as his assistant.

Moholy-Nagy was then perhaps the most widely respected, and the most versatile, expatriate Hungarian artist in Europe. After the war he had moved to Berlin and become a member of the artistic avant-garde, enjoying particularly close contacts with the Russian Constructivists. Later, he served on the faculty of the Bauhaus, first in Weimar and then in Dessau. In 1928 he returned to Berlin and became interested in making films, completing his first one, *Marseille Vieux Port*, in 1929. That same year he helped to organize the Deutsche Werkbund's mammoth "Film und Foto" exhibition in Stuttgart, providing a cross-section of the most exciting developments that had taken

place in European and American film and photography during the previous
decade.

In Berlin, György Kepes filled for Bandi the role of mentor that Kassák had
filled in Budapest. Through Kepes, who was in daily contact with Moholy-
Nagy, Bandi continued his initiation into leftist politics and socially committed
art. Practically every day he ate either lunch or dinner at the boarding-house
room that Kepes shared with his girlfriend, Chaja Goldstein, a dancer, and
in which friends gathered for impassioned political and artistic discussions that
went on for hours and hours.

Bandi may not have had any direct contact with Moholy-Nagy, but through
Kepes he at least received a distillation of that seminal artist's ideas. He may
not have read all the books that were then creating sensations in Berlin, and
he may not have seen all the avant-garde German and Russian films that were
being shown in the city, but through Kepes and his friends he became aware
of all these things, learned at least the gist of their contents, and came to
understand something of their significance. Furthermore, he would have been
made aware of the latest political crises and interparty squabbles that were
shaking the foundations of the Weimar Republic—though it must have been
nearly impossible for anyone to keep up with all of the factions and alliances
that shaped the political situation. By 1931 German politics had become so
convoluted that the German Communists had even persuaded themselves that
a Nazi takeover would be the best thing that could happen to Germany and
to the cause of international Communism. As long as the Social Democratic
Party maintained any significant power, they argued, the workers, who did
not perceive the true evils of the party, could not be mobilized into revolt.
If, however, the Nazis came to power, their evil would be so apparent that
the proletarian revolution would necessarily follow in short order.

But Bandi knew that, as a foreign, leftist, cosmopolitan Jew, he epitomized
all that the Nazis hated and wanted to destroy. He was thus first and foremost
a passionate anti-fascist: whoever directly opposed fascism was his friend; whoever
didn't was his enemy. Years later he wrote of his time in Berlin: "Although
. . . I was still attracted by the general aims of socialism, I became even more
opposed to the Communist Party, which, in my opinion, seemed to be fur-
thering Hitler's rise to power."

Given this position, it was entirely natural that he should attend some of
the lectures then being given in Berlin by the outspokenly anti-Stalinist and
anti-fascist Marxist philosopher Karl Korsch, whose basic teachings had much
in common with Kassák's.

In 1926 Korsch, who had risen to a high position in the German Communist Party, was expelled for his criticism of Stalin. He then began to work closely with the independent, leftist trade unions. Throughout the late 1920s and early 1930s, in trade-union halls, "alternative" schools, and even the homes of such friends as Bertold Brecht, Korsch lectured and conducted discussion groups. In his educational programs of 1931 and 1932, when Bandi heard him, Korsch warned that the Nazis were perfectly capable of gaining absolute power in Germany and that once they did so their position would be unassailable. He vigorously criticized the German Communist Party for its adoption of the dangerously naïve slogan "After Hitler, Us!" The Communists, of course, dismissed his warnings as the rantings of an excommunicated heretic.

Like Kassák, Korsch favored an idealistically anti-authoritarian (which is to say anarchistic) society. As far as he could see, all hope for such a society in the Soviet Union was dead, and the prospects for Germany were not much better. There was, however, a nation in which a new and promising revolutionary experiment was just beginning. On April 12, 1931, the people of Spain had gone to the polls and elected a republican government. Two days later King Alfonso XIII abdicated, and Spain was proclaimed a republic. The nation's large and militant revolutionary factions immediately began to clamor for radical reforms.

In June 1931 Korsch was invited to Madrid to attend the congress of the Confederación Nacional del Trabajo (CNT), a powerful organization of anarchistic trade unionists (anarcho-syndicalists). He was very excited by what he saw and, upon his return to Berlin, published an enthusiastic article about the possibility that Spain could develop a non-Soviet-allied, non-Stalinist form of Communism. Whether Bandi actually read Korsch's article, heard Korsch talk about Spain, or only heard Korsch's views second-hand, it was probably Korsch's ideas that planted the seed of what would within five years grow into his own passionate involvement with the struggles of the Spanish Republic. Indeed, when Capa went to Spain shortly after the outbreak of the civil war in 1936, he made a point of seeking out the anarcho-syndicalist divisions that were fighting around Córdoba. In photographs taken a few minutes before Capa shot the most famous picture of his entire career, of a soldier collapsing onto the ground, we see that the soldier was wearing a cap embroidered with the initials "CNT."

Bandi had come to Berlin to study not at the university but at the Deutsche Hochschule für Politik. The Hochschule was a liberal school founded in 1920 to provide—as an alternative to the classical, theoretical programs of the German universities—the practical political training the new generation needed to rebuild a nation devastated by war, economic disaster, and political turmoil.

As an institution of the political middle, the Hochschule at first excluded both Communists and Nazis from its faculty and student body, although by the early 1930s the students were quite evenly divided in their loyalties among the Centrists, the Social Democrats, the Communists, and the Nazis. The school was remarkable in that it was one of the very few places in Berlin— or, for that matter, in all of Germany—where one could witness orderly debates between opposing factions. In a gesture of forced and futile optimism, one German magazine published a photograph of such a debate at the Hochschule (a photograph that contrasted dramatically with the usual pictures of street fights) and commented in the caption, "Things can also work this way." But, alas, not for long.

Although Bandi had his Abitur certificate, he didn't need it for the Hochschule, whose founders had close ties to the heavily working-class Social Democratic Party; the school's doors were open to anyone who wished to advance himself, whether he had graduated from a Gymnasium or not (only one-third of the students had). In addition to its regular curriculum the school had a full program of evening classes and lectures. Tuition was kept low, and there was a close rapport between students and the first-rate faculty that was unusual at German universities. All in all, the Hochschule was considered a radical school, an intruder in the stultifyingly reactionary, elitist, and hierarchical world of German higher education. (By the late 1920s, several years before the Nazis had begun to draw huge numbers of votes in parliamentary elections, German universities had become hotbeds of Nazism. By 1931 as many as half of all German university students were Nazis; violent attacks on Jewish professors and students had become so frequent that Bandi would probably never have considered going to a German university.)

Bandi registered at the Hochschule on October 27, 1931. Housed in a four-story, nineteenth-century version of an Italian Renaissance palazzo that had originally served as an architecture academy, the school had one of the best journalism departments in Europe. Nonetheless, Bandi's friends do not remember him as an ardent student. He had always been restless and found it hard to sit still through dull lectures or to do a lot of assigned reading. But being enrolled at the Hochschule did have some advantages. His student identification card entitled him to a substantial fare reduction on the city's streetcars and subways and admitted him to a student cafeteria where he could get a decent meal for very little money. It could also provide justification for his being in Berlin in case the police ever became inquisitive.

Bandi managed to live quite easily on the small allowance his family sent him each month. His room may have been dingy and smelly, but it was also very cheap. György Kepes and Chaja Goldstein gave him many meals, as did Eva Besnyö. And his tuition was low. Even after paying for his basic expenses, he must have had something left over for pocket money, for in his student identification picture he looks quite prosperous. His moderately long black hair is combed straight back from his forehead, and he is spiffily dressed in a suit jacket, tie, and sweater: a radical in bourgeois clothing. Indeed, the face that smirks at us from that photograph hardly looks like that of an astute, politically committed young firebrand. Rather, he looks like an arrogant wise guy, a joker, trying to appear too sophisticated to take seriously the process of school registration.

He was not to remain even a modestly comfortable bourgeois for long. Toward the end of 1931 the Hungarian economy, which had already suffered badly in the first years of the Great Depression, collapsed almost overnight, and Julia wrote to tell him that the family could no longer send him his monthly allowance. Since his returning to Budapest was still out of the ques- tion, he would have to get a job—not an easy thing to do when the unem- ployment rate is over thirty percent and you don't speak the language of your adopted country well. (Bandi had spent so much time with his Hungarian friends that he hadn't had much need or opportunity to practice his German.) Suddenly he found himself completely without money. His friends were very generous, but times were hard for everyone, and they couldn't possibly afford to feed him all the time. As for paying the rent, Bandi managed to stall his landlady, Frau Bohen, with excuses and promises.

As he grew hungrier and hungrier, he discovered a new advantage of his room off the kitchen. Every day Frau Bohen gave her pet dachshund a veal cutlet, which Bandi would snatch away as soon as she was gone. The fat, spoiled dog soon became so thin, and its coat so lackluster, that its mistress took it to a veterinarian and was dumbfounded when he told her that the dog was suffering from malnutrition. Now suspicious, Frau Bohen kept the door open a crack to watch what happened after she left the kitchen. When she saw her lodger wresting the cutlet from the dog, she leapt in and screamed at Bandi, frightening him so badly (or so he later claimed) that he jumped out a back window. Since he could never muster the courage to return and collect his belongings, he lost everything.

Finding himself without a place to live, he resorted to looking up his mother's cousin, Piri Moscowicz, the wife of a successful industrialist. It was undoubtedly because his relative seemed so hopelessly bourgeois and because he was relishing his independence that he hadn't bothered to look her up earlier, but now, swallowing his pride, he went to her apartment. No one was home, so, weak from hunger and exhaustion, he just curled up on the floor in the hallway, and went to sleep until Piri returned. He lived in her apartment for a couple of weeks and then disappeared as suddenly and as mysteriously as he had appeared.

Bandi had to start making some money. For advice he turned to a professor at the Hochschule whom he had gotten to know quite well and asked him whether he should go into agriculture or photography. (The idea of Bandi working as a farmer, or even as an agricultural manager, seems preposterous.) Capa himself later gave the simplest and most obvious explanation for his final decision: "While pursuing my studies, my parents' means gave out, and I decided to become a photographer, which was the nearest thing to journalism for anyone who found himself without a language." He thus joined the legions of expatriate Hungarians who discovered in music or in visual arts such as painting, photography, and film a variety of universal languages in which they could communicate effectively wherever they found themselves.

One day, before having definitely made up his mind, Bandi went to Eva Besnyö and asked her, "How is this photography? Do you like it? I'm thinking of doing it myself." Eva, still something of a traditionalist, replied, "But you'll have to study photography, and you haven't any money." She was rather shocked by Bandi's casual attitude; to her, photography was something for which you had to have a real vocation and years of training.

But Bandi knew that the new cameras were so easy to use that you needed no special training; to become a photographer, all you needed was to acquire a camera. When he explained his predicament to György Kepes, Kepes said that he had an extra camera—a 6 x 9 cm format Voigtländer that he had received in payment for designing the show window of a camera store in Budapest—and that he would gladly give it to Bandi on extended loan. In possession of a camera, Bandi was now a photographer. All he had to do was find a way to make some money.

The winter began badly," wrote Capa of the winter of 1931–32. "*Au fond* I had never thought that poverty had anything to do with shoes. But now when I look at poor people, I glance at their feet. The gray stones of Berlin were wet from the rain. I had always loved the feel of rain on my face, but now the rain, without touching my face, went right to my shoes. Before the rain, everyone had admired my shoes. My mother had bought them before I left home, and we were sure that they would last for years. They had been made for the mountains, but my mother said that a young man of seventeen could wear them without concern in the city. That was only a few months ago, and in this city in which I still had trouble finding my way around, the days had come to seem like an endless succession of Sunday afternoons. But this time it was really Monday, and I was hurrying to start my first job." That job was in the darkroom of the photo agency called Dephot, short for Deutscher Photodienst (German Photo Service). Simon Guttmann, the man who ran it and who hired Bandi, was to become one of the most influential in a succession of mentors.

Before founding Dephot in 1928, Guttmann, who was apparently born in Budapest in 1890, had for many years been active in German avant-garde art and radical politics. He was living in Berlin in 1910, when he founded the vanguard theater Die Neue Bühne. He was then also a member of the literary and philosophical group called Der Neue Club, for whose occasional evenings of avant-garde entertainment (entitled Neo-Bombastic Cabarets) Expressionist artists designed posters and programs, and writers belonging to the group read poetry and offered skits.

At the outbreak of World War I, many of the members of this rarefied circle, including Guttmann, moved to Zurich, where they joined with other artists from all over Europe and created the perversely playful, anti-art movement they named "Dada." Hans Richter, one of the principal Dadaists, recalled in his memoirs that Guttmann, though not actually a member of the Dada group, almost always sat at the Dada table in the Café Odéon, where James Joyce and Lenin were also among the regular customers. Richter called Guttmann "one of the quickest and best conversationalists" he had ever known and said that his brilliant ideas "poured out of him in full panoply and at a precipitate rate, as though he were afraid that if he held them back for even a fraction of a second, he might forget them."

Guttmann returned to Germany at the end of the war, became involved with the Spartacists (a group of radical Socialists who formed the nucleus of the German Communist Party), worked in an art gallery, wrote as a free-lance journalist, and ran a news-photo agency. In 1928, with the financial backing of Alfred Marx, the son of a wealthy industrialist, he recruited two photographers and a darkroom man, rented an apartment in a building on the corner of the Friedrichstrasse and the Jägerstrasse in Berlin to serve as an office, and announced the establishment of Dephot.

It was, as Guttmann remembers it, his interest in esoteric Judaism that led to his first meeting with Bandi Friedmann, at a discussion group led by a numerologist named Dr. Oskar Goldberg. Guttmann had known Goldberg (whom Hans Richter described as "rather alarming," "uncouth," and "daemonic") ever since the days of Der Neue Club and the Neo-Bombastic Cabarets. By the 1930s Goldberg was claiming that numerology and other mysteries of the Cabala could make one a "supernatural revolutionary," with such power that it would no longer be necessary to worry about the exhaustion of the world's natural resources.

In view of Bandi's lackadaisical initiation into Judaism, it is difficult to see what he was doing at meetings of the Goldberg circle—unless, of course, someone had advised him that he might get a line on a job that way. In any case, he attended several meetings without saying a word before he finally introduced himself to Guttmann and asked for a job with his agency. Guttmann was somewhat reluctant, but he tried to help fellow Hungarians whenever possible, and when his darkroom man said he could use another helper, Bandi was hired.

He found the atmosphere at Dephot charged with excitement. Photographers were setting off for or returning from assignments all over the world, there were constantly pressing deadlines, and everyone willingly worked long hours. The formality and the systematic organization characteristic of German offices of that time were almost totally lacking. And yet somehow everything got done.

At the center of this apparent chaos was Simon Guttmann himself. He was a small man—some people called him "The Homunculus," while others said he reminded them of a spider—with angular features, a high forehead, a dapper mustache, and piercing eyes behind the thick lenses of his wire-rimmed spectacles. The well-groomed mustache contrasted incongruously with his shabby manner of dressing, usually in old, crumpled suits with buttons missing. Still a brilliant conversationalist, he bubbled over with so many ideas for photographic reportages that editors came to depend on him and were thus willing to put up with his difficult, eccentric personality. Once, for instance, Guttmann went to see an editor of *Der Welt Spiegel*, the weekly pictorial supplement of the daily *Berliner Tageblatt*, and found her wearing a dress decorated with epaulets; disliking their military overtones, he picked up a pair of scissors and simply cut them off.

By 1931, Dephot represented an impressive list of photojournalists, including Umbo, Felix H. Man, Harald Lechenperg, Walter Bosshard, and Kurt Hübschmann. Of these, Bandi became quite friendly with the first two while he was working at the agency. (Only later would he get to know Lechenperg and Bosshard, who were away on assignment most of the time.)

Umbo (born Otto Umbehr in 1902) had gone to work in a coal mine near Essen when he was eighteen, but in a year was studying design at the Weimar Bauhaus. In 1923 he went to Berlin, working at odd jobs—as house painter, clown, commercial and theatrical designer, assistant to the journalist Egon Erwin Kisch, and camera assistant to Walter Ruttmann during the making of his landmark film, *Berlin: The Symphony of a Great City*, a dawn-to-midnight portrait of the metropolis. Combining his interests in design, journalism, and film, Umbo became a highly versatile photographer, specializing at Dephot in portraiture and advertising photography, but also carrying out many assignments for reportage and experimenting with Surrealism. He was bohemian, leftist, playful, and completely lacking any sense of the value of money— a real Dada figure; he even had a wildly decorated Dada car.

If Umbo directed Dephot's portraiture and advertising work, it was Felix H. Man who was the agency's star photojournalist. Born Hans Felix Sigismund Baumann in 1893, he studied painting in Munich and Berlin before World War I. As an officer in the German army during the war, he used a Kodak to make an intimate record of life in the trenches; and in the 1920s, working as an illustrator for the house of Ullstein, the largest publisher of periodicals in Germany, he again used a camera, this time to make studies for his drawings. When Ullstein published some of the photographs, Guttmann saw them, was impressed, and approached him about working for Dephot. Before quitting Ullstein, Baumann did a trial reportage, which Guttmann sold to the *Münchner Illustrierte Presse*, the principal rival of Ullstein's *Berliner Illustrirte*. Baumann published his story under the pseudonym Felix H. Man, and when he joined Dephot soon thereafter, he decided to adopt his new name permanently.

Man's special genius was directed toward the quirks and oddities of the daily (and nightly) world of the city and toward people of all kinds, from unemployed workers to great artists. He photographed everything from concerts to factories and from the pleasures of Berlin's Luna Park to the sufferings of unemployed coal miners in the Rhineland, but his most famous series of photographs is "A Day in the Life of Mussolini," published in the *Münchner Illustrierte Presse* early in 1931. One picture especially, showing Mussolini standing at his desk in his grand-ballroom-sized office with its trompe-l'oeil painted columns, devastatingly exposed the Italian dictator as a megalomaniac dwarfed by the deceptive sham of his ambitions.

But the man who was Bandi's closest friend at Dephot was not a photographer at all; Ladislaus Glück was Guttmann's economic manager, assistant idea man, and "roving editor," accompanying photographers when they went out on assignments and writing the text for stories. Born László Fekete (or Tölgy) in Budapest, he had been a member of the radical Galileo Circle as a student and soon thereafter had been appointed an official in Béla Kun's short-lived Communist regime. During the 1920s, under the name Peter Koester, he edited the illustrated weekend supplement to the *Berliner Börsen Courier*. At Dephot, under the name Glück (his continuing involvement with the Communist Party was apparently the reason for all his aliases) he encouraged Bandi and helped him out whenever he could; several years later, when their paths crossed in New York, Bandi repaid his debt of gratitude.

Although Bandi started out as a darkroom assistant, he soon found himself doing all sorts of jobs: answering the telephone, delivering photos to editors, and even carrying equipment for photographers on assignments. (Guttmann called him the *laufbub*, the German equivalent of "gofer.") He was working long hours, but his financial troubles were far from over. In fact, he was still desperately poor. But getting a job at Dephot, even in a menial capacity, was a little like being admitted to a secret society. Bandi was now in daily contact with some of the most innovative and successful photojournalists in Germany.

On paper, Dephot's finances looked reasonably healthy, but there were constant cash-flow crises; sometimes the firm didn't even have money for stamps. Stories went around about how Guttmann would visit friends and ask them to lend him a few marks—and then in the course of conversation mention that he had just sold a story for 2,000 marks. Guttmann often had to pawn some of the firm's cameras and darkroom equipment, and even when money finally came in from publishers, it was eaten up quickly by rent and expenses. (In the fall of 1932 Dephot went bankrupt, but Guttmann was able to restructure the firm under the name Degephot [Deutsche Photogemeinschaft].)

As the youngest and most recently hired employee, Bandi was the last to get paid. But he was nothing if not resourceful: the office had to be heated through the winter, and he discovered that he could buy coal cheaply from the central depot, haul it in buckets to the office, charge less for it than the regular delivery service would, and still make a profit of something like two or three marks a week—a pittance, but still enough to make the difference between getting by and not getting by.

After having stayed at Piri Moscowicz's apartment for a couple of weeks, Bandi found a miserably cold and bare attic room that at least allowed him to regain his precious independence. He never had any money to pay his rent, but he had his charm. Day after day, week after week, he managed to persuade his landlady that he would be able to pay her any day. But he knew that even his charm had its limits and did his best to avoid his landlady whenever possible. He would sneak out very early in the morning, work twelve hours or so at Dephot, attend an occasional evening class at the Deutsche Hochschule für Politik, and then spend hours talking with friends at György Kepes's room or in a café before sneaking up the stairs to his room. He could go on studying at the Hochschule only because the school had a sliding scale of tuition fees; no one was ever barred from classes due to inability to pay. Bandi's student identification card carries validating stamps for both the winter semester of 1931–32 and the following spring semester of 1932.

Felix Man recalls that Bandi "was very bright and intelligent and liked by everybody, and as he was very poor but handsome the girls [who worked] at Dephot used to bring him sandwiches." Or sometimes Bandi would ask one of the photographers to lend him a few pfennig so that he could get a cheap bowl of pea soup for lunch. And every once in a while, he would hit the jackpot. If Simon Guttmann was in the right mood when a big check finally arrived, he might decide to put practical considerations aside and treat the whole staff to a meal at the Café Jaedicke, whose location near the offices of Ullstein and the other big publishing firms made it the preferred hangout of journalists. On his own, Bandi gravitated toward the Romanisches Café, headquarters of the avant-garde and of the Hungarian émigré community, where he could usually find someone in the bohemian crowd to treat him to a meal or at least a cup of coffee. Failing that, he discovered that a glass of water with lots of sugar dissolved in it could keep him going until something better came along.

During the winter of 1931–32, the streets saw a great deal of campaigning, demonstrating, marching, and interparty fighting as March 13, the date set for the presidential elections, drew near. The Nazis, believing that victory for the party and its candidate Adolf Hitler (who didn't even become a naturalized

German citizen until two weeks before the election) was at last possible, mobilized whole armies of members to hand out broadsides, to hold mass rallies, to march through the streets singing the "Horst Wessel Lied," and to rough up the opposition.

Street fights were frequent. They gave vent to frustration and hatred, but they accomplished nothing politically. Accordingly, Bandi and a group of his leftist friends decided that they could most effectively hurt the Nazis by making them look ridiculous. Since the weather in Berlin in early March was still very cold, they began to go out at night and pour buckets of water on the streets through which they knew the Nazis would be marching the next day. They hoped that the sight of hobnailed boots slipping uncontrollably on icy streets would make a mockery of the Nazi marching song, whose opening lines went:

> The flag held high, the ranks tightly closed,
> We march on with firm, courageous steps.

Having already fallen afoul of the police for political activities in Budapest, Bandi was understandably nervous about his participation in this guerrilla warfare; if he was caught—either by the police or by the Nazis—the consequences would be grave. This awareness made him slightly paranoid. One day, when he and György Kepes were out walking, they encountered a demonstration in progress. The sight was so commonplace that neither of them gave it much notice, but suddenly, without warning, the police swept down upon the demonstrators. Bandi instinctively took flight, and Kepes, not quite knowing why, ran after him. The police, who react to a running man as hounds react to a fox, pursued them. Somehow the two young men eluded the police and found their way to the top floor of an apartment building, where Kepes lectured his friend on the virtues of keeping a cool head.

Supported by the Social Democrats, the conservative incumbent Paul von Hindenburg won the elections, and three days later he outlawed both the major uniformed Nazi groups, the brown-shirted SA and the black-shirted SS. For a moment it looked as though Germany might rid itself of the fascist curse. But two months later, after a change of advisers and a change of heart, Hindenburg rescinded the ban on the Nazi paramilitary groups. Back in their uniforms again, the Nazis filled the streets of Berlin with redoubled fury. There were so many bloody street fights among the Nazis, the Communists, and the Social Democrats during the summer of 1932 that, in effect, a state of civil war prevailed in Berlin. When parliamentary elections were held at the end of July, the Nazis emerged with a huge majority—almost 100 seats more than the second-place Social Democrats.

Eva Besnyö, horrified by the atmosphere in Berlin, left to spend the summer in Hungary, and not long afterward, György Kepes became seriously ill and went home to Transylvania to recuperate. Feeling more and more alone in an increasingly hostile city, Bandi shifted his need for love to a prostitute whom he had first seen on his first day of work at Dephot. As he later told the story (undoubtedly embellishing it somewhat) he was rushing to get to work on time on that gray, windy morning when he saw her, a beautiful woman with shoulder-length blond hair, wearing an elegantly simple gray suit, standing on the corner right outside the Dephot office. She looked more like Greta Garbo than like a streetwalker. "Berlin," Capa wrote, "seemed suddenly friendly." The woman, unfortunately, was not. Her price was a firm five marks, and she could easily see that even such a small sum was beyond the resources of this young boy, with his unruly mop of jet-black hair, a soiled leather jacket, and worn knickers. With the coming of poverty, Bandi had quickly lost his sleek, well-dressed look.

Undaunted, he continued to daydream about the woman on the corner. Although he knew very well that she was a prostitute, he felt certain that he could find true happiness in her arms. She became a symbol of everything he lacked in Berlin. All he needed in order to have her to himself—for a few minutes at least—was five marks. Five marks!

With the arrival of spring, Bandi's main source of income disappeared: the Dephot office no longer needed the coal he had hauled all winter. Then one day a registered letter arrived from his two aunts in New York.* In it, like a gift from the gods, were two ten-dollar bills, which Bandi promptly converted into eighty marks. He suddenly felt like a millionaire.

The first thing he wanted to do was give his nagging landlady her come-uppance. Peeling off bills as though there were plenty more where those came from, he disdainfully paid her the entire fifty-five marks he owed her in back rent. To his chagrin, she evicted him on the spot; once even, she wanted to stay even. Only then did Bandi realize that if he had paid her just half of what he owed her, she would have let him stay on—he would have had her on his hook. Years later, reminiscing about this episode, Capa wrote that he lost his shelter and his belief in morality at the same moment.

---

* Two of Julia Friedmann's sisters, Gladys and Lenke, had moved to New York. Lenke married a man named Ignacka Herskovits, who had a successful business manufacturing orthopedic inner soles. These relatives occasionally sent Bandi small amounts of money.

Having, in effect, thrown away fifty-five marks, Bandi resolved to make the most of what was left. He would spend fifteen marks on improving his appearance, five on love, and the remaining five marks he would put aside as capital. The first thing he did was to replace his threadbare knickers with a pair of gray flannel slacks. Then he headed straight for the public baths and soaked in hot water for an hour until he finally felt clean. Next he stopped at a barbershop and had his hair cut neatly. His fellow workers at Dephot were so impressed by the transformed Bandi who finally showed up for work, several hours later, that they didn't dare send him out on any errands that day, and when he asked for permission to leave early, at five-thirty, no one questioned his right to do so.

All day long, working in the darkroom, he had imagined the romantic things he would say to the girl of his dreams, who now, at last, was within reach. Would she even recognize him? He was almost frantic with anticipation. On the stroke of five-thirty he left the office and ran downstairs, out the door, and around the corner. She was gone.

She had stood near that corner for the past six months, in all kinds of weather and at all hours. Now that he had come to claim her, she was gone. In a state of shocked disbelief, he gazed at the clock across the street. Where could she be? Perhaps just in the café. As he turned and looked in a shoe-store window, a particularly elegant and comfortable-looking pair of brown leather shoes caught his eye. He looked down at his old, leaky mountain boots, then again at the elegant shoes in the window, and said to himself, "They would go nicely with my new trousers."

At six, just before the store was to close, Bandi looked around quickly one last time to see whether his girl was coming back and then went in and bought the shoes, which cost nine marks, fifty pfennig. He was left with fifty pfennig in his pocket. As soon as he left the store, he glanced in the window again, to reassure himself that he had made the right choice. And then he saw her reflection. She was back at her station. When Bandi turned toward her, she looked at him and smiled. He stood for a moment looking at her, and then he began to run.

Out of money, out of his room, deprived of the friends who had been so generous to him, Bandi spent many nights during the summer of 1932 sleeping on park benches. But in the middle of this hot, depressing, politically terrifying summer, something happened that was to change the course of Bandi's life. Harald Lechenperg sent back from the Punjab the rolls of film he had shot at the Maharaja of Patna's wedding. They were to be developed and printed at Dephot before being delivered to Ullstein. Bandi, working in the darkroom, became so excited when he saw the contact sheets that he rushed out with them, hammered on the translucent glass pane of the door to Guttmann's office, and burst in, exclaiming that these were the greatest photographs he had ever seen.

Now, one simply did not burst into Simon Guttmann's office. Although Guttmann has in recent years insisted that Dephot was a community of equals in which there was no boss, he was, in fact, rather autocratic. His office was sacrosanct; *no one*, not even a member of the staff, was allowed to enter unless he had first telephoned or—better yet—written for an appointment. Yet in burst Bandi.

Ordinarily, Guttmann would have screamed mercilessly at anyone invading his privacy, but he was charmed by Bandi's spontaneous enthusiasm. Lechenperg's photographs were, indeed, excellent—and Bandi's appreciation of them convinced Guttmann on the spot that this young darkroom assistant had the makings of a first-rate photographer; he lent Bandi a Leica and began sending him out on simple assignments. Dephot was never a spot news-photo agency; instead, its photographers concentrated on human-interest stories, which were sometimes but by no means always linked to current events. Nevertheless, the agency could always use the money that an occasional news story of local interest might bring in.

Pete Petersen, who, like Ladislaus Glück, was a "roving editor" at Dephot, recalls that early on Guttmann sent Bandi to cover a swimming meet. When Bandi showed the photos to his boss, Guttmann said they were awful and bawled him out, criticizing his work mercilessly. Afterward, Petersen, who thought the photos were quite good, asked Guttmann why he had been so hard on Bandi. Guttmann replied, "Well, I can't just tell him he's a master."

Gradually Guttmann sent Bandi out on increasingly important assignments. Guttmann, Glück, Petersen, and the established Dephot photographers all gave him advice and criticism and taught him the rudiments of building up a good reportage. In his spare time, Bandi wandered around Berlin, photographing whatever caught his eye.*

Toward the end of November, Guttmann gave Bandi his first big assignment. Capa later wrote that one day, while he was still working in the darkroom at Dephot,

---

* One of Bandi's Berlin reportages (about people looking at an exhibition of artist Heinrich Zille's work) appeared in *Der Welt Spiegel*, March 12, 1933, p. 3. The rest of his work from this period has disappeared.

the newspapers carried a story that Trotsky would speak in Copenhagen. My bosses were excited—but, when they looked around, they saw they had sent all the photographers out to cover events that were happening in Germany. I was the only one there. They said, "Go!"

Leon Trotsky, however, didn't just suddenly show up in Copenhagen and announce that he was about to make a speech. For the more than three years since his expulsion from the Soviet Union, he had been stranded on one of the Princes Islands, about an hour and a half by steamer from Istanbul; he had been unable to get a visa for the United States or any European nation, but in the autumn of 1932 a group of Danish students had invited him to speak, assuring him that their government had promised to grant him an eight-day visa. Trotsky was skeptical, but he was determined to escape from his isolation, even if only briefly, so he applied for the visa, and much to his amazement, received it. Accompanied by his wife and three secretaries, he sailed from Istanbul on November 14, two weeks before he was due to speak in Copenhagen.

Although he tried to travel incognito, the European press quickly learned of his voyage and dispatched reporters and photographers to chronicle his less-than-stately progress. The newspapers were full of reports and rumors. No one could believe that Trotsky could possibly be traveling all the way from Turkey and back simply to deliver a lecture to some Danish students; the idea seemed preposterous. The newspapers agreed that the lecture must be a pretext—surely Trotsky was rushing to a meeting of his disciples from all over the world to plot the overthrow of Stalin. In fact, much less melodramatically, he hoped only that the Danish government might allow him to take permanent refuge there or that, once in Europe, he could persuade some other government that his presence was not to be feared.

In his version of the Trotsky story, Capa implies that he had been nothing more than a darkroom boy when suddenly his big chance came along entirely by accident, but in fact Guttmann had been grooming him for months; he has recently said that he would never have sent Bandi on such an important assignment if he hadn't been confident of his abilities. He persuaded a *Welt Spiegel* editor (the same woman whose epaulets he had once cut off) that his young protégé could do the job, and, to make the trip to Copenhagen as financially worthwhile as possible, he lined up an assignment for him from Ullstein as well: to photograph the American film comedians Laurel and Hardy, who would also be visiting the Danish capital.

Having arranged these assignments, Guttmann sent Bandi off to Copenhagen. As Capa told the story years later:

> My departure was a comedy. I got an old passport and no visa. They bought me a first-class ticket and I traveled stylish like a minister. When the conductor came to inspect the passport and visa—I took out a menu card from a restaurant and gave it to him among many other important-looking papers—and he was baffled at first— but I talked faster and more than any first-class passenger he ever had and he nodded finally and passed on.

This, of course, is a variation on the story that Bandi's father loved to tell. In 1932 Bandi possessed a valid Hungarian passport, but it is quite possible that for one reason or another he was unable to obtain a visa; so there may be an element of truth in his account.

Trotsky had a busy day on Sunday, November 27, before lecturing the Danish students. He had traveled far and wanted to make the most of the attention focused on him. To disseminate his ideas as widely as possible, he had prepared French, English, and German versions of his speech, delivering the French version that morning before the camera of a French filmmaker and, his itinerary kept secret, broadcasting the English version to the United States in the afternoon. Finally, that evening, he went to the Copenhagen Stadium—the Sport Palast—to address an audience of 2,000 on "The Meaning of the Russian Revolution."

Fearing a Stalinist assassination attempt, Trotsky was escorted by a guard of 200 mounted and foot policemen to the stadium, but the precautions turned out to be needless, for not even a single heckler showed up. Nevertheless, wrote Capa,

> no one could take pictures, because Trotsky never wanted to be photographed. There were photographers from all over the world with their big box cameras—but none could get in. I had a little Leica in my pocket so no one thought I was even a photographer. When some workers came to carry long steel pipes into the chamber, I joined them—and my little Leica and I went to look for Trotsky.

The truth of the matter is that Capa borrowed this last detail from an episode that occurred in Paris in May 1936, when he found himself unable to gain admittance any other way to a meeting at which Léon Blum was speaking. In Copenhagen, Bandi had a ticket for Trotsky's lecture and just walked in like everyone else. But that doesn't make such a good story.

Capa's comments to the contrary, Trotsky doesn't seem to have been notably camera-shy. He had allowed himself to be photographed during his journey, and he had cooperated fully with the French filmmaker earlier on the day of his speech. He had also allowed himself to be photographed at the radio microphone. But he was naturally worried about security. A gun could possibly be brought into the hall inside a big box camera, just as American gangsters used violin cases to carry their machine guns. Furthermore, Trotsky was a great oratorical showman. He would not have wanted his speech interrupted at some dramatic climax by the popping of flashbulbs. Bandi's Leica, however, was small and needed no flash.

Trotsky began his lecture by asking two questions: "First, why did this revolution take place at all? And, second, has the revolution stood the test?" While dealing with the latter, politically more sensitive of these questions, Trotsky—who not once in his entire speech mentioned Stalin by name—pounded his fist on the podium, gesticulated wildly, and snarled at the current state of the Soviet Union. It was one of his most brilliant and impassioned performances as a public speaker, and Bandi, positioned close to the podium, managed to snap a dramatic series of photographs that show, better than any others ever published, the power of Trotsky's oratorical charisma. *Der Welt Spiegel* gave them a full-page layout—a most auspicious debut for the young photographer. *

4

Bandi's heyday at Dephot (by then, Degephot) didn't last long. On January 30, 1933, the advisers of the senile President Hindenburg persuaded him to appoint Hitler as chancellor. That night the Nazis staged an enormous torchlight parade, a terrifying display of mass fanaticism. By then Bandi, obviously not an "Aryan," was already being jeered at and accosted in the streets. Herr Pieck, the doorman of the building in which the Dephot offices were located, wore his SA uniform to work every day, and it was clearly only a matter of time before he stopped merely giving Bandi dirty looks and started denouncing him. By remaining in Berlin, Bandi was placing both himself and Dephot in danger.

---

* No trace of a Laurel and Hardy story has ever turned up.

Trotzki betritt
das Rednerpult

Photographische Ausdrucksstudien von seinem Vortrag auf
einer sozialistischen Studentenversammlung in Kopenhagen

„Ich will nicht leugnen,
dass mein Leben in nicht
ganz geregelter Weise
verlief. Die Gründe da-
für sind jedoch eher in
den Zeitverhältnissen
zu suchen als in mir."

„Die Gesetzmässigkeit
der Ereignisse erkennen
und in dieser Gesetz-
mässigkeit seinen Platz
finden, ist die erste
Pflicht des Revolutio-
närs."

„Jeder echte Redner
kennt Augenblicke,
wo aus seinem Mun-
de etwas Stärkeres
spricht, als er selbst
in seinen gewöhn-
lichen Stunden ist.
Das ist „Inspiration".
Sie entsteht aus der
höchsten schöpfe-
rischen Anspannung
aller Kräfte. Das Un-
bewusste erhebt sich
aus tiefen Höhlen und
unterwirft sich die
bewusste Gedanken-
arbeit, verbindet sich
mit ihr zu einer hö-
heren Einheit."

Die Texte sind Leo Trotzkis
Autobiographie „Mein Le-
ben" (erschienen im S. Fischer
Verlag, Berlin) entnommen.
Aufnahmen Friedmann-Degephot.

The end came on February 27, when a fire gutted the Reichstag, the German parliament building. Hitler accused the Communists of arson, outlawed the Communist Party, and declared a state of emergency that allowed him to assume dictatorial powers. That day thousands of leftists began to flee Germany. Simon Guttmann advised Bandi to leave at once. He went straight to the Jewish philanthropical organization that had helped him on his way to Berlin, and they gave him train fare to Vienna. *

Upon his arrival, he moved into the flat in the semi-suburban 18th Bezirk that Dephot photographer Harald Lechenperg shared with his mother. Lechenperg, who was always ready to do a favor for Simon Guttmann, was back from the East and not only invited Bandi to stay at his apartment but hired him as his assistant. Bandi quickly became a member of the family. He found in Lechenperg's household the kind of stimulation and camaraderie he had enjoyed at György Kepes's in Berlin. With Lechenperg, his mother, and their friends, Bandi would sit around the table after dinner, drinking tea, eating peanuts, and talking for hours. Lechenperg's mother liked the young Hungarian but got so tired of hearing his political opinions that she asked whether he wouldn't agree to limit them to one hour an evening.

The political events taking place that spring in Vienna and the rest of Europe provided more than enough material for an hour's discussion every night. Less than a week after the Reichstag fire, the Austrian parliament had suspended itself, and the Austrian chancellor, Engelbert Dollfuss, had taken advantage of the situation to seize power. On the morning of March 7, the Viennese awoke to learn that Dollfuss had banned public meetings and demonstrations and had instituted censorship of the press. A week later, when members of parliament arrived to resume their suspended session, they found the doors of the parliament building barred by police. In the meantime, German parliamentary elections gave the Nazis an even larger majority than ever.

Although Hitler was an Austrian by birth, he and his party were not well loved by the Austrian government in 1933. Devoutly Catholic and justifiably afraid of Hitler's Pan-Germanic ambitions, Dollfuss allied Austria with Catholic Italy against Protestant Germany. Through the spring of 1933, while Bandi was in Vienna, Dollfuss devoted his energies to building up what was

---

* As the bearer of a valid Hungarian passport, Bandi was free to leave Germany. The Nazis were eager to capture as many leftists as possible, but they were sufficiently afraid of the Hungarian government (and sufficiently hopeful of an eventual alliance) that by and large they kept their hands off Hungarians.

soon to be launched as his "Fatherland Front," anti-German and anti-Nazi but still deeply fascistic. Anti-Semitism was on the rise in Vienna but it was not yet nearly as virulent as in Germany. For the moment, Austria was a fairly safe, if not altogether comfortable, haven.

Fritz Goro, assistant to the director of the *Münchner Illustrierte Presse,* and his wife were vacationing in the Tyrol when they heard about the Nazis' parliamentary victory and decided to remain in Austria, abandoning everything they had left behind in Munich. Soon after they arrived in Vienna, Harald Lechenperg invited them to stay with him.

At that time Goro, who was later to become one of the world's finest science photographers, was only an enthusiastic amateur. He had shot quite a few photographs in St. Anton and now hoped to sell them, for his money was running out. Lechenperg assigned the job of developing and printing the film to his young assistant—Bandi Friedmann—who developed them so carelessly and scratched them so badly that they were completely unsaleable. Goro was, of course, furious, but Bandi could get anyone to forgive him for anything. To compensate for the loss, Lechenperg drove to Munich in the Model-A Ford he had driven from Bombay to Berlin earlier that year and retrieved some of Goro's important papers from his apartment. The German border guards were so impressed by the car's Indian license plates that they just clicked their heels and let Lechenperg across, both going and returning.

After two or three weeks in Vienna, Goro made arrangements to work for the photographer Hug Block in Paris, and he and his wife set off for the French capital.

Early in June, not long after the official proclamation of Dollfuss's "Fatherland Front," Bandi took a steamer down the Danube to Budapest. During the almost two years since he had been forced to leave home, the Hungarian Left had been rendered so utterly powerless that the government no longer regarded it as much of a threat. In the political climate that now prevailed, Dezsö Friedmann was able to obtain permission for his son to return, apparently on condition that he refrain from all political activity.

We can only wonder whether Bandi saw Kassák that summer. (Arthur Koestler, who was in Budapest at the same time, wrote that Kassák was free "to edit, at his table in the café, his Marxist quarterly. The police did not bother about Communist *littérateurs,* so long as they remained *littérateurs* and had no contact with the one potential enemy, the underground Party.")

Certainly he was not deterred from seeing his friend and fellow graduate of the Munkakör, Kati Deutsch, who, having lived in Berlin for two years, had also left immediately after the Reichstag fire. By this time, she, too, had been drawn to photography as a career and was studying with Pécsi, the photographer under whom Eva Besnyö had served her apprenticeship. Bandi used to stop by Pécsi's studio almost every morning to watch, to chat, and to gossip.

Bandi found his family suffering great economic hardships in the wake of their salon's bankruptcy, and living in an apartment smaller and less conveniently located than their old one. Julia, Dezsö, and László continued making dresses, but without all the trappings and employees they had had before. Although he stayed with his parents, Bandi, as always, spent as little time at home as possible, especially since he had managed to get a job that took him far afield. The Veres travel agency, directly across from Gerbeaud's famous café on the Vörösmarty ter, one of Pest's most elegant squares, had hired him to make scenic and picturesque photographs of Budapest—its buildings and its daily life—to be reproduced in brochures. This work kept him very busy, for he was paid not per picture but per meter of 35mm film (26 negatives). Just as he used to occupy the family bathroom for hours soaking in the tub, now he monopolized it as his darkroom, and it was always festooned with long strips of film hung up to dry.

That summer Bandi photographed many of the notable sights of Budapest. Among them, a family friend remembers, were people sitting on the steps of the Pest quai, eating slices of watermelon. She recalls that Bandi made tender, bittersweet photographs of these people, who were too poor to sit and eat in the cafés along the adjacent Corso. The photos have disappeared.

The photographic highlight of Bandi's summer came with the International Jamboree that brought thousands of Boy Scouts from all over the world to Gödöllö, the town seventeen miles northeast of Budapest where the Hungarian kings had had their summer palace. Admiral Horthy now spent his summers at that palace, and it was he who invited the scouts to set up their tents in the royal park. Bandi's photographs of the Jamboree have not survived. But one photographer who saw the contact sheets in Paris the following winter recalls that the pictures weren't very exciting. Bandi had asked him to try to sell the photos to the French press, but he didn't succeed.

Whatever the restrictions on his contact with leftists, Bandi spent a great deal of time that summer with his old friend and fellow activist Csiki Weisz. Like Csiki, Bandi felt himself collared, leashed, and muzzled by his family and the government and was also eager to leave. Finally they decided to strike out for Paris together, and soon after the Jamboree closed on August 15, they boarded a Danube steamer. Csiki had no money, but Bandi had accumulated enough money to pay their fares as far as Vienna.*

Because Harald Lechenperg was off on another one of his trips to the East, Bandi and Csiki did not stay in his apartment. Instead, they stayed with a fat, warm and generous woman known to everyone simply as Tante Marthe. She and her equally fat and kindly sister had become good friends of Kassák's during his Viennese exile, and ever since then they had made their small apartment available as a sort of hostel for his followers, often—in those days when young leftist intellectuals were crisscrossing Europe in their search for a safe and stimulating haven and when Vienna was one of the most important way stations—bedding down as many as a dozen young people at any given time. Although Tante Marthe and her sister had no money, there was never any question of paying them for their hospitality. To feed everyone as cheaply as possible, they would serve an enormous bowl of white bean salad with oil and vinegar dressing for dinner.

To make some money for the next leg of their trip, Bandi got a job as a photographer for a news-photo agency that supplied photos on a daily basis to several Viennese newspapers. He went out on routine assignments, covering events of mostly local interest, but he didn't work very hard. Instead, he spent a lot of time with Csiki, wandering aimlessly through the streets and sitting in the parks. When, after a month or so, they became impatient to move on, Bandi didn't have enough money for their train fares; so he took several of the agency's cameras and pawned them, thoughtfully leaving the pawn tickets on a desk in the office. He supplemented this money by paying a visit to Rozsi Strasser, who was such a loyal customer of the Friedmanns' dressmaking salon that even after moving to Vienna she would return to Budapest a couple of times each year to have new clothes made. As a letter from Julia had asked her to do, Mrs. Strasser gave Bandi a loan. Well bankrolled, he and Csiki set off for Paris.

---

* It is not true, as has been claimed, that because they were due for compulsory service in the Hungarian army Bandi and Csiki had to leave Budapest clandestinely or on tourist visas that authorized only brief visits abroad. There was no compulsory military service in Hungary at that time. Bandi and Csiki would have been eligible for regular exit visas. Indeed, the Hungarian government was quick to grant exit visas to known leftists, for it was glad to get them out of the country. Bandi left Hungary with a passport valid for ten years. U.S. State Department records indicate that he still held his Hungarian passport in 1940.

The train pulled into the Gare de l'Est on a cold, rainy September day. Neither of the young men knew Paris, and neither of them spoke more than a little French. But Bandi, who at this point began to call himself "André,"* wasn't worried. During his year at Dephot he had easily become fluent in German; he learned languages quickly and would soon master French.

André and Csiki had been told that the best place to find a cheap room was in the Latin Quarter, near the Sorbonne. They found one on the top floor of the Hôtel Lhomond on the Rue Lhomond, between the Panthéon and the Rue Mouffetard. It was a poor hotel, too sleazy even to be listed in either the telephone book or the business directory. The room had faded, densely patterned floral wallpaper, two enameled iron bedsteads, a dilapidated armoire, and a flimsy washstand, with a cheap pitcher and basin. But they weren't bothered by the austerity, for the room was to be nothing more than a base of operations. They intended to spend as little time in it as possible.

Of all the cities in the world, Paris must surely be the worst in which to be hungry and penniless—as André and Csiki found themselves when their money ran out after a few weeks. Practically every block has its boulangerie, its patisserie, its butcher, its charcuterie, its cheese store, its fruit and vegetable market, its café, its restaurant. The aromas alone could drive a hungry man mad.

When they could get them, which was by no means every day, André and Csiki lived on fried potatoes and eggs that they cooked on a small alcohol burner in their hotel room. When they couldn't buy potatoes and eggs, couldn't get credit in any stores or restaurants, and couldn't borrow any money, André would try—usually successfully—to charm a Hungarian chocolate vendor he knew into giving him some chocolate on credit. And when even that failed, he would, as a last resort, fall back on his Berlin trick of subsisting on sugar dissolved in water.

---

* Bandi's name appears as "André Friedmann" on his Deutsche Hochschule für Politik registration card, but he didn't make regular use of the name until he reached Paris.

As their desperation and their command of French increased, André and Csiki grew bolder. Unwilling to beg and unable to earn, they decided to steal. They would locate a grocery store with a single clerk, ask for something that had to be fetched from a high shelf, and, while their victim was up on a ladder, stuff their pockets and run. The plan worked quite satisfactorily.

The next step was to get bread. One day, standing outside a bakery, André hatched a plan. He told Csiki, "I'll go in and lean over the counter, blocking that horrible fat woman's view. While I ask her for some kind of fancy roll that she won't have, stand behind me and push as many rolls into your pocket as you can. She won't notice you because I'll have all her attention."

Once in the shop, André broke into his voluble, heavily accented, ungrammatical French. Behind him Csiki grabbed some big rolls, but their size and his nerves hindered his efforts to get them into his pockets. Looking up, he caught the reflection of the *patronne*'s vigilant eye in a mirror hanging on the wall directly across from her. Dropping the rolls, he kicked André and ran. André, not immediately grasping the situation, stood there for a moment until he heard the *patronne* begin to scream, "Police! Voleurs!" He caught up with Csiki, and for what seemed like hours they ran frantically, knowing that if they were caught they would be deported as undesirable aliens. They ran until they collapsed from exhaustion, and by then the police were nowhere in sight.

Having realized that stealing from food stores was too dangerous, André and Csiki decided to try fishing in the Seine. They had spent many hours strolling along the quais, watching the old men who patiently dangled their lines in the river, and speculating on the miserable quality of fish that would swim in such dirty water. Now, however, they could no longer afford such squeamishness. Borrowing a rod from a friend, they sat down on the quai to wait for a nibble, and eventually their enterprise was rewarded with two tiny, muddy fish, which they stealthily exchanged for two larger ones they found in the bucket of a sleeping fisherman. Back at their hotel, when they discovered that they had no fat to cook the fish in, André set out to borrow some and returned with a bottle of brilliantine that a neighbor assured him was a perfectly acceptable substitute for cooking grease. The meal for which they had had such high hopes ended up tasting of river mud and cheap perfume. In contrast to such nauseating fare, starvation seemed not so bad.

Soon André was forced to swallow his pride and look up some of his older acquaintances and relatives in Paris. After having ruined Fritz Goro's photographs in Vienna, it must have been with some trepidation that he got in touch with him, but Goro, who was living in photographer Hug Block's rather luxurious apartment while Block was away on vacation, was forgiving and took pity on André's predicament, which was really only a little worse than his own. He invited André home for a meal or two, and although the meals consisted mostly of potatoes that he had to help Goro's wife peel, André was grateful.

Another place in which he occasionally sought refuge was the apartment of his mother's cousin, Szeren Fischer, whose husband Béla, a Rumanian artist and interior designer, had fallen in love with Paris while working on the Rumanian pavilion at the 1925 Exposition des Arts Décoratifs. Béla was a dreamer, never very successful or concerned about success, and the family lived very simply on a street near the Madeleine that was known mainly for its prostitutes. (André used to joke that he liked to visit so that he could ogle the girls promenading in the street.) An enthusiastic amateur photographer, Béla had built a darkroom in the family's apartment, and André would go there sometimes to process his film, eat a meal, borrow some money (which Béla could ill afford to lend), or simply to see Béla and Szeren's little daughter Susie, on whom he would continue to lavish affection, gifts, and advice for the rest of his life.

Even when André managed to borrow some money, it never lasted very long. Remembering the lesson he had learned from the Berlin landlady who had turned him out as soon as he paid his bill, he was very reluctant to spend money on practical necessities. If he had any money, he felt compelled—in a gesture that was surely half genuine generosity and half ostentation—to spend it on food and wine for his friends. There can be no doubt that he was very generous, but it seems likely that André, the homeless refugee, used his generosity to win and hold the friends whom he so desperately needed in order to maintain some sense of security, of belonging, of being needed. On the other hand, he was a committed socialist. With all his borrowing, sharing, pooling of resources—even stealing—perhaps he felt that he was simply putting socialism into action in his own small-scale way. In any case, André always seemed to need more money, and, after he had been in Paris long enough to meet some relatively prosperous émigrés, he perfected certain ingenious techniques for borrowing it.

In Montparnasse he ran into Geza Korvin, an old schoolfriend from Budapest, and suggested that they look for a soft touch. André, who had developed quite a reputation for borrowing, knew that anyone who saw him coming would try to avoid him, so he suggested that he walk up one side of the street while Korvin walked up the other: if a prospective victim crossed to avoid André, he would be caught by Korvin. The scheme worked well.

Korvin and André would sometimes meet for breakfast at the Café Capulade, on whose huge zinc bar every morning there was a basket piled high with croissants. They would each take a croissant, eat half of it, and make sure that the waiter noticed it. Then, as soon as he turned his back, they would stuff the remaining halves into their mouths, grab another croissant each, and gobble half of it, so that when he turned around again, they would seem to be still holding the original croissant. Repeating this procedure several times, they would end up with three or four croissants for the price of one.

Of course André and Csiki could never pay the bill for their hotel room, but fortunately the law did not allow a proprietor to evict his tenants for failure to pay. He could, however, turn off their electricity, gas, and water, and, if that failed to produce results, he could confiscate their belongings as collateral. Although the two young men would give the proprietor of the Hôtel Lhomond a few francs now and then to persuade him that they weren't total deadbeats, week by week they fell more and more hopelessly behind in their payments, and eventually they began removing their shoes to sneak in and out. When caught, André would turn on his charm and wriggle out of the predicament with stories of rich aunts in America who had promised to send him money, of checks that were due to arrive from Budapest any day, and of prospects of work. After a few months of living like this, their friends announced that André and Csiki had established a new record for non-payment of rent. Pleased by this notoriety, they pressed their luck even further. Always eager to help anyone in trouble, they would offer asylum in their room to every homeless émigré they encountered. As word of this got around, their room began to overflow with Hungarian photographers, Rumanian painters, Polish students—whoever needed a place to sleep. The sagging beds were seldom empty, day or night, and those who couldn't find room in one of them simply stretched out on the floor. Often, when André and Csiki came in at the end of a late evening, they would have to wake up the occupants of their beds, but one night they found two gentlemen with heavy black beards, who, when they were awakened, remained silent and refused to budge. The next morning the two strangers rose, dressed, and departed—all without saying a word or even acknowledging the presence of anyone else in the room. No one had any idea who they were. Perhaps the proprietor, taking his cue from André and Csiki's casual attitude toward sharing their room, had decided to cut his losses by renting the room for a night to two travelers so desperate for lodging that they were willing to put up with such peculiar conditions.

Finally, the proprietor lost all patience. Early one morning, while Csiki was still lying in bed, he burst in and proceeded to remove everything he could find. Fortunately, André had gone out very early that morning with his camera—so at least they would still have one suit between them, as well as the means of making some money, if André ever got an opportunity to use the camera. They stayed on at the hotel for a few days, but it was a terrible nuisance that only one of them could go out at a time. Finally, realizing that the proprietor was angry enough to report them to the police, they decided to "shoot the moon"—to sneak out of the hotel, leaving behind all their impounded possessions and all their debts, never to return. André managed to borrow some clothes and shoes for Csiki, and one at a time they slipped quietly out of the Hôtel Lhomond.

After that they would occupy a hotel room for a few weeks, until they had stretched to the limit their excuses for not paying, then "shoot the moon" and move on to new quarters. They grew accustomed to having no possessions and living, as it were, off the land. This worked until one wily proprietor raided their room in the middle of the night and confiscated their shoes, so that they couldn't leave without paying him. In desperation, André cabled Imre Rona, a Hungarian émigré not much older than himself who had a photo agency in Amsterdam and who, on his frequent trips to Paris, would give André small loans and take him out for big dinners; Rona bailed them out.

André was trying hard all the while to find work, making the rounds of newspapers, magazines, and photo agencies, but, except for his photographs of Trotsky, his portfolio was not impressive. Moreover, the competition was very stiff, for half the émigrés in Paris seemed to be trying to make a living as photographers. For the first few months André's efforts to find work were completely in vain. To save face, he would tell his friends that he considered the need to work an utterly absurd nuisance, something dreamt up by the small-minded bourgeoisie. And when he saw how hard some of his friends worked for very little money, he would chide them, saying, "You're ridiculous. Why do you work at these little things that bring in no money? You must wait for the big things, the big event, which you can sell. You work so hard now—and for what? You're still starving."

As poor as they were, André and Csiki—like all the émigrés who sought refuge in France—had to maintain a desperate charade of respectability for the authorities. The law required them to go to the Préfecture de Police at regular intervals to demonstrate that they had some substantial means of support, yet as refugees they were not allowed to have full-time jobs. France was still in the throes of the Depression, and it was unthinkable that foreigners should be given work until all Frenchmen were once again employed. The refugees had two legal choices: they could take on free-lance assignments, or they could demonstrate that they were receiving money from friends or relatives living outside France. Since few could get either money from home or enough free-lance work to support themselves, they resorted to tricks. They would, for instance, have their families send them money orders that they would show to the authorities and then return uncashed. Or someone would borrow a thousand-franc note from a rich friend, hold on to it just long enough to get his papers renewed, and then return it—or pass it on to another needy refugee. One such note is said to have passed through some forty hands, becoming well worn and looking suspiciously familiar to the police inspector, before it found its way back into the hands of its original owner. However poor a refugee in Paris might be, he simply couldn't afford not to keep his papers in proper order. One needed a valid *carte d'identité* for all kinds of everyday transactions, from renting a hotel room to pawning possessions at the city-run Crédit Municipal.

André did his best to hold on to his camera through thick and thin, so that he would have it if an assignment finally came along. Furthermore, the camera hanging from his shoulder announced to the world that he was a photographer, or at least an aspiring one. It identified him as a man with a profession, and it was an enviable status symbol. But sometimes things got so bad that he was forced to pawn it, usually at the Crédit Municipal on the Boulevard de Port-Royal. George Orwell, who had recently pawned some things there, described the interior as a "large, bare room like a school class-room, with a counter and rows of benches." When a customer entered, he deposited his pledge on the counter, was assigned a number, and sat down to wait. Eventually a clerk would call out, for everyone in the room to hear, "Numéro such and such, will you take x number of francs?" It was take it or leave it; anyone who tried to argue would have his pledge instantly refused. When André's less tactful friends asked him what had happened to his camera, he would reply, in Parisian argot, that it was "chez ma tante" (at my aunt's house) or "au clou" (on the nail), referring to the nails on which the numbers were hung in the pawnshop.

During those bad times when his camera was in hock, André grew discouraged and depressed, fearing that he would never be able to develop his career, that he would be trapped in a life of poverty, hunger, and flight. Everyone knew that war was certain to come sooner or later, and André was afraid that war would mean the end for him, a stateless alien. Already, what he found in the streets around his hotel was not greatly different from what he had left behind in Berlin. Paris—and especially the university quarter—was infested by uniformed fascist leagues, as eager for violence as were the Nazis. Fortunately, no single league was as strong as the Nazis were in Germany; factional disputes kept the royalist Action Française, the Mussolini-inspired Solidarité Française, the Bonapartist Jeunesses Patriotes, and the militaristic, anti-republican, anti-Semitic Croix de Feu as divided as the parties of the Left.

The members of the leagues were mostly students and fanatics, but the economic and political situation was leading more and more of the normally conservative bourgeoisie to seek radical solutions. Ever since the Depression had finally hit France in 1931, the French had been toppling one government after another in a frantic search for leaders who could extricate them from the crisis, and when all this shifting of power led to more chaos rather than less, many Frenchmen—fearing especially for the value of the franc—simply lost faith in the democratic process and began to long for an efficient, benevolent dictatorship.

On top of everything else, in this atmosphere of instability and low-grade hysteria, the Parisians found their beloved city invaded by Germans. World War I had ended only fifteen years earlier, and many French men and women still hated on principle anyone who spoke German. It didn't matter that these Germans and German-speaking émigrés from Eastern Europe were peaceful refugees from Nazism and not an invading army. They were foreigners, Jews, and intellectuals—all of them Communists, or so it seemed.

The refugees now had to find their own place within Paris and create a sense of community for themselves. Most of them, having no furniture, lived in the cheap hotels of the Left Bank. Montparnasse became Paris's foreign quarter, its German and Eastern European ghetto, where one heard more German, Hungarian, Russian, Czech, Rumanian, and Polish than French.

The cafés of Montparnasse, and especially those at or near the intersection of the Boulevards Montparnasse and Raspail, were the social centers of the émigré colony. Foremost among them was the Café du Dôme, whose caned chairs and small, round, marble-topped tables spilled far out onto the sidewalk of the southwest corner of the intersection. The Dôme was to Paris more or less what the Romanisches Café had been to Berlin—émigré center, meeting place, employment bureau, forum for the latest ideas, and home away from home of the avant-garde.

Because their hotel rooms were small and shabby, the refugees couldn't bear to spend much time in them, let alone entertain friends in them—and so the cafés became their communal living rooms and social clubs. During the day they went to read the newspapers, to play chess, to write novels, diaries, articles, and letters; indeed, as one of the services included in the price of a cup of coffee, the management provided stationery printed with the café's letterhead. In the evening they went to the cafés to meet their friends, to argue about art and politics, and to try to dispel the feelings of loneliness, hopelessness, and vulnerability that could attack even the most resilient and enterprising. Surrounded by his friends, André could at least temporarily banish his haunting sense of futility and begin to laugh. Only those who knew him best ever saw him as anything but light-hearted, charming, resourceful, and optimistic.

But the cafés were oases of sociability in a hostile city. For the most part, language barriers and the xenophobia of the French kept the refugees isolated in a world of their own. One organization that both typified that isolation and tried to overcome it was the Schutzverband Deutscher Schriftsteller im Exil (Protective Association of German Writers in Exile), whose first public function, held in September 1933, was a German-French Friendship Evening. When Alfred Kantorowicz, one of the founders of the SDSE, met André in Spain during the Civil War, he recalled having seen him at meetings of the SDSE, which were held in the basement-level Café Mephisto on the Boulevard St.-Germain. Since André spoke German and had never completely abandoned his ambition to be a writer, his attendance was natural. Officially the SDSE was politically neutral, but it was in fact run by a Communist caucus that included Kantorowicz, Arthur Koestler, Egon Erwin Kisch, Gustav Regler, and Bodo Uhse, with all of whom André would eventually have some contact. At a typical meeting, one of the caucus members or a guest writer might read from his works, or else someone would lecture on issues or work of current concern: Kisch on "Theoretical and Practical Questions of Reportage," Kantorowicz on "Literature That Prepares for War," or Paul Westheim on the political photomontagist John Heartfield.

The meetings of the SDSE certainly satisfied some of André's need for exposure to eminent intellectuals, but for making friends he depended above all on the Dôme. Among the struggling young émigré photographers whom he met there was Gisèle Freund, who had fled Germany on a few hours' notice after learning one morning in May 1933 that she was to be arrested that night. She smuggled out, at great risk, her photographs of fellow students who had been beaten up by the Nazis. In Paris, Freund, who had been a student at the famous Institute for Social Research in Frankfurt, studied sociology at the Sorbonne and supported herself by making photographic portraits and reportages, finally combining her two pursuits in her thesis on the sociology of photography in nineteenth-century France. Freund went on to a distinguished career as a photojournalist and historian of photography. During the late 1940s and the early 1950s, she renewed her friendship with André, who by then was Capa, and she became associated with Magnum, the photo agency of which he was one of the founders.

Another young photographer whom André met at this time was Hans Namuth, now famous for his portraits of artists. In July 1933, the eighteen-year-old Namuth was arrested by the Gestapo for distributing Communist leaflets in Essen, thrown in jail for about ten days, and released only when his father appeared at the police headquarters in his SA uniform. In September he went to Paris on a two-week tourist visa and stayed, living in the Latin Quarter and working as a dishwasher. He first met André on October 22, 1933, his twentieth birthday; to celebrate, they and a few other friends pooled their meager funds and made the rounds of the cafés.

More important to André—then and for the rest of his life—was a brilliant, sensitive, amusing, polyglot, multi-talented Pole named David Szymin (pronounced as if spelled "Shimmin"), who was known to all his friends as "Chim" (pronounced "Shim"). Born in Warsaw in 1911, Chim was the son of a leading publisher of Hebrew and Yiddish books. In addition to a precocious interest in literature, politics, and Judaism, Chim had shown such talent as a pianist that until his late teens he seriously considered making a career of music; but because his father wanted him to study the technical side of publishing so that he could join the family firm, he went off to Leipzig in the fall of 1929 to begin a three-year program in printing techniques, graphic arts, and photography. In 1932 he made his way to Paris, where he enrolled at the Sorbonne to study chemistry, intending to prepare for research on printing inks and lithography. But soon he found himself in the same predicament André had gotten into in Berlin; his family was so badly hurt by the economic crisis that they could no longer afford to send him money for tuition and living expenses. Instead, they suggested he get in touch with David Rapaport, a family friend who ran a photo agency in Paris. Chim did so and soon found himself a committed and modestly successful photojournalist.

It is difficult to imagine two young men less likely to become best friends than André and Chim. André was gregarious, rambunctious, and quite uninterested in anything to do with Judaism. Chim, on the other hand, was shy and courtly, and he felt the weight of Jewish tradition on his shoulders. He had the temperament of a rabbi or of a Talmudic scholar, and the analytical mind of a mathematician or of a chess player (which he was). Although André mingled with serious writers, he preferred to read mystery stories, while Chim, who was fluent in German, French, and English, favored James Joyce and Romain Rolland. And, in contrast to André's dark, romantic good looks, Chim's looks were decidedly owlish. He was of medium height but seemed short; his face was round, his forehead was high, his nose beakish, his lips full, and his eyesight so bad that he had to wear glasses with very thick lenses. And yet Chim was blessed with that wonderful, elusive quality of angelic physical charm that is given only to those who are both very intelligent and very gentle.

André and Chim soon became inseparable—*copains*, chums, almost brothers. Their friends spoke of them as the sun and the moon. But André did not

Robert Capa's parents, Dezsö and Julia Friedmann, Budapest, 1910.

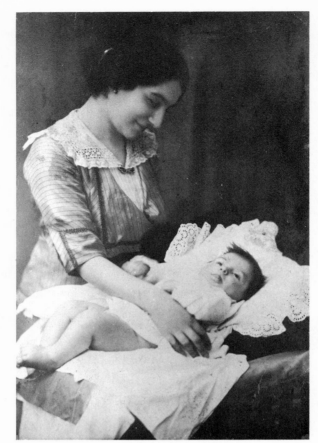

Capa and his mother, 1913–14.

c. 1914.

c. 1916.

Capa with his parents and family friends, Budapest, c. 1917.

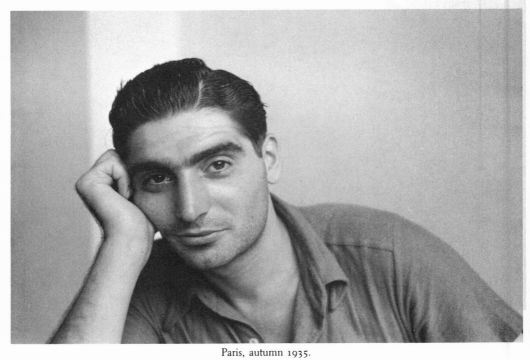

Capa's student registration card, Berlin, 1931.

Paris, autumn 1935.

Paris, 1934–35.

Gerda Taro and Capa, Paris, autumn 1935.

Gerda at the Guadalajara front, Spain, July 1937.

Gerda, Paris, 1936.

Gerda at the Córdoba front, Spain, September 1936.

Gerda's monument in Père-Lachaise Cemetery, Paris.

dominate the friendship; on the contrary, the two young men saw themselves as very different but equal. André had unbounded respect for Chim's intellect, for his moral judgment, and for his eye. He always said that Chim was the better photographer, and took Chim's advice and criticism very seriously. Furthermore, when they met, Chim was already far more successful than André, for he spoke French well enough to break into French journalism and had managed to get a job as a staff photographer for the Communist weekly newspaper *Regards*, thereby setting an example for André to live up to. For his part, André teased Chim into relaxing a bit, imparted some of his Hungarian charm, and taught him to get along with all kinds of people—all of which was of great help to Chim in his work, for, like André, he specialized in very direct, candid photographs and so had to be able to put his subjects at ease.

André and Chim had such a profound influence on each other that if one looks through a collection of their early photographs, it is often very difficult to guess who took which. From André, Chim acquired self-confidence and learned to be aggressive enough to get close to his subjects. From Chim, André learned that although a photojournalist has to be aggressive, and even callous, in order to get into position to take the most dramatic photographs, all his efforts will be wasted unless, at the actual moment of taking his picture, he can replace his boldness with sensitivity and tenderness.

During the first several months of their friendship, Chim kept telling André about his extraordinary friend Henri Cartier-Bresson. But somehow Cartier-Bresson always seemed to be away or busy. Quite tall, with a large head that appeared to balance rather precariously on his thin neck, and with eyes full of intelligence and vulnerability, Cartier-Bresson was, indeed, an extraordinary young man. Born in 1908, he was the son of a wealthy Norman family in the thread and textile business. After studying at the great Lycée Condorcet (whose alumni included Marcel Proust and André Malraux), Cartier-Bresson went on to Cambridge in the fall of 1928 to read literature for a year.

He had used a Brownie box camera as a child, and during the 1920s he had developed a passionate interest in painting, studying in 1927–28 with the Cubist André Lhote. It was in 1931, after contracting blackwater fever on a hunting expedition in the Ivory Coast and returning to Marseilles to recuperate, that he became really serious about photography. He was attracted to Surrealism, and in the super-realism of photography, which froze actions in a way alien to ordinary experience, revealing odd and disturbing or humorous juxtapositions, he found what was for him the perfect medium. Because he was independently wealthy, Cartier-Bresson could afford to pursue his Surrealistic visions in France, Spain, Belgium, Italy, and Germany during 1932 and 1933.

It is no wonder that it took Chim several months to arrange a meeting in Paris between André and Cartier-Bresson, but once it took place, they became fast friends.

As a wealthy, highly educated, almost aristocratic Frenchman, Cartier-Bresson appeared to be precisely the sort with whom most émigrés could never hope to form an intimate friendship. But he was an independent spirit, a rebel from his class; he didn't care that André and Chim were foreigners. Like Chim, Cartier-Bresson admired Joyce and Rolland, and, in addition to shared tastes in literature, the two young men had the same reserve, the same delicacy, the same inclination toward secrecy, the same grace and wit. And they both felt the need to have contact with André's untrammeled high spirits, his optimism, his unorthodoxy, his street-smartness, his charm, his ease with people, his spontaneity—all qualities that are refreshing and often enviable to those who are intellectual, studied, self-conscious, and analytical.

When André, Chim, and Cartier-Bresson sat at the Dôme together, they rarely talked about photography—certainly not in terms of techniques or aesthetics. André much preferred to talk about the girls he was going out with—or wanted to go out with. When they discussed photography at all, it was mostly about ideas for stories, about making contact with editors, about making money. Chim had a regular but small income, André had practically no income at all, and Cartier-Bresson, out of pride and political conviction, wanted to be independent of his family's wealth. Although he was trained as an artist and always thought of himself as an artist who happened to use a camera, he wanted to be published in the pictorial press. The wily André advised him, "If you are labeled a Surrealist photographer, you won't go any further. You won't have an assignment; you'll be like a hothouse plant. Call yourself a photojournalist and then do whatever you like."

But the favorite topic of conversation among the three friends was politics, about which they had endless and lively arguments. Chim would almost certainly have had to be a Communist Party member in order to have his job on the staff of *Regards*, and Cartier-Bresson is said to have had the kind of enthusiasm for the Left that only someone from the upper classes who feels guilty about his privileges can manifest. One of André's friends from that time recalls that it was said that Cartier-Bresson would not answer the telephone in the morning until he had read *L'Humanité* and fully mastered the official line for the day. Nevertheless, his feelings about the party must have been complicated by its official denunciation of Surrealism as a decadent form of idealism and Freudianism. As for André, he was still basically a skeptic, although the French party's war against fascism drew him closer to Communism than he had been in Berlin. Like Chim and Cartier-Bresson, he went to meetings of the party-affiliated Association des Ecrivains et des Artistes Révolutionnaires, but he didn't work for the Communist press until the Communists united with the more moderate parties of the Left in a front against fascism, and he never joined the Communist Party. When one of his friends would put pressure on him, telling him that unless he joined, the sincerity of his hatred of fascism could be called into question, André would evade the real issue by replying flippantly, "The girls in the party are too ugly. They all have ugly legs. How can I spend my time with them?" The truth of the matter, however, was that Kassák, Korsch, and his own observations in Berlin had taught him that the Communists were not to be trusted unreservedly. They had furthered the cause of Nazism in Germany, and, as long as they were obsessed with fomenting dissension that could precipitate a revolution, there was no telling what damage they might do in France.

6

André didn't have to wait long to see the kind of havoc the Communists could create, for during January 1934, both the Communists and the fascists did their best to exploit the repercussions of the Stavisky scandal—in which several high government officials were implicated in attempts to cover up a huge swindle involving municipal bonds—as a pretext for revolution. Demonstrations that ended as riots became an almost daily affair, and at the end of the month Premier Camille Chautemps was forced to resign.

While Paris was in pandemonium, however, André's own situation became a bit more settled, for he got a job with Hug Block. Among the first to make professional use of the Leica, Block was publishing his reportages in all the most prestigious French, British, and German magazines. Because he had so many contacts in the European press, he founded a small agency—the Agence Hug Block—to distribute the work of other photographers along with his own, and he hired Fritz Goro to manage it. Block himself was so much in demand as a photographer that he needed an assistant to carry his equipment, help with the developing and printing of his work, and sometimes even take photographs at his direction. Despite Goro's bad experience with André in Vienna, he suggested that Block hire him, and although Block was not particularly impressed by the young Hungarian's portfolio, he gave André the job, "off the books," of course.

As Capa later told the story, he began to work for Hug Block on Tuesday, February 6, 1934, the day on which the Chambre des Députés was to reconvene to vote on the new cabinet. The fascists had announced that they would mount a demonstration so huge that while the new premier, Edouard Daladier, was proposing his cabinet inside the Palais Bourbon, the Chambre would hear the shouts of the protesters massed outside. The various factions of the Left mobilized for enormous counterdemonstrations.

The day was unseasonably warm and humid, threatening rain. In anticipation of violence, municipal employees removed from around the trunks of all the trees near the Palais Bourbon the heavy iron grilles that Parisian mobs have traditionally ripped up and hurled at charging troops of police. At Hug Block's apartment in a large fin-de-siècle building on the Right Bank just off the Pont Mirabeau, friends stopped by or telephoned to report the latest developments. Finally, shortly before six o'clock, Block told André to grab a camera and lots of film and come with him. They drove to the Cours-la-Reine, parked their car, and then advanced toward the Place de la Concorde on foot. The sun had gone down, and the temperature had fallen rapidly. An icy fog hung over the thousands of protesters who were massing in the square. On the Pont de la Concorde, which led across the Seine to the Palais Bourbon, were stationed six big police trucks, a cordon of foot policemen five deep, and two hundred mounted police. At first the restless crowd was strangely quiet, but soon groups began to chant slogans and to sing the "Marseillaise." The police repulsed several attempts to cross the bridge. Then, at about 6:20, the crowd surrounded a bus, forced its passengers to get off, broke its windows, and set it on fire. When the police and firemen tried to extinguish the fire, the mob pelted them with stones and anything else they could get their hands on, including metal chairs and grilles from the adjacent Tuileries gardens. Within a few minutes the riot had turned into a full-scale battle. Mounted police with drawn sabers charged into the crowd, and the rioters attacked man and horse alike with broomsticks in which they had implanted razor blades.

The scene must have evoked in André intense memories of a similar, though considerably smaller and tamer, riot in Budapest, and it was surely for the joy of vicarious revenge that he cheered when he saw a rioter hit a mounted policeman squarely with a hurled rock. Block immediately scolded him, explaining that the police were defending the republic against the fascist enemy—but André's reaction had had nothing to do with the politics of the moment.

Once darkness fell, the situation on the square quickly grew worse. Since the rioters had knocked the bulbs out of most of the streetlamps, the only light came from torches and fires, casting grotesque shadows onto the walls of surrounding buildings. The rioters regrouped for a determined charge on the bridge. The police fired. Several rioters were killed, many others wounded. Nearby cafés were transformed into first-aid stations. Snipers climbed up into the bare chestnut trees along the Cours-la-Reine in order to get better shots at the police on the bridge. André wanted to get closer to the action and, apparently giving no thought to his safety, started to push into the crowd. But Block wisely counseled him, "There is nothing you can do except get badly hurt. It's too dark to photograph," and André prudently heeded his advice. This was André's first lesson in calculating a risk to his life for the sake of his work. By midnight the rioters and police alike were exhausted, and when the casualties were counted, sixteen rioters and one policeman were found to have been killed, 500 rioters and 400 policemen to have been wounded. Lesser disturbances continued for several days.

The Soviet Comintern was slow to digest the lesson of Germany. Finally, however, in June 1934, pragmatism demanded that partisan differences within the Left be put aside temporarily, at least long enough to defeat fascism, and Moscow accordingly directed the French Communists to make overtures to the Socialists. The latter, having grown accustomed to the attacks, slander, and treachery of the Communists, feared a wolf in sheep's clothing. Nevertheless, a month later, on July 27, the Socialists and the Communists signed a pact of unity—the foundation for the Front Populaire, whose meetings and celebrations André was to photograph extensively.

While the French Left was consolidating itself, André was engaging in his own battles with Hug Block. He resented having to work for Block when he wanted to be acquiring a name—and the rewards of fame—for himself. Furthermore, he made no secret of his resentment. Block recalls that André was openly arrogant, scornful, and sarcastic toward him. Many of Block's reportages had a distinctly leftist edge of social criticism, but André accused Block of not being committed enough to the Left. Then he accused Block of cheating him out of some money, and there were disagreements about who deserved the credit for certain story ideas. Block found André tough, cynical, and sharp. Inevitably they clashed. Eventually they had several big fights—real explosions with a lot of shouting—and came close to hitting each other. After a few months, André left and went his own way.

It must have been sometime around the spring of 1934 when André Friedmann met André Kertész, who was then one of the most successful and highly respected photographers in France or, indeed, in all Europe. Like Block, Kertész belonged to that small circle of photographers whose work was in constant demand by the editors of every major continental and British picture magazine. But while André had apparently been jealous of Block, he found in Kertész a man who could follow Kassák, Kepes, and Guttmann in his succession of father figures and mentors, all of them Hungarian. Born in Budapest in 1894, Kertész bought his first camera in 1912, and, while serving in the Austro-Hungarian army during World War I, made a touching, intimate documentation of the everyday life of soldiers. After the war, though working in a stock brokerage, he continued to photograph, publishing his work for the first time in 1917. Having decided to make a career of photography, Kertész moved to Paris in 1925 and, within a few years, had a large circle of friends that included Mondrian, Colette, Brancusi, and Man Ray, of whom he made memorable portraits. In addition to portraiture and his sensitive observations of Parisian life, Kertész pursued his career in photojournalism. In 1928 he bought a Leica and found it to be easy to handle, inconspicuous, and fast. The resulting photographs were so beautiful and conveyed such a powerful sense of immediacy and intimacy that editors were captivated by them, even though they generally disapproved of small-format negatives, which were difficult to retouch. When V*u*, the French answer to the great German picture magazines, was founded that year, Kertész became one of its principal contributors. During the early 1930s, he greatly influenced many of the young photographers working in Paris, among them Henri Cartier-Bresson, Chim, Brassaï (whom Kertész instructed in the techniques of night photography), and André Friedmann.

When André asked Kertész to help him find work, Kertész gave him some printing to do, but the results were not satisfactory. Furthermore, André was irresponsible and unpunctual; if it was raining when he woke up in the morning, he was likely to stay in bed. But, although Kertész was disappointed in André's performance in the darkroom, he could see that he had great potential as a photographer. For the moment, however, he was able to get him only a few unimportant assignments from small photo agencies.

Through the first half of the summer of 1934, André drifted from small job to small job—assisting in a darkroom here, perhaps selling an occasional picture there. But in August the kind of big job that he insisted was the only kind worth doing came his way at last. Two cousins, Kurt and Hans Steinitz, both émigrés from Germany, had recently founded a photo agency, Agence Centrale. Hans wrote the texts and captions for the picture stories, while Kurt handled distribution. Since neither of them knew anything about the technical side of photography, they hired as their darkroom technician a Hungarian named Taci Czigany, who happened to be a very good friend of André's. It was either Taci or Gisèle Freund, a cousin of the Steinitzes, who told André that Agence Centrale was looking for a photographer to do a reportage on the newly fashionable Riviera resort of St.-Tropez. The agency couldn't afford to pay the fee and expenses that a well-established photographer would demand, so they were looking for someone young, with talent, who would do the job more for the experience than for the money. Hans Steinitz recalls that André gave the impression of having a deep-rooted conviction that he could do what he set out to do. And he had an irresistible smile. With his charm and his apparent determination to succeed, he must have seemed perfect for the job. The Steinitzes gave him an advance to cover his expenses, equipped him with a fine, medium-format Plaubel Makina camera—then favored by the press because it was very compact when folded up and because it took a pack of twelve sheet films instead of single plates—and sent him off to the Riviera for a few days.

A week or so later, there was still no sign of André back in Paris, nor had Agence Centrale received any report on his progress or plans. The Steinitzes began to worry. Even after they cabled him there was no word from St.-Tropez. Finally a package from André arrived at the agency's office, but, inexplicably, it contained strips of 35mm film, not the sheets of film the Plaubel took. Furthermore, the images on the films were terribly amateurish; they were incorrectly exposed, badly lighted, and awkwardly composed. They were, in short, unfit for publication. The Steinitzes felt they had been betrayed. They were also, quite naturally, anxious about their Plaubel camera.

When André eventually returned to Paris, he was full of excuses and explanations. The Riviera was horribly expensive, much more so even than Paris. In order to get the real feel of St.-Tropez he had had to spend a great deal of money. His advance had lasted no time at all and he had been forced to pawn the Plaubel, but he still didn't have enough money. Then, one day, he left his clothes and his Leica on the beach while he went in for a swim, and when he came out, he found that everything had been stolen. Somehow or other he managed to borrow another Leica, which he proceeded to ruin by using it under water: he had been so captivated by what he had seen while swimming in the clear waters of the Mediterranean that he had decided to try to capture those beauties on film. The catalogue of disasters went on and on. André felt that he couldn't be held responsible for what happened, but his employers felt otherwise. As far as they could see, André had had a good time at their expense and had totally failed to keep his part of the bargain. They made it clear that they would never give him a job again.

Only a few months after it had been founded, Agence Centrale went out of business. Although André's St.-Tropez fiasco certainly contributed to the agency's collapse, his charm prevailed, as always, and Kurt Steinitz forgave him—at least to the extent of being willing to help him when he had film to develop and print. Since the Steinitzes had paid the rent for the agency's premises in advance and had invested in darkroom equipment, they decided to make their facilities available—for a fee—to photographers who didn't have their own darkrooms. For small jobs, André used his uncle Béla Fischer's darkroom, but his uncle had only a manual print drier, and even with the help of the entire family, including his little cousin Susie, there was a limit to how much André could handle there at any one time. The attraction of the Steinitz darkroom was that it had a drum drier that could handle large numbers of prints within a short time. André occasionally received large orders for prints from Pete Petersen, one of his friends from Dephot, who had a firm specializing in publicity photographs for the European automobile industry. Petersen and his partner soon found themselves traveling all over Europe for such clients as Rolls-Royce, Citroën, Shell, and Pirelli, but although Paris was more or less their base of operations, they didn't have their own darkroom there and they hired André to develop and print their work. Sometimes they would arrive in Paris in the late afternoon and inform him that they needed several hundred prints by early the next morning; he and Taci would work all night to get the job done. Darkroom work bored André but he was always glad to get work from Petersen, because he got paid well and immediately. Little of this money, however, seems to have found its way into the pockets of the Steinitzes, who kept many of André's negatives as security against money he owed them. He never paid them, and they eventually threw the negatives out.

7

In September 1934, Simon Guttmann visited Paris and looked up his young protégé. Guttmann, whose Hungarian passport made it possible for him to divide most of his time between Zurich and Berlin, told André that he could get him some work shooting publicity photographs for Swiss firms.

One of those assignments called for André to pose a pretty, blue-eyed, athletic, Germanic-looking girl with short, blond hair on a park bench. Since none of the girls he knew was suitable, he had to find someone who fit that description and persuade her to pose for him. Sitting at La Coupole one afternoon, drinking coffee with a few friends, was a girl who fit the bill perfectly; André went over to her and introduced himself. The young woman, whose name was Ruth Cerf, invited him to sit down and offered to buy him a cup of coffee; she could see just from looking at him that he had no money. André explained his problem: he needed her to pose for an hour or so in a little square in Montparnasse that had lots of trees. To reassure her that he was legitimate, he showed her a few photographs he had with him; finally she agreed to pose the following afternoon.* But since she really didn't like the idea of being alone with a guy she'd just met, she persuaded her roommate, Gerda Pohorylles, to come along. Gerda was to be the greatest love of André's life.

Gerda, who bore a remarkable resemblance to the then popular film actress Elisabeth Bergner, had hennaed light chestnut hair that she wore boyishly short. Her plucked eyebrows arched high over her gray-green eyes. She was short—about five feet, one inch—but she carried herself with such style that she seemed taller. And although she was as poor as André, she always managed to look quite elegant.

Gerda's personality was as striking as her appearance. Her friends describe her as having been vivacious, amusing, clever, and quick. She was *mignonne*. She seemed intensely alive. She had a lovely smile, and she seemed incredibly light on her feet, like a little deer. However, others— people who may have had some reason to be jealous of the happiness that she and André found together—emphasized the ambitious, cunning, and shrewd aspects of Gerda's character. To them she seemed pushy. Her smile seemed a bit calculated. She was a *garçon manqué*, a little red fox.

Gerda Pohorylles was born in Stuttgart on August 1, 1911. When she was about seventeen, she moved with her comfortably middle-class family to the Gohlis section of Leipzig, where her father, a Yugoslavian Jew, established a wholesale egg and vegetable business. Gerda attended a commercial school and learned secretarial skills, and through her boyfriend, a handsome young

---

* Ruth Cerf Berg recalls that just before World War II, after she had married and moved to Berne, she received a prospectus from a French-Swiss life-insurance company illustrated with photos for which she had posed for Capa in Paris. The first in the sequence of three photos showed her with a man and a child. The second showed her grief-stricken, with the child on her knees and a photo of her dead husband in her hands. The third showed her smiling as the mailman handed her an insurance check.

Russian medical student named Giorgio Kuritzkes, she became interested in leftist politics. It was in a leftist circle in Leipzig that she met Ruth Cerf.

When Hitler came to power in 1933, a friend of Gerda's family who lived in Stuttgart urged her to leave for Paris, paid for her train fare, and gave her money for French lessons. Gerda and Ruth Cerf went to Paris together that fall and found a room in a Finnish woman's apartment in Montparnasse. (They didn't like the woman, but the room was cheap and reasonably pleasant, and they had kitchen privileges.) Gerda got a part-time job working as a secretary for the child psychiatrist Dr. René Spitz. Ruth worked for an organization that helped émigrés. Neither of them made much money. On cold Sundays, when they didn't work, they would stay home in bed all day and read in order to conserve calories.

Many of Gerda and Ruth's friends from Leipzig made their way to Paris during 1933 and 1934, and before long the two young women had practically reconstituted their old circle, which began to frequent the Café Capulade, where André and Geza Korvin used to filch croissants. The circle's political mentor was Boris Goldenberg, who belonged to the Sozialistische Arbeiter Partei Deutschlands (German Socialist Workers' Party), a group of left-wing Socialists who had split from the Social Democratic Party to found their own party in 1931. Gerda and her friends didn't belong to the SAPD, but their political views, in general, were in sympathy with those of the party: liberal, socialist, and anti-Soviet.

Gerda's political affiliation, or lack of one, is a matter of dispute. Pierre Gassmann, who worked for several leftist publications as a photographer and darkroom man, says that he remembers seeing Gerda at meetings of the German Communist Party in Paris. Similarly, Maria Eisner, for whose photo agency Gerda worked from late 1935 until the middle of 1936, recalls that, although she always felt that Gerda was something of a petite bourgeoise at heart, she was nevertheless a "rabid and registered Communist," who tried to get André to join the party. On the other hand, Ruth Cerf states categorically that Gerda was never a member of the Communist Party.

The romance between André and Gerda did not blossom immediately. She already had a boyfriend (Willi Chardack, a medical student), and André may still have been involved with a German fashion photographer, Regina Langquarz, who worked for *Vogue* and signed her photographs "Relang." André and Relang went out together for a while during 1934, and she had a darkroom that he sometimes used. Like Gerda, Relang had short red hair, but Relang's was flaming red. When the black-haired André and the red-haired Relang walked down the street together, they made a very striking couple.

Although they did not at once become lovers, André and Gerda soon became good friends. He was accepted into the circle from Leipzig and she became, in effect, his manager. She advised him on how to dress and how to groom himself, she made lists of things he had to do, she evaluated story ideas for him, and she encouraged him to be more serious about his work. Her advice and encouragement were by no means wasted.

8

At about this same time André met a young man who went simply by the name Gorta and who worked for the photo agency Anglo-Continental, founded by Fritz Goro and Maria Eisner.* An aspiring journalist, Gorta was a striking, Dostoyevskian figure, very thin, with startlingly large eyes and an unruly mane of straight black hair that was always falling over his face. He was a very good-natured fellow, an astute observer of political events, and a good writer. During September 1934, Gorta received an assignment from Vu to go to the Saar and interview as many different sorts of people as possible— from leading industrialists to coal miners—and report on the prevailing moods and attitudes. He invited André to go along to take photographs.

The Saar was very much on the minds of Frenchmen that fall, for a plebiscite in which the Saarlanders would decide the political fate of their region had been scheduled for January 13, 1935. Since the end of World War I, the coal-rich, highly industrialized, predominantly German-speaking Saar had been administered by France under the supervision of the League of Nations. The Saarlanders were now to decide whether to maintain the status quo, to become officially part of France, or to reunite with Germany, which, although its economy was in no position to develop the Saar or to improve the hard lot of its miners and steel workers, promised full employment and higher wages.

---

* Gorta was the agency's liaison with the American agency Black Star, which began to represent André in the United States at this time.

André and Gorta arrived in Saarbrücken during the last week of September. As André photographed it and Gorta described it, the city might just as well have already been in Nazi Germany. Flags, banners, and posters bearing swastikas were everywhere. In the cafés, restaurants, stores, and factories, virtually everyone greeted their friends with the Nazi salute and a cry of "Heil Hitler!" Indeed, Gorta remarked that anyone who greeted another person simply by saying "Bonjour" or "Guten Tag" was, in effect, committing a revolutionary act.

André got some excellent shots of workers relaxing, talking, drinking— many of which were cropped for publication in Vu so that they looked as though they had been shot in extreme close-up, when, in fact, they were shot from some distance. On the main street of Saarbrücken, lined with Nazi banners so long that they reached practically from third-story windows to the sidewalk, he photographed pedestrians and bicyclists stopping to read the huge list of supporters that the Nazis posted to intimidate their opposition. (The lists were padded with the names of thousands of people who were long since dead, and even many of the living signed up only out of fear.) And while Gorta interviewed them, André took pictures of the leaders of all the pro- and counterunification factions.

Vu ran the Saar story in two parts. The first, published in the issue of November 7, 1934, was entitled "The Saar. Warning: High Tension" and carried the byline "Text and Photos by Our Special Envoy Gorta"—even though most of the photographs were really André's. (They appear on his contact sheets, on the same rolls of film with photographs for which he subsequently received credit.) Undoubtedly angered by Vu's failure to give him credit (for whatever reason), André demanded and got it for the second article, which carried the byline: "Interviews and Photos by Our Special Envoys Gorta and Friedmann." Published in the November 21 issue of the magazine and entitled "The Saar: What the Saarlanders are saying . . . and for whom they will vote," the article was given an exceptionally dynamic layout, incorporating a lightning-bolt motif into the title and positioning all the text and photos diagonally on the page. Belated though it was, his French debut was impressive.

Although the Saar reportage was well received, André could never seem to get enough work.

Paris is getting worse day by day [he told his mother in November], and, even though I've started to work again, success is very far away. So I've decided that from February 15th on I'll move my headquarters to London, where the prospects are better. I have three good friends there (one is a famous Dephot photographer). I'm through with the bohemian life and am ready to make a fresh start.

The famous photographer from Dephot to whom he refers is surely Felix Man, who had run into him in Paris in September and given him some advice about his work. Another friend—"acquaintance" perhaps more accurately reflects the nature of their relationship at that point—was Stefan Lorant, former editor of the *Münchner Illustrierte Presse*, who had just founded *Weekly Illustrated* in London with Man as one of its principal contributors. As it turned out, Lorant left the magazine in December. When André heard the news, he abandoned his plan.

Compared to what it had been a year earlier, André's situation in Paris was actually quite comfortable. He wasn't working steadily, but at least his random assignments were bringing in some money, and he had a decent room on the top floor of a hotel on the Rue Monsieur-le-Prince run by a congenial couple. As he later told the story, he and two other young Hungarians who were friends of his* had been living in the hotel for some time when the *patronne* came to them one day and said, "You're such nice boys . . ." It turned out that she wanted a grandchild, and her married son, an invalid, couldn't give her one. She explained that if one of them was willing to stand in, everything could be arranged. The three Hungarians drew straws; one of André's friends got the short straw. The son then left town until his wife became pregnant; once that was accomplished, there was to be nothing more between her and the young Hungarian surrogate. All this must have taken place about December 1934 or January 1935, for in October 1935 André wrote to his mother, "A little grandchild was born at the hotel, and, when I have no money for the rent, I take him for a promenade."

At the end of January 1935, six months after her son László had died from his rheumatic heart condition, Julia, still grief-stricken, set out from Budapest to visit her sisters in New York. She felt she needed a change; she was hoping to move the whole family to America and was going there first as an advance scout. Finding that she liked New York, she got a job in the garment district and stayed for a year. While she was away, Dezsö supported himself by acting as a middleman for fashion designs (some of which André sent him from Paris), and Kornel finished up his studies at the Madách Gymnasium.

André was usually not much of a letter writer, but while his mother was

---

* During 1934, Csiki had met a young woman and married her. He was, therefore, not one of these young Hungarians.

in New York he wrote her a long series of letters that give us some exceptionally candid glimpses of his life during that period. That the letters were addressed to his mother of course limits their frankness in regard to his love life and explains all the assurances of seriousness and respectability, as well as all the promises and apologies in respect to the regularity of his correspondence. But even these distinctly filial touches—in contrast to what we might expect from one whose public façade was so much that of a bohemian, devil-may-care, prodigal son—add to the intimacy of the self-portrait that emerges.

André had much that he could report very proudly to his mother that spring, for he was, as he put it, about to become a member of the international press. Simon Guttmann and Henri Daniel (Guttmann's associate in Paris) had drummed up a couple of assignments for him to do in Spain and were trying to negotiate an advance that would make his trip possible.

But rather than boast of his triumphs, André tended to regale his mother with picaresque accounts of his problems, disasters, and near-misses, of which he had plenty. The biggest problem before setting out on his trip was to get a new camera—not an easy thing, he explained, "because money isn't coming in from anywhere." But, oddly enough, he says elsewhere in the same letter that a Parisian agent had just paid him for a story he had done and that he had used the money to buy a suit.* That a new suit took precedence over a new camera suggests how important an appearance of prosperity was becoming to him. The lesson of the Pest boulevardiers had not been wasted on him: nothing succeeds like the illusion of success.

Given his preoccupation with clothes, it's quite appropriate that André earned a few francs that spring by posing for a sketch that appeared in the fashion magazine *Le Jardin des Modes* published by Lucien Vogel, who also published *Vu*. The sketch turned out, however, to be completely unlike André's actual appearance. He had to put on a white cotton athletic shirt, blue shorts, and sneakers and sit on a bicycle. The artist who signed himself or herself "Libis" proceeded to transform him into a blond-haired, teenaged boy who looked more like a young English lord than a Hungarian refugee. A friend recalls that André told her that he found the whole business something of a lark.

On March 25, on stationery from the Café du Dôme, André wrote to his mother,

---

* That payment was possibly for the story André did, apparently at this time, on the Norman pilgrimage town of Lisieux. The surviving prints are stamped "Agence Anglo-Continental."

This has really been a difficult birth. I am starting out in three days. Naturally I don't even know where my head is. I still don't have a camera, and there won't be very much money either, but this is a last chance, and I must make the most of it. Yesterday I received a letter from Ullstein saying that they have transferred 1,000 francs advance, but, because of exchange complications, this will not arrive until three weeks from now. So the first stretch of my trip will be very difficult.

That André would accept assignments from Ullstein demonstrates just how desperate he was. In August 1934, Joseph Goebbels, Hitler's minister of propaganda, had forced the Ullstein brothers, who were Jewish liberals, to sell their firm for a pittance and flee Germany. The major Ullstein publications were continued under Nazi direction, and soon flattering photographs of Hitler, Goering, and Goebbels were appearing quite regularly on the cover of the *Berliner Illustrirte Zeitung*, for which André was now going to make a couple of reportages.

Several arguments must be advanced in his defense. First of all, the re-portages he was planning had nothing whatsoever to do with politics; one was to be about the home life of a boxer, the other about a balloonist. Secondly, the assignments for the *Berliner* were arranged by Simon Guttmann, whom André trusted and respected. André probably told himself that if Guttmann thought it was all right, then it must be so; after all, many former Dephot photographers—among them Umbo, Harald Lechenperg, and Walter Boss-hard—were still having work published quite regularly in the *Berliner*. And, finally, André simply couldn't afford to refuse any assignments. As errors of judgment—and even betrayals of principles—go, this one of André's, though morally ambiguous, seems relatively innocent in cause and harmless in effect.

Waiting until practically the last minute, André juggled his finances on the day of his departure and somehow or other managed to buy—or at least to make a down payment on—a new Leica. It helped matters somewhat that when the editors of *Vu* learned that André was about to leave for Spain, they asked him to stop in Toulouse on the way and do a story for them, for which they gave him a small advance. But no sooner did he arrive in Toulouse than new troubles began.

I finished the first reportage after a great deal of difficulty [he told his mother], but it came out very well. First the police arrested me, because of my picture-taking, but, thanks to my *Vu* accreditation, the Chief of Police apologized and invited me to lunch.

Like a cat, André always landed on his feet, although his acrobatics were not always as graceful and effortless as he made them sound. Here he mentions his arrest and its aftermath very casually, as though it had all been a big joke. Not until he returned to Paris in June did he elaborate on his original story, telling his mother that there had been "great commotion" on account of his Toulouse reportage. When the police arrested him, they threatened to throw him out of the country, and even when he returned to Paris more than two months later, the matter had still not been entirely settled. André had to spend three days trying to clear up the situation, but at least in the end received a promise of an official press card to prevent such mishaps in the future. As for what he photographed in Toulouse to create such a furor, that remains a mystery. The Paris papers had reported that on Sunday, March 24, a gang of fascists had raided an anti-fascist meeting in Toulouse, killing one man and wounding several others. Perhaps André's reportage had something to do with the aftermath of this incident. Whatever its subject, Vu never published the story, because, as André wrote to his mother, "one editor doesn't want to run any more about politics."

Having extricated himself from his predicament, André went on to San Sebastián, where he did a story on the daily life of boxer Paolino Uzcudun, whose third fight with the German champion Max Schmeling was scheduled to take place in Berlin on July 7. André's reportage concisely documented both Paolino's strength and his gentleness and juxtaposed his humble origins with the comfortable estate he had bought with his earnings as a boxer.

From San Sebastián, André went on to Madrid, where he encountered yet another setback.

> I had an appointment yesterday with an airplane inventor* who has a really magnificent invention [he wrote]. At last I got in to see him and immediately asked him about his machine, to which he replied that he isn't interested in it any longer and that I shouldn't bore him with it. Now he's discovered a very interesting relationship between the South African Negro and the Chinese languages—but I told him, "This I cannot photograph" . . . at which point he threw me out!

While in Madrid, however, André did manage to photograph Lt. Col. Emilio Herrera, one of Spain's most famous pilots, who was preparing for a record-breaking balloon ascent to an altitude of 25,000 meters (82,000 feet). Herrera was planning to wear a deep-sea diver's suit, which would allow him

---

* Juan de la Cierva, a Spanish mathematician who, in 1923, invented the first successful rotary-wing aircraft, the "autogyro," which was a forerunner of the helicopter. He flew across the English Channel in an improved model in 1928.

to use a wicker gondola instead of the pressurized steel gondola that was usual for a high-altitude ascent. André photographed him checking his equipment and only afterward realized that he should also have taken some pictures of him with his family, but he got a chance to do so several weeks later when, after ruining many of his exposures in a Madrid darkroom, he had to shoot the story all over again. Even then he worried that if Herrera didn't break the record, the story would be killed. He needn't have worried on that score, for although Herrera's actual ascent (when and if he made it) seems to have passed unnoticed in the international press, *Vu* gave André's reportage a good layout and the *Berliner Illustrirte* used it as a cover story.

Aeronautical inventions and record attempts were very hot news during the 1930s, just as aerospace programs were to be later. The leading French illustrated daily paper, *Paris-soir*, devoted an entire half page every week to a column entitled "The Aeronautical Week," and hardly a day passed without some aeronautical item or other appearing on the paper's front and/or back pages. *Vu* and *Regards* regularly featured aeronautical stories, and even *L'Illustration*, the French counterpart of the conservative *Illustrated London News*, frequently found room between its articles on châteaux and old-master paintings for extensive coverage of aeronautical developments. And at least three German photographers—Ernst Udet, Willi Ruge, and Wolfgang Weber—were making a lucrative specialty of aeronautics. It was in this atmosphere that André photographed Emilio Herrera and tried to photograph Juan de la Cierva.

Having covered the great parade in Madrid celebrating the fourth anniversary of the Spanish Republic on April 14, André proceeded to Seville for Holy Week, that city's observance of which has been described as being simultaneously the most sacred and the most profane festival in all of Europe. Throughout the week before Easter, the streets of Seville are filled with caballeros and grandees on horseback, with mantilla-clad señoritas in antique carriages, with Gypsies, flamenco dancers, toreros, mummers in exotic costumes, thousands of drunk and boisterous tourists, young boys throwing firecrackers, and, dominating it all, spectacular religious processions. André photographed everything and joined in the festivities, as much as his dwindling funds allowed him to. Compounding his problem was Don José Filipo Octavio de Toledo, a relative of the family with whom he was staying.

Don José [André related in a letter to Gerda] has taken this week off from work. Why should he work when his distinguished friend can pay? If Don José will just shell out a little, then I can remain his distinguished friend and at the end of the week I'll still be a member of the international press.

He managed to get only twenty pesetas out of Don José ("I am only a petty thief," he told Gerda), but at last a letter from his mother enclosing a ten-dollar bill from his aunts reached him. "Without it," he wrote, "I would be in the sauce."

Soon after he returned to Madrid, André received word that Guttmann had sold his story on Paolino Uzcudun to the *Berliner Illustrirte* for a sum large enough to earn out his advance and cover his expenses; from that point on, all the money he made from his trip would be profit. So, with typical irresponsibility, André stopped working and headed straight for Barcelona and the nearby seaside resort of Tossa de Mar, where the father of one of his old girlfriends owned a pension. The very pretty former girlfriend and her equally pretty sister were both there, and their father liked André so much that he offered him free lodgings for the entire summer. Guttmann, who wrote to say that he and Ullstein were "very, very satisfied" with André's stories, approved of the plan and suggested that his protégé open "a small atelier" in Tossa for the summer. André liked the idea and began to make plans. He would first go back to Paris for a few weeks to take care of some business and do a couple of stories; then, about July 1, he would return to Tossa for two months to work and to finish the novel he had begun to write. (Geza Korvin recalls that André lent him two or three chapters of the novel, typed on pink paper. It was a romantic novel, and, according to Korvin's judgment of those early chapters, not very good. Korvin never got around to returning the manuscript, and eventually he lost it.)

But André didn't spend the summer in Tossa, after all, for when he returned to Paris, something even more appealing came up. He would first cover the Bastille Day celebrations in Marseilles (while there, he also photographed a forest fire that was raging nearby; he got close enough to singe his hair) and then go to Cannes to meet Gerda, Willi Chardack (whose affair with her had turned into a friendship), and Raymond Gorin, a friend of Chardack's from medical school. After they met up, the four friends went to the island of Sainte-Marguerite, in the Iles de Lérins, a few miles offshore from Cannes. On this beautiful, sparsely inhabited island, in whose fortress-prison the original Man in the Iron Mask is said to have been incarcerated, they camped near the ruins of a tower and roughed it, living on canned sardines. It was during that summer, while basking in the sun, swimming, and exploring ruins, that André and Gerda really fell in love.

Early in September, the four friends, deeply suntanned, returned to Paris. André had only two francs left, but he told Kertész, in Hungarian, "Never before in my life have I been so happy! Now only the pick and the spade [*kapa*] could separate Gerda and me."

9

On September 9, 1935, a few days after his return to Paris, André wrote his mother a long letter to bring her up to date on his affairs. He claimed to have sent her a postcard every week during the summer and one long letter, but she had received nothing and was furious. To assuage her, André wrote at some length about his new respectability and new plans:

> Naturally, as always, I haven't got a cent—so back to the hotel. In any case, I've taken a front room on the street, and the landlady can hardly recognize me. Imagine, Mother, my hair is short, I'm wearing a tie, my shoes are shined, and I appear on the scene every morning at 7 o'clock. And, what's even more surprising, I get home by nine every evening. In one word, I'm through with bohemian life.

He went on to tell his mother that Gerda was a very good influence on him and that she was helping him greatly with his work. He was starting to do a few minor assignments again, and she was typing up the stories in French, German, and English.* Though discouraged about how little money he was making, he was excited about working with her and was even beginning to teach her to use a camera.

Before long, they were not only working together but living together as well, in a modern but inexpensive one-room apartment near the Eiffel Tower. In informing his mother of this development, André rationalized that "since

---

* André later told a friend that Gerda "had learned her English from Dos Passos' 1919. The thing on John Reed. Deeply moved, she went off to a new life." (Jay Allen, preface to *Death in the Making*.) That book, published in 1932, the second in Dos Passos' *U.S.A.* trilogy, with its long passages of impressionistic, unpunctuated, stream-of-consciousness writing, hardly seems suited for use as an elementary English reader. But since the four-page section on Reed ("the last of the great warcorrespondents [sic] who ducked under censorships and risked their skins for a story") begins less than ten pages into the book, it isn't totally implausible that Gerda got that far. We can, however, only wonder how much Gerda's fascination with Reed influenced André and to what extent (if at all) she thought of herself as his Louise Bryant—whom Dos Passos didn't mention. (Coincidentally, Capa and Reed shared the same birthday; Reed was born on October 22, 1887.)

it's now possible to eat at home, it makes living cheaper," and he went on to assure her that he and Gerda were "mainly independent comrades."

Late in October he wrote, "After spending so much time looking for jobs for myself [he had tried in vain to find someone to send him to cover Mussolini's invasion of Abyssinia], I finally found one for Gerda. She is selling pictures for an agency,* and, because she's so pretty, editors buy from her." A few weeks later he reported that he had at last managed to find two regular part-time jobs for himself as well. He didn't specify what the first one was, but the second was a two-afternoon-per-month position as the picture editor for a Japanese monthly published by the Paris office of the Mainichi Press; he was paid the really quite generous salary of twenty dollars a month. (He got the job through two young Japanese, Hiroshi Kawazoe and Seiichi Inouye, whom he had met in Cannes during the summer; after they all returned to Paris in the fall, they became close friends.)

While working for Mainichi, André was able to do a reportage that he had wanted to do for more than six months, ever since he had seen an article about sport parachuting in the Soviet Union in the March 16 issue of *L'Il-lustration*.† As soon as he saw it, he showed it to several friends, saying, "Here's my kind of story! I could do it so well! But I'd like to jump, not stay behind in the plane the way this guy did. My pictures would be much better."

The recklessness of the jump, the element of risk, the sheer thrill of hurling oneself from an airplane, plummeting through space and then floating gently to earth, all appealed greatly to André's love of gambling and adventure. He vowed at once that he would go to the Soviet Union to photograph the parachute school. He would strap his camera to his body, jump, and photograph all the way down—the pictures couldn't help being sensational. At that time, however, he was just about to leave for the south of France and Spain, and when he returned to Paris in the fall and tried to get a Russian visa and an advance, he was unable to obtain either. Instead, he found a parachuting school outside Paris that was run by a former acrobatic pilot named Denois. Since his own camera was in the pawnshop, he borrowed a Leica from Mainichi.

---

* The agency, Alliance, had been founded by Maria Eisner that fall, after the disbanding of Anglo-Continental.

† Parachuting had remained little more than a curiosity until about 1930, when the Russians recognized its military potential. The Soviet government then began to subsidize massive training programs. In his article accompanying the photographs in *L'Illustration*, Henri Bouché stated that the Soviets had declared that during 1935 "Russian youth must accomplish a million parachute descents." Their goal was that "a Russian should leap from an airplane as easily as one alights from a streetcar."

André told his friends that he had jumped—and, indeed, his reportage was cleverly constructed to make it look as though he had—but he actually shot his story without jumping or even going up in a plane.*

Although André had advanced his career considerably during the past year, the letters he wrote during the fall and winter of 1935 reveal a highly ambivalent attitude toward photography. On the one hand, he enjoyed working with Gerda and was encouraged by Kertész's praise of his latest pictures. He was so optimistic that he told his mother, "It is my opinion that Kornel should learn photography, for eventually I'll be in a position where I can help him." On the other hand, however, he was hoping to be able to give up photography altogether and get into filmmaking.

The jump from still photography to film was a natural one, and during the 1920s and 1930s, a number of distinguished photographers, including Moholy-Nagy, Paul Strand, Charles Sheeler, Ralph Steiner, Man Ray, and Henri Cartier-Bresson,† turned to film, either to supplement their photographic work or to replace it. Most of the photographers who made the transition did so because they felt frustrated by the aesthetic limitations of still photography. But André felt most bitterly frustrated because he couldn't make a decent living from photography. Much of the time he couldn't get any work at all, and, when he finally was given an assignment or two, he found himself working very hard for too little reward—much praise, perhaps, but very little money. The cinema represented an opportunity to win fame and fortune.

After having hit an economic and aesthetic low point late in 1934, the French film industry, structurally transformed, had entered an exceptionally exciting and productive period by the middle of 1935. In the early 1930s the need to purchase expensive sound equipment at a time when money was extremely scarce had put the major French film companies under the control of the banks and other investors whose interest in cinema was strictly financial; by the end of 1934 they had killed the studios by forcing them to churn out the cheapest possible potboilers. The death of these giants cleared the field for a host of independent producers, who ushered in a brief period of indi-

---

* Seiichi Inouye recalls that André sold the story to *Paris-soir*, but research has failed to locate it. A set of vintage prints is preserved in the files of Capa's estate.
† In 1935, while André was trying to break into the French film industry, his friend Cartier-Bresson was in the United States studying filmmaking with Paul Strand, who, in that year, worked with Ralph Steiner and Leo Hurwitz on Pare Lorentz's film *The Plow That Broke the Plains* for the U.S. Resettlement Administration. After his return to France in 1936, Cartier-Bresson worked as an assistant to director Jean Renoir during the making of *La Vie Est à Nous* (Life Is Ours, a film sponsored by the French Communist Party) and *Une Partie de Campagne* (A Day in the Country).

vidualism and creative freedom. The influx of new money, as well as the general feeling of political optimism and commitment fostered by the newly formed Front Populaire, made the period from 1935 to 1937 a very good one for the French film industry. Directors such as Jacques Feyder, Jean Renoir, Julien Duvivier, Marc Allegret, and Max Ophuls made impressive and successful movies during these years. And it was their world of commercial films, not that of documentaries, which André was eager to enter.

As early as September 30, 1935, in a letter in which he reports that his photographic work was beginning to pick up, he told his mother,

> Today I had the first conference concerning the cinema, and things look favorable. Through the lady lawyer, I met the Chargé d'Affaires for cinema at the Ministry of Culture. Today I went there with the last story I did in Marseilles, and he liked it very much. He said he'll introduce me at some film studio. Naturally, this will take some time.

The lawyer was a woman with whom André had been very friendly—though apparently not romantically involved—at least since the spring of that year. He never mentions her name in his letters, and no one seems to remember it. He does, however, mention that she was married, and he repeatedly refers to her generosity; besides trying to help him get started in the movies, she often fed him and gave him money for photographic materials.

That December was an exceptionally difficult month for André, especially since he and Gerda were not living together. The apartment near the Eiffel Tower had not worked out—though whether for emotional or financial reasons is not clear—and so he moved into the large apartment near the Cité Universitaire shared by Hiroshi Kawazoe and Seiichi Inouye, both of whom were also aspiring filmmakers.

On top of (or perhaps partly because of) his separation from Gerda, André was feeling discouraged about photography, and Christmas only made him feel even worse. "Toward Christmas," he told his mother, "the homeless fall into a bad mood." But by that time he had reason to be feeling rather happy, for he had some good news to report:

> Next week I'm going to have a tiny film part, and after that I'll get into a studio as an assistant without pay. This is the end of photography. I've had enough, and now I'd rather suffer with something else. . . . The lady lawyer was discovered by Paramount yesterday, and she got a contract immediately. Naturally, the joy is great, and, of course, I'll jump, too, since she is such a good friend. . . . Now I'm

really preparing for the final struggle. I must get into the movies, because with photography I have no hope.

10

Although his movie job fell through, André's depression didn't last long, for early in January he and Gerda moved back into a hotel together, and at the beginning of February Simon Guttmann came through with some assignments. On February 7 André wrote his mother, "Although we are living together again, we're so busy that we barely see each other. We're not starving, but materials cost a lot. Nevertheless, the fact that I'm finally working again makes me very happy."

Things got even better the following month when André began to work on a regular basis for Maria Eisner's agency, Alliance. In return for doing three reportages a week he received a monthly advance of 1,100 francs, of which 500 went for materials and expenses. Since Eisner was paying Gerda 1,200 francs a month, between them they had an income which, though modest in absolute terms, must have seemed quite princely after their former deprivations. But they really earned their money; early in April André told his mother, "In the past four weeks I haven't slept more than five hours a night. We get up early and run around all day, and at night we manufacture an article."

That spring's election campaign and its aftermath gave André lots to cover, but since he could never have earned his advance on the strength of his political stories alone, he devoted much of his energy to reportages about such aspects of Parisian life as market streets, the Louvre, and the Bourse. One of the most appealing and amusing of these stories deals with a subject that was very close to his heart: efforts to break into the movies. The Ciné Crochet was held in a suburban open-air arena on whose stage virtually anyone with talent (or with delusions of talent) could perform before a movie camera and a live audience. At the end of each act the audience would register its approval or disapproval with a show of hands, not to mention cheers and catcalls. The screen tests of those the audience liked would be passed on to talent scouts from the various film studios. André focused on a succession of couples who hoped to follow in the steps of teams like Fred Astaire and Ginger Rogers or Jeanette MacDonald and Nelson Eddy. Some were young, eager, and self-confident, while others looked like old troopers from the music halls or even members of the suburban petite bourgeoisie who had fallen on hard times and were looking to the movies for a way out. Clearly, André sympathized with their hopes and failures.

André was working hard and making decent money, but he still wasn't satisfied, so he and Gerda devised a plan. Right in the middle of a letter dated April 7, between details of his income and the news that he intended to move with Gerda into a better hotel at the end of the month (they moved into the Hôtel de Blois on the Rue Vavin, across from the Dôme), André quite casually told his mother,

> I am working under a new name. They call me Robert Capa. One could almost say that I've been born again, but this time it didn't cause anyone any pain.

As he later told the story (of which, naturally, not all the details hold up under careful scrutiny), he and Gerda decided to invent a rich, successful American photographer named Robert Capa. André, who would pose as Capa's dark-room man, would actually take the photographs that Gerda would sell as Capa's. If an editor wanted to meet Capa or speak to him, Gerda would make up an excuse for his elusiveness. The particulars of the arrangement are virtually impossible to sort out, since "Capa" was conceived partly as an imaginary character, an alter ego, and partly as a pseudonym for André to adopt—although, despite what he had written to his mother, he didn't begin to introduce himself as Capa until after the outbreak of the Spanish Civil War.

The trick worked well at first—or so the story goes. Gerda, as the agent for the "fabulously successful" Capa, managed to convince Parisian editors that she would be insulting her client's international reputation if she sold his photographs for less than 150 francs apiece, three times the going rate. Editors gladly paid the asking price for "Capa's" photographs, the very same pictures for which they might have refused to pay even fifty francs had they realized they were the work of the struggling emigré André Friedmann. It was really true, after all, that nothing succeeds like the illusion of success.

Although André surely relished the idea of pulling a fast one on editors who had previously rejected his work, he actually had a more practical reason for selling his pictures through a ruse: there was another photojournalist named Friedmann working in Paris. Georges Friedmann, a well-established photographer on the staff of the daily *L'Intransigeant*, occasionally sold pictures to Vu and other magazines where André was trying to get his own work published, and that situation must have led to some confusion, since magazines that gave photographers any credit at all generally gave only the last name. When, for instance, Vu published André's photographs of the Saar simply under the name "Friedmann," many people must have assumed that they had been taken by Georges. In an attempt to avoid such confusion (and to hide his Jewishness from the editors of the *Berliner Illustrirte*), the younger Friedmann had signed his work "André" during 1935, but he decided that using only his first name made him sound like a hairdresser, at which point he and Gerda came up with "Robert Capa." He did, however, continue to use the credit line "Photo André" from time to time until the end of the 1930s, especially when he had sold a story to one magazine as an exclusive and wanted to sell the outtakes to another publication. Also, when he photographed on visits to Paris during the Spanish Civil War, he would often publish the pictures under the names "André" or "Fried" in order to hide the fact that he—"Capa"—wasn't continuously at the front.

There are several rather far-fetched stories about the derivation of the name "Capa," but André himself later claimed that he had derived the name from Frank Capra's.* Capra had achieved international fame as the director of such films as *Platinum Blonde* (1931), *American Madness* (1932), and *Lady for a Day* (1933)—and his masterpiece, *It Happened One Night*, with Claudette Colbert and Clark Gable, had not only won the Academy Award for the Best Picture of 1934 but had also won Oscars for its director and its two stars. As a young man who still hoped to break into the movies one day, André must have realized that a pseudonym so similar to the name of one of Hollywood's leading directors could be quite advantageous—as, in fact, it later proved to be, when people would grant interviews and issue invitations to Capa, confusing him with Capra.

André claimed that the name "Robert" also came from the movies: from the actor Robert Taylor, who in 1936 was starring as Greta Garbo's screen lover in *Camille*. Like "Capa," "Robert" was easy to pronounce, easy to spell, and easy to remember. On the other hand, the whole name was so difficult

---

* One unlikely story asserts that the name originated in André's remark that only the pick and the spade [*kapa* in Hungarian] could separate him from Gerda. (Why, when he was very much in love with Gerda, would he choose a name symbolizing death and separation from her?) Another explanation has it that André often used the Hungarian expression "Now I'll grab the spade [*kapa*] handle and succeed." (He had, indeed, used the expression in a letter to his mother—but that was almost a year before he took his new name.) Some say that the name arose because he had been nicknamed "capa" (the shark) as a youth, but his family and his closest Hungarian friends recall no such nickname—

to pin down in terms of national origin that Gerda could not only tell French editors that Capa was an American but also tell American editors that he was a rich, successful French photographer. And when André went off to Spain, his new surname sounded conveniently Spanish, especially with the simple conversion of "Robert" to "Roberto." This cosmopolitan ambiguity must certainly have appealed to André: "Robert Capa" was a perfect name for a stateless person.

At the same time, Gerda took an almost equally cosmopolitan pseudonym for herself. Henceforth she would be not Gerda Pohorylles but Gerda Taro, a name borrowed from a young Japanese painter living in Paris, Taro Okamoto. Like "Capa," the name "Taro" was easy to pronounce, to spell, and to remember—and it too was rich in associations. Most obviously, the name sounds like "tarot," with its connotations of fortune-telling and Gypsies. Furthermore, "Gerda Taro" sounds a bit like "Greta Garbo," who in 1936 was at the peak of her fame. Gerda must have relished even this tenuous link with the star who epitomized the sophisticated and mysterious femme fatale on the screen, and, of course, the allusions to the stars of *Camille* in their new names gave the romance between André and Gerda glamorous, mythic—and prophetically tragic—overtones.

Anyone who adopts a pseudonym is telling the world a fiction about himself, but, like most fictions, it reveals much about the teller. In André's case we are reminded that he loved to amuse his friends with embellished tales of his adventures, tales with at least some basis in fact, tales that he told over and over until he himself must have believed them to be true. His invention of an alter ego confirmed the transformation of his public image that he had been making for over a year, ever since meeting Gerda. The long-haired, unkempt, unshaven Gypsy wearing an old dirty leather jacket had—at least on the surface—transformed himself by the spring of 1935, when he set off for the south of France and Spain. He had told his mother then that he had become a "gentleman" who was "washed, cleaned, and pressed," wearing a new suit. That fall, after his romance with Gerda had really blossomed, he reported over and over again in his letters that he was so neatly dressed and groomed that his friends hardly recognized him. Indeed, André said that he hardly recognized himself; he had come to look like

---

which, in any case, would be pronounced "tsapa." As for the claim that the name was chosen at random from the Paris phone book, the 1936 directory did list a Helène Capa as well as a perfume shop called "Capa" and a distributor of paper products called "C.A.P.A."—none of which seems likely to have provided inspiration for a name that was devised with the intention of ensuring success. It has also been said that André Friedmann (literally "peace man") needed a disguise, a cloak ("capa" = "cape" in Spanish), when he went off to cover the Spanish Civil War, but the name was devised several months before the war broke out.

"a petit bourgeois from Buda." By February 1936 he had gotten an "American-style" haircut (although he said it ruined his looks), and he was wearing a raincoat that one of his Japanese friends had brought him from London. He was even wearing a felt hat.

The new clothes and the haircut were, however, something of a disguise. As André himself pointed out in one letter, he was a "false petit bourgeois." In a sense, it was not André Friedmann who wore the fine clothes and had his hair cut short; it was a fantasy figure who embodied the fulfillment of André's own wishes and of the demands that his mother and Gerda were making on him. At the time of his invention, Robert Capa was all that André was trying to be—or at least trying to seem. Capa was rich, successful, glamorous, and American. André was not yet any of these, but he had set his sights on becoming all of them.

Throughout the rest of his life, the ego and the alter ego—André and Capa—coexisted. Right from the beginning this dual identity must have complicated his relationship with Gerda, who sometimes called her lover André and sometimes Capa. It was as though they had a ménage à trois, and it was clearly Capa—the fantasy figure—of whom Gerda was especially fond.

André strove very hard to *become* Robert Capa, and he almost, but not entirely, succeeded. The longer he played the part of Capa, the more completely he grew into the role, but Capa always remained the construction of his fantasy, even after the fantasy had become reality—when André/Capa really had become successful, glamorous, and American. At heart he remained André Friedmann, although he kept that part of his personality very private. Robert Capa was the embodiment of the destiny he had set for himself, yet André Friedmann seems always to have remained somewhat uncomfortable with—and even skeptical of—that destiny.

11

The French left-liberal, anti-fascist coalition known as the Front Populaire (which united the Communist, the Socialist, and the misleadingly named bourgeois Radical-Socialist parties) promised such sweeping social and economic reforms that, at least for a few months before and after the elections that took place in the spring of 1936, it infused its supporters with euphoric optimism and filled its opponents with dread. A great many conservative Frenchmen recalled that very shortly after the electoral victory of a left-liberal coalition in 1914, World War I had broken out and Germany had invaded France. Now there was again much cause for worry about a German invasion. England's refusal to help France stop Hitler's remilitarization of the Rhineland in March 1935 raised fears that the French could not count on their most powerful ally, and the failure of the League of Nations to stop Mussolini's aggression in Abyssinia demonstrated the ineffectiveness of that organization as a peacekeeper.

To make matters worse, there was the example of Spain, which had elected a Popular Front government in February 1936. That spring the government tried to steer a moderate course, while honoring some of its more radical campaign promises, such as partial autonomy for Catalonia and land reform, but the far Left declared that the election results had constituted a mandate for revolution. Assassinations, riots, and anti-Catholic vandalism proliferated. The turbulence so frightened the conservative, Catholic, and rightist elements in France—and gave their press such dramatic evidence of what could happen in the wake of a Front Populaire victory—that it jeopardized the Front's chances of success in the upcoming elections.

To counter such alarming news and to report on the progress being made by the coalition government, *Regards* sent Chim and writer Georges Soria to Spain in April, but before he left, Chim persuaded the editors to hire André to cover the Front Populaire campaign for them. The work presumably did little to improve either his reputation or his income—for many of his pictures ran without credit, and Maria Eisner recalls that *Regards* paid so little that it was last on her list of publications to which she would try to sell stories—but André threw himself enthusiastically into it, for much more than money and reputation was at stake. It seemed that a Front Populaire victory could halt the spread of fascism and perhaps even bring about its downfall.

Hardly a Sunday went by that spring without a huge Front Populaire march through the streets of Paris: a protest march, a commemorative march, a strike march, a march to demonstrate solidarity with some cause or other, a march in memory of leftist martyrs, a march to celebrate a victory. Hundreds of thousands of people routinely turned out, many of them carrying flags, banners, and placards, and André photographed them passionately, whether he was right in the thick of things, recording the ardent faces, or teetering precariously on a rooftop, positioning himself for shots that would convey a sense of the vastness of the crowds.

As the elections approached, he photographed Parisians of all sorts—

students, policemen, businessmen, bourgeois couples—studying the posters that the various parties put up all over the city, pointing out details, arguing, and trying to decide how to vote. And on Sunday, May 3, the day of the election run-offs, he photographed voters in St.-Denis, an area in the northern part of Paris with a mix of workers and petite bourgeoisie. In front of the *mairie* people were holding heated discussions and speculating about the outcome; inside André photographed the voters' faces—registering determination or doubt—as they submitted their ballots to the official who checked to see that they were properly filled out.

In the evening he photographed the crowds who had gathered in the Place de l'Opéra to watch the election results projected onto screens. Although the Front Populaire hardly won by a landslide, the peculiarities of the electoral system nevertheless gave the coalition close to two-thirds of the seats in the Chambre des Députés. And since the Socialists had won the plurality of seats, it was clear that a Socialist would become the new premier. The natural choice was Léon Blum, who had long led his party's delegation in the Chambre. Blum, a Jew and a distinguished man of letters, had become something of a hero, a living martyr, after having been savagely attacked and nearly killed by French fascists in February.

Most French workers—who were still very badly paid and badly treated—voted for the Front Populaire primarily because the coalition promised them the right to collective bargaining, paid vacations, and a shortening of the work week with no reduction in pay. As far as they were concerned, the elections were tantamount to a national referendum on these issues, and once the Front Populaire had won, they felt the victors should carry out the will of the people immediately. Why wait a month until the newly elected Chambre could convene and a new cabinet be formed?

On May 26, after Blum and the leaders of the other coalition parties had made it clear that they intended to take no action until they were sworn in, the great wave of strikes began that nearly brought French industry to a standstill. Two days later, the 35,000 workers at the Renault works in the Parisian suburb of Boulogne-Billancourt began an around-the-clock sit-in strike, occupying their factory as though it were a besieged town. The organizers allowed the women, children, and old men who worked in the factory to leave, but everyone else, whether or not they supported the strike, was forced to remain. Even the plant's administrators were locked in.

It was the Renault strike that really captured the imagination of the Left and that prompted André and Chim (who had just returned from Spain) to grab their cameras and rush to see what was happening, but when they arrived at the main gate that first day, they learned—as did many other reporters and photographers—that the strikers weren't letting anyone in. Later on, virtually anyone could obtain a pass from the Confédération Générale de Travail that would admit them to the occupied factories, but that first day at Renault, the strike leaders were adamant: absolutely no one was to be allowed entry. Nevertheless, André charmed his way into the factory that night and managed to take a few photographs of workers sleeping beside their machines.* Over the course of the next several weeks both he and Chim made extensive reportages on life in various occupied factories, where the workers passed the time by singing and dancing or by sitting on top of the surrounding walls, drinking wine and talking to their friends and families gathered outside.

By June 4, when Blum and his cabinet were sworn in, some 350,000 workers were on strike in the Paris region, and another 700,000 throughout the rest of the nation. Rumors of an imminent nationwide general strike—and even of a revolution—created widespread panic. The next day, after the cabinet had had its first meeting, Blum spoke on the radio to assure the strikers that he would give top priority to their demands. He was as good as his word, railroading the necessary legislation through Parliament during his first week in office. But still the strikes continued.

About June 12, a week after the big Paris department stores had gone on strike, André went to the Galeries Lafayette's rooftop terrace, where the strikers who weren't playing cards, reading, knitting, or listening to the radio were sleeping. Judging from the number of sleepers, the initial excitement of the strike had long since worn off. But camaraderie remained strong, even in sleep: in one photograph a young woman sleeps with her head on a friend's lap, and in another, five young women are all slumped together as they sleep sitting on a bench.

On Sunday, June 14, two days after the metal workers—by far the largest group on strike—had finally accepted the settlement proposed by the government, more than 100,000 Parisians filled the seats and lawn of the Stade de Buffalo for a jubilant victory rally sponsored by the Communist Party, which had not instigated or even encouraged the strikes. In fact, the more it had begun to look as though the strike movement would turn into a workers'

---

* In its issue of June 3, 1936, Vu published an illustrated article entitled "The Strikers' First Night." Although all the photographs are credited to Isaac Kitrosser, who claimed to be the only photographer to gain admittance to the Renault factory that night, at least one (showing two sleeping workers) appears on the same roll of film as other photographs of the strike for which André received credit elsewhere. Because the Renault strike ended temporarily the next day, May 29, there was no second night on which André could have taken a picture in time for publication in Vu. The strike resumed on June 4.

revolution, the more firmly the party leaders had urged the strikers to return to work, for Stalin had made it clear that he wanted his most powerful western European ally to be strong and united in order to deter Hitler from invading the Soviet Union. But now that the strikes were ending, the party was eager to take credit for the gains the workers had won.

By three o'clock on that warm, sunny afternoon, the stadium was packed, and everyone was wearing at least a touch of red—a red scarf, a red tie, a red flower, a red ribbon. As usual, André and Chim seemed to be everywhere, mingling with the crowd to catch smiling faces and telling gestures, darting around the official podium during the speeches, and scurrying around, under, and onto the raised, cross-shaped runway during the parade. At one point, a banner appeared that evidently forced André to compromise between his desire to photograph all that was happening and loyalty to one of his best friends. He framed his image so that only half of the banner—the left half, bearing the name "Cartier"—is visible. The right half, which surely bore the name "Bresson," is cut off by the edge of the picture. Like thousands of other workers in the French cotton industry, the employees of the firm of Cartier-Bresson had gone on strike.

At the end of June, André—like many other photographers and reporters— traveled to Geneva to cover a special session of the League of Nations at which Haile Selassie, the deposed Emperor of Abyssinia, was to make a plea for harsh international sanctions to punish Italy for its invasion of his country. André, of course, was hoping for sensational exclusives, but the League, nervously trying to protect Haile Selassie and such other high-ranking emissaries as Léon Blum and British Foreign Minister Anthony Eden, rigidly controlled the press. After photographing the delegates getting out of their cars and entering the Assembly building, the journalists were all herded into the press gallery in the Assembly hall.

On Tuesday, June 30, just as Haile Selassie was about to begin speaking, a group of Italian journalists in the crowded press gallery stood up and began to whistle and to yell insults and denunciations at him. A few of their neighbors tried in vain to force the obstreperous Italians to sit down and be quiet, but finally the police arrived, collared them, dragged them from the press gallery, and restored order.

The disruption was obviously an important story that could have international repercussions, especially since the Italians were all prominent journalists and editors who had undoubtedly acted with the permission—and perhaps even at the instigation—of their government. But practically the entire press corps had the story, and now Haile Selassie was finally about to begin speaking. No one thought it worth missing the Emperor's long-awaited speech just to watch a few bad-mannered fascists being carted off to the police station. No one except André.

Apparently he had been watching one of the journalists who had tried to suppress the Italians—a Spaniard, whom the police, assuming him to be one of the troublemakers, arrested. André recognized the mistake and realized that there might be a story in it—the only story of which he was likely to get exclusive coverage—so he followed the Spaniard and the policemen out to the street. The journalist proclaimed his innocence all the way, until finally in the back seat of an open car the policemen on either side of him clapped their hands over his mouth and then gagged him before they drove off. (The misunderstanding was cleared up at the police station, and the Spaniard was released.)

André—who was still trying to hide the fact that he was taking the pictures that were being published under the name Robert Capa—later claimed that Lucien Vogel, the editor of Vu, noticed him following the wrongly arrested Spaniard. Several days later, when André's story reached his desk in Paris, Vogel telephoned Gerda, and when she told him that the story would cost three hundred francs, he replied, "This is all very interesting about Robert Capa, but tell that ridiculous boy Friedmann who goes around shooting pictures in a dirty leather jacket to report to my office at nine tomorrow morning." Thus, we are asked to believe, André Friedmann's ruse was discovered and he *became* Robert Capa. But whether or not things happened exactly that way, Vogel bought the story and gave it a full page in Vu. The credit line reads "Photos Robert Capa."

André's story created a sensation. The incident in itself was hardly earth-shaking, yet it symbolized—better than any other photographic story to come out of the League's special session—what had really happened in Geneva. In the article opposite André's story in Vu, Madeleine Jacob wrote, "Whatever sins [Haile Selassie] will have to place in the balance at the Last Judgment, he will have suffered much from the injustice, the hypocrisy, and the cow-ardice of the League of Nations." In the episode of the Spaniard being arrested and gagged by the Swiss police, André captured in dramatic, graphic terms the equivalent of what the League coolly and discreetly did to Haile Selassie during the rest of the special session.

A week after his return from Geneva, André was on the road again for Alliance, this time to the town of Verdun, about 130 miles northeast of Paris. On the

1. Les journalistes italiens viennent de siffler. Dans les tribunes et dans la salle le public et les délégués se lèvent pour protester.

2. Curieuse méprise. Un journaliste espagnol s'élevant avec force contre un de ses collègues italiens, est pris pour un Italien et emmené violemment par la police...

LES INCIDENTS
DE GENÈVE
VUS PAR VU

3. Malgré ses protestations renouvelées, il est conduit au commissariat.

4. Les gendarmes lui ferment la bouche...

5. Et pour plus de tranquillité le bâillonnent. Cette méprise s'est heureusement terminée au poste où le malheureux Espagnol a été relâché tout de suite.

6. Le surlendemain des incidents causés par les Italiens un journaliste israélite tchèque se suicidait en pleine séance pour attirer l'attention du monde sur la tragique situation des Juifs en Allemagne.

twentieth anniversary of the longest battle of World War I—a battle in which the French and the Germans each lost well over 300,000 men—Verdun was to be the site of a massive demonstration in support of a lasting peace. Altogether, some 20,000 men who had fought on various fronts during the war came to Verdun from fourteen nations (including France, Germany, Great Britain, the Soviet Union, and the United States) to pledge their commitment to peace. Many of them brought their sons; as many as 50,000 non-combatants attended.

That night André photographed in Verdun's military cemetery, which was illuminated by hundreds of floodlights, as each former combatant stationed himself behind one of the white crosses and placed a bouquet on the grave at his feet. A solemn, anguished silence hung over the crowd. Suddenly a cannon boomed. Speakers at the four corners of the cemetery called out, "Cessez le feu!" The giant floodlights were shut off, plunging the crowd into darkness. After several minutes of total silence, a child announced over the public address system, "This is for the peace of the world." There were no speeches, but all of the participants, speaking in their own languages, swore an oath to protect the peace for which the men at Verdun and elsewhere had died.

It was all for nought. The ceremony at Verdun, in fact, marked the end of Europe's nineteen-year peace. On Sunday, July 19, five days after André had returned to Paris to photograph the delirious Bastille Day festivities celebrating the Front Populaire victory and the triumphant settlement of the strikes, the Parisian papers carried the news that a rightist military rebellion had broken out against the Spanish government. Within four months André would hear Pétain's famous rallying cry of Verdun—"Ils ne passeront pas!"—translated into Spanish—"¡No pasarán!"—ringing through the streets of a Madrid besieged by fascist troops.

12

In its broadest outlines, the Spanish Civil War pitted the Left and its duly elected Popular Front government against the Right—a coalition of fascists, monarchists, and Roman Catholics led by Gen. Francisco Franco. Because the Right received a great deal of aid (troops, advisers, and materiel) from Germany and Italy, anti-fascists all over the world saw the Spanish Civil War as their first opportunity to confront international fascism with more than words; until then, they had had to stand by in mounting frustration while the governments of the western democracies pursued policies of appeasement.

As soon as news of the outbreak of the civil war reached Paris, Capa (as he now began to introduce himself) undoubtedly made the rounds of editors, just as he had at the start of the Italian invasion of Abyssinia. But now there was a difference: his recent political coverage had brought him recognition and respect. Furthermore, he and Gerda wanted to go to Spain together as a team.* Gerda had been practicing photography for some time, and now she was ready to work as a full partner, not merely to type captions and articles to accompany Capa's photographs. They had two cameras between them, a Leica and a Rolleiflex. Capa would mainly use the Leica, Gerda mainly the Rolleiflex.

Just then Capa received word that his mother was finally due to arrive in Paris. In May she had traveled from New York to Nice, where she had gotten a job working for a furrier, an old friend from Budapest. In June, Kornel joined his mother in Nice, having completed his studies at the Gymnasium. Now they were to come to Paris. The visit was intended to be brief, for Julia, certain that another world war was approaching, was eager to emigrate to the United States with Kornel—and with Capa, too, if she could persuade him— as soon as her sisters there could arrange for the necessary papers. Dezsö had decided to remain in Budapest.

The family reunion was not a happy one, for Julia and Gerda took an intense dislike to each other, and Julia was horrified by her son's plan to cover the civil war in Spain. To make matters worse, it soon became clear that there would be a long wait for the papers from America. Kornel wanted to study medicine, but he didn't speak French, and as he realized that he and his mother would be in Paris for some time, he apprenticed himself to a Hungarian photographer named Emeric Fehér and took a room in the Hôtel de Blois, where Capa taught him to make prints in a darkroom improvised in a bathroom across the hall. There, for almost a year, Kornel printed Capa's negatives at

---

* One legend has it that Capa was in Barcelona when the war broke out, on assignment to cover the Workers' Olympiad (a competing leftist version of the official 1936 games in Berlin). In fact he was not; originators of the story apparently confused Capa with Hans Namuth, who was on assignment for *Vu*.

night, and every morning he carried the wet prints, wrapped in newspaper like a package of fish, to Fehér's studio, where his pay consisted entirely of the right to use the electric print drier on his lunch hour. He was finally fired for using too much electricity.

At the beginning of August, despite his mother's protests, Capa found a way to get himself and Gerda to Spain. Lucien Vogel was planning to fly a group of journalists to Barcelona; from there they would spread out to cover the civil war for a special issue of *Vu*. He invited Capa and Gerda to join the expedition.

The flight ended in minor disaster, for a mechanical failure forced the plane to make a crash landing in a field some distance from Barcelona. Vogel and one of the reporters both broke their right arms, but Capa and Gerda emerged unharmed. As for the plane itself, when mechanics concluded that repairs would take some time, Vogel, in a gesture compounded of munificence and impatience, gave it to the Catalonian government, thereby doubling the size of its air force.

Arriving in Barcelona on August 5, two and a half weeks after the outbreak of the war, Capa found the city radically changed since he had been there in the spring of 1935. After the swift suppression of the local military uprising, this comfortably bourgeois city, capital of prosperous, industrial Catalonia, had undergone a proletarian revolution. Factories, stores, and restaurants had been taken over by their employees; managers who refused to cooperate with the new order had been imprisoned or shot. Thousands of workers swelled the ranks of hastily organized militia groups, and the streets and cafés were filled with these very unmilitary soldiers, most of them dressed in civilian clothes or whatever pieces of uniform they could assemble. They wore cartridge belts crossed over their chests, and the rifles slung over their shoulders were often nearly antiques. Many of the militiamen wore boiler suits, and these dark blue, one-piece coveralls became a sort of uniform. Civilians, too, wore work clothes on the street. To wear a business suit—or even a tie or a felt hat—was to risk arrest as a "fascist bourgeois."

The anarcho-syndicalists of the Confederación Nacional del Trabajo (CNT) constituted by far the largest faction in Barcelona; by their sheer numbers they held the real power in the city. Passionately anti-militaristic, they agreed to fight in loosely organized and almost totally undisciplined militias only to advance the cause of their revolution. Although Karl Korsch had interested Capa in the CNT, the fanatical anarcho-syndicalists of northeastern Spain were notoriously hostile to outsiders, often threatening to shoot visitors, and Capa and Gerda accordingly stayed away from them.

Like the anarcho-syndicalists, the semi-Trotskyites of the Partido Obrero de Unificación Marxista (POUM), a brother party of the Sozialistische Arbeiter Partei Deutschlands that had so interested Gerda and her Leipzig friends, supported the government in the civil war only because a Loyalist victory was a prerequisite for revolution. Also like the anarcho-syndicalists, they opposed a regular, centralized army in favor of militias. Politically the POUM was even more extreme than the CNT, but its leaders and militias were hospitable to visitors.

The third major faction in Barcelona was the Partit Socialista Unificat de Catalunya (PSUC), which, though ostensibly the unified Socialist-Communist party, was dominated almost totally by the Communists, who declared that all thoughts of revolution must be put aside until fascism had been completely destroyed, not only in Spain but throughout Europe. Because the PSUC controlled the supply of Russian arms, it gained control of the central government and was eventually able to suppress both the CNT and the POUM. Although Capa and Gerda's sympathies tended at first to keep them away from the PSUC, they did photograph a well-disciplined unit of PSUC militiawomen drilling on a beach outside Barcelona. French and British magazines were clamoring for pictures of Spanish militiawomen, who were still very much a novelty. There were women in the CNT and POUM militias, but the only all-female unit seems to have been this PSUC one.

While they were in Barcelona, Capa and Gerda photographed people in the streets and cafés, children playing on barricades, and requisitioned cars with factional initials crudely lettered on their doors speeding recklessly by. They also photographed manifestations of the city's intense anti-religious feeling. Churches were smoldering everywhere, and those that had not been set afire by angry mobs at the outbreak of hostilities were now being methodically burned by the anarchists. The gutted interiors were used as garages or as warehouses for the confiscated property of the rich.

At the Barcelona railroad station they photographed soldiers bound for the Aragón front bidding a last farewell to their wives and sweethearts. Then, after a week or ten days in the city, they themselves drove out to that front in an official press car.

By mid-August the situation in mountainous Aragón was stalemated, as it would remain for more than a year. The fighting amounted to little more than occasional skirmishes—most of them at night, which, of course, was no good for photographers—and much of the front was completely inactive. Capa later wrote in his book *Death in the Making* that they first found the front near a village which, "like so many in Spain," was called Santa Eulalia, but there was apparently nothing to photograph there except a group of militiamen and one militiawoman on maneuvers. Capa claimed in his captions that bullets from the enemy hiding across a broad ravine were whizzing past the soldiers as they bounded down a stubble-covered hillside, but that seems rather unlikely, for other photos show the soldiers—and even Gerda with her Rolleiflex—casually standing around on the hillside.

On the nearby Huesca front, Capa and Gerda photographed militiamen camping in improvised shelters, manning machine-gun and artillery posts, and even—because things were so slow—helping farmers on nearby collectivized farms harvest and thresh their wheat. Then the photographers drove southwestward, and for an excellent reason: the language in which they both were most comfortable was German, and there were many German émigrés (most of whom had been in Barcelona for the Workers' Olympiad) serving in the militias between Huesca and Saragossa. They visited the village of Tardienta, headquarters of the German Communist Thälmann Centuria, but they spent most of their time with the POUM column that had its headquarters in Leciñena, about twelve miles northeast of Saragossa.* Leciñena had been taken in a surprise night attack during the second week of August, but since then there had been very little fighting, and the bored soldiers lay around in the terrible heat most of the time. The Insurgents conducted daily air raids, but only one bomb—a largely ineffectual one at that—had hit the village. It was hardly a situation conducive to making exciting battle photos, so Capa and Gerda focused instead on the strong faces of the militiamen as they danced in the evening, drank wine streaming from flasks held at arm's length, and listened to their leader, Manuel Grossi, addressing them from a balcony.

After a week or so, they left the Aragón front and proceeded to Madrid, which was then in great danger. Although Loyalist troops were successfully blocking the Insurgent advance through the Guadarrama mountains a short distance to the northwest, a large Insurgent army was rapidly approaching the capital from the southwest, and Insurgent planes had begun bombing, though the air raids had not yet done much damage. The city was bracing itself for the worst. One photo by Gerda, showing workmen constructing a protective, beehive-like dome of bricks over the fountain of Cibeles, sums up the situation.

Capa and Gerda were naturally eager to photograph Loyalist victories, but the Guadarrama front was stalemated and prospects southwest of the capital looked very bleak. There was, however, one front from which the news sounded highly encouraging. During the second half of August, the Madrid government

---

* It was with this POUM militia that George Orwell would serve that winter. (See his *Homage to Catalonia*.)

had begun an offensive—its first major offensive of the war—to take Córdoba back from the Insurgents. Day after day the government reported new advances, even claiming—falsely—that its troops had entered the city. If one wanted to photograph Loyalist victories, the Córdoba front was apparently the place to be. It was also there that one could see the most idealistic of the CNT militias in action.

On their way south Capa and Gerda stopped at Talavera de la Reina, but the situation there seemed hopeless and journalists were not allowed to visit the front. They also stopped at Toledo, where at the outbreak of the war the Insurgent Colonel Moscardó, threatened by a large Loyalist force from Madrid, had barricaded himself along with 1,000 of his troops, several hundred women and children, and 100 leftist hostages into the Alcazar, the huge and virtually impregnable fortress-palace that dominates the city. Now, at the end of August, the Loyalists still had the Alcazar under siege. Asturian *dinamiteros*, coal miners expert in the use of dynamite, were preparing to dig two tunnels so that they could lay explosive charges under the fortress's west wall, but the tunnels would take a couple of weeks to complete. Meanwhile, very little of any importance was happening. Capa and Gerda continued south, resolving to return when the tunnels were finished.

On the afternoon of September 5, Hans Namuth and Georg Reisner, who had traveled from Madrid with the Swiss journalist Franz Borkenau, photographed the terror-stricken inhabitants of Cerro Muriano as they were fleeing an Insurgent air raid. Cerro Muriano was a front-line village from which the CNT militia had planned to launch a drive toward Córdoba, eight miles to the south, early that morning. Only later, when Namuth saw Capa's pictures in Vu showing some of the same people he and Reisner had photographed along the same road, did he realize that Capa and Gerda had been there too.

Establishing the fact of Capa and Gerda's presence in Cerro Muriano on the afternoon of September 5 has a double significance, for not only does it identify the location where Capa made a powerful series of photographs of refugees, but it also provides the most important clue we have for pinpointing the place where he made the most famous photograph of his entire career— the one ostensibly showing a Loyalist militiaman at the moment when the shock of being hit by an enemy bullet registers on his body and he begins to collapse into death. On the vintage prints preserved in the files of Capa's estate with their original chronological numbering, the numbers on the sequence of pictures to which the Falling Soldier belongs immediately precede those of the Cerro Muriano refugee series. It is, therefore, very likely that Capa shot his Falling Soldier picture at or near Cerro Muriano, on or shortly before September 5, 1936.*

One year later, on September 1, 1937, three days after he had arrived in New York for a visit, Capa gave an interviewer from the New York *World-Telegram* an account of the circumstances in which he had made his already famous picture. Capa said that he and the man whom he was to photograph

> were on the Córdoba front, stranded there, the two of them, Capa with his precious camera and the soldier with his rifle. The soldier was impatient. He wanted to get back to the Loyalist lines. Time and again he climbed up and peered over the sandbags. Each time he would drop back at the warning rattle of machine-gun fire. Finally the soldier muttered something to the effect that he was going to take the long chance. He clambered out of the trench with Capa behind him. The machine-guns rattled, and Capa automatically snapped his camera, falling back beside the body of his companion. Two hours later, when it was dark and the guns were still, the photographer crept across the broken ground to safety. Later he discovered that he had taken one of the finest action shots of the Spanish war.

Although Capa claimed that he was alone with the soldier on the hillside, the image of the Falling Soldier belongs to a sequence that shows the man in question among a group of soldiers (several of whom, like the Falling Soldier himself, are wearing caps embroidered with the initials "CNT") jumping across a gully and firing over the far edge of that gully.

When the Falling Soldier photograph was first published—in the September 23, 1936, issue of Vu—another photograph, showing a man in a further state of collapse, was reproduced directly below it on the page. Although some writers have claimed that both photographs show the same man, careful examination leaves no doubt that they show two different men. The Falling Soldier is wearing a white shirt and what appear to be khaki trousers; from each shoulder a strap runs straight down to a cartridge box at his waist; and he flings his gun away as he falls. The man in the other photograph is wearing a one-piece boiler suit; the straps running from his shoulders to his cartridge boxes cross at the center of his chest; and he seems to hold his gun firmly as his arm twists behind his back. Another photograph shows the two men lined up with some of their comrades and waving their rifles. The man who was

---

* For an account of that day's fighting at Cerro Muriano, see Borkenau's book *The Spanish Cockpit*, pages 158–65.

to become the Falling Soldier appears at the far left; the other is the third from the left.

If one then looks carefully at the ground in the Falling Soldier photograph and in the variant image and compares the configurations of prominently upstanding stalks, it becomes obvious that the two men are shown falling on almost precisely the same spot. (The Falling Soldier is about one foot closer to the photographer than is the man in the other picture.) We may well then ask why it is that although the two men fell within a short time of each other (the cloud configurations are almost identical) in neither picture do we see the body of the other man on the ground.

There has, of course, been a good deal of controversy about whether or not Capa posed his famous picture. Glaring inconsistencies in the three published accounts given by British journalist O'Dowd Gallagher (who claims to have been sharing a hotel room with Capa at the time, but who probably didn't even meet the photographer until the fall of 1938) allow us to dismiss his claims to the effect that Capa posed his picture in northern Spain; but the questions raised by the visual evidence are not so easily dealt with. It is possible that as soon as one man was hit, his comrades rushed to his aid and moved the body, only to have a second man hit on the same spot moments later—although in aiding the first victim, the men would almost certainly have trampled the grass. Or perhaps the man in the famous picture was the first to fall, and, as he did so, slid forward outside the frame of the second picture.

The fact is that we shall probably never know exactly what happened on that hillside. Capa told several friends stories about making the Falling Soldier photograph, but those accounts conflict—at least in the retelling—and don't throw much light on the questions raised by the visual evidence. As for the account in the *World-Telegram* (the only account written down while Capa was giving it), the photographer stated at the end of it:

No tricks are necessary to take pictures in Spain. You don't have to pose your camera [i.e., pose your subjects]. The pictures are there, and you just take them. The truth is the best picture, the best propaganda.

In any case, it seems rather improbable that proud soldiers would have agreed to stage photographs that purported to show their deaths. If it had been a question of intentional fakery, it seems more likely that all involved would have preferred to stage pictures of victory. But in the end, after all the controversy and speculation, the fact remains that Capa's Falling Soldier photograph is a great and powerful image, a haunting symbol of all the Loyalist soldiers who died in the war, and of Republican Spain itself, flinging itself

LA GUERR

PHOTOS CAPA

Le jarret vif, la poitrine au vent, fusil au poing, ils dévalaient la pente couverte d'un chaume raide.. Soudain l'essor est brisé, une balle a sifflé — une balle fratricide — et leur sang est bu par la terre natale...

PHOTOS CAPA

CIVILE EN ESPAGNE

COMMENT
ILS
ONT FUI

...e une scène calquée sur la Bible, la vision de ces ...s fugitives au visage douloureux évoque les exodes ...iques de l'Ancien Testament. PHOTO CAPA

Longeant les rails infinis, les enfants, insoucieux, croient à une promenade joyeuse, mais leur mère, d'un long regard, contemple une dernière fois le village embrasé.
PHOTO REISNER

C'est la migration du peuple d'une province tout en- tière, au pas lent des mulets lourde- ment chargés, parmi les cris des enfants, sous le dur soleil.
PHOTO CAPA

Peut-être vivaient-ils heureux, peut-être coulaient-ils des jours paisibles dans un calme village... La guerre civile est venue et avec elle le désespoir, l'écroulement d'un foyer dans la misère. CAPA

Solitaire, les larmes coulant sans bruit sur ses joues, cette pèlerine emporte avec elle tout son humble bien.
PHOTO CAPA

bravely forward and being struck down. To insist upon knowing whether the photograph actually shows a man at the moment he has been hit by a bullet is both morbid and trivializing, for the picture's greatness ultimately lies in its symbolic implications, not in its literal accuracy as a report on the death of a particular man.

Capa and Gerda were among the hundreds of reporters, photographers, newsreel cameramen, government officials, and sightseers who gathered in an olive grove just outside Toledo early on the morning of September 18 to watch as the Loyalists detonated five tons of TNT under the west wall of the Alcazar. At 6:31 the fortress seemed to erupt like a volcano, but its defenders, who had caught wind of the plan and pinpointed the tunneling by listening to the ground with stethoscopes, had huddled at the far side of the fortress, where they withstood the blast virtually unharmed. When the Loyalist troops swarmed over the rubble, the defenders repelled the attack.

Ten days later Franco's army arrived in Toledo and relieved the Insurgents in the Alcazar. The siege was the greatest struggle in which the two sides had as yet engaged, and the Insurgent victory gave rise to widespread pessimism. If the Loyalists couldn't hold Toledo, how could they hold Madrid? And if Madrid fell, wouldn't the Republic fall with it?

Undoubtedly disheartened by these prospects, Capa and Gerda returned to Paris by way of Barcelona during the last week of September. They had not been able to photograph a single Loyalist victory, and now it looked as though there would be none at all. And yet—signaling an irony that would haunt Capa throughout his career—even out of such a discouraging situation they had emerged with many photographs that brought them a measure of personal success. *Vu* had published many of their pictures in its special and regular issues; *Regards* had published others; and a few had appeared in *The Illustrated London News* and the *Berliner Illustrirte*. These sales must have made them a good deal of money, although most didn't do much for their reputations, for Capa received credit for only some of his photographs and Gerda received none for hers. But the publication of the Falling Soldier in *Vu* with his credit line more than compensated for the anonymity elsewhere, for the picture was widely hailed as the most exciting and immediate shot of battle action ever taken.

13

Although Capa was on his way to becoming a great war photographer, and to being recognized as such, he apparently felt that the situation in Spain was too hopeless to make it worthwhile for him to return. If he was captured, the Insurgents would probably disregard his claim to journalistic immunity, and, in any case, he wasn't interested in taking pictures of Loyalist defeats.

So during October, while the arrival of Franco's army in Madrid was expected daily, Capa returned to political reporting, covering a Communist rally in Strasbourg and the tumultuous congress of the deeply split Radical-Socialist Party in Biarritz, among other events.

His photographs of Alsatian women in traditional dress giving the Front Populaire salute at the Strasbourg rally had great potential as propaganda for the Left, for it was widely believed that the predominantly Catholic and German-speaking Alsatians, horrified by accounts of anti-Catholic atrocities committed by leftists in Spain, felt little sympathy for Blum's government. But when one of the photos was used on the cover of the October 14 issue of *Vu*, the image was cropped to transform it into a close-up of one woman, and all indication of her gesture was removed. Ironically, the editors then captioned the cropped photo "The True Face of Alsace." The article inside accused the Communists of stirring up trouble in Alsace and strongly implied that the "true face of Alsace" belonged to a rightist. The explanation for this unexpected distortion is that because of its outspoken position in favor of the Spanish Republic, *Vu* had lost so many advertisers that Lucien Vogel had been forced to sell his magazine at the end of September; the new owner shifted its editorial position considerably to the right—a move whose implications Capa apparently failed to consider when he sold his story.

The following week the editors of *Regards* took evident delight in reproducing the offending cover of *Vu* alongside Capa's uncropped photograph. *Regards*, however, was in no position to criticize, for on the back cover of its October 15 issue, to illustrate its story on the "tragic destiny" of girls who had gone astray, it had reproduced a photograph that Capa had taken of Gerda. So much for the journalistic integrity of the time. As for Capa and Gerda and their friends, they must have considered the picture a marvelous joke.

By November 6, when Franco's army finally reached the outskirts of Madrid, the populace was thoroughly demoralized. Few preparations had been made for defense, and the Loyalist garrison was small and poorly equipped; the city's fall seemed inevitable. But at the last minute, the exhortations of a few inspiring leaders—coupled with the full realization that an Insurgent victory would mean a rampage of torture, rape, and slaughter—roused the Madrileños to fanatic determination to resist. Pouring into the Casa de Campo, the vast park west of the city through which Franco was clearly planning to attack, they began to dig trenches and throw up barricades of mattresses, doors, and even suitcases taken from the checkroom of the nearby North Station and filled with dirt. Virtually every able-bodied man and woman took up whatever arms they could find or improvise.

When the fighting began on November 7, the Loyalists—soldiers and civilians alike—answered the fire of the most advanced German machine guns with the blasts of crude shotguns; they ran out in front of tanks to attack them with sticks of dynamite and bottles of gasoline lighted from the tips of cigarettes (for matches, like just about everything else, were in short supply); and they struggled to hold their lines at whatever cost. For anti-fascists all over the world, the battle of Madrid took on mythic overtones; it was a struggle between the forces of good and the forces of evil. If Madrid fell, so would the Spanish Republic. But if the city stood, then perhaps it really would become, as the Loyalist slogan promised, "the tomb of fascism."

On the first day of fighting the Loyalists managed to block the advance in the Casa de Campo, but from their positions the Insurgents were able to lob heavy shells into downtown Madrid, and their planes were now bombing the city with horrible effectiveness. The next morning, almost miraculously, as it seemed to the beleaguered Madrileños, the first of the International Brigades appeared, made up of volunteers from nearly every country in Europe (very few Americans having yet arrived). They had been in the midst of training at Albacete but rushed to the aid of the Loyalist troops when it became clear that every available man, no matter how poorly trained or equipped, was needed to defend Madrid. The arrival of this force of about 2,000 men gave an incalculably great boost to morale and enabled the Loyalists to halt the Insurgent advance. On November 15, however, a renewed Insurgent attack in the Casa de Campo managed to cross the Manzanares and occupy several buildings in the University City, where one of the fiercest battles of the entire civil war began.

Capa states in *Death in the Making* that he arrived in Madrid on November 12, but his memory must have erred, for much evidence indicates clearly that he arrived on November 18—without Gerda, for whom he perhaps felt that Madrid would be too dangerous. As soon as news of the city's heroic resistance reached Paris, Capa must have begun trying to get an assignment to go there, but it wasn't until November 14 that *Regards* (which was now his principal employer) gave him a letter to the Spanish ambassador in Paris, urgently requesting a visa. On the sixteenth the paper gave him a letter of introduction stating that for the period from November 18 to December 5 he was to be its only special envoy in Madrid, and a postcard he sent to Gerda from Toulouse, the principal way station for flights to Spain, was postmarked on the seventeenth. Capa presumably flew to Valencia and then (since other forms of transportation were rarely available) hired a taxi for the drive to Madrid.

On the night of November 17, as on the preceding night, Insurgent air raids turned Madrid into an inferno. Incendiary bombs started fires all over the city—except where Franco's prosperous supporters lived, for the General had declared those districts exempt from bombing. The light of the fires enabled additional waves of bombers to make out targets on which to drop high explosives. Because of the hollow-tile construction of many of the city's buildings, a single bomb could easily rip through an entire six-story structure as though it were built of cardboard. Hundreds of people were killed or badly injured, but the Madrileños were not demoralized; on the contrary, the raids infuriated them and further strengthened their determination to resist.

When Capa arrived on November 18, fires were still raging throughout the city, and the streets were filled with people migrating from their damaged homes to other parts of the city, carrying mattresses, bundles of clothing, and whatever other few personal belongings they had managed to salvage from the ruins. Still another raid came that night, and the shrieks and moans of the injured could be heard long after it had ended. For Capa (who during October had photographed a Parisian civil defense rehearsal in which fireworks realistically simulated explosions, while onlookers took the whole thing as a joke), the reality of the first intensive aerial bombardment of a European capital must have come as a terrible shock.

Capa worked on two major stories while he was in Madrid: one on the fighting in the western outskirts of the city and one on the plight of people who had lost their homes in the air raids. It was easy to go back and forth from one story to the other, for getting to and from the front was simply a matter of riding a streetcar. Along with soldiers returning from a day's rest, Capa paid his five centimos and rode out to the battle.

He spent a good deal of time his first week with the XIIth International Brigade, whose commander, a lively and charming man who used the *nom de guerre* General Lukacz, was a Hungarian, and whose political commissar, Gustav Regler, had been a leading figure in the Association of German Writers in Exile. Capa sought them out almost immediately upon his arrival in Madrid, and early on the morning of November 19, when Lukacz was sending out a patrol to explore the no-man's-land northwest of Madrid (he had only a plan of the city torn out of a Baedeker), he told Regler to take Capa along.

> The young man [wrote Regler] disliked the noise of the shells which soon whistled over us, though they exploded far in the country. Later he asked leave to change his pants, saying with humor that it was his first battle and that his bowels had been weaker than his feet.

During the ensuing battle in the farm buildings around the fortified manor house known as the Palacete de la Moncloa and in the neighboring model farms of the university's agricultural school, Capa attached himself to the XIIth Brigade's Thälmann Battalion, the nucleus of which was formed by the German Communists of the Thälmann Centuria, which he and Gerda had visited on the Aragón front in August. Some of his photographs show small patrols exploring the farm buildings, never knowing when they might stumble upon an enemy detachment in a stable or a granary, but most show the men who had already occupied buildings and turned them into small fortresses, reinforcing the walls with sandbags and knocking holes in the walls through which to fire their machine guns. He also went out by the slaughterhouses, which lay further to the west in the no-man's-land between the lines, where he photographed Asturian *dinamiteros* as they used a small catapult to hurl their grenades across the old animal enclosures into the enemy lines. The idea that former slaughterhouses for animals were now slaughterhouses for men appealed greatly to Capa's sense of war's grotesque irony.

On November 20 dense rain clouds sheltered the city from enemy planes, but the shelling by Insurgent artillery in the Casa de Campo continued and, if anything, grew worse. The telephone company building, the Telefónica, then the tallest building in Europe and the location of the government's press offices, made an excellent target in its own right and enabled the Insurgents to get their bearings for the entire Gran Vía area of central Madrid. The following ten days of cloudy and rainy weather, accompanied by icy winds from the north, protected the city from aerial bombing but brought on an epidemic of colds, bronchitis, and pneumonia among the shelterless, poorly clothed, and starving populace and made life in the trenches even more miserable than usual.

It was probably not until about a week after his arrival in Madrid that

Capa paid an extended visit to the University City proper, where he found the XIth International Brigade engaged in a holding action. He spent most of his time with a company of the Commune de Paris Battalion in the Medical School, an immense, rambling building situated on high ground in the eastern section of the campus. Some of the very worst fighting had taken place there, and skirmishes continued, but most of Capa's photographs show only the watchfulness, the camaraderie, and the pluckiness of the French and Belgian volunteers who had settled in to defend the building.

Capa later claimed that he had joined a group of sixty-five militiamen in one of the university buildings two hours before the Insurgents attacked. For two days, so he said, they were stranded in one wing, until Loyalist troops finally succeeded in rescuing the sixteen who remained alive. But although Capa got a few dramatic shots of the defenders of the Medical School in action, the surviving images support no such tale; evidently he felt he had to provide exaggerated tales of danger to accompany his photographs, no matter how strong they were in their own right. He was, of course, taking enormous risks just by being in Madrid and visiting the front lines at all, even during a lull, and he was getting many superb pictures, but that wasn't enough for him; his exploits had to sound (even if they couldn't always actually be) in proportion to the reputation of Robert Capa, whose exaggerated identity was made up in the first place. And, anyway, the always shrewd Capa knew that the more he could persuade his editors that he had placed his life in danger to get his photographs, the more they would feel bound to pay him. The fabrication of his legend was no longer simply a matter of entertaining his friends, it was also a matter of business. The legend paid off.

But it didn't interfere with his growing realization that there was more to war than just action and adventure. His pictures of Madrid make it clear that he was beginning to understand that the truth about war was to be found not only in the heat of battle, in the official show, but also at the edge of things, in the faces of soldiers enduring cold, fatigue, and tedium behind the lines and of civilians ravaged by fear, suffering, and loss. Capa was always— throughout his entire career—primarily a photographer of *people,* and many of his pictures of war (even those taken in the midst of battle) are not so much chronicles of events as extraordinarily sympathetic and compassionate studies of people under extreme stress.

Some of his most memorable photographs of the defenders of Madrid were, for instance, taken far from immediate danger, behind the lines, where soldiers sought refuge from the constant damp cold in holes covered over with whatever materials they could scavenge, and where they read, played chess, and wrote letters during their hours of inactivity. For years Capa himself had

UNE MAISON
EVENTREE.
QUI ABRITAIT
3 OU 4 FAMIL-
LES. UN BUF-
FET RESTE.
SEUL TEMOIN
DE LA VIE
DISPERSEE

DEUX FEMMES
DANS LA RUE
DEVASTEE,
DEUX IMAGES
DU DEUIL.

LA CAI

UNE VOIE DU QUARTIER DE VALLECAS, LE BELLEVILLE
DE MADRID, OU QUELQUES RUES ONT ETE TOTALEMENT
DETRUITES PAR LE BOMBARDEMENT DES FASCISTES.
UNE FAMILLE EMBALLE QUELQUES OBJETS, UN MATELAS
DES HARDES SUR UNE CHARRETTE. L'EXODE COMMENCE
LES PHOTOS DE CES DEUX PAGES ONT TOUTES ETE
PRISES DANS CE QUARTIER

TOUT   CE
QU'UNE FAMIL-
LE A PU SAU-
VER DE LA DES-
TRUCTION

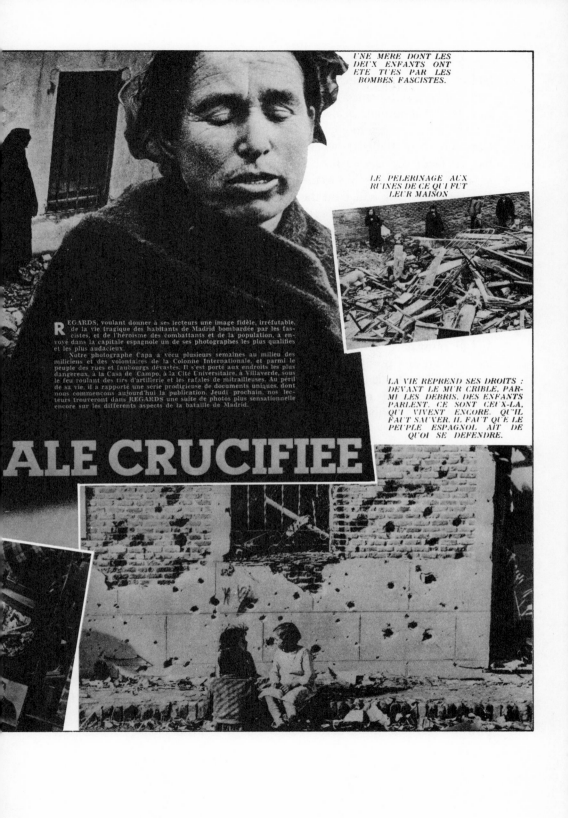

UNE MÈRE DONT LES
DEUX ENFANTS ONT
ÉTÉ TUÉS PAR LES
BOMBES FASCISTES.

LE PÈLERINAGE AUX
RUINES DE CE QUI FUT
LEUR MAISON

R EGARDS, voulant donner à ses lecteurs une image fidèle, irréfutable,
de la vie tragique des habitants de Madrid bombardée par les fascistes, et de l'héroïsme des combattants et de la population, a en-
voyé dans la capitale espagnole un de ses photographes les plus qualifiés
et les plus audacieux.
Notre photographe Capa a vécu plusieurs semaines au milieu des
miliciens et des volontaires de la Colonne Internationale, et parmi le
peuple des rues et faubourgs dévastés. Il s'est porté aux endroits les plus
dangereux, à la Casa de Campo, à la Cité Universitaire, à Villaverde, sous
le feu roulant des tirs d'artillerie et les rafales de mitrailleuses. Au péril
de sa vie, il a rapporté une série prodigieuse de documents uniques, dont
nous commençons aujourd'hui la publication. Jeudi prochain, nos lecteurs trouveront dans REGARDS une suite de photos plus sensationnelle
encore sur les différents aspects de la bataille de Madrid.

LA VIE REPREND SES DROITS :
DEVANT LE MUR CRIBLÉ, PAR-
MI LES DÉBRIS, DES ENFANTS
PARLENT. CE SONT CEUX-LÀ,
QUI VIVENT ENCORE. QU'IL
FAUT SAUVER. IL FAUT QUE LE
PEUPLE ESPAGNOL AIT DE
QUOI SE DÉFENDRE.

...ALE CRUCIFIÉE

had to adapt to harsh circumstances and so must have identified with these men; he later commented in reference to his pictures, "The war had become routine; the abnormal, as always, had become normal."

The same seemed to apply to the victims of the air raids in the working-class suburb of Vallecas, where he photographed black-clad women with haggard faces who, despite the bombings and terrible food shortages, managed to laugh among themselves as they stood in line for their tiny rations. But the homeless who took refuge on the platforms of the Madrid subway could not bring themselves to laugh. Capa's photographs of them lying on mattresses or sitting on benches in the Gran Vía station show only fear, sadness, resignation, and boredom.

There was, however, some cause for rejoicing, for by the time Capa left Madrid on December 5, it seemed certain that the city would not fall. For the moment, there was nothing more for him to cover—and in any case, his visa and letter of introduction were about to expire. Furthermore, he had promised to get his pictures to *Regards* in time for the December 10 issue, and he must have wanted to work on the layouts so that the pictures would have the greatest possible impact.

When he returned to Paris, his photographs created a sensation. *Regards* devoted much of its next four issues to them, even publicizing them on the cover of the December 10 issue with the headline:

THE CRUCIFIED CAPITAL:

the prodigious photos

of

CAPA

OUR SPECIAL ENVOY TO MADRID.

Inside the editors said, "*Regards*, wanting to give its readers a faithful, irrefutable image of the tragic life of the inhabitants of Madrid, bombarded by the fascists, sent one of its most qualified and audacious photographers to the Spanish capital. . . . At peril of his life, he made a prodigious series of unique documents."

By the end of December his pictures had been featured in four spectacular layouts in *Regards*, as well as on the cover of the *Zürcher Illustrierte*, and several had been given a spread in *Life*—his first appearance in the magazine with which he would have the most important affiliation of his career. (*Life* had just begun publication at the end of November.) Early in January the British *Weekly Illustrated* devoted several pages to his photographs, and even

Vu bought quite a few pictures, although after his experience in October Capa must have reserved the right to approve the layouts. He could now make such demands, for he was at last becoming something of a celebrity.

14

The editors of *Regards* were so pleased with Capa's pictures that they sent him back to Madrid in January. The trip, however, was anticlimactic; very little of interest was happening at that time. He made a few photographs and returned to Paris. But a few weeks later, in the middle of February, he went back to Spain, this time with Gerda. They headed for Almería, a white-washed town on the Andalusian coast to which many thousands of refugees from Málaga and its environs had fled.

The Insurgents had taken Málaga on February 8, and because they had wanted to avoid the fierce resistance of a trapped civilian population, they had left open one escape route, the coastal road to Almería, 150 miles to the east. Tens of thousands of people set out on the five-day trek, most of them on foot, clutching children and a few possessions, some leading overburdened donkeys or mules. The sun was brutal during the day, and the nights were cold. There was little food. Many quickly wore out their shoes. The road was lined with those who had collapsed from pain, hunger, and exhaustion.

Then, in an act of wanton brutality that anticipated the bombing of Guernica, the Insurgents pursued the refugees with tanks, strafed them from planes, and shot at them from ships that approached close to shore. Along some stretches, the road was like a shooting gallery: on one side a cliff fell to the sea, on the other rose a high, solid wall of stone. There was nowhere to hide. Thousands died on the road. But even for those who reached Almería, the ordeal was not over. On the evening of February 12, by which time the streets were choked with sleeping refugees, Insurgent planes bombed the town.

In Almería itself, as well as in Murcia, to which some of the refugees had been transported, Capa and Gerda concentrated on scenes very similar to those in the Madrid subway stations, though even more wrenching. Here people were camping on the pavement, completely without shelter. Old women and children were huddled together on piles of sacks and blankets. The heads and feet of many were wrapped in bandages. The faces of even the youngest children, usually oblivious to tragedy, registered despair.

Judging by the photographs that survive from this trip, it appears that Capa and Gerda arrived in Almería after the exodus itself had ended. As they drove westward on the road to Málaga, they encountered a few stragglers, but the photographs that Capa published in *Death in the Making* as having been taken on the Málaga–Almería road had actually been taken at Cerro Muriano the previous September. The flight from Málaga had become a symbol of Insurgent cruelty, but no one had heard of Cerro Muriano, so Capa captioned his photographs for maximum impact. He obviously did so for the sake of propaganda, not to take credit for having covered an event for which he actually arrived too late.

After a week in the hills between Almería and Málaga, where they saw no fighting, the photographers proceeded to the Jarama front, where the Insurgents were trying to cut the Madrid–Valencia highway, over which all supplies for the capital had to be transported. By the time Capa and Gerda arrived, however, the Loyalists safely held the highway—at least for the time being. The photographers went out to Arganda, where a key bridge had been hotly contested, and they visited the International Brigades' operational headquarters in Morata de Tajuña, but there was no action. Nor was there any when they returned to Madrid and visited the elaborate system of trenches, tunnels, and caves that the Loyalists had dug around the Insurgent-held Clinical Hospital in the University City.

Then, almost immediately, Capa left for Paris—without Gerda—arriving in the French capital on the morning of March 2. He went because he had been offered a job as staff photographer for *Ce Soir*, a newly founded afternoon paper designed to compete with *Paris-soir* (it even blatantly copied *Paris-soir*'s format, devoting its back page entirely to photo-stories, both news-related and human-interest). *Ce Soir* proclaimed itself an independent paper, but it was in fact Communist-run, although it was aimed not so much at party members (who were served by *L'Humanité*) as at fellow travelers and supporters of the Front Populaire. The paper's editor-in-chief, Louis Aragon, whom Capa had met in Madrid in November, was a well-known Communist, but to support the paper's claim to political independence he hired, or published contributions by, many non-Communists.

Capa's primary commitment was now to *Ce Soir*, but since his contract allowed him to sell photographs to other publications as well, he continued to have his work published in *Regards*, *Weekly Illustrated*, *Life*, the *Schweizer Illustrierte Zeitung*, and elsewhere. With so many contacts of his own, he felt he no longer needed Alliance to handle his work and instead set himself up in business. He rented and moved into a studio in a new building at 37 Rue Froidevaux, across the street from the Cimitière du Montparnasse, and hired Csiki to do his developing and printing. He even had stationery printed up with the letterhead "Atelier Robert Capa."

His work was going well, but it appears that by this time his romance with Gerda was not. There can be no doubt that Capa still loved her intensely, but as she began to win respect for her work, she began to demand more professional independence and they began to spend more time apart than together. The most tangible evidence of their changing relationship is the succession of bylines with which they stamped prints of their photographs. At first, all of Gerda's pictures were lumped together with Capa's and published under his name, which she must have resented, as she must have resented being left behind in Paris while he went to Madrid to cover the siege; but for the work they did jointly in February they had a stamp made up to read "Reportage Capa & Taro," and prints of the pictures she took alone in March are stamped "Photo Taro"—the byline under which she then finally began to have her work published regularly in *Ce Soir* and *Regards*.

As her professional independence and standing grew, so, apparently, did her emotional independence—all of which surely made her all the more attractive to Capa, who neither wanted nor could afford to be tied down in a conventional marriage. (He had, after all, been rebelling against family life since the age of ten.) Not only would Gerda not try to hold him back when he had to leave for a dangerous assignment, she would go with him. Rather than limit him, she would push him, encourage him to take risks, and they would do great work together.

It appears that sometime during the spring of 1937 Capa asked Gerda to marry him and that she refused. (He later told a married photographer who worked with his wife that such a marriage struck him as ideal and that he envied him. He also said that if Gerda had lived, they would have had such a marriage.) Later in life he would consider marriage to three other women, but in each case it was the woman who wanted to marry and Capa who resisted. He loved Gerda as he never loved any other woman, for she offered the possibility of a love that would not curtail his freedom. The trouble was that she was now offering him more freedom than love, and for once in his life he became possessive—which made her resist him all the more, for she was unwilling to let emotional demands interfere with her suddenly burgeoning career.

Soon she was telling friends that she and Capa were *copains* (buddies), not lovers. After only about a year and a half of being lovers, they had returned—against Capa's will—to a relationship much like the one they had the first year after they met. Only now, in addition to being close friends, they were occasional partners, sometimes traveling, working, and perhaps even sleeping together—though apparently only when it suited Gerda to do so. Capa was very much in love and very frustrated.

His sense of frustration could only have been exacerbated by the first assignments he did for *Ce Soir*: a parade of Paris's Laurel and Hardy fan club, the Salon des Artistes Indépendants, a gala costume benefit for the Union des Artistes at the Cirque d'Hiver, and the opening of an agricultural exposition. It must have been something of a shock to go from Spain to such routine trivialities, but Capa could reassure himself that he was doing such stories only to kill time and to earn his salary between more important assignments.

After three weeks of this work, something more interesting finally came up: an inspection tour of the French-Spanish border, across which France had prohibited the shipment of arms or passage of volunteers. Capa and *Ce Soir* reporter Charles Reber spent a day exploring the area around Perpignan, and then, on the morning of March 26, set out on the drive to Andorra. Against Reber's advice, Capa insisted on wearing a Spanish militiaman's jacket he had bought in Madrid, and he stubbornly carried a large box containing a whole arsenal of flashbulbs that looked like little bombs. Reber pointed out that after one look at Capa's jacket, every policeman and customs officer they encountered would assume that they were volunteers trying to cross the border, and once they saw the box of flashbulbs, they would be sure they had captured a couple of arms smugglers. But Capa maintained that he would need the warm jacket up in the snow-covered mountains, and he insisted that the flashbulbs were indispensable for the practice of his profession. In any case, he was confident that his charm and fast talking could get them out of any difficulty that might arise.

He soon had a chance to test his claim, for at the first checkpoint they came to, the guards took one look at him and started to congratulate themselves on having made a real catch. "Never have I seen authorities examine papers so thoroughly," wrote Reber. "Each guard in turn took our documents and looked at them every which way. We had to come up with some treasures of diplomacy in order to convince these brave representatives of the customs that we were simple journalists and that we had not the slightest intention of joining the militia or smuggling contraband." Finally—and rather reluctantly—the guards let them pass. Capa's reaction to the whole episode was that he thought the guards didn't have much sense of humor.

Over and over again as Capa and Reber drove up into the Pyrenees, the scene was repeated. Finally they reached the town of Porté, from which, twice a week, a troop of ten skiers made the trip to Andorra to carry provisions and mail to the French garrison that, at the request of the tiny republic, had been stationed there since the outbreak of the Spanish Civil War.

Soon after Capa and Reber left their car in Porté and started to walk up the steep road to the Puymorens pass, the skiers came into view, and Capa threw himself into photographing them from every position: standing, kneeling, even lying in the snow to get the most dramatic shots. But at that moment a policeman who had followed the two journalists from town, his suspicions having been aroused by Capa's jacket, pounced and demanded both their papers and an explanation. Only partially satisfied by their assurances and credentials, he told them he would let them go—but only if Capa destroyed his film of the skiers on the spot. Capa did so, but, never one to accept defeat, was soon out chasing after the ski troop to replace his lost photographs.

From Andorra, Capa and Reber went by way of Toulouse to the Côte Basque, where they spent several days investigating the clandestine fascist "embassies" in Hendaye, Biarritz, and St.-Jean-de-Luz, returning to Paris about April 1. The trip was interesting, but it produced few good photographs, and, in any case, it was peripheral to the main story. Capa was eager to get back into Spain itself, where fighting had flared up again on the Jarama and Guadalajara fronts. On April 5 he obtained from the office of the under secretary of state in the French Ministry of Foreign Affairs a letter asking the passport office to issue him papers for a trip to Madrid and Valencia as a reporter for *Ce Soir* and for Metro-Goldwyn-Mayer News.* But before he could leave for Spain, *Ce Soir* sent him with a team of three reporters and a sketch artist to Brussels to cover a parliamentary by-election that was to take place on Sunday, April 11. The election was actually of little importance, but the international press had blown it up into a symbolic struggle between fascism and democracy, for Léon Degrelle, leader of the fascist Rex Party, had decided to run against the liberal Paul Van Zeeland for the vacated seat. Capa duly photographed rallies, campaign gimmicks, posters, and, after the election, Van Zeeland's victory parade. The editors of *Ce Soir* were apparently pleased, for they ran his pictures on the front page almost every day for a week and on two days devoted the entire back page to them.

With this obligation fulfilled, Capa returned to Paris and a few days later left for Spain with Gerda, who had come to Paris at the end of March for a brief rest. Arriving in Madrid, they established themselves in the Hotel Florida,

---

* No evidence of Capa's ever having made either stills or newsreel footage for MGM News has yet come to light.

which journalists favored because of its proximity to the press office in the Telefónica. That proximity also had an unpleasant drawback, however, for occasionally an Insurgent shell aimed at the Telefónica would land on the hotel, doing little damage besides breaking windows and blowing out the water-heating system, but nevertheless shaking up the residents.

Among the journalists staying at the Florida was Ernest Hemingway, who had arrived in Madrid late in March to collaborate with John Dos Passos (whose novel 1919 had made such an impression on Gerda), Dutch documentary filmmaker Joris Ivens, and Ivens's young Dutch cameraman John Fernhout—who was then married to Eva Besnyö—on a film eventually entitled *The Spanish Earth*. Ivens and Fernhout were mostly off filming in a small village, but Hemingway remained behind in the city, where he spent much of his time with two men, Herbert Matthews of *The New York Times* and Sefton Delmer of the London *Daily Express*, with whom he formed something of a triumvirate: Hemingway playing the part of the burly, macho intellectual in his beret and wire-rimmed glasses; Matthews, tall, lanky, shy, serious, and one of the most meticulously accurate and thorough reporters in Spain; and Delmer, six feet tall and weighing over 200 pounds, who looked to Hemingway like a "ruddy English bishop."

Matthews was to become one of Capa's closest friends, as they continued to encounter each other on various fronts during the civil war and World War II. But Capa's friendship with Hemingway was to have an even greater significance: the photographer later was to write that soon after their first meeting, he "adopted [Hemingway] as a father." The arrangement was apparently mutually satisfactory, for Hemingway always relished the role of the brave, wise, omniscient father figure, and, as a writer famous for his war exploits and his knowledge of Spain, he was a perfect mentor for this young man making a name for himself covering the Spanish Civil War. For his part, Capa, who was always something of a cynic, must have realized that a friendship with Hemingway could only help his own reputation.

After about a week of visiting the once again stalemated fronts outside the city, it became clear to Capa that the really exciting news was going to come not out of Madrid but out of Bilbao. After the Insurgent setback on the Guadalajara front northeast of Madrid, Franco—eager to gain control of the iron ore, coal, and industry of the north—had decided to move the bulk of his forces from around the capital and send them against the Basque provinces.

Capa wanted to leave for Bilbao at once, but his papers were valid only for Madrid and Valencia, and, in any case, there were no planes flying the route between Madrid and Bilbao, between which lay a huge expanse of Insurgent-held territory. So he returned to Paris with Gerda to get new papers and to confirm his assignment with the editors of *Ce Soir* and *Regards*.

They arrived in Paris on April 22 or 23, and while he was waiting for arrangements to be made, Capa did several assignments for *Ce Soir*, including coverage of the May Day parade and demonstrations. That day he took several pictures of Gerda looking especially happy and chic as she bought the traditional sprig of lily of the valley that was supposed to guarantee happiness for the coming year. In fact, Gerda had less than three months left to live, and much of that time she and Capa would spend apart.

A few days later Capa, without Gerda, left for Biarritz and then flew from there to Bilbao in a small French plane. The enemy patrolled the route regularly, but, until it was discovered that the Insurgent blockade at sea was largely ineffective, there seemed to be no safer way to get into Bilbao.

By early in May, Insurgent troops were approaching the city from the east along a broad front. Having taken the defenseless towns of Durango and Guernica after merciless bombings, they had come to the range of low mountains that served as Bilbao's last natural line of defense, and on May 7 they attacked Mount Solluve, one of the most strategically important of those mountains. According to *Ce Soir* reporter Mathieu Corman, who was with Capa during the battle, German planes strafed the Basque trenches on the lower slopes, while Insurgent tanks advanced, firing, until they were stopped by roadblocks. At dusk, *dinamiteros* tossed grenades under the stalled tanks, and when the men in the undamaged tanks nearby saw what was happening, they backed up and fled. Even so, over the course of the next several days the Insurgents secured Mount Solluve.

After that first day of battle, Capa spent most of his time documenting life in the beleaguered city itself: women reinforcing the city's fortifications with mountains of garbage, the farewells as women, children, and old men boarded the French and British ships that had run the blockade to evacuate them, and the daily routine of air raids. Alerts that culminated in minor raids became so frequent that mothers and their children took to spending the time between them sitting on sandbags outside the shelters; there the women talked and knitted while the children played. But others had to run frantically for shelter when the sirens sounded. Capa calmly remained aboveground photographing until the streets were empty.

On May 12, after he had photographed a gasoline dump fire started by Insurgent bombs, Capa was driven out to the Bilbao airfield in an official Packard, its siren clearing the way. There he handed the pilot of the plane that was about to take off for Biarritz a package of film to be rushed to Paris.

BILBAO
SOUS

Anxieusement, il scru-
te le ciel, guettant
l'approche des incen-
diaires...

REPORTAGE PHOTOGRAPHIQUE de CAPA

Un instant
d'accalmie, en-
tre deux com-
bats farouches.

Ci-dessus : u
basque donn
à boire à un
turien venu
Bilt

Ci-contre, à ga
une bombe a
feu o un dépô
sence. Avec un
me inouï, les h
vont à l'approc
flammes pour e
crire l'incendie
tant des pellet
terre.

FEU

Les avions allemands survolent la ville. L'alerte a vidé les rues. Sur la grande place déserte, la bouviere est reste seul avec son âne chargé de provisions.

Sauver l'enfant, la chair de sa chair !

Premier hululement de sirène. C'est le commencement de l'alerte.

: des jeunes de Bilbao ... de la terre ... fortifications ... ture de fer itale basque.

... le refuge.

ANTONIO ALVAR

LUBRIFICANTES ATLANTIC

Permanencias Infantiles el hombre de mañana

The next day the first of his vivid photographs of the battle of Mount Solluve appeared in *Ce Soir*.

By May 15 it looked as though Bilbao were about to fall, and the minister of information announced that one last plane was leaving for Biarritz. Capa, who wanted to stay, gave all his exposed film and all his cameras except for one Leica to reporter S. L. Shneiderman, Chim's brother-in-law, to take on that plane. But Capa didn't stay in Bilbao very long, for it soon became evident that the city would hold out a while longer, and in the meantime there was little happening that he hadn't already photographed. On the night of the seventeenth he left in a fishing boat that ran the blockade, arriving in Bayonne the next day, just in time to join Shneiderman and his wife in the horde of photographers and reporters assembled in the British consul's office for Jessica Mitford's wedding to Esmond Romilly, at which there were so many photographers using flash that one French newspaper called it a "mariage au magnésium."

After that welcome diversion from the anguish he had observed in Bilbao, Capa went on to Paris, where he had to see his editors and once again obtain papers for traveling in Spain. Unhappy with the restrictions imposed on him by *Ce Soir*, and bored by the work he had to do for the paper in Paris, he asked to be released from his contract. His request was granted on condition that he give *Ce Soir* priority on the French publication of his photographs. At once he went to the Time Inc. office to talk to Richard de Rochemont, the brilliant, Harvard-educated chief of European operations for *The March of Time*, the journalistic film series founded and produced by his brother Louis. Capa, who knew nothing about cinematography, managed nevertheless to persuade de Rochemont to lend him an Eyemo—a small, hand-held movie camera—with which to shoot some footage in Spain for *The March of Time*. De Rochemont gave him a quick lesson in using the camera, offered a small advance against publication of his photographs in *Life* (he was also head of Time Inc.'s Paris bureau), and sent him on his way.

Capa must have left Paris almost immediately after getting his letter of safe conduct from the Spanish ambassador on May 26, for by the thirty-first he and Gerda (who had been in Valencia on her own) were together at the Navacerrada Pass, near Segovia, to cover the abortive Loyalist offensive that Hemingway described in *For Whom the Bell Tolls*. On the first day of the battle Capa and Gerda, working side by side, exchanged the Eyemo and a Leica back and forth for shots of tanks maneuvering, officers studying maps and talking on field telephones, and men advancing; both handled the movie camera in a manner that is essentially photographic rather than cinematic, using it to make shots of only a few seconds' duration that seem like extended stills. Very few shots were of any use to *The March of Time*.

Back in Madrid, which was enduring some of the heaviest shelling of the entire siege, they photographed and filmed *dinamiteros* using guerrilla tactics in house-to-house fighting in the southwestern suburb of Carabanchel, and they covered the state funeral of General Lukacz, who had been killed on the Aragón front on June 12 when his car was hit by an enemy shell. But more important than anything happening in or near Madrid was the Loyalist resistance to an Insurgent drive toward the rich mining region around Peñarroya, Pozoblanco, and Almadén. Accordingly, Capa and Gerda headed south, arriving on June 24 at the Chapaiev Battalion's headquarters near Peñarroya, where they met Alfred Kantorowicz, the unit's political commissar. Kantorowicz thought Capa looked familiar, but the photographer had to remind him that they had met in Paris at the Association of German Writers in Exile. Kantorowicz also had some trouble identifying Gerda, whom he had previously seen only in the public rooms of Valencia hotels, where she had always been very stylishly dressed. Now she was wearing "trousers, a beret pulled down over her beautiful red-blond hair, and a dainty revolver at her waist."

On their first day with the battalion, Capa and Gerda filmed and photographed a mock attack. Kantorowicz wrote in his diary that the staff and troops headquartered behind the lines "all had to wear their helmets and carry their rifles, and Capa arranged a whole attack scene: an imaginary fascist position was stormed as the men, with terrifying roars and passionate battle-lust, leapt and bounded double-time into victory." Capa, he added, "was very pleased with the result." The photographs are probably those *Ce Soir* published as showing an attack on the village of La Granjuela. This dramatic series of pictures shows men advancing along a dirt road into a tiny country village, a scenario that may well have been a re-creation of what had actually happened at La Granjuela on April 5, when the battalion had captured it. Such dramatic re-enactments of events were by no means unusual in *March of Time* films, for Henry Luce himself had ordered the series directors to use "fakery in allegiance to the truth" whenever necessary. When Capa told Kantorowicz that the footage of the staged battle would appear more authentic on the screen than footage of an actual battle would, he was probably echoing advice that Richard de Rochemont had given him.

It was certainly not for lack of courage that Capa and Gerda staged the attack on La Granjuela, for the next day they went out to the front lines, where a heated battle was raging. When Gerda heard that one Polish company was disappointed that they couldn't be filmed because it was too dangerous to approach their position during the day,

nothing could hold her back as she tossed her camera on to her shoulder and, with profligate foolishness, in broad daylight, ran across the 180 meters [to the position] without cover. A few daring ones followed her. It was the time of the siesta; the fascists seemed to be sleeping. All went well. Gerda Taro filmed at length the position and the comrades of the second company. It was almost with force that the men held her and Capa there until dusk [when it would be safe to return to the main lines].

Soon after this trip to Peñarroya, Capa—who no longer had an agent to handle such matters—returned to Paris to sell their pictures and to turn their film over to Richard de Rochemont, but Gerda remained in Madrid. Capa would never return to Madrid, nor would he ever again see Gerda alive.

15

Gerda remained in Spain as one of *Ce Soir*'s correspondents at the congress of the International Association of Writers for the Defense of Culture, but on July 10, with the two-week conference only half over,* she cabled her editors to request permission to cover the new Loyalist offensive west of Madrid. Permission was granted.

Upon her arrival in the capital, she moved into the bustling headquarters of the Alianza de Intelectuales Antifascistas Españolas. Housed in a former palace, the Alianza was run by poet Rafael Alberti and his wife Maria Teresa León, with both of whom Gerda had become very friendly. She had also become very friendly with Ted Allan, the nineteen-year-old political commissar of Dr. Norman Bethune's blood-transfusion unit.† For his part, Allan had fallen in love with Gerda. But then so had several of the foreign corre-

---

* The congress opened in Valencia on July 4, proceeded to Madrid on the sixth for three days, and then returned to Valencia for several days before moving on to Barcelona and finally to Paris for the closing session.
† Bethune, an eminent Canadian surgeon who was pioneering the use of sodium citrate to keep blood fresh for transfusions at the front, had hired Geza Korvin to make a film (*Heart of Spain*) to use for fund-raising. Capa and Gerda had seen Korvin in Madrid in April and through him had met Allan.

spondents in Madrid. Claud Cockburn, a tough, skeptical, and satirical British Communist who was writing for the London *Worker* is said to have moved into the Alianza in order to be near her, and there are rumors of a liaison between her and the Czech-German journalist Egon Erwin Kisch, who was then the most famous and influential Communist reporter in Europe. But Gerda wasn't interested in getting very involved with anyone, for she was reveling in her independence and in her new sense of herself as a highly respected photojournalist who easily won friendship and affection. In tributes written after her death, colleagues and Loyalist officers whose units she had visited spoke over and over again of her warmth, her charm, her bravery, and her infectious joy. "La Pequeña Rubia," the little redhead, as the soldiers called her, was welcome at every front, for the presence of this young woman, so petite and so girlishly gay that she seemed to be barely more than a child, suggested to the men that perhaps things weren't so bad after all. Judging from accounts of Gerda's exuberant bravery on the field of battle, it seems that she was transferring much of her former passion for Capa to her work, to her career, and to the fate of the Spanish Republic.

At dawn on July 6, a Loyalist force of some 50,000 men had begun an offensive push toward Brunete, where two roads crossed that were crucial for the flow of supplies to the Insurgent troops in the Casa de Campo and the University City. Because they took the Insurgents by surprise, the Loyalists were able to advance rapidly on Brunete, capturing the villages of Quijorna and Villanueva de la Cañada on the way. But massive Insurgent reinforcements soon arrived to begin a battle far bloodier than any other yet fought in the civil war. As more than 100,000 thirst-tortured men fought for three little villages on the dusty Castilian plain, in temperatures that often exceeded 100° F in the shade, attacks alternated with counterattacks; nobody ever seemed really certain exactly who at any given moment held which village, or which part of a village, or which stretch of ground. The confusion was so great that each side occasionally bombed or shelled its own men. The slaughter was prodigious.

It must have been about July 12 when Gerda was finally able to get to Brunete, for her first photographs of the captured town appeared in *Ce Soir* on the fifteenth. When she arrived, houses were still burning, tanks were rolling through the streets, and the Loyalists were engaged in dangerous house-to-house searches for the remaining Insurgent snipers. By the time she ate supper with an artillery battery of French, Belgian, and Italian volunteers in a wheatfield outside of town, she had taken some of the most dramatic pictures of her career. But the photograph that created the greatest stir in the press was not an action shot at all. It showed three Loyalist soldiers standing in front of a wall in whose masonry was embedded a ceramic plaque bearing the name "BRUNETE." The photograph was a trophy, for it offered indisputable proof that the Loyalists had actually taken the town.

The following week Gerda returned to the front, this time with her friend and admirer Claud Cockburn, who later wrote that as they were sitting in a field, under machine-gun fire from German planes, they

> arrived at the conclusion that we had, this time, very little chance of getting out alive. She then stood up and began to make photographs of the planes, saying, "In case we do somehow get out of this, we'll have something to show the Non-Intervention Committee."

Gerda's reckless bravery may reflect a feeling that she had expressed to Cockburn a few days earlier. "When you think of all the fine people we both know who have been killed even in this one offensive," she said, "you get an absurd feeling that somehow it's unfair still to be alive."

When Capa left Madrid to return to Paris, he had given Gerda the *March of Time* movie camera to use. She threw herself into the film project with characteristic and, indeed, martyr-like enthusiasm. Cockburn wrote that on July 22, by which time the Insurgents had begun a massive counteroffensive, Gerda,

> after having worked all night on her film, had to run thirteen kilometers carrying her film camera in order to reach the exact point in the lines where she believed she could make the most useful shots. That evening she arrived [back at the Alianza] exhausted but saying, "Tomorrow I'll get up at six so I can get better shots."

During the morning of Saturday, July 24, Insurgent troops, supported by artillery, tanks, and planes, blasted the Loyalists out of Brunete in what Herbert Matthews described as fighting of "enormous violence." That afternoon, however, the Loyalists were able to regroup and attack Brunete again, gaining a toehold by dusk; in a bitter struggle after nightfall, they managed to regain much of the village.

The next morning Gerda, who was planning to leave for Paris the following day and wanted one last chance to get some spectacular action shots, set out for Brunete with Ted Allan, but by the time they reached General Walter's headquarters, it was almost one o'clock in the afternoon. Although Gerda had gotten to know the general on previous visits to the Brunete front and at the Navacerrada Pass, he was not well disposed to them when they arrived. Despite

Gerda's insistence that she simply *had* to photograph the action that day, he ordered them to leave the area immediately. In five minutes, he warned them, all hell would break loose.

Allan was ready to obey, but Gerda had no intention of doing so, and she persuaded him to go with her to some shallow dugouts on a hill nearby. Soon the Insurgent artillery started up, and Insurgent planes began to attack; some of the hundreds of bombs they dropped on the Loyalist lines during the next hour fell uncomfortably close to the dugout into which they had managed to squeeze themselves. Gerda took pictures all the while. Then came strafers, and still she photographed. One of the planes apparently saw her camera glinting in the sun and swooped down right overhead; she shot a picture of the neat row of dust explosions the bullets made as they hit the ground. Gerda's sangfroid gave Allan the impression that she had been through all this before. And of course she had; she told him that he would get used to it, too.

Under the continuing heavy barrage of bombs, artillery shells, and strafing, the Loyalist troops in and around Brunete panicked, broke ranks, and began to flee—a fatal mistake, for once they were out in the open, the planes could attack them all the more effectively. Near Gerda and Allan's dugout some soldiers made an attempt to halt the retreat by threatening to shoot anyone who tried to get past them. Gerda jumped out of the dugout and started shouting at the retreating men, exhorting them to re-form their lines. The men, realizing that the planes had at last stopped coming over, obeyed.

At about 6:30, having walked all the way to Villanueva de la Cañada, north of Brunete, Gerda and Allan saw General Walter's large black touring car speeding in their direction and hailed it. The general wasn't in his car; instead, there were three wounded men in the back seat. Gerda tossed her cameras onto the front seat, and she and Allan jumped—in the best tradition of American gangster movies—onto one of the running boards. She was certain that she had gotten the best photographs of her life that day, and she wanted to celebrate with a bottle of champagne when they got back to Madrid. Then she would leave for Paris in the morning.

Suddenly a Loyalist tank that was careering wildly out of control bore down on them. The car's driver swerved to avoid it, but it was too late. The tank sideswiped the car, mangling Gerda and Allan. Eventually they were taken to the American field hospital at El Escorial, where the doctors operated on Gerda during the night. They thought she would make it, although she was suffering badly from shock and would probably limp for the rest of her life if she survived. It was about six o'clock on that morning of Monday, July 26, when she died.

In the middle of July, Capa had told Gerda on the telephone that he was
trying to get Richard de Rochemont to send them to China for *Life*. The
Japanese garrison in Peking had claimed that while they were engaged in field
maneuvers at the Marco Polo Bridge on the night of July 7, they were fired
upon by the Chinese. The Japanese government, which had been looking for
a pretext to declare all-out war on China, promptly did so. Gerda was enthusiastic about going to China and said that she would return to Paris on the
twenty-sixth to begin making preparations. For his part, perhaps Capa imagined that the long sea voyage and radical change of environment might help
to bring him and Gerda closer together again.

When Gerda failed to show up in Paris as planned, Capa tried to call her
at the Alianza to find out why she had been delayed and to give her the news
that the *Life* assignment had come through. But no one at the Alianza knew
what had happened to her.

The next morning Capa rose early to go to the dentist, and on the way
there he bought a copy of *L'Humanité*. Sitting in the dentist's chair, he opened
the paper to the third page to read the column of short reports from Spain,
the last of which bore the headline:

A French journalist

Mlle. Tarot

is reported to have been killed

during a combat near Brunete.

The one-sentence report, dated July 26, read: "It is rumored, although it has
not been possible to obtain any confirmation whatsoever, that a French journalist, Mlle. Tarot, was killed today, during a combat in the region of Brunete." Later that morning Louis Aragon, whom Georges Soria had telephoned
from Madrid, told Capa that the reports were true.

That night Capa, Ruth Cerf, and Paul Nizan, a *Ce Soir* editor, left for
Toulouse, where Gerda's body was supposed to be flown, but when they
learned that international law forbade the transport of the dead across borders
by plane, they returned to Paris. The remains were eventually driven to

Perpignan, just over the French border, and then put on a train for Paris. Shortly after 8:30 a.m. on Friday, July 30, the coffin, still covered with flowers from Madrid and Valencia, where the body had lain in state, arrived at the Gare d'Austerlitz. When Gerda's father, who had rushed to Paris, began to chant in Hebrew, Capa was so overcome by emotion that Seiichi Inouye and Aragon's wife, Else Triolet, had to take him away. He was absolutely devastated by his grief. Until the funeral he remained in his studio, weeping and refusing all the food and drink that Inouye brought him.

The funeral procession from the Maison de la Culture, where the body had lain for two days, to the Père-Lachaise Cemetery* began at ten-thirty on the morning of Sunday, August 1, which would have been Gerda's twenty-sixth birthday. Despite the bitter absurdity of her having been killed by a Loyalist tank in what was essentially a horrible traffic accident on the periphery of battle, the Communist Party had declared her an anti-fascist martyr and had organized a spectacular procession, with flowers, music, banners, and thousands of mourners. Aragon later wrote that Capa, "by my side, cried, and, when the cortege halted, hid his eyes on my shoulder." The pick and the spade now indeed separated him from the woman he loved most in his life.

In death Gerda found the fame she had craved in life. She was hailed as a heroine, a latter-day Joan of Arc. Tributes poured in to *Ce Soir*, and the paper printed them all. The editors, who for more than two weeks dragged out the coverage of the last days of Gerda's life and her funeral, made limitless claims for her heroism and for the thoroughness of her coverage of the civil war, even going so far as to claim that she had recently spent much time on the Bilbao front (she hadn't been there at all) and publishing a photograph that Capa had made in December as one of Gerda's last photographs of Madrid. French girls took Gerda as their idol and formed organizations in her memory. An article in *Life* did much to spread her fame as "probably the first woman photographer ever killed in action." She became so well known in death that when, in 1938, a Philadelphia bubble-gum company issued in its packages a set of 240 cards illustrating "True Stories of Modern Warfare," a card devoted to Gerda's death was among them.

Capa was totally bereft. Overcome by grief, he began to drink heavily. He

---

* According to *Ce Soir* (May 30, 1938, p. 8), Gerda's monument—a horizontal block topped by an Egyptian-style marble bird and bowl and a double cube bearing her name, dates, and a brief text about her death—was sculpted by Alberto Giacometti. Her grave was located near the Mur des Fédérés, the memorial to the Communards. The lease for the plot expired several years ago; since it was not renewed, Gerda's monument was removed and apparently destroyed.

was tortured by feelings of guilt for having introduced Gerda into the profession that led to her death as well as for not having been with her on that last fatal day. Occasionally he grew so hysterical that some of his friends were afraid he might kill himself; when he disappeared for several days, some feared he had done so.

He had actually fled to Amsterdam, for Paris was so full of painful memories that he felt he had to escape. He showed up unannounced at the studio where Chaja Goldstein, who had been György Kepes's girlfriend in Berlin, now lived with her husband, Theo Gusten. After having been out of touch for several years, Capa and Chaja had recently encountered each other in Montparnasse, and though they had never been especially close friends, Chaja sensed that Capa had come to view her as a sort of older sister. When he arrived in Amsterdam, he told Chaja and her husband the story of Gerda's death, and they invited him to stay in the little room over their studio. They took care of him for several days, and finally, Chaja accompanied him back to Paris.

Ted Allan, still convalescing and on crutches, arrived in Paris soon afterward and Capa paid him a visit at his hotel. Apprehensively Allan asked him, "Don't you realize that I loved her?" but Capa replied, "So what? How could you help it?" and persuaded him to come and stay in his Rue Froidevaux studio, where he took care of him for a week. The two men, bound by their love for the dead woman, talked about returning to Spain or going to China to work on a book together. And when, on August 20, Capa sailed on the *Lafayette* to New York to see his mother (Julia and Kornel had left Paris for New York early in June), Allan, who was going home to Toronto to recuperate, went with him.

Capa became even closer to Gerda in death than he had ever been in life. She had been his lover for only a relatively brief time; before and after that period they had been *copains* and partners. In death, Gerda became Capa's wife. Now that she was dead there was nothing to stop him from telling people that they had been married, and undoubtedly he felt as closely tied to her as if they actually had been. When he went to China in 1938, he took along a small valise completely filled with prints of a picture he had taken of Gerda, and he gave a print to everyone he met, telling them that she had been his wife and claiming that he had been with her at the time of her fatal accident. That was evidently how he felt things *should* have been, and he was not going to defer to mere facts. Life was so absurd, what did it matter if he changed a few details?

Much of what this young man of twenty-three had experienced and seen had taught him that it was dangerous to let oneself get too attached to anyone or anything; to do so was obviously to risk terrible grief. His exile at seventeen had separated him from his family. In Berlin and in Paris he had learned still more about impermanence and loss; and in Spain he saw death, loss, and flight everywhere. It was apparently the nature of families to be torn apart, of loved ones to be lost, of homes and possessions to be abandoned in flight. And yet he had allowed himself to become deeply attached to Gerda, only to lose her.

Capa later said that when Gerda died, his own life came to a kind of end as well; he felt he had little of any real value left to lose, and (we may infer) he chose to keep it that way. Henceforth he would remain, at some deep level, detached from family, friends, women, money—indeed, from life itself. They were all to be enjoyed as fully as possible, but only in the present moment. There could be no strings attached, no promises for the future. (His dread of commitments showed up even in so small a matter as meeting for a drink; he was *always* late, often by as much as an hour or more. He knew that no matter how irritated his friends might be, he could quickly charm them into forgiveness.) So fully did he enjoy his friends, and they him, that most thought him a man who loved life and threw himself into relishing its pleasures. But, despite his belief that it was inconsiderate and in bad taste ever to appear anything but charming and gay (he held to this rigid, gentlemanly code as meticulously as any aristocrat ever did), his closest friends sensed another side of him, the part that remained André Friedmann, who had been deeply wounded by Gerda's death and remained profoundly grieved.

Never again would he let himself become so vulnerable; he would remain unattached. Having nothing to lose—so his reasoning went—he would be protected from further loss. It seems at first a selfish position, and yet Capa, always considerate in his own peculiar way, apparently felt that to allow others to become overly attached to a man in his profession was to set them up for loss and grief. As long as he remained free, he and those about whom he cared (his very distancing was, after all, a measure of his care) would remain safe. Ironically, on the one hand, his detachment gave him an air of extraordinary freedom that made him more attractive than ever; on the other hand, maintaining his detachment against all temptations, he inevitably found that the price of his protection from loss was isolation and loneliness, even when he was surrounded by his most congenial and amusing friends.

17

Capa traveled to New York primarily to see his family for consolation, but he also had some business to take care of. Since he was dissatisfied with the Black Star agency, which had been representing him in the United States, he went to Pix to talk to Léon Daniel, whose brother Henri had been one of his first agents in Paris. Daniel was so eager to handle Capa's work that he not only offered very acceptable terms but also agreed to hire Cornell (who had Anglicized his name) to work in the agency's darkroom, as well as to give Capa's Dephot friend Ladislaus Glück (who was again using the name Peter Koester) a job writing captions.

The next order of business was to try to get a contract from *Life* giving him an advance against a guaranteed minimum number of pages per month. Reaching such an agreement was so important to him that after talking to the editors (with Daniel as interpreter, since Capa spoke no English—a circumstance that made him feel, he wrote, uncomfortably like a country cousin) he stayed in his hotel room for three days and nights waiting for their call.* Finally the call came; he would get his contract, and, since he was in New York, the editors wanted him to begin working at once on some local stories: one on an American Legion parade and one on Stillman's Gym, famous as a training ground for champion boxers.

When he took his photographs of the gym to *Life*, the editors were pleased with his conception of the story and his choice of subjects, but because he hadn't used flash to illuminate the dark interior, the pictures were murky. Despite his ostentatious carrying of a box of flashbulbs on his trip along the French-Spanish border, Capa didn't really know how to use flash properly. In desperation he turned to his old friend André Kertész, who had been living in New York for a year. Kertész went to the gym with Capa and showed him what to do. The second batch of pictures turned out well, but *Life* ended up not running the story anyway.

---

* Wanting to be as close as possible to the *Life* offices, then located in the Chrysler Building, he had checked into the Hotel Bedford on East Fortieth Street, only two blocks away, as soon as he arrived in New York. Ted Allan, who was also acting as his interpreter, stayed with him.

As important as the *Life* contract was to his livelihood, more important
from an emotional standpoint was the matter of publishing a book of his and
Gerda's photographs of the Spanish Civil War that would serve both as propaganda for the Republic and as a memorial to Gerda. After the house of
Covici, Friede accepted his proposal, he enlisted Kertész to lay the book out
and Jay Allen, a journalist he had met in Bilbao in May, to write a preface
and translate the captions. Capa dedicated the book, *Death in the
Making*, to Gerda, "who spent one year at the Spanish front, and who
stayed on."

By the time Capa returned to Paris in November, he was much recovered
and became involved with a beautiful young Arab woman whose first husband,
so rumor had it, had found her in a North African brothel. She was as lithe
and dangerous as a tiger, with jet-black hair, skin the color of amber, and a
ferocious temper. She was the perfect woman for him at that moment, for
she offered friendship with much laughter (they teased each other, he calling
her "sale arabe" and she replying "sale juif" or "sale bandit," a pun on his
Hungarian nickname), and she offered sex with no strings attached (she was
evidently bisexual and, according to some, was still working as a prostitute).

She also offered the excitement of danger. Once, as they were sitting at
the Select (which had replaced the Dôme as Capa's regular hangout), one of
Capa's joking taunts went too far; knocking over their table, the woman jumped
up, grabbed him by the neck, and started to choke him. The storm passed
quickly, but for several days Capa carried the marks of her nails on his neck.
She frightened him a bit, but at least her intensity, her humor, and her air
of danger could take his mind off Gerda for a while.

Even such a lover, however, couldn't provide enough adventure to satisfy
Capa. He was eager to throw himself back into his work and to find an anodyne
in the danger and camaraderie of the front. He was, therefore, pleased when
Joris Ivens and John Fernhout invited him to accompany them to China,
where they were going to make a film about the Sino-Japanese War. They
asked him along both because they felt the trip would help him to recover
further from Gerda's death and because they hoped that his connections with
Life would prove useful. Capa, craving adventure and also welcoming the
chance to salvage some of his original plan and to learn more about filmmaking, readily accepted.

Since they weren't leaving until late January, he wanted first to make a
quick trip to Spain, although complications then arose with *Ce Soir*. Finally,
after frustrating weeks of waiting while editors and agents postponed decisions
(in the meantime, he did a story on Belgian coal miners with Chim), he left
for Barcelona about December 19 with the intention of making a short film

on schools, hospitals, and other services for children—only to change his plans as soon as he arrived. *

On the morning of December 15 the Loyalists had begun a massive assault on Teruel, a walled town in the bleak mountains of southern Aragón that the Insurgents clearly planned to use as the jumping-off point for their campaign to drive a corridor through to the Mediterranean, thereby separating Barcelona from Valencia and Madrid. The Loyalists hoped that their offensive would not only stop the Insurgent push to the sea but also provide the psychologically decisive victory that the Brunete offensive had failed to yield.

Capa arrived at Teruel on the twenty-first and accompanied a detachment of the audacious *dinamiteros* he admired so much as they spearheaded a direct attack on the town, finally blasting their way in with grenades. A Loyalist victory apparently assured, Capa rushed back to Valencia that evening to send off his scoop. There he encountered the triumvirate of Hemingway, Matthews, and Delmer, who were driving to Teruel and back each day in Matthews's huge old car.

Of the next three days, on each of which Capa drove with his friends to Teruel, Matthews wrote:

> We [watched] the civilians pouring out in pitiful groups and columns and the soldiers gradually cleaning up all but [the most] stubbornly defended buildings. . . . We saw tanks and armored cars maneuvering and firing until snipers and machine-gun nests were silenced; machine-gun crews being rushed on to roofs and high angles; dynamiters making the last charge while windows were kept under streams of fire to protect their advance; soldiers creeping up from every side to dash into houses. . . . The [Civil Governor's palace] was set afire, and it made a tremendous blaze. There were dead bodies all over the place, bodies of men and of mules, and there was no time to clean up the streets.

Every evening the journalists returned from the horrors of Teruel to the comforts of Valencia. In contrast to what they were witnessing during the day, Hemingway's posturings at the hotel must have seemed more grotesque than

---

* Before leaving New York, Capa had received an advance of $100 and the loan of a film camera from the Medical Bureau of the North American Committee to Aid Spanish Democracy. He had agreed that within three weeks he would take at least 200 photographs and several reels of film showing Medical Bureau activities and American hospitals in Spain, but he never took them. A year later he was still trying to pay back the advance in bits and pieces, grumbling that the Bureau had used so many of his Spanish photographs without paying him that he shouldn't have to reimburse them.

ever, but Capa could never afford to pass up a saleable story—and a story about Hemingway would always sell. So he photographed the writer taking a swig from a bottle of Scotch for breakfast, checking his maps, preparing the day's provisions, and conferring with Soviet novelist Ilya Ehrenburg. Because Hemingway had just finished writing his play *The Fifth Column*, much of it set in the Hotel Florida in Madrid, Capa always claimed that this series of pictures was actually taken there. They almost could have been (and probably wouldn't have looked much different if they had), but they weren't.

Capa spent Christmas Eve driving with his friends to Barcelona, where Hemingway left them to return to the States. Then, on New Year's Day, Insurgent newspapers and radio stations claimed that their side had retaken Teruel, despite the blinding snowstorm and crippling cold that made fighting an even more hellish ordeal than usual. Because communication lines around Teruel had been knocked down, not even military officials in Barcelona could deny the claims with certainty, and so on the morning of January 2, Capa and Matthews set out to investigate. Twenty miles outside Teruel they came to a steep pass in which two feet of snow had ensnarled hundreds of army cars and trucks in an enormous traffic jam. Despite the best efforts of the huge work force dispatched to handle what one officer called "one of the principal episodes of the battle," it took Capa and Matthews from eleven in the morning until seven-thirty in the evening to cross the three-mile pass.

The interim [wrote Matthews] was a confused and rather agonizing nightmare of heaving, straining, grinding upward yard by yard, with the car swaying from side to side and the wheels unable even to turn on the slippery surface. We were bruised from innumerable falls, since it seemed almost impossible to keep one's feet for more than a few minutes; we were blue with cold, and famished and terribly tired, but so was everybody else, and somehow we all sooner or later got to the top of Puerto Ragudo.

Our reward came when, after we had coasted down to Barracas, some Carabiñero officers with whom we had become friendly on the way up invited us into their headquarters for the night. That meant a cheerful, blazing fire in a peasant's hut, a marvelous feast of dried salt codfish, bread, wine, and coffee, a pleasant chat on war and women and home, and a few hours' sleep, rolled up in a rug before the smoldering fire.

The next morning Capa and Matthews found that although the Insurgents had gained a great deal of ground and had battered the town relentlessly for several days with artillery and aerial bombing, most of Teruel was still in Loyalist hands. The largest concentration of Insurgents was in the charred ruins of the Civil Governor's palace; after blasting away the façade, Loyalist soldiers swarmed over the rubble and into the building, where ensued, wrote Capa, who scrambled after them,

> a grenade battle without mercy. All the walls seemed to have been mined; explosions resounded everywhere. Dominating the dry reports of revolvers, between the rare seconds of silence that followed the explosions of grenades, one heard rising from the heart of the building cries of "¡Arriba España!" [the Insurgent rallying cry] and the groans of those unfortunates whom the Insurgents had taken as hostages. . . . One advanced with extreme prudence. . . .

By the time Capa left Teruel that evening to return to Paris, the Loyalists held the palace, and by the end of the week they again held the entire town, but they would not hold it for long. By the end of February, the Insurgents would retake Teruel, and on Good Friday, Franco would reach the sea.

The editors of *Regards* were so excited by Capa's photographs of Teruel that when they published the first of two dramatic layouts the headline read:

"Regards" presents
the photos taken by CAPA
of the
Victory of Teruel.

Ce Soir, too, in the headline of the article he wrote, put Capa's name above that of Teruel.

Teruel was also his first major story in *Life*. The magazine devoted five pages to the photographs, but the editors felt they had to defend their decision to publish them, since pictures of the horrors of war had previously provoked letters full of "dismay and outrage" from many readers. Far from soft-pedaling the photographs of Teruel, the editors wrote that "even the best pictures cannot show war in all its horror and ugliness. . . . No pictures can convey the sounds that come from a thousand dying men or the smells that come from a thousand dead men." They concluded that "the love of peace has no meaning or stamina unless it is based on a knowledge of war's terrors."

Capa himself would never have made such grandiloquent claims. In his view, it was an absurd and treacherous world, and nothing he or anyone else did could change that fundamental truth. He had no illusions about his photographs putting an end to war or anything of the sort. And, after the disillusioning collapse of idealism in Spain (the brutal Communist suppression of the POUM had begun that spring), he had little faith in political change; things would always be essentially the same, and there would always be terrible wars. All you could do was try to help individuals caught up in war—and even then there was little more you could do than try to raise their spirits for a moment, perhaps flirt a little, make them laugh; you could give them cigarettes and candy (which he always carried for that purpose); and you could photograph them, to let them know that somebody cared. And perhaps someone who saw the pictures might be moved to do something, however modest. Only a fool, he felt, would expect anything more.

18

By the time Capa returned to Paris, having stopped in Barcelona for a few days, he had only two weeks to get ready to leave for China—which would have been plenty of time if his financial arrangements hadn't suddenly grown complicated. The editors of Ce Soir had promised to underwrite his trip, but now they changed their minds and decided to give him only a small advance, and Ivens (who would be flying to Hong Kong from the United States) cabled that he couldn't give him any advance at all. As it was, the film budget was very tight; Ivens and Fernhout were each going to receive a salary of only fifty dollars a week. But Ivens finally agreed to pay Capa's expenses in China if Capa would himself arrange to pay for his passage there and back. Even with the advance from Ce Soir, to which were added one from Simon Guttmann, one from Pix, and his retainer from Life, Capa was short of money. Hemingway later boasted that he sent Capa two hundred dollars for the trip.

When Capa and Fernhout sailed on the Aramis from Marseilles on January 21, 1938, it turned out that on board was another pair of young men setting out to cover the war in China: W. H. Auden and Christopher Isherwood. Though friendly, Capa and Fernhout didn't spend much time with them, for the two Englishmen seemed so terribly serious. Isherwood later wrote of Capa and Fernhout—with a distinct tone of admiration—that

with their horse-play, bottom-pinching, exclamations of "Eh, quoi! Salop!" and
endless jokes about *les poules*, they [were] the life and soul of the second class.
Capa is Hungarian, but more French than the French; stocky and swarthy, with
drooping black comedian's eyes. . . . Fernhout is a tall, blond young Dutchman—
as wild as Capa but slightly less noisy.

On February 16, after stops in Port Said, Djibouti, Aden, Colombo,
Singapore, and Saigon, the *Aramis* arrived in Hong Kong, where Capa and
Fernhout met up with Ivens. They paid a brief visit to Sun Yat-sen's widow
and then flew to Hankow, the temporary seat of Chiang Kai-shek's government.

Since the conservative Chiang had—though only under duress—formed
an alliance with the Chinese Communists to fight the invading Japanese, the
war in China was widely considered the eastern front of the war that was being
fought in Spain: the war between the international Popular Front movement
and the international fascist movement. As in Spain, the Popular Front alliance was a most uneasy one. In China, however, it was not the Communists
who had the upper hand. Chiang held the real power, except in the north-
western city of Yenan, where the Communist Eighth Route Army, under the
political leadership of Mao Tse-tung, had established itself.

Because it was Madame Chiang, her husband's most trusted lieutenant,
who would give—or withhold—permission for the film team to travel to key
fronts and to visit the Eighth Route Army, Ivens had enlisted actress Luise
Rainer (whom Mme. Chiang admired greatly for her starring role in the film
The Good Earth, released the previous year) as a principal in the corporation
he organized to sponsor his film. He also counted on Capa's *Life* connection
to win Mme. Chiang's support, for *Life* publisher Henry Luce, born in China
of missionary parents, was a leading Sinophile. But Ivens's precautions back-
fired. Mme. Chiang was so impressed with the film team's connections that
she became convinced that their film (which was eventually entitled *The Four
Hundred Million*) would be extremely influential in the United States. Great
care would thus have to be taken to ensure that it presented China in the
most favorable light possible. There could be no shots of backwardness or
poverty, of military inefficiency or of the hated Communists. To make certain
that her will was obeyed, Mme. Chiang assigned a high-ranking military man
to control the movements of the film team and to supervise an entire corps
of spies and censors. John Fernhout recalls that whenever they visited Mme.
Chiang, she would let them know how effective her spies were by asking,
"Did you have a good time at so-and-so's last night?"

For six weeks, Mme. Chiang kept the film team in Hankow. Ivens very
much wanted to make a film—or at least a long segment of one—about the

life of a child soldier (a "little red devil") in the Eighth Route Army, but he could never admit such a thing to her. Instead he had to try to find excuses for heading toward the northwest, hoping that he could eventually break free of her network of spies and censors and make a dash for Yenan. But Mme. Chiang was not to be fooled.

Those six weeks in Hankow were especially frustrating for Capa, who felt that because Ivens wasn't paying him any salary, but only expenses (which amounted to considerably less than five dollars a day), and because he had paid his own passage out of his advances, he shouldn't be bound too tightly to the others. But Ivens had told the Chinese that Capa was only a member of the film team, not a free-lance photographer, and he was therefore prohibited from traveling on his own. While Ivens waited for travel permits, Capa also had to wait, doing stories in Hankow for which he needed no special permission, and when the film team was finally granted permission to travel, he had to stay with them at all times; he was not allowed to return to Hankow to send off a scoop. Furthermore, because his photographs were officially regarded as publicity stills for Ivens's film, they were subject to much stricter censorship than the photographs of free-lancers, who were actually given quite a lot of liberty.

The only reportage of any interest that Capa was able to do in Hankow was on a big parade on March 12 that was simultaneously celebrating Sun Yat-sen's birthday and some minor victories on the northeastern front. Much of the rest of the time he spent—either alone or with John Fernhout—in the bars and the White Russian cafés on Dump Street, where all the journalists congregated while waiting for something to happen.

Finally, at seven o'clock on the morning of April 1, the film team and its army of censors, spies, and equipment- and supply-carriers boarded a train bound not for the northwest but for the Suchow front in the northeast, where the Chinese showed signs of stopping the Japanese advance. Although anti-aircraft guns had been mounted on the roofs of the railroad cars, everyone was relieved that the overcast weather, which kept the Japanese bombers away, made them superfluous. (The Japanese had decided that the only way to conquer China was to capture the railroads and to use them to create a network of control over the sprawling nation; until then they would do their best to hinder Chinese use of the railroads. Traveling a great deal on trains, Capa came to recognize their importance, calling the war "a war of railroads." In fact, he did a long reportage on the role of military transport trains, refugee trains, and armored trains in the war.)

The next day in Chengchow, which had been largely evacuated after Japanese bombers demoralized the population, the film team met the other

journalists who would accompany them to Suchow: Archibald Steele of the
Chicago *Daily News*, Irving Epstein of the United Press, and Walter Bosshard,
the former Dephot photographer of whose Far Eastern exploits Capa had
heard so much but whom he had not met until now. Bosshard was covering
the war for the *Neue Zürcher Zeitung*, for Ullstein, and for Black Star
(from whom *Life* was buying many of his pictures). A dapper man who,
with his neatly trimmed mustache, bore a distinct resemblance to Dezsö
Friedmann, Bosshard was to become both a friend and a nemesis of Capa's
in China—a nemesis because he was a competitor for space in *Life* and
because, by reaching Yenan, he preempted Capa's hoped-for scoop for the
magazine.

Also traveling with the group was Capt. Evans Fordyce Carlson of the
United States Marines, President Roosevelt's personal observer in China. Ivens
remembers Carlson (who later became famous as the leader of "Carlson's
Raiders") as "a tall, solid Protestant, simple, sober, and rather reserved, yet
with warm human qualities that are unusual in a military man." Carlson,
who quickly developed a warm friendship with the members of the film team,
gave Capa his first acquaintance with the breed of American officer whom he
would come to admire and befriend during World War II.

The train from Chengchow pulled into Suchow at dawn on the morning of April 3, and at three o'clock the following morning they arrived at the
old farm that served as the field headquarters of Gen. Sun Lien-chung,
commander of the Twenty-sixth Route Army. There they would remain for
several days, while fighting raged within earshot around the walled town of
Taierhchwang.

During the first day, the group went to an artillery observation post to get
a glimpse, through binoculars, of the Japanese lines; the enemy, noticing the
activity, gave them a special welcoming barrage of artillery fire. After dinner,
as they sat around in a barn, Ivens and Fernhout sang Dutch sailor and love
songs, Carlson played "I've Been Working on the Railroad" on his harmonica,
and Capa sang songs of the Hungarian plains "in a hoarse, melancholy voice."
The next day, blessed with fine weather and bright sunshine, Ivens and Fernhout shot the first feet of their film at a forward observation post and gave
Capa his first lesson as second cameraman. He was also learning something
else that would be more useful to him in the long run; he was learning to
speak English, the common language of the group. He would later joke that
he had "won his English in a crap game in Shanghai."

Although the film team was now close to the front, it was little better off
in terms of opportunities to film—or to photograph—battle action than it had
been in Hankow. If anything, it was even more frustrating to be able to hear
fighting going on in the distance and to see troops and materiel moving up

for what was clearly a major battle, and yet be unable to get close to what was happening. For three days the Chinese met Ivens's request for permission to go to the front with the reply, "The Honorable Guests are welcome, and we admire their courage . . . but we can't possibly allow guests to be in danger."

Even had they been allowed at the front, however, they wouldn't have been able to film or photograph the decisive fighting, for it took place at night, when the effectiveness of the superior Japanese technology was reduced and the effectiveness of Chinese machine guns in close fighting was increased. Indeed, the final attack was led by the Chinese 31st Division, whose machine-gunners were so famed for their night assaults that they were called "sleep robbers."

At six o'clock on the morning of April 7, an officer, bursting with excitement, awakened the whole group to announce that during the night the Chinese had driven the Japanese out of Taierhchwang. Not only was it the first major Chinese victory of the war, it was also the first time in history that a Japanese army had suffered a frontal defeat.

Until eleven o'clock that morning the film team waited frantically for transportation to Taierhchwang—but the Chinese weren't going to let them get near the town until it was certain that no pockets of snipers remained and that there was no immediate danger of a Japanese attempt to retake the town. When the group finally arrived in Taierhchwang, they found a scene of overwhelming desolation: buildings reduced to piles of rubble, streets strewn with bodies, trees stripped of their branches—and even of their bark—by machine-gun and artillery fire. But on the ramparts were Chinese soldiers proudly waving the Nationalist flag.

Life laid out Capa's pictures of troop maneuvers in and around Taierhchwang in such a way as to suggest that he had gone to the front with the 31st Division at dusk on April 6 and had remained with them throughout the night of battle. Even more misleading was the accompanying text, which claimed that Taierhchwang's name would be added to the list of "small towns famous as turning points in history—Waterloo, Gettysburg, Verdun." The victory at Taierhchwang turned out to be more valuable for propaganda than for any lasting strategic importance; the Japanese soon retook the town, and Suchow fell to them at the end of May.

The victory at Taierhchwang did much to raise Chinese morale, but when Capa returned to Hankow on Easter Sunday, April 17, his own morale was very low. He complained in a letter to Peter Koester,

> In general, I am the "poor relation" of the expedition, and this is causing me plenty of difficulties. . . . They are very fine fellows, but the movie is their private affair

(and they let me feel that), and the still pictures are completely secondary. . . . The pictures of Taierhchwang are not bad, but it really isn't easy to photograph well if you have a big film-camera on your back, four censors around, and then have to help the film operator . . . I have to photograph to the side and don't have much time to do it, either.

He wistfully told Auden and Isherwood, who were then also in Hankow, that he would "like to get back to Paris for the Fourteenth of July and dance in the streets" and then return to Madrid, and in a letter to Kertész he grumbled that he hadn't had a good Chinese meal since he left Paris.

Waiting around in Hankow while Ivens mounted a second campaign to get permission to go to the northwest, Capa became friendly with Agnes Smedley, a forty-eight-year-old American journalist and radical activist whose boyishly short hair and rare combination of romantic political idealism and effective practicality undoubtedly reminded him of Gerda. Like Gerda, Smedley had great personal charm and charisma, which put her at the center of the journalistic community in Hankow. The daughter of a Colorado mineworker and a washerwoman, Smedley was largely self-educated. In 1919, after having become involved with Communism and with the movement to liberate India from British rule, she went to Germany, where she eventually became a correspondent for the prestigious *Frankfurter Zeitung*, which sent her to China in 1928. She had remained there, becoming a passionate and valued supporter of—and prolific propagandist for—the Chinese Communists. She was also an extraordinary humanitarian, going to great lengths to obtain medicine and clothes for the poor and wounded of China. Her ministrations on the streets of Hankow became a familiar and much-admired sight.

Capa was a frequent visitor to Smedley's apartment, a small oasis of comfort and sociability in a huge and otherwise completely deserted former military headquarters. He cultivated her friendship not only because her personality was irresistible but also because he was determined to get to Yenan—with or without Ivens—and Smedley, who was very close to Chou En-lai, then Mao's representative in Hankow, could pave the way.

At last permission came through for the film team to travel to the northwest, though not to Yenan. Ivens and Fernhout left Hankow on April 29, with Capa to follow two days later. The delay was lucky for Capa, as he shot one of the most widely published of his Chinese stories on the day they left, which was the thirty-seventh birthday of Emperor Hirohito of Japan. To celebrate, the Japanese had planned a big air raid on Hankow that would focus on the

Hanyang Arsenal. When the alarm sounded, early in the afternoon, Chinese pursuit planes were already in the air, and so, instead of running down into the shelters, many of the Chinese who had been eating lunch on Dump Street stood outside the restaurants to watch the hour-long battle. Capa caught on his film the crowd's expressions of anxiety, followed by outbursts of joy as twenty Japanese planes were shot down. Seen side by side with the pictures he had taken during an air battle over Madrid in November 1936, the photographs convey a strong sense of the universality of war, and lend graphic support to the claim that Spain and China were two fronts of the same war. Even the defending planes were the same in both places: Russian-made.

Although the Chinese declared the air battle a victory, the price was horribly high: twelve Chinese planes were shot down, and in the slums surrounding the arsenal (which had been emptied some time before) a thousand civilians were killed or injured.

Capa caught up with Ivens and Fernhout in Chengchow and proceeded with them by train westward to Sian, a walled city that, from the outside, looked like an enormous penitentiary. Inside were dirt streets lined with shacks and ruins, all constantly swept by clouds of dust from the Gobi Desert. Isherwood, who had been there a few weeks earlier, thought the city smelled of murder.

For two weeks the film team was held in virtual room-captivity in the city's incongruously ultra-modern luxury hotel, and when Ivens requested a truck to take them to Yenan, his request was—naturally—turned down. He then tried another tactic, asking to be allowed to film the Great Wall, for he had figured out that to get to the nearest segment, they would have to drive through Yenan. But Mme. Chiang's agents thwarted him again: they would give him permission only to film a stretch of the Wall to the west, beyond Lanchow, not one to the north. Taking what they could get, the film team set out for Lanchow.

Because the railway line ended in Sian, they traveled westward along the old Silk Road in a bus. In temperatures of over 100° F they had to keep all the windows open, but then such awful clouds of dust were sucked in that it was like being inside a vacuum cleaner, and they all had to wear towels over their faces with only narrow slits cut for their eyes. From time to time, as howling winds covered the road with dunes of sand, the bus would get stuck and everyone would have to get out and push. When they finally reached the Great Wall, after a six-day ordeal, they found that that particular section had crumbled so badly that it looked like just one more huge sand dune.

Before leaving for Lanchow, Capa had learned to his great dismay that Bosshard had already been to Yenan. On top of that, Ivens finally abandoned his own efforts to get there; he would make his film without any footage of the Eighth Route Army. But Capa was unwilling to be deprived of what he hoped would be his most important story. Counting on Bosshard's visit to Yenan having been too brief to "shoot him down," Capa made arrangements with the Communist representatives in Sian to go to the northwest by himself in July or August, after he had finished his work with Ivens.

Upon his return to Hankow about June 15 (he went alone, since Ivens had come down with mumps and would have to remain in Sian for several weeks), Capa wrote Koester that the six-week trip had been "the world's most idiotic and painful." On top of the ordeal of boredom, frustration, heat, and dust, the primitive film-processing lab in Hankow had ruined one of his best reportages—a story on the peasants and fishermen who ferried Chinese troops across the broad Yellow River on goat-skin rafts and crude boats. In the brutal heat of a Hankow summer, the emulsion of the improperly fixed film began to melt as the huge wooden drying wheel to which it had been tacked was spun around. The accident was a strange prefiguration—even in its amphibious subject—of what would happen to his negatives of the Allied landing on Omaha Beach on D-Day in 1944. Furious and frustrated, there was nothing Capa could do but go to Dump Street and get wildly drunk.

As the Japanese advanced on Chengchow—the crossroads of the two major railway lines of northern and eastern China and gateway to the Hankow region—Chiang Kai-shek ordered the dikes of the Yellow River blown up. The flood, which halted the Japanese only temporarily, inundated eleven cities and four thousand villages, destroyed the crops of three provinces, and rendered two million people homeless. Capa rushed to Chengchow and beyond, where he shot many powerful pictures of refugees migrating to dry land. He was so pleased with the results that he exclaimed in the letter he wrote to Koester on July 4, "At eight o'clock this morning, after a six-day-and-night trip, I returned from the floods—and the report is sensational!" He had even been able to get some shots of improvised ferries to replace those that had been ruined.

An hour and a half after his return he was with Ivens and Fernhout at a meeting of Chiang Kai-shek's Supreme War Council. It was the first time Chiang had ever allowed such a meeting to be filmed or photographed, and it was the first meeting from which were absent the Germans whom Chiang had hired in 1931 to advise him on military training and strategy. Capa's photographs of Chiang seated at the head of a large, map-covered table while he listened to the reports of his officers were widely published.

The next day Capa covered the departure of the German advisers, whose recall Japan, which had signed the Anti-Comintern Pact with Germany in

1936, had been demanding since the outbreak of the war with China. Germany had agreed in May, but the advisers—retired officers, four of them Jews—were no longer subject to military orders and not fond of Hitler. Germany could force them to return home only by threatening to deprive them of their citizenship and property if they failed to comply. Finally, on July 5, the advisers, led by Gen. Baron Alexander von Falkenhausen, a "tall, suave, icy-cold strategist," whose traveling companion was a cocker spaniel, reluctantly boarded a train in Hankow. After photographing the farewells on the station platform, Capa shinnied up a telephone pole to get a shot of the enormous Nazi flag that had been spread out on the roof of the Germans' car to ward off Japanese bombers.

After this brief but fruitful flurry of activity (during which he also did stories on Mme. Chiang's social work and on a meeting of the Communist committee in Hankow), Capa went through one of the most trying periods of his trying stay in China. The death of the mother of Mme. Chiang's chief liaison with the film team brought work to a complete stop for ten days. Capa came down with dysentery, and in his weakened condition he couldn't tolerate the 100° F-plus heat. ("If it's not the runs, then it's the sweats, and I can hardly stand up," he complained to Koester.) In the midst of all this frustration and discomfort, Bosshard returned to Hankow with good pictures of at least half the people and activities Capa was hoping to photograph in Yenan. On top of that, Ivens told Capa that he would have to accompany him and Fernhout to Canton and Hong Kong. Capa had understood that when the filmmakers left Hankow he would be on his own at last and free to head up to the northwest, where he felt there were still enough important stories to justify the long and arduous journey, providing that *Life* wanted the pictures "very badly." Otherwise, he told Koester, he would be happy to leave China as soon as possible.

There was also disturbing mail from New York and Paris. At the end of almost a year of hard work, Capa had cleared—after payment of his debts and expenses—only sixty dollars from Pix! Although *Life* had already published several of Capa's stories from China, editor Wilson Hicks was being cagey about committing himself further. The editors of *Ce Soir* were angry because they discovered that they weren't always the first French editors to be given a look at Capa's latest stories, and Capa's agent in England, a Mrs. Muir, was so angry about infringements on her territory that she was threatening to sue. Moreover, there were problems with Simon Guttmann, who had burst into Capa's studio just as the photographer was leaving for Marseilles. "It was his idea," Capa wrote to Koester, "that my atelier, my future, and my Chinese trip all belonged to him. I talked him out of that pretty energetically." Now Guttmann was giving a hard time to Csiki, who was manning the darkroom in Capa's studio while Ruth Cerf typed captions (sometimes, when Capa's captions got lost in the mail, fabricating them entirely). All this led Capa to tell Koester, "We shall detach Guttmann. I am sorry, but he leads to the craziest things, and I wrote to tell Csiki not to allow himself to be terrorized." To his credit, Guttmann sold the *Schweizer Illustrierte* a ten-page cover story of Capa's China photographs that must have brought in a handsome sum.

Prompted by these muddles and mishaps, Capa hatched a plan to break free from all his encumbering agents. On July 27 he wrote to Koester:

> I am starting here the organization of a few young photographers, and I shall continue the same in Europe. . . . I don't know what is happening with Cartier[-Bresson] and Chim. Something could also be done with them, and Csiki would be the one to find out. I would like it if we could form some sort of organization, but in no case would I want it to be a regular agency. Furthermore, the Paris atelier is my private headquarters. . . . Currently all I can do is to teach a few young men here to do good work, which will have significance only after my departure.

That letter contains the germ of Magnum, the photographers' cooperative that Capa was to found in 1947 with Cartier-Bresson, Chim, and several other friends. Right from the beginning, Capa saw the projected organization as a sort of fraternity with the responsibility not only of representing its members in their business dealings but also of initiating young photographers into the profession of photojournalism—as Guttmann and the photographers at Dephot had initiated him. Koester was to be the businessman of the organization, as he had been at Dephot. Alas, he had died of tuberculosis four days before Capa wrote his letter; Capa received the news several weeks later in a letter from Cornell.

On July 19 Japanese bombers aimed for the first time at civilian areas of Hankow; until then they had aimed at airfields, railroad lines and depots, and other military targets, killing civilians only through careless aiming. When the alarm sounded, Capa photographed people running toward the small European quarter, as they always did, just as the poor of Madrid had sought safety in wealthy neighborhoods. (In August, when the crowds seeking refuge grew so large that there was almost as much danger from crushing as from bombs, the French consul ordered a stout picket fence laced with barbed wire built around the quarter. Once it was filled with as many people—both European and Chinese—as was deemed safe, the gates, guarded by tanks and by soldiers armed with machine guns, were closed.)

After the raid Capa went with Ivens and Fernhout to the hardest-hit area to film and photograph the heroic efforts of the fire brigades and the grim work of those searching for bodies buried under the rubble and ashes. Although he took some extraordinary pictures that day, Capa protested to Koester,

> Unfortunately, my reportage is quite imperfect, because our "movie expedition" had an appointment elsewhere, and after ten minutes of work they dragged me back to the hotel. And so the story is incomplete. I wanted to finish it the next day (they now come over daily), but on the 20th there was only an alarm, no bombing.

There is an unmistakable—and chilling—note of disappointment in that last sentence. And Capa realized it. A few days later he wrote to Koester,

> Slowly I am feeling more and more like a hyena. Even if you know the value of your work, it gets on your nerves. Everybody suspects that you are a spy or that you want to make money at the expense of other people's skins.

He then expressed an idea that he would adopt as an ironic motto of a sort: "The war photographer's most fervent wish is for unemployment." But was it really? Of course he hated war and was appalled by the horrors he saw and photographed; nevertheless, photographing war was what he did best, and it was bringing him the success for which he had struggled so hard. As for being a hyena, he knew as much about loss and grief as most of those he photographed, and, far from being an impassive voyeur who merely observed from a safe vantage point, he cared deeply about the outcome of the war against fascism and was always ready to risk his life to get great photographs.

Because Ivens wanted to get some footage of air raids on a great modern city, he had decided to go to Canton, which was being heavily bombed. On the morning of July 21, Capa, Ivens, and Fernhout set out on the four-day train trip; once there, they rented the top floor of the city's tallest building, a fourteen-story hotel, and waited for the bombers to appear. They felt terribly brave, for such a building made an outstanding target, and the top floor was, naturally, the most vulnerable (and, for that reason, also the cheapest). Only later did they learn that they had been in the safest place in town; the Japanese had earmarked the hotel for its General Staff headquarters and had ordered their bombardiers not to damage it.

In the middle of August—having gotten their footage of the air raids, and having filmed the peasant reserves, armed only with spears, who were to aid regular troops defending the coast—Ivens and Fernhout left for the United States to edit their film. Capa was on his own at last. His plan was to return to Hankow by way of Nanchang, where, he wrote, he could photograph "the river, the mountains, guerrillas, fliers, and tanks—in one word, everything." In Hankow he would document preparations for the defense of the city and then fly to Yenan to do a story on the Anti-Japanese Military and Political University ("the guerrilla academy"). After that, he would return to Hankow to cover the battle for the city, which by that time would probably have begun in earnest. Then, finally, at the end of September, he would leave for Paris.

But the Chinese authorities insisted that Capa, now that he was officially a free-lance photographer, must register, apply for travel passes, and get an interpreter in Hankow before proceeding to Nanchang. In Hankow he saw his friend Captain Carlson, who had recently spent several weeks in Yenan and, while there, had taken many photographs. Together they cooked up a plan: Capa would sell Carlson's photographs to Pix (giving full credit to Carlson) and integrate them with the pictures *of* Carlson he had taken on the trip to Taierhchwang. Published together, the two sets of pictures would imply that Capa had traveled with Carlson through the northwest; there was no longer any need for him to make the long trip himself.

While in Hankow, Capa met another extraordinary American officer, Col. (soon to be General) Joseph W. Stilwell, the military attaché whose acerbic criticism of stupidity and incompetence earned him the nickname "Vinegar Joe." Stilwell, a rough-and-ready, totally forthright and unpretentious officer of the old school, was, like Carlson, sympathetic to the Chinese Communists, whom he found to be "uniformly frank, courteous, friendly, and direct." He also liked Capa and noted in his diary that the photographer was "quite a guy."

At midnight on September 6, Capa and six young Chinese photographers—presumably the ones he had been teaching in Hankow—arrived at the army camp near Nanchang, some 150 miles southeast of Hankow, where Stilwell was spending the night. After they were awakened at dawn the next morning by Japanese planes overhead and guns firing nearby, Stilwell joined Capa and his "gang" (as the colonel called them) for cocoa, and Capa decided to join up with Stilwell for the remainder of his trip. Along the road that first day they saw "pack transport coolies—exhausted men—curled up to die," but the closer they got to the front, the warmer the welcome they got from military officers. The following morning Capa and Stilwell shared a breakfast of cheese and moldy bread and then climbed a mountain from which they had a panoramic view of "a sea of rocky hills with scrub brush" that could be held indefinitely. Stilwell noted that it was "hot as hell and hard going" that day. Late that afternoon he set out to return to Hankow.

In Hankow those last few weeks before the city fell to the Japanese, there was a close bond of camaraderie within the community of international journalists, who called themselves "The Hankow Last Ditchers." In addition to Capa, there were his friends Agnes Smedley, Archibald Steele, and Walter Bosshard, as well as such newer friends as Yates McDaniel of the Associated Press, Mac Fisher of the United Press, Freda Utley of the London *News Chronicle*, and Jack Belden, a romantically idealistic and mercurially moody man of twenty-eight who had recently been fired by the United Press for disregarding orders from the home office. Captain Carlson and Colonel Stilwell were honorary members of the group.

Those last weeks in Hankow were like an Irish wake that went on and on while the victim was still dying. There was no longer any talk of Hankow's becoming the Madrid of China. Everyone knew that the city would fall soon. The question was *how* soon. But while they waited, and while thousands died all around them from the Japanese air raids, the correspondents enjoyed themselves as best they could. They met for meals at the Navy YMCA, where a "crowd of Chinese and foreigners gathered to eat the cheapest Western-style food in Hankow." If they wanted alcohol and fancier food, they went to Rosie's, where at least some of the patrons had pretensions to glamour. After dinner they often went to the movies. (One cinema-owner obviously had a macabre sense of humor, for only weeks before the Japanese descended on the city he featured *The Last Days of Pompeii*.) During the day, the United Press office in the Lutheran Mission served the "Last Ditchers" as a clubhouse. When the sirens wailed, the journalists would all go up to the roof of the mission to watch, and when the raid was over, they would all rush to the scene of the damage.

Among the "Last Ditchers" were a couple of newsreel cameramen who, so Capa complained, also shot stills and then would "sell their negatives to the AP for two cents." Complicating matters further, the journalists' practice of traveling in a pack made it very difficult for Capa to get exclusive shots of anything. But he had taken steps to ensure that he stood out from the crowd. Back in July he had written to Pix asking them to "send immediately twelve rolls of Kodachrome with all instructions about how to use it, filters, etc., . . . in short, all I should know, because I have an idea for *Life*." By September the film had arrived in Hankow, and Capa was able to shoot some effective color photographs of the aftermath of an air raid.*

Capa left Hankow—and China—about ten days after his return from the Nanchang front. The fall of Hankow seemed imminent, although the city miraculously managed to hold out for another month, until October 25.† Capa, who was eager to return to Spain, felt that there was no point in remaining in Hankow unless he could get a big exclusive spread in *Life* out of it. When he learned that Bosshard, with whom he would surely have to share the story in *Life*, was planning to stay to cover the battle and the inevitable Japanese takeover,‡ he started for home. He was in Hong Kong by September 22. Unwilling to waste a month at sea, he flew from there to Paris, a journey of several days.

Back in Paris, he was full of stories—many of them perfectly true, others hardly based on fact at all. According to one of the latter that surfaced in print a few years later,

> when Capa was in China last, he had an appointment to meet a guerrilla general, at an appointed hiding place, thirty days from then. He hopped off a truck on the Burma Road and waved goodbye to his friends. Capa had no money, but only his camera, a Hungarian passport, and a 30-day visitor's visa which had expired . . . [sic]. He crossed through the Japanese lines and arrived at the General's headquarters, only 3 days late—but with $600 he had won from Chinese officers with whom, en route, he had played poker.

The only elements of truth in the entire story are that he had been in China and that he had had a Hungarian passport and a camera.

Just about the time Capa returned to Paris, a Hollywood movie was doing much to foster, or to reflect, a certain amount of skepticism about the activities

---

* These may well be the first photographs of war ever taken in color. Kodachrome 35mm film had come on to the market less than a year before, and, since editorial (as opposed to advertising or art) photographs printed in color were still exceedingly rare in magazines, hardly any photojournalists yet bothered to use color film. *Life*, however, devoted two pages to Capa's color photographs of Hankow (October 17, 1938, pp. 29–30).

† In its issue dated October 26, *Ce Soir* published a layout of Capa's photographs of Hankow air raids with text (not by Capa) that implied that the photographer was still in China.

‡ Bosshard, who had the protection of a Swiss passport, did indeed remain in Hankow until the end. Although he made many remarkable pictures of the fall of the city, *Life* did not feature his photographs but rather those of an American named Paul Dorsey, who had been accompanying the Japanese troops and who entered Hankow with them (*Life*, December 12, 1938, pp. 15–19).

of newsmen in China. *Too Hot to Handle*, released in October 1938 and starring Clark Gable and Myrna Loy, opened with shots of a newsreel cameraman (Gable) faking footage of an air raid on a Chinese town that looks much like Taierhchwang. The film goes on to develop the character of the newsman as a debonair, courageous, ruthless, mischievous, reckless, high-spirited, and sweet-talking fellow who delivers the goods and then drinks champagne for breakfast. We can only wonder to what extent—if at all—Capa and the character played by Gable influenced each other. In a few shots, Gable looks uncannily like a portrait of Capa that had been published in *Time* the previous February; he is even holding an Eyemo movie camera, just as Capa is in the *Time* photograph. The *Time* article—a review of the exhibition of Capa and Gerda's Spanish Civil War photographs at the New School in New York—mentioned that Capa was currently in China. Was art imitating life, or the other way around?

19

Capa's return to Paris was not as happy as he had hoped it would be, for soon after his arrival there was disheartening news: on the last day of September, in an effort to appease Hitler and to avert war, England and France had signed the Munich Pact, giving the Sudetenland to Germany. Seeing that he could not count on his western European allies, Stalin began at once to make overtures of friendship to Hitler. Among his first gestures in that direction were his withdrawal of Russian advisers from Spain and his agreement that the International Brigades should be disbanded. Neither gesture had great military significance, for the Russians left behind a large number of well-trained Spaniards, and the foreign volunteers had dwindled—largely because of extremely heavy casualties—to a mere 6,000 men. Symbolically and psychologically, however, the departures of the Russians and of the volunteers were debilitating to the Spanish Republic, which now felt itself pitted alone against the vast resources of international fascism.

Exhausted and discouraged though he was by his trip to China, Capa felt a deep obligation to cover the demobilization of the foreign volunteers, for whom he had developed such admiration and affection, and so on October 16, in the hills near Falset, a few miles east of the Ebro River, he photographed them as they marched in their final review before a group of open trucks that served as reviewing stands. Because he didn't realize until too late that one of his cameras was malfunctioning, many of the exposures he made that day were ruined, but fortunately he had taken enough good pictures with his other camera to comprise a moving reportage.

On October 25 Capa and Chim (who had joined his friend in Barcelona) drove out to Montblanch, where government and military leaders were to bid farewell to a large delegation of volunteers of all nationalities. From a balcony, Prime Minister Negrín, André Marty (commander of the International Brigades), and Generals Rojo, Modesto, and Lister addressed the men, assuring them that they had not fought in vain. As they listened to the speeches and sang the anthem of the Spanish Republic, the volunteers were filled with emotion; it was on their strong, good faces—registering determination and hope as well as sadness and anxiety—that Capa focused.

Four days later he and Chim covered Barcelona's bittersweet farewell parade for the volunteers. Fearing that the Insurgents would seize the opportunity for an air raid, the government kept the starting time a secret until 4:10 in the afternoon, twenty minutes before the march was to begin, when loudspeaker trucks drove through the city broadcasting the announcement. As squadrons of fighter planes patrolled the skies, some 250,000 people lined the Diagonal to cheer the departing volunteers and to fill their arms with flowers.

Earlier in the war Capa had gravitated toward the German, Hungarian, and French volunteers, but now, having learned English in China, he began to associate more with the Americans and the British. At the Hotel Majestic, the press headquarters in Barcelona, where they spent much of their time while waiting for the League of Nations commission that would supervise their departure from Spain, Capa became particularly friendly with several members of the Abraham Lincoln Battalion, including poet Edwin Rolfe, Capt. Leonard Lamb, and Maj. Milton Wolff, the battalion's appropriately Lincolnesque young commander. But not all of the new English-speaking friends he made at the Majestic were men: Diana Forbes-Robertson, an Englishwoman, and Martha Gellhorn, an American, were to become two of his closest lifelong friends. Neither of them was ever his lover, but with each he had a flirtatious sort of brother-and-sister relationship.

Forbes-Robertson, whom everyone called "Dinah," was the twenty-five-year-old wife of former New York *Herald Tribune* correspondent Vincent

("Jimmy") Sheean, author of the best-selling memoir *Personal History*. Fifteen years younger than her husband, Dinah was overwhelmed by his older and extremely knowledgeable circle of friends in Barcelona. She felt left out and wondered what right she had to be in the war-torn, famine-stricken city; she saw herself as just one more mouth to feed.

Then Capa, who was Dinah's age, turned up. He must have seen at once beyond her upper-class charm and beauty (she had been born into one of the great families of the English theater) to her intelligence, her strength of character, and her warmth. A day or two after their first meeting, Capa found her sitting forlornly in the lobby of the Majestic while everyone was scrambling to arrange transportation for the day's visit to the front, and she confessed that she felt like a misfit.

> Then [she recalls] Capa said, "I take you." (He always dropped various parts of speech. He spoke good and funny English—inventive English. He handled it beautifully. He always managed to say what he wanted to say.*) So he said to me, "We go Propaganda Ministry. We find so-and-so." He dragged me along in the bus or the tram to the Propaganda Ministry, where we found Constancia de la Mora, the magnificent woman who was Director of Propaganda. Capa simply said, sweepingly, "Dinah would like to do something about Spain. She would like to write or speak or whatever you want. Find something."

Almost before she knew it, Forbes-Robertson was launched as a writer and lecturer who did much to aid the cause of Spanish refugees and children. This experience began her long writing career. "Capa had that extraordinary 'including' thing that made me feel his friend," she recalls. "He was the first person who made me feel I had every right to be there. He changed my life."

Martha Gellhorn was Hemingway's lover, but they spent much time apart, traveling independently, for Gellhorn had her own work to do and Hemingway was still trying to hide the fact that all was far from well between him and his wife, Pauline.† Despite her glamorous, blond, movie-star looks, and her upbringing in a prosperous St. Louis family, Gellhorn was already a tough journalist—though some saw her toughness and slanginess as a pose to impress Hemingway, about whom she actually had mixed feelings. She was drawn to

---

* These qualities are equally evident in the letters he wrote to his family from this time on. His pidgin English has been left intact in quotations from them throughout the rest of this book.

† Although Gellhorn had been with Hemingway in Madrid in April 1937, Capa had not gotten to know her at that time.

his talent and to his great appetite for experience, but she bitterly resented his patronizing attitude. In revenge, she and Capa would sometimes tease him about his military pretensions and call him "Scrooby" or "The Pig." Although Hemingway didn't have much of a sense of humor about himself, he would tolerate the teasing of this pair, for he loved Martha and had grown fond of Capa.

Capa saw a good deal of Hemingway during November, but one day was especially memorable. On the fifth, a bright autumn day, Capa drove with Herbert Matthews and Jimmy Sheean out to the bridgehead at Mora la Nueva, on the east bank of the Ebro River, where they had arranged to rendezvous with Hemingway, Col. Hans Kahle, and Henry Buckley of the London *Daily Telegraph*. A week earlier Franco had begun a major offensive against the Loyalists on the west bank, where the situation had been stalemated since July, but, despite heavy shelling, General Lister and his Vth Army Corps were still holding out. Since the Mora bridge had been destroyed by enemy bombs, the journalists would have to cross by boat, even though the crossing would be difficult, for the Insurgents had opened the dams in the north, hoping that they could make the river so deep and its currents so rapid that the Loyalists would be trapped on the west bank.

After successfully crossing in a boat whose four oarsmen Hemingway paid with cigarettes, they found the town of Mora de Ebro a total ruin. Capa photographed one house that had been virtually cut in half by a bomb, although, remarkably enough, the blast had left a table and two chairs on the second floor undisturbed. Observing this, Hemingway remarked, "That shows what you've got to do when a bombing starts. Just sit down at the table. Easy."

The journalists found Lister at his headquarters, but he soon asked them to leave, for a massive retreat was about to begin. Recrossing the river then turned out to be considerably more dangerous than crossing it had been. The boat was manned by only two oarsmen, one of whom, wrote Sheean, "was a scrawny peasant, probably undernourished for months, who did not look quite equal to the task ahead of him. Nor was he: for halfway across that twisting, treacherous river, with its sudden shallows and swift deep alternating currents, the boat began to veer sharply down toward the spiky wreck of the bridge." Hemingway, at last, had an opportunity for real heroism; he grabbed the failing oar and pulled for dear life, getting them safely across.

The next night (November 6), in an effort to divert the Insurgents from the battle at Mora de Ebro, Loyalist troops waded across the Segre River, a tributary of the Ebro, some forty miles to the north. When word of the offensive reached Barcelona early on the morning of the seventh, Capa headed straight for the front. He found it southwest of Lérida, near the town of Fraga, where the fighting was especially heavy. In this barren, rocky, hilly terrain, as thousands of men made a last, futile attempt to thwart the imminent Insurgent victory on the Ebro, Capa made some of the most dramatic front-line battle photographs of his entire career. In shots of men running forward, crouching in shallow caves or behind piles of rocks, and helping wounded comrades to the rear, we can almost believe that we smell the acrid fumes of gunpowder and feel the earth shaking as shells explode nearby—sometimes so near that they actually caused Capa's camera to shake at the moment of exposure.

The pictures were sensational. *Life* gave the story two pages (and claimed that Capa had waded across with the troops on the first night, even though he was really at a party in Barcelona with Hemingway, Malraux, and the Sheeans); *Regards* gave it five pages and the back cover; and Stefan Lorant's new British magazine, *Picture Post*, devoted eleven pages to the photographs, hyperbolically calling one of them (of several men taking refuge under a rock overhang as shells explode close by) "the most amazing war picture ever taken." The magazine prefaced the story with a nearly full-page photograph of Capa, under which ran the caption: "The Greatest War-Photographer in the World: Robert Capa."

During the second half of November, the cumulative strain of his work caught up with Capa, as he told his mother in a letter from Paris dated December 10:

> After my return I was so sick that for a while I had an absolute breakdown. Now I am perfectly all right, and my morale has improved. I am going tomorrow to the forest of Fontainebleau to rest for a day and a half (I get big vacations), but I'll celebrate Christmas at the front, *comme il faut.*

Capa did not in fact manage to spend Christmas at the front, for he was still too exhausted to work. However, when he returned to Spain on about January 10 he went out to the Catalonian front to photograph Lister and his men. There was a lull in the fighting, and he came away without any exciting action photos, but he did get some fine studies of soldiers' faces. He never again returned to the Spanish front lines; from then until he left Spain he stayed in and around Barcelona, focusing mainly on the terrible plight of the refugees fleeing before the relentless Insurgent advance.

The mood in Barcelona was almost exactly what it had been in Hankow the previous September. Although there were hopes that Barcelona might follow Madrid's heroic example in defending itself, the realists correctly sur-

THIS IS WAR !

The pictures on these and the following pages were taken during the great battle of the Ebro. They tell the whole story of a counter-attack by Government troops. But they are not presented as propaganda for, or against, either side. They are simply a record of modern war from the inside.

ON a dark and cold October night, between Lerida and Balaguer, there came up from the invisible Segre river a succession of splashes, like fish rising. Fifteen thousand Spanish Government troops were crossing the river. They took less than an hour to get over and immediately spread themselves up and down the farther bank for a distance of some six miles.

For a few hundred yards in front of them the country was flat; sparse bushes and some poplar trees offered a little cover. Beyond, in unending petrified waves, the bare, rocky desert stretched ever upward towards the distant hills. The shivering attackers advanced to the outskirts of the flats and crouched beneath the scarce cover while behind them could already be heard hammer blows upon wood

as the pontoon bridges began to take shape. Thus they waited until dawn.

As the light grew strong each company gathered about its political commissar to hear once more why they were there, for what they were fighting, how they were to reach out for new objectives. By the help of maps each detail of coming events was made clear.

Most of what the commissars had

to say was already known Spanish Government military lay down that each soldier mu explained not merely his own but the meaning of the actio whole, and its importance to th for which he is asked to figh must never go into battle l automaton moved by words o mand. He must think for and accept necessity because he

1 THE STAFF PLANS THE ATTACK
Back behind the front a group of officers of the Spanish Government forces plan the final details of their counter-attack on Franco's men. they work with their maps and telephones, reports keep coming in to them from patrols sent out the night before.

ON THE PHONE TO H.Q.

fore going forward the officer has a last
lk to army headquarters, hears how
matters are going in other sectors.

3 **THE COMMISSAR SPEAKS**

The political commissar, an Asturian
sailor, addresses the men. Beside him is
the officer-in-charge, a former solicitor.

4 **PREPARING FOR THE ATTACK**

A few more cartridges crammed into
the pouch, a hasty examination of rifle
and bayonet . . . they move forward.

5 **ON THEIR WAY UP TO THE FIGHTING LINE**

The men begin to file forward. Kit has been whittled down to a bare minimum—their weapons, a water-bottle and a few cigarettes, are all most
of them take with them. Food will come up to them later on by mule.

mised that the hungry, exhausted, poorly armed city, which was now being heavily bombed and from which thousands had already fled to France, could offer little resistance. Capa would have found the situation unbearable if it were not for the intense camaraderie and esprit de corps of a small group of "last ditchers," among whom were Herbert Matthews and Martha Gellhorn (who had remained after Hemingway had gone home).

During the night of January 12, Barcelona was plastered with posters announcing the general mobilization of all men up to the age of fifty for the defense of Catalonia, and by noon on the thirteenth the mobilization centers were filled to overflowing. That afternoon Capa went to one such center, a stadium on the outskirts of town. In his poignant series of photographs of the men with their families, he captured the fear, the gravity, and the resignation of the farewells. He also caught the nervousness of men checking and double-checking their equipment; the tenderness of last-minute attentions, such as that of a woman sewing a button on the back pocket of her husband's trousers; and the shyness and eagerness with which the men, having said goodbye to their families, began to strike up new friendships with their comrades.

Two days later, on January 15—a sunny, unseasonably warm day—Capa was out on the coastal road south of Barcelona photographing the refugees who had waited until the last minute to abandon Tarragona. Suddenly, out of the beautiful, blue sky, Insurgent planes swooped down over the road to machine-gun the helpless refugees who had piled so many of their possessions onto carts that they had to help their emaciated mules by pushing from behind. Hundreds of women and children had gone as far as they could on foot, until they were forced by exhaustion to stop by the side of the road and hope that a friendly truck might give them a lift. But there were few friendly trucks and many hostile planes. The road soon flowed with blood and was strewn with the refugees' possessions. Perhaps the most harrowing of the photographs Capa took that day was a series that show an old woman who miraculously survived unscathed an attack that killed everyone else in her group as well as her dog and her two mules. Capa found her circling her cart endlessly in a state of total, uncomprehending shock.

To accompany his reportage about refugees—both those who reached Barcelona and those who didn't—Capa wrote:

> I have seen hundreds of thousands flee thus, in two countries, Spain and China. And I am afraid to think that hundreds of thousands of others who are yet living in undisturbed peace in other countries will one day meet with the same fate. For during these last three years that is the direction in which the world we wanted to live has been going.

And after describing a beautiful, dark-eyed young girl he had photographed as she sat despondently on a pile of sacks in front of a Barcelona refugee center, he wrote, "It is not always easy to stand aside and be unable to do anything except record the sufferings around one."

By January 21, Heinkel bombers had become an even more familiar and dreaded sight than ever in the skies over Barcelona. Often a respite of no more than fifteen minutes separated the raids, day and night. The constant pounding shattered the nerves of even the coolest correspondents. The noise—and fear— kept everyone awake until they finally collapsed for a few hours from nervous exhaustion. Martha Gellhorn recalls that on one of those terrible nights, Capa kept her company in her hotel room. The two of them sat there in the dark, shivering from the cold, she in a sweater and he in the reversible, camel's-hair-lined raincoat he had bought in New York. Gellhorn considered the double-breasted coat, with its mother-of-pearl buttons, rather vulgar, but Capa said he had always wanted such a coat, and now, if he had to die, he was going to die wearing it.

Herbert Matthews had agreed to take Capa and two English reporters, William Forrest and O'Dowd Gallagher, with him when it came time for the final departure from Barcelona, and in anticipation he had been grooming his car "like a faithful battle-horse." Finally, at about one o'clock on the morning of Wednesday, January 25, Matthews received the alarming news that the Insurgents had already crossed the Llobregat River, less than ten miles to the west. Together with Capa and Gallagher he went to the Censor's Office, where Capa photographed the other two sending their last dispatches from the city by candlelight. Within an hour they had finished packing the car and, with Forrest, left the city on the coastal road heading north.

That morning they had a "heavenly breakfast of fruit, bread and butter and much steaming coffee" at the American Embassy in Caldetas, where the Americans who were to be evacuated on the cruiser *Omaha* had gathered. The editors of *Life*, greatly concerned about Capa's safety, had obtained permission from the U.S. State Department for him to leave on the *Omaha*, but he was determined to document the mass exodus of refugees and stayed with Matthews and the others as they drove on to Figueras, the last major town before the French border.

On the road, the journalists "overtook thousands and thousands of refugees, in carts, on mules, afoot, begging rides in trucks and cars, and always wearily struggling forward to that inhospitable frontier which still remained grimly closed to them"—for the French had not yet agreed to allow the refugees to

enter France. Capa shot many rolls of film along the way, his pictures du-
plicating some of the pathetic scenes he had already photographed along the
road between Tarragona and Barcelona.

In refugee-choked Figueras, where the government was hastily trying to
set up temporary offices, the journalists found a scene of "appalling chaos."
At the improvised press office Capa encountered Jimmy Sheean, who had
just arrived from Paris on the train, and when Sheean announced that he was
planning to go with Malraux to take a look at the situation in Barcelona, Capa
said he would like to go along. That afternoon the two of them looked everywhere for Malraux, but they never did find him.

Capa spent the next several days in Figueras, photographing refugees in
the town and on the nearby roads. At night he slept in the press office, together
with Sheean, Boleslavskaya (the chief *Pravda* correspondent), and a few other
journalists. The first night, announcing that he had at last found a good use
for propaganda, Capa built himself a bed of propaganda leaflets. The second,
after hearing that Barcelona had fallen, he slept on a table and snored louder
than anyone Sheean had ever heard.

On January 28, along with some of the first of the 400,000 men, women,
and children who were eventually to cross the border, he left Spain for the
last time. Although Madrid would hold out until the end of March, Capa's
coverage of the Spanish Civil War was finished. He was exhausted and profoundly depressed, and could bear to see no more.

20

For the past year American and British magazines had been heaping praise
on Capa. In January 1938, when *Life* published his coverage of Teruel,
the editors called him "one of the world's best news photographers." The
following month *Time* called him "one of the world's great photographers,"
and in October, in a review of a Walker Evans book and exhibition, the
magazine commented, "There are perhaps half-a-dozen living photographers
who are seriously and solely engaged in making the camera tell what concentrated truth they can find for it. One, the oldest, is Alfred Stieglitz. Another

is a Hungarian war photographer, Robert Capa." (Among the others were Evans and Cartier-Bresson.) In June, *Weekly Illustrated* called Capa's coverage of China "the most vivid picture story of the year," in honor of which the editors, giving Capa a prominent byline, said that the magazine "gladly breaks, for once, its rule of photographic anonymity." Then in December came the *Picture Post* story calling Capa "the greatest war-photographer in the world." And finally, though privately, the crusty Wilson Hicks of *Life* wrote him at the end of January to say, "I know your modesty will not lessen when I tell you that you are the No. 1 war photographer today."

Capa richly deserved all the praise. He had made an extraordinary body of photographs, distinguished from most other pictures of the war by the great compassion and intelligence they reflected, by their respect for the dignity and tragedy of their subjects, by their directness, and by their powerful graphic impact. But he was neither gratified nor encouraged, for Gerda's death and the fascist victory made the personal success with which he had emerged from the war seem hollow, bitter, and even shameful.

It was also useless now that there was, for the time being at least, no more war for the world's greatest war photographer to cover. In order to make a living he would have to resume doing the kind of routine stories he had done earlier, even though to do so would be not only boring but also—now that he had his image as a man who thrived on adventure and danger to maintain— somewhat embarrassing. It was becoming increasingly clear that the situation was only temporary. ("In Paris things are very bad," he told his mother. "Everyone is scared to death of Hitler.") But for the moment he had been granted the wish he had made, perhaps rashly, in China: he was unemployed as a war photographer.

A few days after returning to Paris he wrote his mother, referring to Cornell's recent professional debut, "I hope that the young Capa is a great photographer, for the old one is in eclipse. . . . I have a great desire to do films again, and there are a few meager possibilities." Perhaps they had something to do with director Jean Renoir or documentarian Robert Flaherty, who were having dinner together in a Paris restaurant when Capa walked in on his first night back from Spain. Renoir, who had met Capa through Cartier-Bresson, invited him to join them, and soon the photographer was holding forth with an account of the horrors and the chaos he had witnessed during the past few days. But Renoir began shooting *La Règle du Jeu* in the middle of February (with Cartier-Bresson working as one of his assistants), and Capa did not become involved in the project.

Capa was so depressed during February that he didn't feel like doing much of anything. ("I was not much in the mood to work," he wrote. "For four weeks I walked around like an idiot.") To make a little money, however, he forced himself to do some lightweight stories for *Ce Soir* and, to make some provision for the future, he made a brief trip to London to talk to editor Stefan Lorant about assignments for *Picture Post*. By early March he was feeling somewhat better—well enough to enjoy escorting Luise Rainer, whom he had met through Ivens, to a white-tie gala. "Imagine how elegant I have become," he proudly joked in a letter to his mother. "Just like a bear in tails."

While he was in London in February, word had come through that the French government (which until then had admitted only Spanish civilians) had finally decided to allow the retreating army of 200,000 Loyalist soldiers to cross the border, although they would be held in internment camps near Perpignan. Lorant immediately assigned Capa to do a story on the camps, but the photographer could not yet bear to face the humiliation that his Spanish comrades were having to endure at the hands of the French, who, he later wrote, "received the exhausted Spanish refugees with the cruel indifference of people who are warm and well fed."

It wasn't until the middle of March that he made the journey to the huge camp on the beach at Argelès-sur-Mer where some 75,000 men were interned. The camp, surrounded by barbed wire and patrolled by mounted Senegalese soldiers who were uncomfortably reminiscent of Franco's cruel Moors, was, as Capa wrote, "a hell on the sand." The French, who had not prepared for such a massive influx of refugees, had barely begun to build barracks when the first men arrived. Now, more than a month later, most of the men still had to improvise their own tents and straw huts. Such shelters, however, gave insufficient protection against the wind-driven sand that inflamed eyes and irritated skin, causing an epidemic of skin sores. To make matters worse, there was no running water, only brackish water from holes dug in the sand.

By the time Capa arrived, boredom had become one of the most serious problems for the men. Occasionally it might be relieved by a visit, but even their family members were not allowed to enter the camp. In some of Capa's saddest photographs of Argelès we see the proud men of the Spanish Republican Army through the chain-link fence against which they press closely to talk to their visitors.

A great series of Capa's photographs that has long been assumed to show an endless line of Spanish soldiers being led by French police across the border in February turns out not to show that at all. The pictures actually show a large group of men being transferred in March from the camp at Argelès to the slightly more comfortable, though still very primitive one at Le Barcarès, on a sandy spit of land twenty miles to the north.

Devastated though he must have been by what he had just seen of the grim aftermath of one war as well as by the news that the Insurgent victory was finally complete (but also no doubt pleased and encouraged by having gotten so many good pictures in the camps), Capa, who had lined up several assignments to make his trip to the south of France as profitable as possible, proceeded to photograph preparations for the next war. After stopping briefly in Marseilles, he went on to the nearby military air schools in Istres, Salon-de-Provence, and Pujaut, where he focused particularly on the training of parachutists. His story was surely inspired by one on a German school for military parachutists that appeared in the February 11 issue of *Picture Post*; as though in angry defiance of the Nazi threat, his reportage counters the earlier one point for point with identical aspects of French training.

In February, at the suggestion of Wilson Hicks, Capa had applied for a Russian visa, but, after his previous experience, he was pessimistic about his chances of getting one. When, in April, it became clear that his pessimism was justified, *Life* and the March of Time Picture Service sent him on the first of three trips to Belgium that would occupy him for most of the spring. His main project was an ambitious reportage on Antwerp, which, one of his captions declared, was *"par excellence* a Socialist city," but he also photographed coal miners in the region around Namur, the Procession of the Holy Blood in Bruges, urban and military leaders in Brussels, and, late in May, Queen Wilhelmina's state visit.

These stories didn't mean much to Capa—or to *Life*, which never ran any of them—and it must have been with a certain relief that he interrupted this work to do a story on Spanish refugee children, whose plight was close to his heart. During the first week of May he went to Biarritz to photograph the orphanages that had been established on five nearby estates (some of them quite grand) by the Foster Parents' Plan for Spanish Children. Each child corresponded with his or her sponsor—among them Eleanor Roosevelt, Helen Hayes, Frances Farmer, Tallulah Bankhead, Archibald MacLeish, Rockwell Kent, and the cast of the Broadway hit *The American Way*—and those who had been "adopted" by a famous person took special pride in that fact. Capa took several photographs of twelve-year-old Lorenzo Murias, who was nick-named "Rooseveltito" in honor of his "foster mother." But what is most striking about Capa's photographs is the dramatic contrast between the comfortable conditions in which the children were living and the absolutely miserable ones the interned soldiers were enduring.

Having spent much of June on an extensive, thoroughly dull story about the Paris Bourse, Capa must have welcomed the chance to have some fun covering the Tour de France for *Match*, which had been a sports magazine until the previous year, when Jean Prouvost, publisher of *Paris-soir*, had bought it and transformed it to compete with *Vu*. Before the cyclists set out from Paris on July 10, Capa photographed the training of a competitor, and, once the twenty-day, more than 2,500-mile-long race got under way, he followed it from the back seat of a motorbike navigated by his friend Taci, accompanied at least part of the way by Hemingway's wife Pauline and her friend Brenda Willerts. Characteristically, he focused more on the spectators, on his fellow journalists, and on the resting cyclists than on the race itself.

If Taci drove the motorbike, it wasn't simply so that the photographer could have both hands free for his camera. Capa had a deep psychological block against driving; whether he was on a motorbike or in a car, driving was a skill he just couldn't master. Nevertheless, although he had failed the test for a French license three times, he kept on trying, and it is not surprising that he had numerous accidents.

In August, when he decided to take a working vacation in the south of France, Capa asked Taci to teach him to drive the old motorbike he had persuaded the editors of *Match* to give him in lieu of cash for his photographs, and, as soon as he felt confident, he set off. All went well until he reached the Midi. Then, as Taci later heard the story, Capa turned a sharp corner too quickly and ran straight into a low wall, was thrown over it, and landed, shaken but unhurt, on the lawn on the other side—to the great surprise and amusement of the owners of the house, who were having tea on the terrace. Utterly charmed by Capa, they invited him to stay for a day or two while his bike was being fixed.

Capa's vacation was interrupted by the news that on August 23 the Russians and the Germans had signed a nonaggression pact. The outbreak of war was now clearly imminent, for there was no longer anything to stop Hitler from invading Poland. On August 26 the French government, fearing that the Communist Party's new pro-Nazi position could be dangerously divisive if France were forced into war, closed down *L'Humanité* and *Ce Soir*. Before dawn on the morning of September 1, German troops entered Poland; two days later Great Britain and France declared war on Germany.

Capa must have had mixed feelings at the prospect of his period of unemployment as a war photographer appearing to come to an end, but he wasted no time before applying to the Press Department of the French Ministry of Foreign Affairs for accreditation. However, because he had been a leading contributor to *Ce Soir*, his application was turned down. Furthermore, the French began to round up both German émigrés and leading Communists for internment in camps in the south of France. While Capa was neither German nor a Communist, he had been active as a member of the German émigré community in Paris and had a reputation as a Communist sympathizer. He had seen quite enough of French internment camps; this was obviously the moment to leave for the United States. His father's death in Budapest that summer had severed his last immediate familial tie to Europe. He would now join his mother and brother in New York.

Because the American quota system favored immigration applications filed in Latin America, Capa applied on September 19 for a Chilean visa.* At the same time, Olivia Chambers of the Paris office of Time Inc. wrote to the United States Lines requesting a place for him on the earliest possible ship leaving for New York. He was, she wrote, going on from there to Chile to do a story for *Life* and would also photograph on board ship.

While waiting for his papers and his passage, Capa photographed French reservists, still dressed in civilian clothes but equipped with knapsacks and blankets, sitting in the cafés for one last *fine* before leaving for duty. On October 15, unsure whether he was trying to escape the war or make his way toward it via a long detour, he sailed for New York.

21

Although the *Manhattan* had a huge American flag painted on each side of its hull to ward off U-boats and another enormous flag painted on its main deck to ward off bombers, some passengers feared that the presence on board of Duff Cooper, who had been British secretary of state for war from 1935 to 1937 and First Lord of the Admiralty until he resigned in protest against the Munich Pact, might lead the Germans to violate American neutrality. But the ship arrived safely in New York on October 21, the day before Capa's twenty-sixth birthday. Having decided not to bother with the inconvenient formality of proceeding to Chile, he remained in New York on a thirty-day visitor's visa.

On board ship Capa had met Geraldine Fitzgerald, who was on her way

---

* Capa later wrote that his Chilean visa described him as a farming expert on his way to improve the agricultural standards of that country.

to Hollywood. Pregnant at the time, she felt ill the first few days out and stayed in her cabin, but her friend Virginia Welles, Orson's wife, kept telling her about Capa. When Fitzgerald finally emerged, in low spirits, he at once set about trying to cheer her up.

> Capa was extremely friendly [she recalls]. He conveyed a sense of inner euphoria. You got the feeling that he wanted to share this euphoria. You couldn't offend him. Some people didn't like his rather wild appearance or his self-confidence and tried to put him down, but after a few minutes they would give up. . . . He always seemed to be having great fun, and people wanted to join in and share the fun.

Like most of Capa's friendships, this one would maintain its warmth despite infrequent contacts. He was to have hundreds of friends spread out all over the world, and whenever he and his friends happened to find themselves in the same place at the same time, their friendships would be resumed, however briefly. What these friendships lacked in the way of constant exercise, they made up for in the intensity of the shared moments of fun. After he left, there were no letters, no postcards, nothing. Then he would suddenly and unexpectedly reappear. When he got into town, he would call up all his friends, and at once there would be a party. Anyone who tried to demand more from Capa soon found that trying to hold on to him was like trying to hold water in a sieve.

Capa made many new friends in New York that fall, among them several members of the *Life* staff. One was Wilson Hicks's assistant, Edward K. Thompson, a likable North Dakotan and brilliant picture editor (he eventually became the magazine's managing editor) who drolly and misleadingly affected the pose of being something of a hayseed. Another was Alexander King, a witty and skeptical illustrator who worked for the magazine as an idea-man. (King, an eccentric bohemian who gave his birthplace as Budapest or Vienna, depending on whom he was talking to, and who, like Capa, was often in hot water with the *Life* editors, later recalled that when things got rough, he and Capa would talk about finding a rich South American to finance a project for them.) Capa also became very friendly with King's young assistant, John Morris, a recent graduate of the University of Chicago. At lunchtime they occasionally went skating together in Rockefeller Center (where the *Life* offices had moved), and this brought back such memories of his youth in Budapest that when, on the way to the rink one day, he encountered John Phillips, a *Life* photographer he had met in Paris, Capa remarked, "Ici j'ai découvert ma jeunesse."

Although Capa was again living at the Hotel Bedford (where he left his door open every morning so that friends could come in and kibitz with him while he soaked in the tub), he frequently went to his mother's apartment on West Ninety-fourth Street for the lively gatherings around the kitchen table at which Julia—whom Cornell's friends called "Mother Goose"—would serve huge pots of *lecsó*, a Hungarian pepper-and-egg casserole. There was inevitably much talk of photography, for Cornell and the friends with whom he worked in the Pix darkroom—among them Yale Joel and Ralph Morse, both of whom, like Cornell, later became *Life* photographers—were full of enthusiasm and ambition and looked up to Capa with awe. Joel recalls that Capa "sensed each person's special capacity and gave encouraging criticism. He sparked our imaginations and was a great influence and example."

Capa received help, too, for his work with *Life* required that he make extensive use of flash, with which he still wasn't comfortable. Cornell, on the other hand, had mastered the technique; some of his sophisticated stop-action pictures of Harlem jitterbuggers had appeared earlier that year in *Match*. Thus, Cornell could teach his older brother a few things, and, in fact, Capa always remained impressed by Cornell's technical abilities. He also relied heavily on Cornell as a go-between in both his professional and his family life, depending on him to handle many of his dealings first with Pix and later with *Life*, to explain the oddities of American manners and business methods, and to take care of Julia. Ever since he was an adolescent, Capa had spent as little time as possible with his family; now, even though his mother was overjoyed to have him living in New York, he had no interest in becoming a more attentive son. For the rest of his life, he would continue to breeze in and out of her life, staying just long enough to regale her with tales of his latest exploits— which only made her adore him all the more.

Another of Capa's overlapping circles of friends centered on Gjon Mili, an Albanian-born photographer whose multiple-exposure strobe pictures frequently appeared in *Life*. Mili, of whom Capa once wrote that he looked and dressed like a scarecrow, was famous for the end-of-the-year parties he gave in his huge loft on East Twenty-third Street, at which an enormous crosssection of the city's photographers, painters, musicians, and writers regularly showed up. Capa and Mili became poker buddies, playing at least once a week with a group of friends that included violinist Alexander Schneider.

Capa also played poker with John Fernhout, who, having divorced Eva Besnyö and married a dancer named Polly Korchein, was living in New York. Robert Flaherty often joined in the games, and it was on one of these occasions that Capa again saw Flaherty's daughter Monica, whom he had met in Paris at the end of January.

Monica Flaherty says that when Capa started chasing her, she resisted him. She wanted friendship; he wanted romance and excitement. Some of Capa's friends, however, got the impression that Monica had fallen in love with him and was hurt and jealous because she couldn't hold on to him. Capa was running around all the time, working, playing poker, and chasing other women; he seemed incapable of focusing on just one woman at a time. (Stefan Lorant says he thinks that on his visits to London Capa went to bed with a number of the *Picture Post* secretaries.) Flaherty, a no-nonsense young woman who was to become a pilot for the Air Transport Command during the war, simply wouldn't put up with his philandering. As for Capa, whenever anyone accused him of being a Don Juan, he would reply, in a tone of great resignation, "I'm afraid I defend myself badly against the women."

Soon after his arrival in New York, Capa began to do human-interest and news-related stories for *Life*, the majority of which were never published. Although he still wasn't happy about this kind of work, his *Life* assignments gave him a crash course in American culture that was certainly more comprehensive and revealing than any citizenship course routinely offered to immigrants. By the spring of 1942, Capa would have seen the United States from New York to California and from New England to Florida. He would have met a cross-section of Americans ranging from politicians to cowboys and from socialites to bartenders. Along the way he would have had a great deal of fun, for Capa never remained a stranger long; everywhere he went he quickly made friends and became at least a marginal participant in whatever event he was covering. And yet, as a thoroughly European young man, he inevitably remained something of an outsider who found the quirks of American society bizarre, amusing, and often refreshing.

One of Capa's most exotically American stories was on an eight-day elk hunt in the mountains of northern New Mexico late in November. To get into the spirit of the occasion, he bought himself a cowboy outfit, complete with boots and leather chaps. "I have become a complete cowboy," he wrote to Cornell, "and I'll soon be catching elephants with a lasso." But while he didn't turn out to be a "complete cowboy" himself (at one point his horse ran away with him on a wild ride down a mountainside), he wasn't at all disappointed by the real cowboys he met on the hunt. Of them he said, "They are big, tough and healthy and have so much fun at whatever they are doing. They don't really give a damn what is happening in Europe." For the moment, he was about as far away from the war as he could possibly be (although not much was happening anyway during this period, which British wags called the "Bore War").

Another quintessentially American assignment took him to Florida early in February to photograph Senator Robert A. Taft, who was making a swing through the state in his campaign for the Republican presidential nomination. In Miami, on the second day of the trip, Capa got a wonderful story. Taft's press agents had decided that the senator's visit wouldn't be complete without photographic coverage of his catching a big fish. But since too much was at stake to leave anything to chance, a dead sailfish was loaded onto his boat. With the boat still tied up, Taft sat in a chair at the stern and posed with a rod so that newsreel cameramen on the dock could get close-ups of him "fishing," and after the boat had gone out a few yards he reeled in the dead fish that had been attached to his line. While the newsreel men took pains to make their footage look realistic, Capa made a point of revealing what was really going on. Some of Taft's campaign managers later held the publication of Capa's photographs in *Life* at least partly responsible for their candidate's failure to win the nomination.

At the end of March, Capa faced a crisis: the immigration authorities—from whom, with *Life*'s help, he had wangled monthly extensions of his visa— refused to extend it any longer; he would have to leave the country almost immediately. There was no way to avoid the necessity of leaving for six months, and for that purpose *Life* had agreed to send him to Mexico on assignment. But if he wanted to be certain that he could return at the end of that period with permanent-resident status—the first step on the way to becoming a cit- izen—he would have to marry an American citizen, which is what he did.

A couple of months earlier, John Fernhout and his wife had introduced him to a beautiful and sophisticated young woman named Toni Sorel. Toni, a tall, dark-haired, intelligent, and attractively tough native New Yorker who had been a leading high-fashion model for *Vogue* and *Harper's Bazaar* and had had several small parts in Broadway shows, was then studying modern dance with Polly.*

Capa and Toni saw each other a few times—nothing too serious. But then, at a wild party on the night of March 27, when Capa announced his predic- ament, Toni, on an impulse, offered to marry him the next day. Since Maryland was the nearest state without a waiting period for a marriage license,

---

* According to the certificate of her marriage to Capa, Toni's real name was Nona Teilenbogen. In May 1940, she attracted a good deal of attention in the press for her role as a fashion model in George S. Kaufman's comedy *George Washington Slept Here.*

they would drive down to Elkton, which, as the first county seat over the Maryland border on the New York-to-Washington highway, had become famous as the place New Yorkers eloped to for spur-of-the-moment marriages. The only trouble was that neither Capa nor Toni had a car, and neither knew how to drive.

As it happened, two of Capa's closest friends at *Life*, Otto Hagel and Hansel Mieth, were waiting for their marriage license. Hansel, who had become an American citizen, was a *Life* staff photographer, but Otto, who had entered the United States illegally by jumping ship, was, like Capa, only on retainer. The magazine's editors were aware of the situation and had promised that if Otto and Hansel got married, they would send Otto on a six-month assignment to Cuba, from which he could enter the United States legally. Late in March, they applied for their license.

On the morning of the twenty-eighth, a cold, rainy day, Capa burst into the *Life* darkroom where Otto and Hansel were making prints and amazed his friends by suggesting an immediate double wedding, that very afternoon, in Maryland. "But who are you going to marry?" they asked. "And what's your big hurry?" When he explained, they reluctantly agreed to drive down to Maryland—even though it was raining very hard and Hansel had to fly to Montana early the next morning on an assignment.

When the two couples arrived in Elkton, after a difficult drive in the rain, they were exasperated to learn that Maryland had just changed its marriage laws; the state now had a three-day waiting period for a marriage license. Furious that they had come all that way for nothing, they piled back into the car for the long drive back to New York. But at the outskirts of town a car pulled alongside, and the two men in it signaled Otto to pull over to the side of the road. They had been tipped off by the county clerk that the couples wanted to get married; taking Capa and Otto aside, they explained that there was a loophole in the new law: there was no waiting period if the prospective bride had a medical certificate stating that she was pregnant. It could all be arranged, for a price.

When Toni and Hansel learned the terms of the deal, they were outraged. No, they absolutely would not submit to this humiliation. But they had come this far, and if Toni didn't go through with it, Capa might not be able to re-enter the country. As for Hansel, if Toni were willing to go through with it, then she might as well too.

The doctor filled out the forms quickly and routinely, asking only for names and ages. Just as the two couples were ready to rush back to the courthouse, the two men who were arranging things told them that the county clerk would grant them their certificates only after they had said their marriage vows before the local minister. To the two non-religious couples, this was almost the last straw. Still, they complied.

Having fulfilled their obligation to the aged, doddering minister, whose equally aged sister served as witness, they raced to the county courthouse, where the clerk, eager for his payoff, had waited for them a full hour beyond the usual closing time. But when Capa and Otto went to pay him, they found that, having already paid off the two arrangers, the doctor, and the minister, they were now short of cash. It took almost every cent that Toni and Hansel had between them to come up with enough to pay the legal and "special" fees. Officially married at last, the two couples didn't even have enough money left to buy themselves a celebratory drink—not that anyone but Capa felt like celebrating.

On the way back to New York, Otto and Hansel quarreled bitterly and then fell silent. In the back seat, when Capa tried to become amorous with Toni, she slapped his face. Angry at being rebuffed, he retreated to pout in one corner of the seat, while Toni wept in the opposite corner. She finally asked to be dropped off in Greenwich Village, and Capa went on alone to his hotel.

Capa and Toni never lived together or consummated their marriage. Toni now says that she simply liked Capa and was doing him a favor by marrying him; she had no interest in the marriage developing into anything serious. Nevertheless, Hansel Mieth recalls that Toni later admitted to her that she had fallen in love with Capa, but that he didn't reciprocate. As for Capa, although he seems to have regarded the marriage simply as a way of getting onto the preferred quota list for re-entry into the States, in his letters to Cornell over the next couple of years he repeatedly referred to Toni not by name but as "my wife." And whether it was out of gratitude, out of guilt, or by the terms of some sort of agreement, Capa frequently instructed Cornell to give her small sums of money—fifty dollars here, a hundred dollars there. Mieth recalls that Toni had agreed to marry Capa in return for his paying for a year's worth of dance lessons, but Toni says that because she was a member of her teacher's company, her lessons were free. Nevertheless, when Capa wrote to her from Mexico during the summer of 1940, the letter began with an apology for not having sent money and followed with his excuses for not having done so. It is entirely possible that Capa had borrowed money from her and was simply paying it back bit by bit, as he did with so many other people.

22

Life sent Capa to Mexico for his six-month waiting period, but he wouldn't simply be passing the time there, for at that moment the country was ripe for Capa's reportorial eye. Mexico was in turmoil—turmoil caused both by the presidential elections scheduled for July and by Nazi *agents provocateurs* who hoped that trouble south of the border would distract the attention of the United States from the war in Europe. In the spring of 1940 Americans were, indeed, very concerned with what was happening in Mexico, and Time Inc. was eager to report on the situation with words, with photographs, and with film.

Capa reached Mexico City via South America toward the end of April. After checking into the small, pleasant Hotel Montejo, he went to the nearby Hotel Reforma to find Holland McCombs, the zestful chief of the Time Inc. bureau in Mexico and the southwestern United States, and *March of Time* director Jack Glenn, an "adventurous, likable, amusing, and insatiably gregarious" Texan. Capa, McCombs, and Glenn quickly formed a "fun-filled brotherhood" and began a "reckless, rollicking spree of fun and frolic and almost brutally bruising work." Capa not only took photographs but also came up with ideas for stories for *Time, Life,* and *Fortune,* did some of the research and reporting for them, and helped McCombs, Glenn, and cameraman Marcel Rebière set up scenes for their *March of Time* film.

> We chased the *politicos* and various stories all over a lot of Mexico [recalls McCombs]. When we were in town, we chased the nightspots, the café society hangouts—where the girls were. We "dated" a lot. Most of the time for the fun of it, but sometimes to try and wheedle information from ladies of all sorts, from all walks of life. Actually, we learned a lot of useful things that way. . . .
>
> After a while, Bob induced Jack Glenn and me to move from our Hotel Reforma headquarters to his place at the Montejo. . . . We and our "staff" sort of took over the Montejo—aided and abetted by [the hotel's friendly management].
>
> We worked so hard and fast that when we quit work, we'd often relax and get drunk in order to relax *more.* On one such evening, Jack Glenn, Bob Capa, and I were tippling too many hot buttered rums in the Montejo bar. I do not remember how it came about, but we decided to have a fight. And we *did*—right out in the middle of the hotel lobby, and

mostly all over the floor. Of course, the tourists were alarmed and called for the management. Dear Pachin Guttiérez [the manager] came prancing into the lobby, took in the situation at a glance, and turned to tell the tourists in a berating voice: "You can't do anything about *this*! That's Mr. Glenn, Mr. Capa, and Mr. McCombs. And I advise you not to try anything with *them*."

The team's first assignment was to report on the activities of Nazi and Communist sympathizers, who, because of the German-Soviet nonaggression pact, were allies. The public aspect of the story was easy enough to cover, for the Left staged a huge May Day parade in Mexico City, but Capa was also able to get some of the inside story. Since some of the most active Communists in Mexico were German and eastern European émigrés whom he had met in Spain, he was able to gain entrée for himself and McCombs to meetings of a group of émigré leftists, exiled Spaniards, Mexican Communists, and fellow travelers at the Caballo Blanco (White Horse), a hacienda on the outskirts of Mexico City. He and McCombs also made contact with the Trotskyites, their ardor greatly fired by the presence of Trotsky himself, who, since 1937, had been living in the Mexico City suburb of Coyoacán. Capa would surely have liked to photograph him again, but Trotsky was in no mood to have anything to do with anyone connected with *Life*. In the fall of 1939 the magazine had commissioned him to write two articles, one a study of Stalin's personality and the other an account of Lenin's death. *Life* published the first but rejected the second (in which Trotsky accused Stalin of poisoning Lenin) as too conjectural, and Trotsky was infuriated by the rejection.

When Capa saw what *Life* did with his story about the Left, he was infuriated too. "It discourages me from photography," he told Cornell. But far more discouraging yet was the news that on June 14 the Germans had entered Paris. "European news is miserable, and it depresses me very much," he wrote. "The world was never as sad as it is now." He couldn't even go out and get drunk, for he was suffering from a case of dysentery. Depressed, discouraged, and bored, he told his old friend Kati Deutsch, who was living in Mexico City, that he was sick of his work and would love to settle down, grow a long beard, and have twelve children.

But with the elections approaching rapidly, Capa couldn't afford to be depressed for long. (A young woman who was staying at the Montejo later recalled Capa's telling her, "Your purpose is never finished, and you must never give up.") Winning the confidence of both candidates (Generals Avila Camacho and Almazán), Capa and McCombs were able to cover the campaigns thoroughly, traveling on their campaign trains and visiting their estates.

Early on the morning of election day, July 7, Capa arrived at the polling place on the Calle Monte Himalayas in Mexico City to photograph one of the oddities of a Mexican election: the battle to gain control of the ballot box. As though offering an incentive to violence, Mexican law decreed that the first five voters inside a polling place should constitute a committee in charge of the voting. Consequently, at dawn each faction gathered an armed force in front of each polling place, ready to storm the entrance as soon as the polls opened. Once established inside, the "committee" would post guards at the doors to prevent supporters of the rival candidate from entering and casting their votes. After a small riot, the Camachistas gained control on the Calle Monte Himalayas, and a while later Avila Camacho himself arrived to cast his ballot.

That afternoon Capa was covering the huge Almazanista demonstration in front of the General Post Office when a group of Camachistas opened fire. It was there, after the screaming, unarmed crowd had scattered and then reformed, that Capa photographed the day's first fatality. The dead man, lying on the pavement, was surrounded by a group composed mostly of young men whose hands were extended toward the victim in a tableau hauntingly reminiscent of an early Renaissance Lamentation.

There were further clashes throughout the afternoon and evening; by the end of the day at least thirty had died and several hundred had been wounded. It was one of the calmest election days Mexico City had ever seen.

The next day Avila Camacho and Almazán both claimed total victory, but the official count wouldn't be announced until September 1, when the new Congress convened. Nevertheless, believing—as did almost everyone else—that the government party's candidate would be the next president, Capa and McCombs went to Avila Camacho's estate in Teziutlán to do a story about him and his family that *Life* could run to coincide with the inauguration on December 1.

As the threat of an Almazán-led revolt grew during August, Capa returned to Mexico City to photograph some of the thousands of tough peasants whom Avila Camacho, in an effort to intimidate the Almazanistas, brought into the city to patrol the streets in open trucks. But the most dramatic and fateful episode of violence that summer didn't involve the presidential elections at all. Late on the afternoon of Tuesday, August 20, a man using the pseudonym Frank Jacson went to visit Trotsky at his house in Coyoacán and plunged an ice pick through the exiled leader's skull. Trotsky died twenty-four hours later, never having emerged from his coma.

As soon as Capa learned of the assassination, he rushed to Coyoacán, but by the time he reached Trotsky's house it had been cordoned off by the police, and there was nothing to photograph. Nor was he able to get any pictures at the hospital. But he did cover Trotsky's cremation at the civil cemetery on

August 27, and, because he was the only Time Inc. journalist present, we can be certain that *Time*'s account was based closely on his report. According to the *Time* article, the heavy steel cart on which Trotsky's body had been placed

> was wheeled to a huge crematory, the door was opened, the body pushed in. . . . As the body of Trotsky entered the furnace, the door jammed, would not shut. Fire licked at Trotsky's black suit, at his hair and wispy beard. They began to blaze. In the terrible heat and light and stench that filled the room, with the fire roaring and smoke pouring out of the open door, his last attendants saw Trotsky burning, his face turning black and shriveling away, his body shrinking so fast that he seemed to be writhing in pain. Natalia Sedova Trotsky was carried fainting to a car.

It turned out that Trotsky's assassin had been living for months across the hall from the Time Inc. contingent in the Montejo. The journalists had taken note of him only because he never said anything, not even "Buenos días," to anyone.

By late September, having completed a series of unexciting assignments on outgoing President Cárdenas, Capa had had enough of Mexico and made no effort to cover the suppression of the Almazanista revolts that had broken out in several Mexican states. At that point he wanted only to get back to the United States. His immigration papers had finally come through on September 5, and on the twenty-eighth he was assigned a quota number: Hungarian First Preference, No. 189. On October 10, accompanied by Holland McCombs, Capa entered the United States at Laredo, Texas, as a permanent resident. Such a simple entry must have seemed anticlimactic to him, for later he often claimed that there had been some last-minute hitch with his papers and that he had hidden in the trunk of the car to cross the border.

23

Capa had gone to such lengths to get his permanent-resident papers not so he could remain in the country but so that he would be free to leave it. By mid-October 1940, however, there was really nowhere for him to go, for the Battle of Britain, the only crucial fighting going on at that time, was clearly drawing to an end. By diverting so many of its planes to raids on London and other large cities, the Luftwaffe had lost its opportunity to destroy the RAF, and although the Blitz would continue throughout the winter and most of the spring with intermittent raids of terrible intensity, the relentless night-after-night attacks on London ended the first week of November. On a purely practical level, *Life* had plenty of coverage of the Blitz and was not about to send Capa to England, and, for the moment, no other magazine seemed interested either.

And so, upon his arrival in New York, he had no choice but to resume working on bread-and-butter stories for *Life*, this time ranging from Republican presidential candidate Wendell Willkie's speech at the *Herald Tribune* Forum to the last day of the New York World's Fair. Some relief from the tedium seemed, however, to be in sight, since Hemingway had just sold *For Whom the Bell Tolls* to Paramount for well over $100,000, the highest price yet paid for film rights to a book, and he had suggested that Capa might be perfect to play the part of Rafael, the Gypsy. Capa, of course, was interested and eager to discuss the possibility. Conveniently, early in November the editors of *Life* agreed to send him out to Sun Valley, Idaho, to work on a major two-part story on Hemingway, who was vacationing there. The first part would focus on the writer's daily life with Martha Gellhorn (his wife Pauline had just divorced him and he was free at last to marry Gellhorn); the second would illustrate passages from *For Whom the Bell Tolls* with Capa's photos of the Spanish Civil War chosen by the novelist. Capa spent about ten days photographing the engaged couple (*Life* claimed that the photographs were taken just *after* their marriage, but they weren't married until November 21, the day after they left Sun Valley), as they shot pheasants, ate dinner with a local farmer, and danced at the quiet Trail Creek Cabin.

It would be a while before casting for the movie began. In the meantime, toward the middle of December, Capa went out to the Midwest to do a story for *Life* on Calumet City, Illinois, the "sin city" in whose 308 nightclubs workers from Hammond and Gary, just across the Indiana state line, spent their Saturday nights. Although *Life* apparently intended the story as an exposé of decadence, it is obvious from his pictures that Capa enjoyed himself as he photographed people drinking, watching the striptease shows, and dancing (most spent so little time in each club before moving on to the next that they didn't even bother to remove their coats). His pictures were quite sympathetic, but he told Ed Thompson that when the mob got wind of why he had come, they sent a couple of thugs to follow him to his train back to Chicago and destroy his films. He claimed that to escape from them he jumped from the

moving train—another episode that sounds suspiciously like something borrowed from a movie. But then Capa himself nearly destroyed his Calumet
City films by accident. Alone in the Chicago office of Time Inc., he put the
films in developing solution and left the darkroom for a smoke. When it was
time to go back in, he discovered that the door was locked and he didn't know
where the key was hidden. Since it was imperative that he get inside immediately, he grabbed a hammer, smashed out the doorknob and lock, and then
stuffed a blanket into the hole to block the light. The story was worth all the
trouble, for *Life* gave it four pages.

From Chicago, Capa wrote to Cornell, "It was a very stupid Christmas.
I sat alone in a hotel room, but now it's over." *Life* kept Capa running all
over the Midwest for another week, shooting such trivial but amusing stories
as a bartenders' union election in Chicago and a party with a hangover theme
in Owosso, Michigan, but one quite unexpected side benefit came out of all
this: on the night train from Minneapolis to Chicago the twenty-eight-year-
old black porter in the bar car struck up a conversation with Capa when he
saw his camera equipment. His name was Gordon Parks, and three years
earlier—after having already worked as a piano player, a lumberjack, and a
professional basketball player—he had decided to become a photographer. He
had tried his hand at fashion photography, but times were hard, and he was
forced to work on trains to make a living. Encouraged and inspired by Capa,
among others, Parks persevered and eventually went on to a long and distinguished career as a *Life* photographer.

Capa returned to New York around the first of the year and spent the next
several months doing routine stories for *Life* ranging from a party to celebrate
the one-thousandth performance of *Hellzapoppin* to the training of volunteer
fire-fighters in Boston. He was now seeing a good deal of Jimmy and Dinah
Sheean, who were as frustrated at being on the wrong side of the Atlantic as
he was. As it had become clear that nothing was going to happen with the
Hemingway movie for quite some time, there was nothing to hold Capa in
the States; and since *Life* still had no intention of sending him abroad, he
was ready to sever his connection with the magazine. So when Jimmy Sheean
got *The Saturday Evening Post* to commission him and Capa to do a series
of articles on various aspects of the British war effort, he jumped at the
opportunity, and, so that Dinah could go along, he proposed that she work
with him on a book about how a single London family was enduring the Blitz.
(Capa would take the photographs; Dinah would write the text.) As one of his
publisher's best-selling authors, Jimmy easily persuaded Random House to
provide a small advance.

Boredom was not the only reason Capa was glad to leave *Life*, for he had developed quite an intense dislike for Wilson Hicks, who, he felt, was trying to hold him down with trivial assignments, was killing too many of his stories, and was constantly trying to cheat him. But when Capa announced that he was leaving *Life* for the *Post*, Hicks was "surprised and shocked." To appease him, Capa accepted a small advance from *Life* and promised that the magazine could have first look at any pictures not used by the *Post*. And because the combined advances from Random House, the *Post*, and *Life* wouldn't cover his expenses, Capa obtained an additional commitment from *PM*, a New York evening paper that was modeled—in format as well as in political stance—on *Ce Soir*.

Because of delays with Capa's papers (he was, after all, still technically an alien, despite his permanent-resident status), Jimmy and Dinah went on ahead to London without him. Finally, during the last week of April 1941, he sailed on a former Norwegian whaling ship that was doing duty as a freighter, its deck covered with the planes and torpedo boats it was transporting to England under the new Lend-Lease policy, in a convoy of forty-four ships.

After arriving in Liverpool with his highly unorthodox portfolio of American "alien resident" papers, a Hungarian passport, and letters of introduction from the publications he was representing, Capa was held for a few days in a Patriotic Camp while his credentials and references were checked out. When he finally reached London in mid-May, he checked into the Dorchester on Park Lane, a hotel especially popular at that time because its modern, wind-resistant steel structure was widely believed to offer the best protection against bombs. "I am living in the biggest hotel, which couldn't be destroyed by twenty-five bombs," he wrote to Cornell, asking him to pass that information along to Julia, adding, with a hint of simultaneous nervousness and disappointment, "and anyway nothing ever happens to me."

Although his affiliation with *Life* was at that point rather tenuous, Capa wasted no time before making himself at home in the *Life* office. On his brief visit to London two years earlier he had become friendly with Dorothy Dennis and Elizabeth Crockett, the two young Irish women who kept the office running smoothly. Now he enlisted "Crocky" to type and polish his article about his convoy crossing, and he gave the film he had exposed on board ship to the *Life* darkroom for developing and printing, even though the story was destined for *The Saturday Evening Post*.

Capa assumed that *Picture Post* would publish the convoy story in England, but when he went to the magazine's office, he learned that Stefan Lorant had moved to the United States. Accustomed to being treated with the deference due him as the "Greatest War-Photographer in the World" (as the magazine had proclaimed him in 1938), Capa was annoyed that the new editor kept him waiting. Finally he stormed out to the nearest telephone booth and called *Illustrated* (successor to *Weekly Illustrated*, which had published some of his photographs in the mid-'30s), whose editor, Len Spooner, told him to come over right away. Spooner promptly bought the convoy story and told Capa he would like to publish his work regularly, thus beginning a close personal and business relationship.

By the time Capa and Dinah got down to work on their book, the worst of the Blitz was over. After the extremely heavy raid on the night of May 10 that destroyed the chamber of the House of Commons, the raids tapered off, and on June 22, when the Germans threw all available resources into their invasion of the Soviet Union, they stopped almost completely. Most of the photographs for *The Battle of Waterloo Road*, as the book was eventually called, were taken during that summer's respite. The book, then, could not be so much about the Blitz itself as about the spirit that had helped the Londoners through the Blitz and that would get them through another if it were to come.

When Capa and Dinah were setting out to find a family on which to focus, someone suggested that they go to St. John's Church in Lambeth, whose vicar, Father Hutchinson, was a vigorous, humorous, and popular man with a taste for the novels of Proust and Hemingway. Capa and Dinah took an immediate liking to him, and he to them; he quickly led them to the Gibbs family, the stalwarts of the one-block-long Whichcote Street, just off Waterloo Road. It would be difficult to imagine a family that could have represented the fortitude, the decency, the good-neighborliness, and the good humor of the London working class better than the Gibbses did. Capa photographed their life in some detail: the tall, strapping Mr. Gibbs at his job as a police guard in an Underground station, Mrs. Gibbs doing her shopping along Waterloo Road, the two of them working in the evening in the local air-raid shelter or Digging for Victory (tending their allotment of vegetable garden) in Brockwell Park.

Dinah had worried that the people of Lambeth might resentfully view her as a sort of "swanky social worker," but she recalls that

Capa utterly took the curse off my accent. He gentled the English working people with his Hungarian accent and made them—and me—relax. He just charmed his way in so that people felt comfortable with him. I remember that when he photographed the Gibbs family eating dinner around their table, he somehow got me practically hanging upside-down with the lights—and yet there never seemed to be any kind of self-consciousness.

An article on Capa that appeared in *U.S. Camera* magazine in 1943 provides further insights into his working methods.

> Capa established friendships [wrote the interviewer] by the simple expedient of being honestly interested and genuinely friendly. . . . He talked [to his subjects], went to their homes, played with the kids, smoked and drank beer with the [men]. Then— he started to take pictures. . . . Sometimes he made a suggestion for some action, . . . [but] he never requested a special pose. Knowing the background of their lives, he could anticipate movements and actions that would tell the story better than he could direct it.

His advice to amateur photographers was very simple and very wise: "Like people and let them know it."

The Gibbses responded, becoming so fond of Capa and Dinah that at the end of the day's shooting they would send them back across the river—to Claridge's and the Dorchester—laden down with vegetables from their plot; they were worried that, living in hotels, their new friends couldn't possibly be getting good square meals.

Some of those vegetables found their way into delicious meals at the White Tower, a Greek restaurant on Percy Street that Capa got started as a lively hangout for the press. Capa and the owner, John Stais, got along famously, and soon, often joined by Dinah, they were making trips into the nearby countryside to bargain for chickens and eggs to supplement the meager rations on which Londoners were then expected to subsist. The fruits of such expeditions improved the restaurant's reputation for good food; Stais's knack for buying cheaply from people afraid that their cellars would be destroyed by bombs enhanced its reputation for good wine and liquor; and the nightly presence of Capa and his friends gave it a reputation for conviviality.

Inevitably, some of the conversation was about photography, and occasionally Capa and Bill Vandivert, a *Life* photographer, would get into an argument about how Capa worked too late in bad light and how he didn't take enough time to set up properly. "I'm not interested in taking pretty pictures," Capa would reply. "I'm anxious to tell story. You never know when things are going to happen. They may happen just as the light goes. I'd rather have a strong image that is technically bad than vice versa."

But Capa and Vandivert agreed more than they disagreed—especially about the idea of forming a photographers' cooperative agency. "Bill Vandivert and I are looking for one more good guy," Capa wrote to Cornell. "We would like to put up a small agency having one fellow in England, one in Russia, one maybe in South America and something in New York."

It was very convenient for the two men to discuss their plans over breakfast every morning in Vandivert's apartment at 39 Hill Street in Mayfair, since Capa had taken the apartment directly upstairs. The management of the Dorchester disapproved of the endless succession of young women Capa took up to his room at night, so he had moved late in June to the Pastoria, a much less stuffy hotel near Leicester Square. But soon after, hearing how reasonably he could sublet an apartment, he moved to Hill Street. The parade of young women, most of them tarts, continued there. Martha Gellhorn observed that "[Capa] clung to tarts, or tarts to [Capa], because he liked them, they were as unattached as he was." He never regarded any of them seriously enough to invite her down to Vandivert's for breakfast.

Often after breakfast Capa and Bill and Rita Vandivert would meet Dinah Sheean in Regent's Park for a few games of tennis before getting down to the day's work, of which there was plenty to keep Capa busy. In addition to the story on the Gibbs family, he and Dinah did stories on Father Hutchinson, on a Home Guard officer, and on air-raid wardens and shelters to round out their book. But of the stories that Capa and Jimmy Sheean were supposed to do together for *The Saturday Evening Post,* only one actually got done: an ambitious story about women and students who had been recruited and trained to fill the jobs in industry and agriculture vacated by men serving in the armed forces.

For *Illustrated* Capa photographed Lord Beaverbrook, the newspaper magnate and former minister of aircraft production who had just been made minister of supply. Len Spooner recalls that Beaverbrook agreed only because he thought he was being photographed by Frank Capra, and Capa did nothing to dispel his confusion. An identical misunderstanding led to Capa's being invited as the guest of honor to a luncheon given by the Lord Mayor.

Late in July 1941, Capa did a story about a daylight bombing raid on France in which one plane was flown by a young American who had volunteered for the RAF. Since regulations then forbade photographers to go along on missions, Capa took pictures of the pilot playing cards with his buddies while they waited for the signal to man their planes. When the planes returned, one was missing—the American's. But it soon showed up, and, although one engine had been shot out and the landing gear was gone, the pilot managed to make a perfect belly landing. Capa rushed out to the field, and when the pilot saw him taking pictures of the wounded men being lifted out of the plane, he asked, "Are these the pictures you were waiting for, photographer?" Capa later wrote, "This sort of photography was only for undertakers, and I didn't like being one. If I was to share the funeral, I swore, I would have to share the procession."

Capa was actually already trying very hard to join the procession. In June, as soon as Germany had invaded Russia, he had applied for a Soviet visa but, true to form, he had gotten no response. He had then written Ilya Ehrenburg for help, but never heard from him either. Now he was determined to use every connection he had to get a visa: he would write to Ehrenburg again; he would write to the influential German Communist writer Bodo Uhse in Mexico (they were friendly enough for him to begin his letter, "Dear Old-Horse Bodo"); and he would enlist the aid of *PM* publisher Ralph Ingersoll, who in the spring had given him a letter calling him "one of America's most important photographers" and saying, "We know him well and have great respect for him." He had planned to remain in London and go on from there to Moscow, but the first three weeks of August were very rainy, and by the time the weather cleared up, all his photography permits had expired. Rather than bother to renew them, he sailed for New York, where he could more easily pull strings and make arrangements for his trip; while there, he could oversee the publication of his and Dinah's book, and he could perhaps even get his agency set up.*

After a "rather short and pleasant" voyage, he arrived in New York on September 4, and two weeks later he rented a studio on the fifth floor of 60 West Ninth Street in Greenwich Village. The apartment had "a skylight all over the roof, a big bed in the corner, and a telephone on the floor. No other furniture—not even a clock." The rent was sixty-five dollars a month.

Although he signed a one-year lease, Capa had no intention of remaining in New York, even if his Russian trip fell through, in which case he planned to return to London and go on from there to cover the fighting in the Middle East. And if not even that could be arranged, he would simply go back to London, where he had made so many friends and could at least get a taste of the war. "After all those months in London," he wrote to Crocky, "I can't get used to New York, and I would like to be back [in London] as soon as possible. . . . Lights and food are very nice for the first few days, but when you get used to them they don't mean a thing."

Getting a visa wasn't the only problem Capa had to solve before he could go to Russia: he had been counting on *The Saturday Evening Post* for an advance, but the editors decided that in view of the number of good pictures available gratis from the Russian government it wouldn't be worthwhile to send a photographer to the Soviet Union. So, reluctantly, Capa got in touch with Wilson Hicks. Margaret Bourke-White had been in Russia all summer

---

* He also had to report to his draft board, which gave him a deferment because of his age.

and had sent some sensational stories to *Life*. Since she was about to return to New York, Hicks was very interested in sending Capa to pick up the beat, and set about trying to help him get his visa.

But before he went anywhere, Capa wanted to organize his agency. On September 23 he wrote to the Vandiverts:

> The boys of whom I was thinking were hired by *Life*, but it seems that [Gjon] Mili, [Dmitri] Kessel, and [Otto] Hagel would play ball, and that would be a pretty good outfit. . . . Hicks was very friendly. I think the best way would be if we could arrange some kind of contract with *Life* which would allow us a good deal of liberty.

Although Capa had vowed that he wasn't going to accept any more trivial assignments from *Life*, he now had several good reasons for doing so—he needed the money, he wanted Hicks's support for the agency and for his Russian trip, and he saw an opportunity to get an all-expenses-paid trip to Hollywood and Sun Valley, two places where he had business of his own to take care of. While covering actor Brian Aherne's trip to the West Coast to raise money for British war relief, Capa investigated the possibility of selling *The Battle of Waterloo Road* to the movies. Although he was able to report to Dinah that "there was a great deal of interest about our book in Hollywood," it is difficult to imagine what kind of movie might have been made from the book, for it has no story line, and in fact it never led to anything.

From Hollywood, Capa went to Sun Valley, where he spent a week photographing and hunting with Hemingway, Martha Gellhorn, and Hemingway's two youngest sons, Patrick and Gregory. The writer was still championing him for the role of Rafael, and, although Capa told Cornell that "Hollywood is no paradise," he was still interested. "I may have to go back for a screen test," he wrote. "The Rafael deal is very timely," his projected trip to Russia apparently notwithstanding. Sam Wood, the film's director and producer, was, however, an extreme anti-Communist, suspicious of anyone who had been involved with the Loyalists in Spain—an odd position for someone about to make a film of Hemingway's novel. Hemingway was trying to get David Selznick to buy the rights from Wood and produce it, with Howard Hawks as director.

When Capa learned that Hawks and Gary Cooper, who had already been cast as the male lead, were to arrive in Sun Valley late in October—along with agent Leland Hayward and his wife Margaret Sullavan—he decided to stay. The stars would transform a routine story into a glamorous one, and Capa would be able to lobby in person with Hawks for the role. Capa did get some good pictures, and *Life* did give the story a good layout, but in the end

Wood retained his rights to the novel and cast the Russian character actor Mikhail Rasumny as Rafael. Nor was that the only one of Capa's hopes to be dashed that fall, for he never did get his Russian visa, and his plans for the agency fell through. He would be spending a lot more time in his New York apartment than he had ever intended to.

24

With America's entry into the war and Hungary's declaration of war on the Allies, Capa's situation grew even worse, for, as an enemy alien, he was forbidden to use his cameras or to travel more than ten miles from New York without a special permit. At first he was allowed to deposit his cameras (he had two 35mm Contaxes, a Rolleiflex, and a Speed Graphic press camera) at the *Life* office, but at the beginning of January 1942 he was notified that if he didn't go at once to the Federal Court House and apply for a temporary work permit, he would have to turn them in at police headquarters. Martha Gellhorn moved heaven and earth to help him get his working papers: she got Virginia Cowles to talk to Henry Luce about the problem and Howard Hawks to ask his friend Shipwreck Kelly to discuss the matter with J. Edgar Hoover; she told Capa that if all that didn't do the trick, she would get in touch with Harry Hopkins, a close friend and adviser of Roosevelt's. So it isn't surprising that Capa got his cameras back in short order, but only to have *Life* assign him more trivial stories. While battles were raging in Russia, in North Africa, and in the Pacific, Capa was covering the military training of the Dartmouth College ski patrol, a Defense Stamp party in Gettysburg, and the opening of the American Theater Wing's Stage Door Canteen in New York.

Since Capa began his book *Slightly Out of Focus* with his receipt of a letter informing him that he would have to turn in his cameras (which he claimed happened in the summer of 1942), a few words should be said here about the reliability of that book as a biographical source. It must be borne in mind that Capa wrote it with the specific intention of selling it to the movies; his first concern was to produce a fast-moving and entertaining story rather than a meticulously accurate account of events. Indeed, he never claimed that the book told the whole truth and nothing but the truth; on the dust-jacket flap he stated: "Writing the truth being obviously so difficult, I have in the interests of it allowed myself to go sometimes slightly beyond and slightly this side of it. All events and persons in this book are accidental and have something to do with the truth." In most cases they have a great deal to do with the truth, although Capa changed the names of some of the principal characters, speeded up the sequence of some events, and embroidered some stories. As he had always done, he tried to make a good story even better.

For instance, he claimed that more or less out of the blue the editors of *Collier's* sent him a check for $1,500 with a letter hiring him for a special assignment in England; he had forty-eight hours to get ready to sail. Capa then (so he claimed) flew to Washington, where, with a combination of charm and good liquor, he persuaded the British press attaché to help him obtain the papers he needed to leave the United States and enter Great Britain. Back in New York the next day, he set about getting all his permits, collecting the final few just in time to make his ship.

In fact, *Collier's* didn't hire Capa out of the blue. Bored with his *Life* assignments and angry that Wilson Hicks wouldn't send him abroad unless he managed to obtain a Russian visa (for *Life* had all the coverage it needed on other fronts), he resumed his old affiliation with Pix. In mid-April 1942, the editors of *Collier's*, believing that the Allies were about to launch an invasion of either France or North Africa from England, hired him through Pix to cover the invasion.

After learning of his assignment, Capa went to Washington not for an afternoon but for a week, staying with Myron Davis, a *Life* photographer he had met in Chicago. Capa proceeded to take over the apartment, occupying the bathroom for hours every morning as he soaked in the tub and read mystery novels. (Davis got the impression that this was his daily rite of passage from André Friedmann to Robert Capa.) He managed to obtain his papers largely because he would be working in England with Quentin Reynolds, the *Collier's* correspondent whose coverage of the London Blitz had made him enormously popular and influential on both sides of the Atlantic.

Accredited to the British Ministry of Information and the Admiralty, and armed with the stamped and seal-embossed document that was to serve as his passport,* Capa was ready to sail on the morning of April 23. There was just

---

* The document was soon crumpled, torn, and taped—which Capa said was all for the best, since papers that looked well used carried more authority and credibility than ones that looked brand-new.

one problem: he had lost his entire $1,500 advance at poker. He had to borrow five dollars from Pix for cab fare out to his ship in Brooklyn, but after reaching England he cabled the agency that he had been playing poker with the officers on board and had won back all the money.

The ship, a former British banana boat now carrying food for England in its hold and dismantled planes on deck, headed first to Halifax, Nova Scotia, where it was to join the large international convoy that it would lead across the Atlantic. When the commodore—who, it turned out, loved the movies—came on board in Halifax and was introduced to Capa, he too confused him with Frank Capra and invited him to accompany him the next morning as he visited the captains of the other ships to brief them. Taking advantage of the commodore's confusion, Capa invited Joris Ivens, in Halifax making a film about Canadian convoy escorts for the National Film Board of Canada, to come along. Although he was fully accredited, all of Ivens's efforts to gain access to a convoy briefing had failed; it was only, as Capa was to find so often during the war, a highly irregular fast play, catching the military bureaucracy off guard, that could cut through the red tape.

The crossing was uneventful until, off the Irish coast, the presence of U-boats was detected, but the destroyer escorting the convoy quickly laid a dense smoke screen that blocked the ships from the submarines' view, and the convoy slipped past unscathed. This episode, minor though it was, gave Capa's second convoy story just enough excitement to make it saleable.

After a picaresque series of misadventures involving British naval, security, and immigration authorities, Capa reached London in mid-May and rented a "messy little service flatlet" just off Fleet Street, overlooking the churchyard of St.-Dunstan-in-the-West. About a week later Quentin Reynolds arrived. Reynolds was a huge (well over two hundred pounds), hard-drinking, garrulous, boundlessly high-spirited Brooklynite who had been the sports editor of Collier's before the war. He loved being a celebrity and played the role to the hilt, taking full advantage of all the privileges to which his prestige entitled him. But even he couldn't immediately get his colleague fully accredited to the United States Army as a war correspondent. The Army Public Relations Office agreed to give Capa a temporary pass to any army base in Britain on which he had an assignment to photograph, but no one—especially an enemy alien—could be fully accredited until he had been cleared by Intelligence.

Since, however, the rumor of an imminent invasion that had taken Capa to England proved to be a false alarm, it didn't matter. For the time being, nothing of any real interest was going on, and the stories that he and Reynolds manufactured to fill space in Collier's and Illustrated until something more exciting came along required minimal, if any, security clearance. During June and July they did stories on Welsh coal miners in the Rhondda Valley (the subjects of *How Green Was My Valley*, which had just won the Academy Award for Best Picture of 1941), on the training of British paratroopers, and on reconstructive surgery in military hospitals. Reynolds, hard-pressed to give his articles some spice, sprinkled them with amusing anecdotes about Capa, telling how, for instance, when he was photographing an operation in which a plastic surgeon was repairing the nose of a young Pole whose face had been smashed by the butt of a German rifle,

> one of the assistant surgeons nudged me . . . and, chuckling, pointed to my mad Hungarian photographer, Bob Capa. We were all, of course, wearing white gowns, caps, and masks, and Capa's usually ruddy face was now a pale gray. The doctor and I helped him out and into an anteroom.
> "I'm blacking out," moaned Capa and, sure enough, he went right out.

Capa had been photographing the horrors of war for years, but this operation was too much for him.

It wasn't until September—after Capa had recovered from the bout of illness that laid him up for most of August (evidently gonorrhea caught from one of his tarts)—that he and Reynolds went to Northern Ireland to cover the build-up of American soldiers and sailors in preparation for the opening of the second front. Capa got some good shots of the faces of black soldiers, but his pictures of military training and of recreation are hopelessly dull. His heart was obviously not in this work.

Unfortunately, because he was still not accredited to the U.S. Army, he was excluded from covering the stories that would have excited him. On August 19, for instance, Reynolds—without Capa—covered the abortive Allied raid on Dieppe. And when the first group of American correspondents sailed from England for North Africa on November 9, the day after the Allied landings in Morocco and Algeria, Capa was left behind. He was not much use to *Collier's* at that point, but the magazine didn't fire him or call him back to New York; in fact, when Reynolds returned to the States early in November 1942, Capa stayed on in England, going at the end of the month to an airbase at Chelveston to do a story on an American bomber group. Except for a striking picture of a gunner in the clear nose turret of his bomber, the photographs largely duplicate—even to one plane's successful belly land-ing—those he had taken the previous year. But that one picture of the gunner made all the difference, for (unknown to Capa) it clearly showed the Norden bombsight, a device so secret that the censors checking the photographs didn't notice anything amiss. It was only after *Illustrated* had printed some 400,000 copies of its December 5 issue with that photograph on its cover that the oversight was discovered. Fortunately, the issue had not yet begun to be distributed; the offending covers were destroyed and a new picture hastily substituted.

Capa claimed in *Slightly Out of Focus* that he was accredited immediately after this incident, for unaccredited civilians could not be tried by a court-martial. In fact, although Capa was cleared of all blame, the incident seems to have delayed his accreditation for several months, and while he waited he went on doing routine stories for *Collier's* and *Illustrated*.

In mid-February 1943, on his way back to London from an assignment, Capa decided to get off the train in Reading and pay a spur-of-the-moment visit to Dinah Sheean's sister Blossom and her husband, F. G. Miles, who owned an aircraft production firm nearby. Dinah and Jimmy had taken Capa along on numerous weekend visits in 1941, and he had become very friendly with Miles, who was "rather tycoonish" and very generous with his money; they were constantly cooking up projects of one kind or another, including some ideas for films, but nothing ever came of them. Not much more had come of the brief romance Capa apparently had that summer with a delicate, exquisitely beautiful young Balinese woman named Olga who was working for Miles Aircraft. When Capa now arrived at the Miles house, Olga, now married, was there with her new husband, Cecil Lewis (not to be confused with the poet Cecil Day Lewis), a World War I flier who had written a very successful book, entitled *Sagittarius Rising*, about his flying experiences. He was now working for the Ministry of Aircraft Production and spending a good deal of time at Reading while learning to fly the new planes. His teacher was John Justin, a very handsome, slender, half-English, half-Argentinian actor who had starred as Ahmad, the deposed ruler, in Alexander Korda's wonderful 1940 film *The Thief of Bagdad*; after that he had temporarily given up his movie career to become a pilot in the RAF.

With Justin was his glamorous twenty-five-year-old wife, Elaine, a ravishing beauty with a most alluring figure, a very feminine and sexy demeanor, and a gorgeous head of hair so strawberry-blonde that Capa nicknamed her "Pinky." As Pinky later recalled, she and Capa "took one look at each other and knew that something was starting." Her marriage with Justin was already on the rocks, but they had been unable to get a divorce.

Pinky's reddish hair was reminiscent of Gerda's, and she had something of Gerda's winning manner, but otherwise the two women were very different. Where Gerda had been tough, practical, ambitious, enterprising, and talented,

Pinky was, as one friend recalls, "dependent and childlike—she could spend an entire morning darkening her eyelashes and believe that she had done something important." But she was beautiful, sexy, and fun to be with—so how could he resist her? Even her frivolousness was reassuring: she was not likely to take him too seriously. And besides, she was caught in her marriage; it would be quite some time before she was in a position to ask *anyone* for a real commitment. Meanwhile, they could have marvelous times together, with lots of laughter and fun. They could even play at having a romance, as long as it remained play. The only problem was that right then Capa needed the excitement of war more than the excitement of romance.

25

He didn't have long to wait. About a week after he met Pinky, he received word that he was at last to be sent to North Africa as a fully accredited photographer/correspondent for *Collier's*. (He was, in fact, to be the only enemy alien accredited to the U.S. Army in such a capacity.*)

Singing "J'Attendrai," which became "their song," Pinky saw him off at Euston Station, where, in the dim, depressing glow of blue blackout lights, thousands of soldiers were saying goodbye to their families and sweethearts. From Glasgow, Capa sailed on a British troopship, arriving in Algiers on March 6, 1943. He then went on to Casablanca to do a story on the U.S. Army Services of Supply, whose men were unloading ships carrying everything from canned rations to partially assembled tanks and jeeps, which they readied for movement to the front on huge outdoor assembly lines. Capa felt that this display of technical know-how and ability to improvise made the SOS the most quintessentially American branch of the army, and he agreed with a French officer who remarked to him, as they watched the operations, "Ça

---

* In 1948 a Hungarian who had apparently changed his name to Eric A. Harris wrote to Capa stating that he had also been an enemy alien accredited to the U.S. Army as a correspondent. Capa does, however, seem to have been the only such *photographer*/correspondent so accredited.

inspire confiance." As well it should have, for Allied supplies and troops were pouring into North Africa at a greater rate than ever, while recent fighting had been disproportionately costly to the Axis in terms of men and materiel, and Allied air and naval forces in the Mediterranean were having great success in cutting the Axis lines of resupply. In his captions Capa astutely observed that the North African campaign had become largely a "war of supplies."

When Capa returned to Algiers, the public-relations office at Allied headquarters provided him with a bedroll, a jeep, and a driver and sent him off toward central Tunisia, where a big Allied offensive was about to begin. As it turned out, this was the offensive that was to bring the North African campaign to a successful close within eight weeks. Capa and his driver raced day and night in an effort to reach the American advance headquarters at Feriana—some four hundred miles from Algiers—to catch the beginning of the American part of the offensive on the night of March 16, but by the time they arrived, the U.S. 1st Infantry Division* had already occupied Gafsa without a fight. The predominantly Italian Axis forces had withdrawn to the hills southeast of the nearby oasis of El Guettar, while the Americans' eastward drive was halted by two days of heavy rains that transformed the terrain into an ocean of mud.

Although Capa was disappointed by the lack of excitement around Gafsa, he wrote to his mother that he was very happy "to be again on some kind of French soil." After the damp chill of an English winter, he had greatly enjoyed the warm sunshine of his first few days in Africa and was delighted by the plenitude of oranges, which were almost completely unavailable in London at any price. Furthermore, he was happy to be at, or at least near, the front; after four years he was finally again in a position to do the work he did best. Besides, he liked the life at the front. "I am glad to be in the field again," he told his mother. "The life is Army life, and it does me a lot of good." It was, wrote Ernie Pyle, the famous Scripps-Howard correspondent whom Capa met in the press camp in Gafsa, "a life consisting only of the essentials—food, sleep, transportation, and what little warmth and safety a man could manage to wangle out of it by personal ingenuity. . . . There were no appointments to keep, nobody cared how anybody looked, red tape was at a minimum, . . . [and] the army accepted us correspondents as part of the family. We knew and were friends with hundreds of individual soldiers. And we knew, and were known by, every American general in Tunisia."

---

* The American II Corps, commanded by General Patton, consisted of three infantry divisions (the 1st, the 9th, and the 34th) and one armored division (the 1st).

The two generals with whom Capa became friendliest were Maj. Gen. Terry Allen and Brig. Gen. Theodore Roosevelt, Jr.; both shared the traits of forthrightness, human warmth, and good humor that he had liked so well in Evans Carlson and Stilwell. Allen, a Texan and a former cavalryman who was commander of the 1st Infantry Division, was a colorful and informal character, as famous for his wildly profane language as for his rather laissez-faire attitude toward battle plans and discipline. Roosevelt, Allen's assistant divisional commander and a son of the former president, was even more easygoing; his men loved him for his bravery, his cockiness, his corny sense of humor, his ability to recite poetry, and for the walking-stick that was his trademark. Two such unorthodox generals were the perfect companions for such an unorthodox correspondent as Capa.

Like Pyle, whose listing of the names and hometowns of individual GIs in his dispatches had made him the most widely read and best loved of all war correspondents, Capa also became friendly with a great many enlisted men (although he had to explain to his editors, who asked him to emulate Pyle, that while he was juggling several cameras, trying to get the best possible shots in the heat of battle, it was often very difficult to ask and write down the names of the soldiers whom he had just photographed). He made every effort to become accepted as "one of the boys," playing poker with them and sharing the dangers of combat; their morale was much improved by the fact that this slightly comic "friendly enemy alien" with his non-regulation uniform (it had been made by a Bond Street tailor who had his own ideas about how an American correspondent's uniform should look) and his heavy foreign accent, equipped with cameras but no weapons, went voluntarily into the front lines. Officers admired Capa for his apparent insouciance and his knack for survival and would invite him along on dangerous missions; they felt that his presence would bring good luck. "I'm getting too popular," Capa once wryly remarked to Time-Life correspondent Will Lang, "and someday this popularity will get me killed." But Lang later said that he "never knew Capa to turn down such an invitation, however dangerous or uncomfortable, as long as it promised exciting photos"—although he kidded reporters that he envied them because "they could write their stories of a battle without ever seeing it, but he, poor Capa, had to risk having his head shot off in order to get his pictures."

Sometimes missions turned out to be a good deal less exciting than they had promised to be. On March 20, after the rain had stopped and the mud had hardened a bit, Capa accompanied the tanks of Maj. Gen. Orlando Ward's

1st Armored Division as they began their eastward push toward the crucial road-and-railway junctions of Station de Sened and Maknassy; to everyone's surprise, they took both objectives with hardly any opposition.

Early on the afternoon of March 22, General Ward ordered his tanks and troops to regroup for a thrust toward the main coastal road. Because the attack was to begin at 11:30 that night, Capa would not be able to photograph it. And, in any case, word had come through that the Germans were moving a crack armored division toward El Guettar. Capa—whose time with the 1st Armored Division had yielded little more than photos of medics and communications men setting up their rear-guard facilities, of men taking breathers under palm trees, and of GIs handing out candy and "shoon gum" to the Arab boys swarming over their jeeps—decided to head back to El Guettar that afternoon. On the way, his luck—the luck that made him so popular—transformed what could have been a fatal mishap into a comic misadventure. As he tells the story in *Slightly Out of Focus*, he got out of his jeep, ran over to a clump of cactus by the side of the road, and was just about to relieve himself when he noticed a little sign that read: "ACHTUNG! MINEN!"

It was his first encounter with buried mines. They were a recent invention, first used extensively in North Africa, where sand and·mud allowed them to be concealed very effectively, without any traces of freshly turned earth. As the Axis forces in Tunisia retreated, they left a trail of mine fields behind them.

> I did not jump [wrote Capa], I did not stir. I did not dare to do anything. I had to do something very badly, but it takes very little to make a land mine go off. I shouted my predicament to my driver. I told him I was standing in the middle of a mine field. He seemed to think the situation very funny. I could see no cause for laughter. I didn't dare to retrace my footsteps, because the mines that had failed to go off the first time might have changed their minds by now. I urged him to drive off and bring back somebody with a mine detector.
>
> I was caught with my pants down. There I was, braving death in a lonely, empty, soundless desert, standing nailed to the sand, behind a stupid cactus bush. Even my obituary would be unprintable.

Hours later (or, at least, what seemed like hours later to Capa), the driver returned with a mine removal squad and with Eliot Elisofon, the *Life* photographer who had covered the 1st Armored Division's advance. The mine squad rescued Capa quickly, but Elisofon, whose rather pompous and egotistical manner Capa found most annoying (mainly because Elisofon had the effrontery to consider himself as great a photographer as Capa considered himself), told the story with great relish in the press camp. Capa later claimed that he was able to live the story down only by sleeping right through an air raid that night.

For the past two days the 1st Infantry Division had been engaged in attacking the enemy forces that had withdrawn from Gafsa to the hills southeast of El Guettar. In response, General von Armin, whose forces near Gabès were under attack from Montgomery's Eighth Army, dispatched the only retaliatory force he could spare: the depleted but still formidable 10th Panzer Division, which began its attack at El Guettar before dawn on the morning of March 23.

Capa, eager to get out to the front to cover his first real battle since the end of the Spanish Civil War, raced to the top of the hill known to the Americans as Hill 336 from its height as given in meters on their topographical maps. There he found the heavy guns of the 5th Field Artillery Battalion and the observation post of the 16th Infantry Regiment's 3rd Battalion.* Before long, German shells began blasting Hill 336, and the American artillery replied, although rapidly diminishing stocks of ammunition on the hilltop limited its effectiveness. The Germans, who had met with little resistance from these same American troops in February, attacked with great confidence, and for several hours that morning it looked as though their confidence were justified. Their infantry swept over the foothills of Hill 336, engaging in fierce hand-to-hand fighting and inflicting heavy casualties on the Americans. Behind the infantry, the tanks advanced relentlessly to the base of Hill 336. There, below the observation post from which Capa was photographing, the tide of battle turned, for the Germans had underestimated the Yanks' new determination and materiel. American mines knocked out eight German tanks, and reinforcements of artillery and tank-destroyer units knocked out many more. Late in the morning the remaining Germans withdrew to regroup. Allied codebreakers intercepted a radioed order for a second attack to begin at 4:45 that afternoon.

In the early afternoon Capa watched from his observation post as Company E of the 16th Infantry Regiment's 2nd Battalion attacked German reconnaissance patrols that had made their way around to the northern flanks of Hill 336. It was his first opportunity to observe in action the unit with which he would eventually choose to land on Omaha Beach on D-Day.

Shortly before 4:45, German dive bombers attacked American positions,

---

* The 1st Infantry Division was made up of three regiments, of which the 16th was one. Each regiment was divided into three battalions, and each battalion into three companies.

and everyone—including Capa—dove for whatever cover they could find. Before the afternoon was over, the Stukas repeated their action twelve times more. Capa wrote on his caption sheet: "I got a lot of dirt in my lenses and scared in my stomach." But however scared he may have been, he managed to get some dramatic shots of the German planes in action.

At 4:45, right on schedule, the German ground forces began their second attack; the Americans, greatly encouraged by the morning's victory, were ready for them. As Generals Patton (with three stars on his helmet), Allen (with two stars), and Roosevelt (with one) watched from the observation post on Hill 336 and directed the action by walkie-talkie, American infantry and artillery routed the Germans, who retreated to the hills after only two hours of fighting. That day the Americans had for the first time in the war won a decisive victory over the Germans.

After a few frustrating days of trying to photograph the grueling but un-spectacular clean-up operations, Capa left to do a story on the Camel Corps of the French Foreign Legion, which was having great success in driving the Italians from southern Tunisia, and, upon his return to El Guettar during the first week of April, he focused not on the fighting (which came to an end on April 7) but on the soldiers' life at the front.

When, in about the middle of the month, the II Corps began to move northward for the final thrust against the Germans, who had been squeezed into a small area around Tunis and Bizerte, Capa decided not to go along. The consensus in the press camp was that Patton's replacement by a complete unknown—Gen. Omar N. Bradley—indicated that the corps was slated for a minor role in the offensive. The correspondents also thought that the con-centration of Axis forces would probably hold out for quite some time. So Capa decided to strike off in search of something more interesting, settling finally on a nearby unit of fighter-bombers. Capa got one great picture, showing a feisty-looking young American pilot named Levi Chase in the cockpit of his plane, on whose fuselage were painted nine swastikas and three fasces, one for each German or Italian plane he had shot down. But otherwise there wasn't much of a story, and when Capa learned that the 301st Bomber Group, the unit whose Norden bombsight had gotten him into trouble, was now stationed at one of the airfields near Constantine, in northern Algeria, he decided to head there. The "Flying Fortresses"—long-range B-17 bombers—of Maj. Gen. James Doolittle's Northwest African Strategic Air Force were then concen-trating on Axis shipping at sea and in ports in Tunisia, southern Italy, Sicily, and Sardinia; a story on their activities would complete Capa's coverage of the Tunisian campaign as a "war of supplies."

When he arrived at Constantine on May 1, he found the planes grounded by bad weather. For four consecutive days, as one mission after another was canceled, he sat around with the men and played poker, at which he lost heavily. But he didn't mind, for he seems to have believed that as long as he lost at poker (the more heavily, the better) he would remain safe, get good stories, and be able to count on Pinky's faithfulness. Somewhat more pragmatically, he used to joke that he could get himself to work only if he lost all his money and so *had* to go out and earn more.

For his story on the 301st Bomber Group, Capa documented twenty-four hours in the life of the crew of one plane, "The Goon." Many of the pictures duplicate those he had taken in England, but during the previous year the rule concerning war correspondents had been changed: he would no longer have to stay behind on the ground.

Although Capa says in *Slightly Out of Focus* that he flew with the 301st Bomber Group on missions over Bizerte, Tunis, Naples, and Palermo (all of which were, indeed, the group's current targets), his contact sheets and typed captions suggest that he flew on only one mission, on May 6, against shipping in the Strait of Sicily. Searching for a target, his Flying Fortress flew so low that it cast a large shadow onto the waters of the Mediterranean, but when at last a munitions ship came into view, the plane climbed to an altitude at which it could avoid as much anti-aircraft fire as possible and then dropped its bombs. As the Fortress flew away, Capa was able to snap a few pictures of what appeared to be a tiny ship, far below, being blown to pieces.*

The next day, when the news came through that the Axis forces, crippled by extreme shortages of equipment and supplies, had collapsed suddenly and that the Americans had taken Bizerte and the British had taken Tunis, Capa immediately set out for Tunis in a jeep. As he rode across northern Tunisia, he photographed the aftermath of battle: the plain wooden crosses in the American cemetery at Béja, the black Iron Cross–shaped markers and engraved propeller blades over the graves in German cemeteries, the wildly twisted wreckage of Axis planes destroyed by Allied bombers at the airfield of El Aouina, near Tunis. When he came to Hill 609, which only a few days earlier had been the scene of some of the hardest fighting of the entire North African campaign, he photographed Arab shepherds leading their flocks past burnt-

---

* In *Slightly Out of Focus* Capa claims that when he flew on a mission over Palermo, "The Goon" limped home after having one of its engines shot out by German fighter planes. He noted on his caption sheets, however, that "The Goon" had been badly shot up on one of its missions but that the damage had been repaired before he arrived at the airfield. The account in the book is probably based on tales that Capa heard at the poker table.

out tanks as they returned to the grazing grounds from which they had fled before the battle.

All along the dusty, sun-baked road to Tunis was an endless stream of refugees driving donkey-drawn carts piled high with their possessions, riding bicycles, or walking, returning from the hills to their liberated city. The procession looked much like those which Capa had photographed early in 1939 on the roads northward from Tarragona and Barcelona—only here the people were happy, not grief-stricken and terrified. Capa was so excited about photographing them that he stood up in his slowly moving jeep to get better shots, but then the jeep lurched suddenly and he fell out onto the road, scraping the palms of both hands. After getting some first aid, he went on taking pictures, with his hands wrapped thickly in gauze.

As he drove across Tunisia, Capa was reminded of the end of the Spanish Civil War not only by the procession of refugees but also by huge, hastily improvised prison camps, into which 250,000 prisoners were herded. The Tunisian camps, surrounded by large coils of barbed wire, looked almost exactly like the internment camp Capa had photographed at Argelès, only now the internees were German and Italian prisoners, not Spanish Loyalist exiles. The mood in the camps was surprisingly cheerful, for many of the men, especially the Italians, were relieved to be through with fighting—so much so that along the roads Capa photographed several groups of Italian soldiers laughing and singing on the way to turn themselves in. The Germans tended to be somewhat more sullen.

After the delirious victory celebrations in Tunis, Capa decided to go back to England to see Pinky. It seemed clear that it would take the Allies a while to prepare for their next invasion, so he could spend several weeks with her and still get to the next jumping-off point without missing anything very exciting. Besides, now that the tide of the war had finally turned in favor of the Allies—and now that he had gotten some good pictures of that turning point—he could afford to take some time out for love.

The inevitable problems with his travel papers delayed Capa's arrival in London until the first week of June 1943, but once he got there he had such a good time with Pinky, who was still living with her husband but evidently separated from him in every other respect, that he was in no hurry to leave. (The only nuisance imposed by Pinky's arrangement seems to have been that Capa couldn't send his letters from the front to her directly; he sent them instead in care of the Time Inc. office, where Pinky—who became the office pet—would read them, making the romance, as Crocky recalls, "public property." Capa's original judgment turned out to be correct: it was all as much a game to Pinky as it was to him.)

Four weeks after his arrival, Capa's vacation was suddenly cut short when he received a cable from New York informing him that his affiliation with *Collier's* would end on July 19.* The editors were pleased with his work, but it had taken almost three months for them to receive the pictures of El Guettar he had sent through regular military channels—and by that time some of the best of them had appeared in newspapers all over the country, for pictures taken at the front could be exclusive only if the photographer left the theater of operations with them. If he turned his negatives over to the military for shipment, the Army had the right to radio its choice to the States; the radioed pictures were then distributed by the wire services. Under the circumstances, *Collier's* decided it made more sense to subscribe to the wire services than to maintain Capa in the field.

Since free-lance photographers could not be accredited, Capa had two weeks to find another job, or else lose his hard-won access to the front. He really didn't have much to worry about, for he could be fairly certain that Wilson Hicks would hire him to work for *Life*; he simply had to swallow his pride and ask Hicks for a job.

There was actually a tremendous advantage in working for *Life*, since

---

* Capa's account of the events following his receipt of the cable—and indeed his entire account of his coverage of the invasion of Sicily—is one of the most heavily fictionalized sections of *Slightly Out of Focus*.

Time Inc., along with the Associated Press, Acme News Photos (the United Press picture agency), and the International Newspaper Syndicate, had joined the U.S. Army-Navy Photographic Pool, members of which got priority on transportation to and at the front, on clearance through censorship, and on shipment of their stories and photos to the States. The member organizations occasionally had to send their photographers out on dull stories the Army wanted covered, but it was a small price to pay for the privileges they got.

Rumor had it that something big was about to happen in the Mediterranean, so as soon as he had cabled Hicks of his availability (and, for good measure, sent *Collier's* a cable appealing its decision), Capa made arrangements to fly to Allied headquarters in Algiers. (Pinky helped him cut through the usual red tape by calling up an officer who had been pestering her for a date; she agreed to have dinner with him if he would get Capa on the next plane. He did.) Capa rushed to Algiers not only because he didn't want to miss a major invasion, but also because he figured that if he were in the field by July 19, he might have a few extra days of grace while waiting to hear from *Life*.

Arriving in Algiers, he discovered that the armada carrying the amphibious troops who were to land on Sicily early on the morning of July 10 had already sailed. It looked briefly as though he had run out of luck, but it turned out that there was one invasion force that had not yet embarked—the paratroopers of the 82nd Airborne Division, who would fly from their bases around Kairouan, Tunisia, on the night of July 9. There was just one problem: Capa had watched a great many parachutists being trained, but he himself had never learned to jump. Still, there was a way out; the Army couldn't very well assign a man without jump training to a parachute unit, but it could assign him to the Northwest African Troop Carrier Command. He would go along in one of the transport planes, photograph the men as they jumped out over Sicily, and return with the empty plane to the base in Tunisia.

Capa claimed in *Slightly Out of Focus* that this plan was put into action on the first night of the invasion, July 9, and that as the paratroopers he photographed landed before the amphibious troops did, his pictures showed the very beginning of the campaign. However, the caption that accompanied Capa's best photograph when the Army radioed it to the States leads us to the realization that the pictures were not taken until two nights later—for it identifies Lt. Col. Charles Kouns, who was the commanding officer of the 504th

Parachute Infantry Regiment's 3rd Battalion.* The 504th, it turns out, jumped on the night of July 11 to reinforce troops fighting around Gela.

Capa's boast of having scooped the invasion seems like a harmless bit of deception, especially since the men he photographed can't have been much less apprehensive than those who had jumped two nights earlier. Insufficient advance warning of the mission led Allied ground and naval forces as well as Axis forces to fire on the planes, shooting down 23 of the 144 that had taken off. (One man, who had asked Capa on the flight out whether it was true that he had come along without being ordered to, exclaimed before jumping: "I don't like your job, pal. It's too dangerous!" In fact, it probably *was* more dangerous to remain in the plane, which had to retrace its way through heavy anti-aircraft fire, than to jump from it.)

But in *Slightly Out of Focus* Capa remarked only in passing that the sky over Sicily was filled with German tracer bullets, for if he still didn't hesitate to tell a story that would make editors feature his pictures, he had by now come to feel that it was undignified to dwell on the dangers he had gone through to get them, let alone to exaggerate those dangers. His exploits and bravery were well known, and now his self-imposed code dictated that he either relate his experiences as comic misadventures or else candidly and simply admit that he had been frightened. No one who wasn't actually present at the time could have any idea of what he had gone through or even, despite his photographs, of the full magnitude of what he had seen—so, he felt, it would be pointless and somehow disrespectful to those who were there to say more.

When the plane landed back at Kairouan about 3 a.m., Chuck Romine, a young public-relations officer who had taken a liking to Capa, was waiting on the field. In the small, suffocatingly hot tent he had rigged up to serve as a darkroom, he helped develop and print the negatives; then, when the prints were ready, the two men jumped into a jeep and tore off toward Tunis. At the press camp there the censors immediately approved the pictures for radio transmission to the States, but—there had to be a hitch somewhere—regulations forbade any mention of an individual photographer's name in the credit line accompanying pictures radioed by the Army. Capa would get no credit for his photographs, and by the time they appeared in *Collier's* the invasion would seem like ancient history.

In his book Capa claimed that while he was at the Tunis press camp that

---

* At that time Army regulations permitted individuals but not military units to be identified in captions, and all insignia, such as shoulder patches, had to be retouched out before photographs could be published.

morning a cable arrived informing the Army that he was no longer working for *Collier's*. He said that Chuck Romine intercepted the cable and immediately arranged for him to parachute with reinforcements into Sicily, where he could evade the Public Relations Office a while longer. The truth of the matter, however, is that Capa still had a week before he would lose his accreditation—and he did not parachute into Sicily at all; as his caption sheets make clear, he went on a supply ship that landed at Licata. (There were limits to Capa's self-deprecation, and going in on a supply ship was obviously more than he could bring himself to admit in his book.) Then, because he wanted to follow through on his story about the 504th, he located the regiment and, on July 17, accompanied it along with the rest of the 82nd Airborne Division to the newly taken city of Agrigento. It was a lucky move, for the next day General Patton, commanding the Seventh Army, included the 82nd in the provisional corps he organized to storm across the island to Palermo. In the midst of such an important campaign, everyone would be far too busy to notice that Capa's accreditation had finally expired.

After Capa had covered the surrender of Palermo's commanding general and the tumultuous welcome the citizens gave the American troops late on July 22, he spent the next day photographing the battered city, but he didn't linger there for long. Nor did he join Patton's eastward push along the coast to Messina, perhaps because he knew he could expect no mercy if the fanatically orthodox Patton found out that he had lost his job. Instead, he decided to strike out after his old division from El Guettar, the 1st Infantry, which was engaged in hard fighting in the interior of the island. He knew that Generals Allen and Roosevelt not only liked him but were so cavalier about regulations that they wouldn't care whether or not he was officially entitled to be covering their campaign.*

But first he had to find them. Rather than wander through the still very dangerous territory between Palermo and the front where the 1st Infantry was deployed, he decided to retrace his steps to Licata and then follow the route the division had taken northward. John Hersey, then a correspondent for *Time*, was in Licata (which he would call "Adano" in his novel *A Bell for Adano*), and Capa persuaded him to go along into the interior. With what Hersey refers to as "his usual grand style," Capa commandeered a jeep for the expedition, and they set out on the night of July 25, reaching division headquarters near Gangi the next afternoon and then going out to join the men

---

* Their lax attitudes would soon cost Allen and Roosevelt their commands; both were relieved by General Bradley on August 6.

of the 16th Regiment, who were pushing toward Sperlinga and Nicosia. It was fairly tough going at first, for the Axis rear guard had orders to delay the American advance at any cost until the rest of the retreating force could be ferried across the Strait of Messina to safety on the Italian mainland. But the young and inexperienced Germans weren't able to hold out for long (Capa afterward photographed some prisoners who had had only a couple weeks of training and had arrived in Sicily just a few days before they were captured), and, as in Tunisia, the demoralized Italians could hardly wait to surrender.

The 16th Regiment found both Sperlinga and Nicosia virtually abandoned by the enemy on the morning of July 28, but such an easy victory raised false hopes for the rest of the campaign. Only five days later, the regiment entered the battle for Troina, a hilltop town dominating a crucial highway, where a seasoned German force had dug in for a fight to the death, surrounding the town with mine fields and establishing an interlocking system of machine-gun nests on the encircling hills; the battle was to be the most difficult in which American troops in the Mediterranean theater had yet been engaged.

The Allies were forced to use unprecedentedly heavy concentrations of artillery fire and aerial bombing at Troina, for tanks were useless in such hilly terrain, and infantry couldn't penetrate the German grid. Such strategy presented Capa with a problem almost as grave, from his standpoint, as that faced by the Allied commanders: he was present at what was obviously one of the most important battles of the Sicilian campaign, but there seemed to be nothing for him to photograph—for the infantry moved only at night, and the artillery barrage yielded little more than shots of a distant town constantly shrouded in smoke. (He later wrote that his pictures "showed how dreary and unspectacular fighting actually is.") But he eventually managed to get some exciting pictures when he accompanied a daring reconnaissance platoon and when he went up in one of the Piper Cubs—nicknamed "Flying Jeeps"—that spotted artillery targets from the air and reported on the accuracy of fire. During Capa's flight more than a hundred guns and a squadron of thirty-six dive-bombers alternated in blasting Troina in a concerted effort to stun the Germans into submission. The flight was dangerous, but Hersey recalls that when Capa told him about it, he made it sound like something one might do for fun on an afternoon at Coney Island.

Finally, early on the morning of August 6, an artillery observation plane confirmed reports that the enemy had abandoned Troina during the night. Entering the town with Herbert Matthews, Capa was reminded of Teruel, another hilltop town whose siege they had covered together, although Troina was as hot as Teruel had been cold. Once in town, they found hysterical and wounded inhabitants who had endured the terrible bombing and shelling, and

Capa, still thinking back to Teruel, took a photograph of a man carrying a severely shell-shocked girl with a bandaged leg—a photo uncannily similar to the one of a man carrying a boy with a bandaged leg he had taken soon after Loyalist troops had entered the Spanish town. The victory at Troina, however, was to be a lasting one.

At Troina, Capa learned that he had scored a personal victory as well. When General Roosevelt arrived in town later that morning, he announced that there was a message at division headquarters saying that Capa was now working for *Life.** Soon thereafter he wrote Crocky to give her the news:

> Wilson gave me a contract: $600 guarantee [per month] and $100 for every page, so if I can make 12 pages a month we will be able to drink champagne, if not we can still drink a lot of Scotch, and if not we can always borrow money. I got a cable from Hicks saying that I am still the great war photographer, and I became very depressed. All that fight and struggle just to please Mr. Hicks makes you feel [as though you were] buying a mink coat for a Bond Street tart.

At least he could afford to chase his blues away with champagne, for that month *Life* devoted seven pages to his Palermo story and eight to Troina.

27

When Capa arrived back in Algiers around the middle of August, he found the city filled with correspondents who had hurried from America and England to cover the invasion of the Italian mainland that was clearly imminent. The ten rooms of the Aletti Hotel set aside for the press were so full that there was no space even for another bedroll on the floor. But a representative of the British Council with a room to himself had invited

---

* Although Capa claimed in *Slightly Out of Focus* that he was hired as a staff photographer at this time, he was actually only on retainer, as he always had been before.

Quentin Reynolds to share it with him, and Reynolds in turn invited Capa to make himself comfortable on the floor. Soon Room 140 was home to nine correspondents—including Ernie Pyle, A. J. Liebling of *The New Yorker*, Jack Belden (a Hankow "Last Ditcher" working for *Time*), Eliot Elisofon, Clark Lee of the International Newspaper Syndicate, and John Steinbeck, who was writing for the New York *Herald Tribune*. On some nights the population rose to as many as eighteen, with late arrivals sleeping on the balcony, in the bathroom, and even in the hall outside the door.

From their balcony the correspondents could see the harbor, in which a fleet of some 700 ships was being assembled to transport the Anglo-American Fifth Army to the Gulf of Salerno, where an amphibious landing was scheduled for the night of September 8. Capa, however, was not to accompany that force, for he had again been assigned to the 504th Parachute Infantry Regiment; this time he was slated to go with its glider-borne troops into an area along the Volturno River, northwest of Naples and forty miles north of the Salerno beachhead.

Arriving at regimental headquarters in the desert near Kairouan at the beginning of September, Capa found the planning and briefing rooms off-limits to correspondents, and the officers bound to secrecy, but on the fourth of the month a few hints were dropped that there might be big changes in the regiment's plans. It was rumored that the new objective might be Rome itself.

The next day, still without any official confirmation of the mission, the correspondents assigned to the 504th—including Richard Tregaskis of the International Newspaper Syndicate and Seymour Korman of the Chicago *Tribune*—were flown to Licata, from which the regiment would depart for the invasion, whatever its objective. * There, little by little, they pieced together details of the new mission. The now friendly Italians had promised to secure several airfields around Rome for American landings; to gain as much protection as possible from German fighter planes, the landings were to be carried out under the cover of darkness. Since there would be time for relatively few transport planes to land, disgorge troops, and clear the range before daylight, many of the men would parachute in.

When the correspondents were at last officially told that they would be landing in Rome, Capa was thrilled. "This would be one of the big scoops

---

* Capa wrote in *Slightly Out of Focus* that he was transferred to Licata on a ship that sailed from Gafsa, but Gafsa is nearly 100 miles from the sea, and Tregaskis says that the correspondents were flown to Sicily.

of the war," he wrote. "While the rest of the photographers were taking pictures of a dreary beach [at Salerno] and maybe a few local mayors, I would catch Mussolini at home."

Late on the afternoon of September 8, as the fully loaded planes were warming up for takeoff, word came through that the mission had been postponed for twenty-four hours; the next evening, as the planes were again loaded and ready to take off, the mission was canceled and the plan abandoned. Terribly disappointed that he wasn't going to "catch Mussolini at home" after all, Capa mourned in a letter to Crocky, "I missed the greatest scoop of anyone's life and am momentarily licked." He felt licked because he was stranded on Sicily while the first Allied invasion of the European mainland was in progress at Salerno—although, in fact, he probably wouldn't have gotten much even if he had been there from the start, for the invasion had begun at 3:30 a.m., and by daylight the worst was over. (George Rodger, one of *Life*'s most seasoned war photographers, covered the landing, but the magazine had to publish drawings to convey any sense of the drama.) And if Capa feared that all of Italy might fall before he could get there, he had nothing to worry about.

The three correspondents didn't sail for the Gulf of Salerno until September 13, arriving two nights later at Paestum, but there was still plenty of combat for them to cover. After spending a few days with the 504th, engaged in heavy fighting around Altavilla, Capa and Tregaskis proceeded to Maiori, in the northern sector of the beachhead, and then up to the crest of the Chiunzi Pass, which dominates the main highway to Naples. Nestled in the deep roadcut at the top, and thus protected somewhat from heavy German artillery on the plain of Vesuvius below, was "Fort Schuster," a stoutly constructed farmhouse pressed into service as an observation post, first-aid station, and command post. "Whisky was offered to us as we sat and talked in the command post, and whisky was necessary," recalled Will Lang. "As each nearby explosion blew open the front door, Capa would put down his glass, raise his camera, and, still seated, photograph the dust and confusion through the doorway, remarking, 'This is the only way to cover a war.' "

After a week at Fort Schuster (by no means all of it spent inside), Capa joined the 82nd Airborne and a division of British tanks on their three-day push toward Naples, entering the city on October 1. Without water, with little food, with no effective civil or military authority, and with thousands of homeless families camped out in its streets, the ruined city—methodically ravaged by the Germans before they abandoned it—seemed to have been plunged back into the Dark Ages. And even more devastation was to come when powerful time bombs hidden by the Germans began going off in public buildings throughout the city. (On the afternoon of October 7, Capa rushed to the central post office after an explosion had killed a hundred people and injured many more.)

Funerals were commonplace, but on his second day in Naples Capa stumbled upon an especially poignant one. Led by one of their teachers, boys from a high school in the Vómero district had stolen guns and ammunition with which to fight the Germans during the last days of the occupation. Now twenty of them lay in the schoolhouse, in coffins so short that the ends had to be left open for their protruding feet. Capa's photographs of the black-clad, grief-stricken women mourning these boys are among his most wrenching of the entire war. Of them he wrote, "Those were my truest pictures of victory."

After the horrors of Naples, Capa welcomed the pleasures of Capri, where he went with Herbert Matthews to photograph the great anti-fascist philosopher Benedetto Croce on October 12. In fact, Capa liked the island so well that he returned there to celebrate his thirtieth birthday with George Rodger, who recalls they were both so exhausted that they spent most of their six-day vacation sleeping.

Rodger, an Englishman who had worked at an astounding variety of jobs before becoming a *Life* photographer, had covered the war from the Cameroons to China and from North Africa to Salerno. Meeting him in Naples for the first time, Capa took an immediate liking to him and was soon affecting a foulard in imitation of his worldly new friend. Together they covered the city's return to life, and inevitably their talk turned to the subject that Capa brought up sooner or later with almost all the photographers he liked: the formation of an agency that would give its members independence and control of the way their work was published. Capa would soon be writing to Cornell, "Maybe we can start something interesting after this war is over. I am bored to be an employee."

In late October and early November, Capa spent a couple weeks with the 504th Regiment as it began its long battle in the mountains north of Naples; by the end of that period, Gen. Matthew B. Ridgway, the divisional commander, had come to admire him so much that he wrote a letter to the editors of *Life* stating that "Mr. Capa, by reason of his professional competence, genial personality, and cheerful sharing of all dangers and hardships has come to be considered a member of the Division."

Capa, however, hadn't liked his taste of mountain fighting, and with the weather growing steadily worse, he was in no hurry to return to the front.

Under the best of conditions it would have been difficult enough for the Allies to storm the German positions around Cassino, where the steep mountains were treacherous outcroppings of rock covered with sparse scrub that offered little cover for attacking infantry. But during the late fall and winter of 1943–44 the men of the Fifth Army had also to contend with bitter cold, with snow on the mountainsides, and with heavy rains that filled the valleys with deep mud. In sodden clothing and with cold, wet feet they manned outposts in terrain so difficult that supplies had to be brought in by mule.

Except for a quick trip to Algiers to cover the Armistice Day celebrations led by General de Gaulle, Capa spent most of November based in a comfortable Vómero apartment he shared with George Rodger and Will Lang, while he roamed Naples with such old friends as Jimmy Sheean and such new ones as director John Huston. And early the following month, suffering from a cold and his annual case of the December blues, he told his family, "The winter at the front is not too agreeable, but we don't always have to be there. I am well off but a bit bored." Even having started at last for the front, he was presented with an excuse not to go on: he sprained his elbow while arm wrestling with another correspondent and had to spend a few days in the Allied hospital in Caserta.

When he finally arrived at the front, on December 18, he went with Herbert Matthews to Mount Pantano, about fifteen miles northeast of Cassino, on whose bitterly contested slopes the 2nd Moroccan Infantry Division, composed mostly of Berber infantrymen and French officers, had recently relieved the American 34th Division. Capa, who had taken a few shots of "Goums" on the Sperlinga-Nicosia front in Sicily, was now drawn to these troops not only because he knew that they would make a fascinating story, but also because his old friend Gen. Teddy Roosevelt, whom Eisenhower had appointed as his chief liaison officer to the French army, was with them.

By December 18 the French had secured the entire western slope of Mount Pantano. Now mule trains could begin to move supplies up to forward positions and burial parties could begin to collect the hundreds of American corpses that had lain for days on the mountainside. Capa photographed many of these corpses (being careful to choose angles from which their faces were not visible, for Army regulations forbade the publication of photographs showing the faces of the dead) and wrote on his caption sheet: "The slope of the mountain with its trees scarred by shell fire, its mud, and dead strewn about, presents the picture most like those scenes of the First World War."

During the week that he and Matthews spent with the Moroccan troops on Mount Pantano and around the little village of Cerasuolo, which they took on December 20, Capa did a long story on the Goums' life at the front.

Then, with many delays caused by heavy rains, he made his way southward to Venafro, where the U.S. 45th Infantry Division had its rear command post—"a series of holes in the mud covered with tents." Largely because of the rain, the front was relatively quiet at that moment, but in a few days the division's 180th Regiment was to launch an offensive. When Capa announced that he was too tired and dirty to wait and asked for a jeep to take him back to Naples, a captain took him to his pup tent and

> opened a barracks bag full of priceless possessions. He fished out a set of fresh underwear, a clean uniform, a pair of shoes, and a bottle of Scotch. An orderly came in and brought three helmets full of hot water. I was washed, shaved, and dressed, and then they cleaned away my last objections with the whisky. The 45th Division must have been awfully keen to get their pictures in *Life* magazine.

Capa was at a forward observation post for the jump-off of the 180th Regiment's attack at dawn on December 30. Soon, when telephone lines between the post and one of the farthest advanced companies were broken, he accompanied two officers as they ran across an open field under enemy fire to convey orders to the men and observe the situation. As they climbed the hill where the company was dug in, German mortar shells burst behind them, and at the top they found the men "pinned down by a terrific barrage." Capa was hit lightly three times by spent shrapnel, which didn't even penetrate his clothing but frightened him, he said, "enough for a Purple Heart." But it was all for nought as far as he was concerned; in a note to the *Life* editors he remarked that his films would "prove again the old truth that in the most dangerous situations you get the least exciting pictures."

Moving southward from Venafro, Capa stopped next at Ceppagna, where the joint U.S.-Canadian First Special Service Force, an elite outfit trained in mountain fighting, had its rear headquarters. He must have been very impressed by what he heard of their exploits, for, despite the fact that they could be reached only by a strenuous all-night climb (the trail was under German observation during the day), he decided to go up after an advance unit. Arriving at the Moscoso Notch early on the morning of January 4, 1944, he took some haunting pictures of women and children fleeing the fighting; one particularly touching photograph shows an American soldier giving a pair of socks he had received for Christmas to a woman whose feet were bleeding from the ordeal. A few hours later, entering the village of Radicosa with a patrol, he got enough good pictures to have made the climb worthwhile. The greatest shows a soldier bandaging the leg of an old shepherd who had been wounded by shrapnel during the fight for the village, his wife and neighbors

LIFE

Vol. 16, No. 5

January 31, 1944

FROM A HILLTOP OVERLOOKING THE LIRI VALLEY THREE INFANTRYMEN OF THE U. S.-CANADIAN MOUNTAIN TROOPS PROTECT AN ADVANCING PATROL WITH THEIR MACHINE GUN

IT'S A TOUGH WAR

Photographs for LIFE by Robert Capa

For months the Fifth Army has inched ahead in Italy. Through mud and mountains it has ground nearer Cassino, chief bastion of the German winter defense line. On Jan. 22, in an amphibious attempt to outflank this line, it landed troops near Anzio northwest of the town of Cassino and only 32 miles short of Rome.

With the troops of the Fifth Army during the battle for the Liri valley on the approaches to Cassino was LIFE Photographer Robert Capa. His pictures, printed here, are grim and unsentimental, but they tell something of what war is like in Italy. They prove that it is a tough war.

When the pictures were taken, the Fifth Army was advancing at the rate of about three miles a week. In terms of the thousands of miles still to go on the roads to Berlin and Tokyo, three miles were insignificant. But for the men who fought for those three

miles they were no mean distance. In the fight some of them died and their bodies lay in the snowy mountain passes near their foxholes. Others were wounded and were brought down steep mountain paths on stretchers to front-line hospitals. But most of them, British and French and American alike, lived somehow through the week. They were the ones who, in spite of their weariness, would fight this week's battles, and next week's, and the weeks' after that.

To these men it seems years ago that they were home. Now all they know and feel is the grinding monotony of war. Day and night they hear the roll of guns, the explosion of mortars, the whine of machine-gun bullets. Their home is among the rocks and snows of the Italian mountains. They are usually wet and hungry, always tired. Most of them have not had a bath or slept in a bed for months. They grumble and they curse and their only dream is of the day

when they will be finished with this chore on the front.

They worry, too, about the home they will return to. They want it to be the same home they left. Last week Secretary of War Stimson reported that these soldiers on the front line in Italy and the South Pacific were worried and unhappy and even angry about what was going on at home. In urging adoption of a national service act, he said: "I can tell you today that the industrial unrest and lack of a sense of patriotic responsibility . . . has aroused a strong feeling of resentment and injustice among the men of the armed forces. If it continues it will surely affect the morale of the Army. It is likely to prolong the war and endanger our ultimate success. Unless we set forth boldly to stamp it out, the hot flame will destroy some of the great love of country which alone can make a man endure the hardship, the pain, and the death which service above self has offered him."

gathered around to watch and assist the first aid. Both the central gesture and the overall composition are strongly evocative (though unintentionally) of a Giottoesque depiction of Christ washing his disciples' feet.

The next morning, with a big snowstorm approaching, Capa decided it was time to leave. Besides, he'd gotten his story; both *Life* and *Illustrated* featured it prominently.

Arriving back in Naples after driving through a nightmarish landscape of shell holes, broken trees, ruins, and abandoned vehicles, he learned that the Army Public Relations Office had chosen him to accompany the commando troops known as the Rangers (whom he had seen in action at the Chiunzi Pass) in an amphibious landing to take place on January 22 at Anzio, thirty miles south of Rome. William Stoneman of the Chicago *Daily News*, who was also picked to go with the Rangers, recalls that he and Capa were "scared to death" when they learned of their assignment. "Capa's first reaction," he remembers, "was to contact the madam of a Hungarian whorehouse in Naples and arrange to buy a case of Spanish brandy to supply a little extra courage for the trip."

The precaution proved to be unnecessary, for the Anzio landings took the Germans completely by surprise. When the first waves of invasion troops landed at two o'clock on the moonless morning of the twenty-second, they met no opposition whatsoever, much to their amazement and relief. Two shore batteries eventually opened up, but they were quickly knocked out by naval guns, and by the time Capa went ashore at daybreak (it would have been pointless for him to go sooner), the Americans had almost completely overcome the small German garrison. Of the 36,000 men who landed at Anzio that day, only 13 were killed and 97 wounded.

Because he had hoped the landings would be spectacular enough to make up for his having missed the beginning of the Salerno invasion, Capa was disappointed and bored by the proceedings. Yale Joel, at that time an Army photographer, remembers seeing him sitting on the hood of a jeep when a lone German plane strafed the beach; everybody hit the sand—except Capa, who stubbornly and disdainfully remained where he was.

The invasion commander Maj. Gen. John P. Lucas's insistence on consolidating the Anzio beachhead postponed the beginning of a full-scale push inland until January 30 (leading Churchill to complain, "I had hoped that we were hurling a wildcat onto the shore, but all we got was a stranded whale"). In the meantime, small-scale attacks were initiated as early as the twenty-fifth. On that day Capa and Will Lang accompanied the U.S. 3rd Infantry Division as it began its push toward Cisterna di Latina, a vital highway and railroad junction fifteen miles northeast of Anzio across almost perfectly flat, relatively treeless farmland (the recently drained Pontine Marshes) that offered little cover except in the model farmhouses that Mussolini had had built. From the abandoned house in which the 2nd Battalion of the division's 15th Regiment had set up its command post, Capa photographed all morning as tanks shelled a nearby house and as infantrymen ran forward to occupy it once the Germans had been driven out. Not all the heavy fire, however, was American. "By noon," wrote Capa, "there was very little left of our farmhouse, and we were busy in a field, rapidly digging model holes which we infinitely preferred to Mussolini's model houses. By evening the house was as level as the surrounding landscape, and our foxholes were so deep that we could stand upright in them without being seen."

Meeting increasingly heavy resistance, the 3rd Division's attack was halted more than three miles from Cisterna on January 27, and by the time Lucas launched his major drive for the Alban Hills on the thirtieth the Germans had rushed troops from other fronts and set up guns in the hills. "The Germans outnumbered us," wrote Capa, "and there was not a square yard of the [beachhead] that they couldn't observe or fill with shells. The newspapermen moved down into the basement of the Press Villa, and we thought twice before we ventured out. . . . There were no new pictures to take on that accursed [beachhead]." Making matters still worse for photographers, the Allies tried to get some cover from German artillery by blanketing the area with chemical smoke.

Capa was willing to endure a certain amount of boredom if he was sure he would be rewarded in the end with a great story—like the fall of Rome. But by the end of the first week of February, it was clear that the Anzio front would remain hopelessly stalemated for some time. (Indeed, Rome didn't fall until June.) Besides, making the very best of a bad situation, Capa had already gotten his story; Wilson Hicks cabled on February 6 to say that he was "pleased beyond measure" with his first shipment of pictures from Anzio. "You're going great guns, Bob," he added. "I salute you again."

Deciding to quit while he was ahead, Capa left at once for Naples and then went on to London. He had had his fill of Italy, where he had endured much danger and difficult conditions to get stories that won him much praise but relatively little money; *Life* published his pictures regularly but rarely gave them quite enough space for him to be able to afford champagne—not that that ever kept him from buying it anyway. Of course he also had a personal reason for leaving: he hadn't seen Pinky in seven months. But a more important—and even more personal—reason was that he wanted to be in England for the invasion of France that the Allies were clearly planning to launch in the near future. More than anything else, he wanted to cover the liberation of his beloved Paris.

28

It is impossible to know exactly to what extent Capa cultivated his romance with Pinky as part of his legend or to what extent, despite his resolution to remain unattached, he had actually fallen in love with her. Certainly, every man at the front had to have a sweetheart back home to talk about over poker, and Capa had to have an especially beautiful one—like Pinky—to maintain his reputation. (Written inside the helmet he wore in Italy was the inscription, "Property of Robert Capa, great war correspondent and lover.") Whatever the case, by the time he got back to London, just in time for the "Little Blitz," they had grown fond enough of each other to move together into a luxurious suite at the Dorchester Hotel.* According to Crocky, who was in New York, Pinky wrote her of the situation: "Capa and I are now 'living in sin' out in the open. . . . I'm very happy and having great fun with the bad little boy who loves me very much and is so sweet to me." She still makes it sound like a play romance, though clearly a most enjoyable one, and although she later told one interviewer, "Capa made me much nicer than I was and much more thoughtful than when I first met him," in the rest of her letter to Crocky she sounds rather like one of the "bright young things" in an Evelyn Waugh satire. Capa, terribly proud of Pinky and always speaking of her in glowing terms to his friends, was lavishing his affection and his money on her, but whenever she mentioned marriage, he would laugh it off. True, he would occasionally ask a friend whether he should marry Pinky (such talk, after all, kept the game

---

* Since *Life* published nothing by Capa between late February and early June, he was getting only his $600 a month advance from the magazine. The high living was paid for by *Illustrated*, which published enlarged, though much delayed, versions of the stories that had appeared in *Life*.

interesting), but as soon as she began to make demands on him he would get annoyed and only half jokingly call her a "pink-haired Statue of No Liberty."

In the carnival atmosphere of London that spring, when everyone was living high while waiting for the invasion of France, Capa and Pinky were caught up in a swirl of parties, poker games, and evenings on the town. After dinner with friends at the White Tower or Le Petit Club Français (the hospitable enclave of the Free French forces, where Scotch—then in short supply in London—was both plentiful and remarkably inexpensive), they might go on to a bottle club for a few more drinks and then back to the Dorchester for an all-night poker game. Among Capa's regular partners were Irwin Shaw, William Saroyan, and directors George Stevens and Irving Reis, all of whom were with a special film unit of the U.S. Army Signal Corps. To the accompaniment of exploding bombs and anti-aircraft fire, Pinky would hover around the table, making amusing remarks, looking beautiful, and keeping the glasses filled with black-market Scotch. The stakes were high enough to keep the games serious and interesting, and Capa lost quite heavily. "Next to myself," wrote Saroyan, "I believe he was the worst player in the London games. It is not unlikely that I am the only player in the world who lost to him."

Capa was surrounded that spring by both old and new friends. Chim (who had Americanized his last name to Seymour) was in London, interpreting aerial photographs for the U.S. Army. John Fernhout was also in town, and Chuck Romine was around so much that some people began to wonder whether there was something more than friendship between him and Pinky. Lee Miller, one of the few women accredited as a war photographer, became a good friend of Capa's at that time, and Edward Steichen came to dinner. And at the bohemian, left-wing salon of Alice Astor Harding he met journalist Michael Foot (later leader of the Labour Party) and renewed his friendship with Claud Cockburn, whom he had last seen in Madrid in 1937.

And then there was the whole Time Inc. crowd, including bureau chief Walter Graebner, *Life* photographer David Scherman, picture editor John Morris, and *Time* correspondents William Walton, Mary Welsh, and Charles Wertenbaker. Capa and Pinky spent many weekends with the "Time Inkers" at "Time Out," the London bureau's country retreat in the town of Little Missenden, near High Wycombe. There they enjoyed good food and good company, walks in the Buckinghamshire countryside, and bicycle excursions to nearby pubs; but the house sometimes got so full that sleeping arrangements involved a good deal of doubling up. Mary Welsh Hemingway recalls one weekend when she spent a miserable night sharing a double bed with Capa and Pinky: "little Pinky on the right, Capa breathing softly but furiously in the middle, I hanging over the left edge until my right side atrophied."

When Saroyan later wrote that he had gotten the impression Capa "was a poker player whose sideline was picture-taking, a business he loathed," he wasn't exaggerating greatly, for that spring the photographer did only one major story, on exiled governments looking homeward. But the rest of his time was not all devoted to pleasure. Late in March he went up to the 82nd Airborne Division's camp near Leicester to make the five training jumps that would qualify him to parachute with the division into France. (It was probably because he feared that the division's mission might once again be aborted at the last moment, as in the Salerno invasion, that he finally decided to go with the more predictable infantry.) He was also among the photographers who gave lectures that spring to the U.S. Army's official photographic unit in preparation for the invasion. He stressed the importance of carrying only equipment that wouldn't interfere with mobility and told the men, "When you're in the fighting, you don't go where there's fire, you go where there are pictures." He probably also passed on the combat advice he had given to Steinbeck before Salerno: "Stay where you are. If they haven't hit you, they haven't seen you. It's only by moving about that you give away your position."

When it became clear that the invasion wasn't going to take place for some time, Capa and Pinky decided to rent an apartment and moved into a furnished penthouse at 26 Lowndes Square. (In wartime London, penthouses—which were especially vulnerable in air raids—were by far the cheapest apartments in luxury buildings.) But they were hardly settled before Pinky had to have an appendectomy. Capa visited her faithfully but confided to his mother, "You know I hate hospitals, and the daily visits are getting me absolutely down." Nevertheless, Capa maintained his sense of humor; it became a standing joke in the Time Inc. office that he was trying to figure out how to put Pinky's operation on his expense account.

To celebrate Pinky's homecoming and Hemingway's arrival in London, Capa decided to give a party on the evening of May 24. Until four o'clock in the morning some forty or fifty friends filled the penthouse, drinking Scotch, gin, and the punch that Capa made by floating brandy-soaked peaches in champagne. It was a marvelous, convivial party, but the next morning Capa received a telephone call informing him that now Hemingway was in the hospital, with a concussion and a badly lacerated scalp. He had accepted a ride back to the Dorchester with Dr. Peter Gorer, who, not quite sober enough to navigate the blacked-out streets, drove his car straight into a steel water tank, smashing Hemingway's head against the windshield. *Life* published Capa's photograph of the writer sitting up in his hospital bed, his head wrapped in a turban-like bandage, but not the shot taken during the same visit showing Pinky lifting Hemingway's hospital gown to expose his posterior.

And so the fun and games continued while the correspondents, packed and ready to leave on a moment's notice, waited for D-Day.

29

The call finally came early on the morning of May 29, 1944. Capa, assigned to the 1st Infantry Division's 16th Regiment—the regiment he'd been with at El Guettar and Troina—proceeded, after several days of briefing at the division's headquarters on a country estate in Dorset, to Weymouth.* There, in the gymnasium of the Coast Guard transport *Samuel Chase*, the regiment's headquarters ship, he found the unit's officers studying a giant sponge rubber model of the section of beach code-named "Omaha," on which every house, every ridge, every tree and hedgerow had been faithfully reproduced in miniature from reconnaissance photographs.† Having evaluated the objectives and abilities of the regiment's companies (Gen. James M. Gavin later wrote that Capa "knew more about judging combat troops and how to fight than most of the so-called experts"), Capa decided to go with Company E of the 2nd Battalion, which was to spearhead the landings on the section of Omaha Beach designated "Easy Red" and push inland to the village of Colleville-sur-Mer. This time, after his disappointments at Salerno and Anzio, he wanted to be certain that he would be in the thick of the action. (Moreover,

---

* Capa was one of four photographer/correspondents chosen to cover the beginning of the invasion. He and Bert Brandt of Acme would accompany the American amphibious troops, George Rodger the British, and *Life* photographer Robert Landry the paratroopers.

† The stretch of Norman coast to be invaded, extending roughly from Valognes to Caen, had been divided by the Allies into five sections, code-named (from west to east) Utah, Omaha, Gold, Juno, and Sword. Omaha Beach was divided into three sections (from west to east) code-named Dog, Easy, and Fox. Each section was divided into two parts: Green (west) and Red (east).

by the time the attack was scheduled to begin, at 6:30 a.m., it would be light enough to photograph.) Following his dictum that "if your pictures aren't good enough, you're not close enough," he would be right beside the first Allied troops landing in France.

At 3 a.m. on D-Day (Tuesday, June 6), by which time the armada had arrived off the Norman coast, a big breakfast of hotcakes, sausages, eggs, and coffee was served on board the U.S.S. *Henrico*, the 2nd Battalion's transport ship. Half an hour later Company E was called to its debarkation station, and at 4:15 the landing craft were lowered into the rough sea for the twelve-mile trip to the beaches. Waves from three to six feet high tossed the boats about, drenched the men (their guns and ammunition were sealed in cellophane bags), and made many seasick (paper bags had been thoughtfully provided for this emergency).

Reconnaissance had incorrectly led the Allies to believe that Omaha Beach would be defended by a relatively small and inexperienced German garrison. But even without the reinforcements that had arrived the day before, the beach defenses would have been formidable. Between the low and high watermarks had been planted dozens of steel and concrete obstacles bristling with spikes and mines. And at the top of the beach, protected by mines and barbed wire and connected by tunnels and deep trenches, was a complex of concrete "pillboxes" and artillery emplacements. Landing at low tide, the first waves of attackers would have to cross some 200 yards of beach blanketed by German fire.

To "soften up" these defenses, the Allies were to pound the beach with heavy naval guns, with aerial bombs, and with rockets fired from ships close in to shore. The naval bombardment was quite effective, but, because of heavy cloud cover, most of the 2,500,000 pounds of aerial bombs were dropped too far inland, and the offshore rockets—which were intended to stun the enemy only three minutes before the first invaders hit the beaches—were fired too early, giving the Germans a chance to recover before the amphibious onslaught began.

When Capa ran down the ramp of his landing craft and into the waist-deep water, he found that

the water was very cold, and the beach was still more than a hundred yards away. The bullets tore holes in the water around me, and I made for the nearest steel obstacle. . . . It was still very early and very gray for good pictures, but the gray water and the gray sky made the little men, dodging under the surrealistic designs of Hitler's anti-invasion braintrust, very effective.

The bad situation was made even worse by the fact that the rough seas had driven many boats somewhat off course, landing too many men in some areas and too few in others, as well as separating men from the officers with whom they had expected to rendezvous on the beach and swamping all but a few of the amphibious tanks that were to back up the infantry. Furthermore, since the off-target aerial bombardment had failed to blast craters in which the men could seek shelter as they advanced, many infantrymen, like Capa— deeming it suicidal to attempt to cross the open beach—sought cover behind the German obstacles. Consequently, the waterline was soon mobbed with crouching, pinned-down men without officers to lead them forward—so mobbed, in fact, that there was no room for the new arrivals who kept disembarking from landing craft. Edward K. Regan, who has recognized himself as the soldier emerging from the water in Capa's most famous D-Day picture, recalls that he "was in the second wave and landed at H-hour plus forty minutes with the expectation that the first wave would have cleared the beach and moved inland. This was not the case, as we found them huddled behind the sea wall with only about twenty-five yards of beach occupied. There was so much chaos and mass confusion that one was reduced to a state of almost complete immobilization."* The news reaching General Bradley on his head- quarters ship sounded so bad that he considered withdrawing the troops from Omaha Beach and concentrating the attack elsewhere.

Finally, discarding the cumbersome raincoat he had been carrying folded over one arm, Capa made a dash for a half-burnt amphibious tank stranded fifty yards ahead. After twenty minutes, by which time the tide had risen up to his chest, he decided that the tank, though providing some cover from small-arms fire, made too good a target for enemy artillery. Behind two soldiers he ran the rest of the way to the beach.

> Exhausted from the water and the fear [he wrote], we lay flat on a small strip of
> wet sand between the sea and the barbed wire. The slant of the beach gave us some
> protection, so long as we lay flat, from the machine-gun and rifle bullets, but the tide
> pushed us against the barbed wire, where the guns were enjoying open season.

With a characteristically ironic pose of nonchalance, he later told Charles Wertenbaker, "It was very unpleasant there and, having nothing else to do, I started shooting pictures." Later, in *Slightly Out of Focus*, he commented,

---

* Regan was in Company K of the 116th Infantry Regiment's 3rd Battalion. The 116th, usually part of the 29th Division, had been attached to the 1st Division for the invasion.

"From the air, 'Easy Red' must have looked like an open tin of sardines. Shooting from the sardine's angle, the foreground of my pictures was filled with wet boots and green faces. Above the boots and faces, my picture frames were filled with shrapnel smoke; burnt tanks and sinking barges formed my background."

In his book Capa claimed that when he finished the roll of film in his second Contax and tried to put a new roll in, he was seized by an almost convulsive panic and ran out to a landing craft that was about to pull away from the shore. But the version of the story he told Charles Wertenbaker (who rendered it verbatim) a couple of days after the event is somewhat different:

> I shoot for an hour and a half and then my film is all used up. I saw an LCI [landing craft, infantry] behind me with a lot of medics getting out and some getting killed as they got out. One place being as bad as another, I waded out and waited in the water for all the medics to get out. Then I climbed aboard and started to change my film. I felt a slight shock and I was all covered with feathers. I thought: "What is this? Is somebody killing chickens?" Then I saw that the superstructure had been shot away and the feathers were the stuffing from the Kapok jackets of the men who were blown up. . . . Then things get slightly confused. I was, I think, exhausted. An LCVP [landing craft, vehicles and personnel] came for the wounded and I went with them.

After the badly listing landing craft had made it back to the mother ship, Capa took a few pictures of the casualties who had been brought back from the beach, and then he went below and collapsed into a bunk. By the time he awoke, the ship was on its way back to England. Arriving in Portsmouth, Capa positioned himself inside the bow doors so that when they opened he could photograph the medics who would presumably be waiting on the dock to receive the wounded. But when the doors opened, standing there was *Life* photographer David Scherman, waiting to photograph the wounded being carried off. The two photographers snapped pictures of each other and had a good laugh.*

Capa immediately gave his films to an Army public-relations officer for transport by courier to London, but in all the confusion, the films didn't reach

---

* *Life* (June 26, 1944, p. 13) stated that it was Scherman who was on board ship and Capa on the dock, but Scherman has confirmed that the *Life* version of the story is incorrect. Scherman clearly recalls that the incident took place in Portsmouth, not Weymouth (as Capa claimed), and that it was the evening of D-Day, not the following morning.

the *Life* office until about nine o'clock Wednesday night. To reach New York in time for the closing of the next issue, the developed and censored pictures had to be on a plane the next morning.

John Morris, *Life*'s London picture editor, was waiting in his office when the films finally arrived, and Hans Wild and Dennis Sanders were standing by in the lab. Morris recalls, "I felt, as did the pool editor from AP, that the whole world was waiting on these pictures. 'Rush, rush, rush,' I told the darkroom." When the negatives came out of the developing solution, Wild told Morris that they were fabulous. Morris responded, "Rush me prints!" A few minutes later Sanders burst into Morris's office, blurting out hysterically, "Capa's films are ruined; they're all ruined." Because of the pressure of time, he had put the negatives in the drying cabinet with the heat on high and closed the door. With no air circulating, the film emulsion had melted. But not quite all was lost. Of the seventy-two images on the two rolls of 35mm film that Capa had shot with his Contaxes during the landing, eleven pictures were printable.* They were, however, slightly blurred; *Life* disingenuously explained in one caption that the "immense excitement of [the] moment made Photographer Capa move his camera and blur [his] picture." In his cable congratulating Capa for the best coverage of the invasion, Wilson Hicks told the photographer that the lost pictures had been ruined by seawater that had seeped into his cameras. Capa did not learn the truth until he returned to London in July.

Ironically, the blurring of the surviving images may actually have strengthened their dramatic impact, for it pervades them with an almost tangible sense of urgency and explosive reverberation. Capa had always said anyway that to convey the excitement of fighting, you should shake your camera a little, and, indeed, the D-Day pictures are no more blurred than some of the best photographs he took at the battle of the Segre River in 1938.

From Portsmouth, Capa took the first ship back to France, but due to a severe shortage of transportation for journalists it was the evening of June 8 before he managed to join his colleagues in Bayeux, which, because the Germans

---

* In addition, the images that Capa had shot with his Rolleiflex before and after the actual landings survived intact. It is not true, as many have claimed, that Larry Burrows, who later achieved fame as a war photographer in Vietnam, ruined Capa's D-Day negatives. Burrows, then eighteen, was indeed helping out in the *Life* darkroom that night, but he was not responsible for drying the developed film.

withdrew to defend Caen, had been captured practically unscathed. At the Lion d'Or, the town's picturesque and cozy inn, one could get a hot bath, a bed with clean sheets, delicious food, and good wine—luxuries unheard of elsewhere in Normandy at that time.

Arriving in Bayeux, Capa was surprised to find his colleagues holding a wake in his honor. A sergeant had reported seeing his body floating in the water on D-Day, and since the press headquarters in Bayeux had had no word of him for forty-eight hours, the report had become official; his obituaries had been released just before his arrival.

Revived by Calvados and the luxuries of the Lion d'Or, Capa spent the next few days covering the consolidation and enlargement of the Allied beach-head, managing incidentally to get a forbidden shot of General Bradley, who had asked his aide to keep photographers away from him while he was wearing a Band-Aid over a lanced boil on his nose. Bradley thought the bandage made him look ridiculous; it does a bit—but in a most engaging way that reveals something of the general's distinctively American forthrightness and down-to-earth character.

Once the beachhead was well established and the conquest of Normandy begun in earnest, Capa and *Time* correspondent Charles Wertenbaker—a warm and worldly man with the bearing of a born general—decided to work together to cover the push up the Cotentin peninsula toward Cherbourg. But first they had to find a way to get to the front. It was a change in the censorship regulations that finally led to a solution; a new ruling allowed that once it was established that the Germans knew a particular division was active in a given area, correspondents were free to identify that division in their dispatches and captions. The competition among divisions for publicity was on, and the 9th Infantry Division immediately set about doing everything possible to make correspondents feel welcome. Not only did it provide correspondents with tents at its headquarters, complete with cots and electric lights, but also, as Ernie Pyle noted, "Correspondents who came with the 9th could get a meal, a place to write, a jeep for the front, or a courier to the rear—and at any time they asked."

Arriving at the division's forward command post, north of the town of Pont l'Abbé, late on the afternoon of June 15, Capa and Wertenbaker found the 9th, together with the 82nd Airborne, pushing across the peninsula in an attempt to cut the Germans in Cherbourg off from their reserves and supplies. Proceeding the next day to St.-Sauveur-le-Vicomte, a key bridgehead on the Douve River, Capa took a series of highly dramatic pictures of paratroopers advancing cautiously along the town's main street, dodging sniper fire and inching past ruined and burning buildings.

For the next two days Capa and Wertenbaker explored the fluid front, managing on June 18 to arrive at the 47th Regiment's 2nd Battalion observation post outside Canville-la-Rocque just in time for a heavy battering by German mortars. After that, while the division spent the next several days maneuvering into position for the final push toward Cherbourg, Capa and Wertenbaker went off to Bayeux for "a lovely hot bath, haircut and shampoo, fresh clothes, and a big steak." (Since Capa rarely shaved in the field, by the time he got back to civilization he usually had a heavy growth of dark stubble that made him look, as William Walton recalls, "rather like a Mongolian bandit.")

They arrived back at the front shortly after noon on Thursday, June 22, and made their way to the forward command post of the 47th Regiment's 1st Battalion as Allied bombers were pounding the unit's first objective in the renewed offensive: the concrete fort at the crest of the Mont-du-Roc, the key to the southwestern section of Cherbourg's outer perimeter of defenses. Once the fort fell, on Friday night, the 39th Regiment streamed past it toward the suburb of Octeville. Wanting to accompany the first outfit to enter Cherbourg, Capa and Wertenbaker set out Saturday morning to find that regiment's forward command post, but they drove for hours—at one point taking shelter in a trench where they played a few hands in their endlessly running gin-rummy game to pass the time—before they finally located it. Soon after falling in with Company L, advancing past farmhouses just outside Octeville, they found themselves in the midst of a nasty battle with German snipers. Capa's captions are considerably more vivid than the photographs he took that afternoon, even though (apparently forgetting momentarily his observation that the most dangerous situations sometimes yield the least exciting pictures) he judged them, sight unseen, as probably his best of the campaign.

> The fields are torn and the infantry takes cover in shell holes and bomb craters [he wrote]. German snipers everywhere. A burned-out pillbox is in the background, and men run quickly over the open fields where the enemy bullets are thick. A well-camouflaged ammunition dump is blown up by our bombing. In the fast growing thick smoke the exploding tracer shells are putting fancy designs. . . . We put up a terrific artillery barrage to smoke out enemy tanks, and our heavy machine guns shoot on open sight of the running enemy. Our shells are hitting 25 to 75 yards ahead of us, and some of the enemy answers land in our midst. We bring up more machine guns, and at the end of the barrage our boys fix their bayonets to clean up the last nests.

With the 39th still pinned down at Octeville, it was the 47th that first entered Cherbourg on Sunday afternoon. But Capa and Werten-

The Greatest War-Photographer in the World: Robert Capa

In the following pages you see a series of pictures of the Spanish War. Regular readers of "Picture Post" know that we do not lightly praise the work we publish. We present these pictures as simply the finest pictures of front-line action ever taken. They are the work of Robert Capa. Capa is a Hungarian by birth; but, being small and dark, he is often taken for a Spaniard. He likes working in Spain better than anywhere in the world. He is a passionate democrat, and he lives to take photographs. Over a year ago, Capa's wife, on her way back to join her husband in Paris, was killed in Spain. She was standing on the running-board of a car when it collided with a tank. Capa went to China and took pictures of the Chinese war, some of which we have already published. To-day, Capa is back in Spain, taking pictures fo. "Picture Post."

Capa with Joris Ivens (*center, wearing beret*) and John
Fernhout (*kneeling*), Hankow, China, 1938.

With Gen. Joseph ("Vinegar Joe") W. Stilwell, China, 1938.

China, 1938.

Washington, D.C., 1942.

Mexico, 1940.

With Ernest Hemingway, Sun Valley, Idaho, 1941.

Polly Korchein and Toni Sorel
(*right*), c. 1940.

Pinky, 1943–44. Inscribed to Elizabeth Crockett's
husband, Alan Reeve: "To my Alan. Sudden death,
wives, bitter insults and Capa shall not come
between us. Elaine xxx."

Capa turning on his Hungarian charm (with an unidentified woman).

Naples, 1943.

Crossing the Atlantic in a convoy, 1941 or 1942.

The evening of D-Day (June 6, 1944),
Portsmouth, England.

North Africa, 1943.

Ready for jump across the Rhine, March 1945.

With George Rodger, Naples, 1943.

Capa (*right*) playing poker with (*from left to right*) an unidentified American officer, William Saroyan, Irwin Shaw, and George Stevens, London, spring 1944 (pencil sketch by Alan Reeve).

Capa (*front row, far left*) with members of the Time Inc. staff who would be covering the Normandy invasion, London, spring 1944. In the first row are Frank Scherschel, Mary Welsh, David Scherman, and John Morris (*second, third, fourth, and sixth from left*); standing are Robert Landry (*left*), Ralph Morse, William Walton, and George Rodger (*second, seventh, and ninth from left*).

With John Steinbeck, about to leave Stockholm for Moscow, 1947.

With Burl Ives and John Huston, London, 1953.

Ingrid Bergman, Berlin, August 1945.

Capa and David Seymour ("Chim"), Paris, early 1950s.

At Longchamps racetrack, Paris,
early 1950s.

Working on "Cavalcade of Fashion" for World Video, Paris, 1948.

Paris, 1951.

Capa with a French officer, Luang Prabang, Laos,
May 1954.

Gen. René Cogny with Capa's casket, Hanoi,
May 1954.

baker, accompanied by Ernie Pyle, didn't get into the city until
Monday morning, when, in the pouring rain, they went along while
men of the 47th's 1st Battalion advanced through the streets toward a
hospital in which the Germans had been holding wounded American
POWs. Most of Capa's pictures of the day were of German prisoners, the
most important of whom was General von Schlieben, commander of the
German garrison in Cherbourg. In an effort to provoke the general into
an interesting expression of anger, Capa announced in German that
he was bored with photographing defeated German generals; in the resulting picture the general looks more exhausted and bored himself than
angry.

Having taken the Cotentin peninsula, the American forces began to move
southward through the western part of Normandy. The advance was badly
hampered both by the terrain—in which the high hedgerows around fields
created what amounted to a crazy-quilt patchwork of little forts—and by heavy
rains that caused much flooding. It was no place or weather for a photographer,
so while the Americans slogged toward Coutances and St.-Lô, Capa, joined
by Wertenbaker, bided his time at the large, comfortable house in Cherbourg
that *Time* correspondent William Walton and CBS correspondent Charles
Collingwood were sharing with Maj. John Palfrey, the Englishman who had
been appointed chief of the city's Allied Police Force. Collingwood put the
salaries of the house's three servants on his expense account, and Palfrey,
with access to the captured German supply dump outside Cherbourg, kept
the house well supplied with good whisky and British cigarettes that the Germans had taken earlier in the war. There were parties almost every night and
plenty of rooms for friends. William Paley of CBS and dramatist Robert
Sherwood—both of them then top brass in the Office of War Information—moved in for a while, and Hemingway showed up to spend a
week.

By July 10 the situation in Normandy had reached a temporary stalemate;
on the eleventh Capa left with Wertenbaker for London, where he had "a
good time and a bad surprise." It was then that he learned the truth about
how his D-Day photographs had been ruined. Although he made a show of
taking the news nonchalantly, he admitted in a letter to his family that he felt
very disillusioned and discouraged, adding that "the little that got printed is
nothing compared to the material which got ruined." To offset this, "Mr.
Hicks at my great surprise offered to me the great honor of joining the staff
and believe it or not $9,000 a year, so I had to accept. I do not like the idea

very much but I have not much choice."* While in London, Capa saw a good deal of Hemingway, also back from Normandy, playwright Garson Kanin, and, of course, Pinky. He had written his mother in June that he was now thinking of asking Pinky to marry him but that he wanted "to sleep and think it over during the next years."

Capa returned to the front just after the breakthrough operation code-named COBRA had begun on July 25. After an Allied saturation bombing inflicted heavy casualties and created great confusion within their ranks, the Germans began to withdraw helter-skelter before the American advance. The way was opening up for the Americans to push along the main roads leading southward from St.-Lô to Avranches, the gateway to Brittany.

Capa followed the 2nd Armored Division through St.-Gilles and Canisy to Notre-Dame-de-Cenilly, which fell with little struggle to the division's Combat Command B on the night of July 27, and for the next couple of days he photographed as the division's tanks and attached infantry herded Germans retreating from the north into a "pocket" between that town and Roncey. *The New York Times* reported that after a group of German tanks and infantry had tried to smash its way past Notre-Dame-de-Cenilly early on the morning of July 29, "piles of German dead lay in the streets and bodies were spread behind almost every house in this town," but Capa's contact sheets show no such horrors; he focused instead on the townspeople as they welcomed the Americans with Calvados and as they attended Mass in their relatively intact church to give thanks for their liberation.

Arriving late on July 30 in Bréhal, which earlier that day had fallen with very little resistance to the U.S. 6th Armored Division, Capa established himself in Le Petit Hôtel, headquarters of the local Resistance. As the apocryphal-sounding (but evidently true) story is told in *Slightly Out of Focus*, after a festive dinner that night with Capa and young members of the Resistance, Maj. Paul Gale of the 1st Infantry Division decided that he and his driver should liberate a town. The coastal resort of Granville, on the road to which the 6th Armored had been turned back by Germans that afternoon, seemed a good choice. Once in Granville the two-man army was joined by the leader of the local Resistance. According to *The New York Times*, Gale sent his driver back to Bréhal for reinforcements and then proceeded to set a German ammunition dump on fire, apparently frightening the Germans sufficiently to send them fleeing. In the morning, when Gale's driver returned

---

* Although Capa's staff position became effective retroactively as of June 15, 1944, he was not listed on the magazine's masthead as a staff photographer until April 23, 1945.

with Capa and three armored scout cars (the only reinforcements he had been able to enlist), they found the town liberated and German prisoners rounded up in front of the hotel owned by the Resistance leader.

For the next several days Capa used Granville as his base of operations, making forays over to the newly taken town of Gavray and down the coastal road to Avranches to photograph the large numbers of German prisoners being taken. Always on the lookout for pictures that would echo his earlier stories, he photographed a column of German vehicles that had been destroyed by American fighter-bombers; the pictures are so startlingly reminiscent of those he had taken in 1939 of the strafed refugees on the Tarragona–Barcelona road that he must have intended them as a sort of testament of revenge for the earlier atrocity.

Meanwhile, Hemingway was playing soldier with the 4th Infantry Division around Villedieu-les-Poêles, fifteen miles east of Granville. Early on the morning of Saturday, August 5, he sent the public relations officer assigned to him, Capt. Marcus ("Mike") Stevenson,* to Granville in a captured Mercedes to pick up Capa, The 4th Division's 22nd Regiment, commanded by Col. Charles ("Buck") Lanham, one of Hemingway's favorite officers, was attacking the little village of St.-Pois, a few miles to the southeast, and Hemingway thought Capa would make good company for the day's action. †

> Papa had it all figured out [wrote Capa]. The regiment had already begun the attack, an hour earlier, from the left flank of the village, and he was sure we could take a short cut and drive in from the right flank without much difficulty. He showed me on the map how easy it would be, but I didn't like it at all. Papa looked at me in disgust and said I could stay behind. I couldn't do anything but follow him, but I made it clear that I was going under protest. I told him that Hungarian strategy consisted of going behind a good number of soldiers, and never taking lonely short cuts through no man's land.

They set out early in the afternoon with Hemingway riding in the sidecar of a motorcycle and Capa and Stevenson following in the Mercedes. All went

---

* Stevenson had been Gen. Teddy Roosevelt's aide until Roosevelt's sudden death from a heart attack on July 12. At the time of his death Roosevelt had been assistant commander of the 4th Infantry Division.

† In *Slightly Out of Focus*, Capa says that they were looking for the 4th Division's 8th Regiment, but the 4th Division history makes no mention of the 8th Regiment at St.-Pois. The 22nd Regiment took St.-Pois on August 5.

well until the motorcycle rounded the last sharp curve before the village. Straight ahead, down the road, was a light German tank. The motorcycle driver slammed on the brakes, and Hemingway flew out onto the side of the road, hitting his head on a rock as he landed—thereby getting, so he claimed, his second Capa-related concussion in a little over ten weeks. Capa and the others were protected by the curve, but Hemingway, lying in a shallow ditch from which "his behind stuck out at least an inch," was in the Germans' line of sight. For two hours they kept him pinned down, and when they finally withdrew, the writer was furious not so much with them as with Capa, whom he accused of having stood by during the crisis waiting to get a photograph of his dead body, instead of going to get help. Actually, Hemingway was probably just angry that Capa had seen him in such a humiliating position— although he also might well have begun to wonder whether the photographer brought him bad luck.

But Hemingway didn't stay angry for long; the next day, joined by William Walton and John Morris, they went off together to spend a week on Mont-St.-Michel, which had recently been liberated and declared off-limits to all military personnel except generals and war correspondents. On the way, Capa met a formerly prosperous farmer who had lost all his animals during the fighting, and when the photographer somehow or other got him a horse, the man was so grateful that he offered to do anything he could for his benefactor. "Invite us to dinner," suggested Capa. The meal was fabulous: rich country-style cooking, a different wine with each course, and between courses—to clear the palate—home-made Calvados. Reaching Mont-St.-Michel after having extricated their jeep from a bomb-crater into which they drove on the way, the men climbed to the ramparts of the ancient monastery to watch with binoculars the tracer patterns and explosions of the fierce counteroffensive the Germans had begun in the Norman countryside around Mortain shortly after midnight.

A convivial group—including Wertenbaker, Collingwood, and A. J. Liebling, as well as Capa, Hemingway, Walton, and Morris—was soon occupying the old Hôtel de la Mère Poularde, and in no time they won over the *patronne*, Mme. Chevalier, who prepared superb meals for them and brought out many fine bottles she had hidden away from the Germans. The greatest delights at the table seem, however, to have come not from the food and drink but from the rubber worm, the left-handed corkscrew, and the plate-tilting device that Capa, Wertenbaker, and Collingwood picked up in a practical-joke shop in Rennes.

Leaving the comforts of the Mont during the day, the correspondents went out to cover the fighting nearby, especially around the heavily defended port city of St.-Malo, twenty miles to the west. On August 8, Capa went with John Morris to photograph the 329th Regiment of the U.S. 83rd Infantry Division just outside the city in the village of La Balue, where a psychological-warfare loudspeaker truck was encouraging the nearby German troops to surrender. When, about twenty minutes after the broadcast had ended, a group of Germans appeared with their hands above their heads, Capa ran forward to photograph them and to ask them what they had thought about the broadcast—to which they replied that they hadn't heard anything; they were just surrendering.

The next day Capa and Morris went with the 83rd as the division advanced along a beach on the outskirts of St.-Malo. Pinned down for six hours at an observation post set up in a harborside café, Capa exchanged reminiscences with six Spanish Loyalists who had joined the local Resistance, and he managed to get a few good pictures of German prisoners. The best shows a French prostitute in slacks and high heels who had decided to follow a column of her captured customers rather than face the wrath of her liberated neighbors.

Capa went back to St.-Malo on August 10, but by then it was becoming apparent that the citadel that dominated the harbor might hold out for some time (it didn't fall until the seventeenth), and he suddenly realized that while he was wasting his time covering a provincial siege, Patton's newly organized Third Army was advancing rapidly on Paris, whose liberation Capa considered—short of the final surrender of Germany—the climactic story of the war.

30

The problem was to figure out which units would be the first to reach the capital. Putting his money on the U.S. XV Corps, Capa followed it through Laval and Le Mans to Alençon, but when it became stalled in the Falaise pocket, he backtracked and joined the XX Corps on the road from Le Mans to Chartres.

As soon as the corps had secured Chartres on August 18, after two days of surprisingly stiff opposition, he proceeded to the town's Préfecture de Police, where members of the Resistance were shaving the heads of women who had run black markets or slept with the Germans. The series he began to shoot there culminates with a photograph of a young woman, who has just had her head shaved, being followed home by a jeering crowd of townspeople; in her arms is the baby she had by a German soldier. Snapped just as a helmeted policeman was apparently making an insulting remark, the picture—in which the supposedly humiliated woman seems transformed into a dignified Madonna tormented by grotesque demons—was to become one of Capa's most famous. It is also one that reveals most profoundly the directness of his sympathy for the sufferings of individuals, regardless of their politics.

At last, on August 23, Capa learned that the French 2nd Armored Division was to spearhead the entry into Paris. Conveniently, he was covering de Gaulle's hasty tour of liberated cities on the road to the capital, and his next stop was Rambouillet, where the division, led by General Leclerc, was waiting. But things were not to be simple, for, arriving in the town and meeting up with Wertenbaker, Capa learned that Leclerc had decided to allow only French journalists to accompany his tanks.

The next morning there was nothing but confusion and frustration among the American correspondents, since Leclerc had moved most of his tanks during the night and was keeping their route secret. After lunch, however, Capa and Wertenbaker were given a tip to head for Etampes, on Nationale 20, the Orléans-Paris road. Arriving there and finding the population celebrating in the streets, despite the rain that had been falling all day, Capa leaned out of the jeep and shouted, "Where are the tanks?" A dozen arms pointed northward. A few miles north of Arpajon they found Leclerc's rear guard.

Delayed until dusk by German defenses between Antony and Fresnes, on either side of Nationale 20, Leclerc halted his forward tanks just beyond Fresnes for the night, but three of his tanks and several half-tracks full of infantry penetrated all the way into the heart of the capital that evening. After dinner in Arpajon with a French journalist and a Resistance woman who had come out of Paris two nights earlier with reports of the fighting and copies of the liberation newspapers (including Ce Soir and L'Humanité, which had resumed publication), Capa and Wertenbaker returned to the edge of the encampment and spread their bedrolls out on the soft, damp earth of a field under a starry sky.

They were awakened at six o'clock the next morning—Friday, August 25—by tanks on the move. Chasing after them, the journalists were stopped at Antony by a barrier of two small trees that had been felled across the road. Guarding the barrier and enforcing Leclerc's order to permit no one to pass was a squad of the division's Spanish Loyalist volunteers, on one of whose tanks was painted the name "Teruel." But once Capa satisfied the men that he had indeed been present at that battle—and was thus one of them—they let the jeep through.*

Capa, Wertenbaker, and their driver (Pvt. Hubert Strickland from Norfolk, Virginia) soon caught up with the rearmost tanks and maneuvered around the entire column, weaving past tanks and through the crowd that spilled out into the road, until only one jeep carrying three French officers was between them and the armored car in which Leclerc stood.

As the French tanks approached the Porte d'Orléans (which on that road was the entry into Paris itself), the Germans offered no resistance, for nearly all but a small garrison in the center of the city had already withdrawn. The greatest impediment to Leclerc's advance was the delirious crowd that from the outer urban districts onward completely filled the streets, parting just enough to let the armored column through at a snail's pace. Chanting "Vive Leclerc!" and "Vive de Gaulle!"—but repeating above all else the cry "Merci! Merci! Merci!"—the throng, composed largely of women, waved handkerchiefs and flags, threw flowers and food, and climbed onto the advancing vehicles to embrace the liberators.

To the best of their knowledge, Capa, Wertenbaker, and their driver held undisputed claim to being the first Americans to enter Paris, passing through the Porte d'Orléans directly behind Leclerc at "9:40 and 20 seconds a.m."

Having followed one regiment of tanks up into the Boulevard des Invalides, they parked their jeep and walked toward the fighting in the streets ahead, where the Germans still occupied the Palais Bourbon, the Ministry of Foreign Affairs, and a few other buildings. From the upper stories, snipers fired on people in the streets—many of them civilians who had come out to watch the excitement. French tanks replied from among the trees of the Esplanade des Invalides; flames and smoke erupted from windows here and there in the classical façades. French marines, firing from behind armored cars and running past entanglements of barbed wire, attempted to enter the Palais Bourbon. White-clad medics rushed forward to rescue the wounded. In the side streets Resistance fighters, wearing civilian clothes and armed with whatever weapons they could find, established themselves in doorways, from which they fired up at snipers. As Germans were taken prisoner, soldiers and medics had to protect them from the wrath of civilians and the Resistance. (When three French marines rescued a German officer from a Resistance group that wanted to shoot him on the spot, Capa remarked to Wertenbaker, "What the Army

---

* Capa did not, as he claimed in *Slightly Out of Focus*, ride into Paris on that tank.

is doing is saving the Germans from the FFI."*) Finally, early in the evening, after the commanding General von Choltitz had been captured, the Germans remaining in the area received orders to surrender.

After spending the next morning photographing collaborationists and making the rounds of the Montparnasse and St.-Germain-des-Prés cafés, which had just reopened, Capa rode with Wertenbaker, William Walton, and Olivia Chambers in de Gaulle's triumphal parade from the Arc de Triomphe to Notre Dame that afternoon. (Chambers, who had worked for the Paris bureau of Time Inc. before the war, had remained in the city throughout the Occupation.) Getting out of his jeep and jumping up onto its hood, Capa photographed a soldier standing in the open turret of his tank, saluting, with tears streaming down his face; then, running to the head of the parade, he got a wonderful shot of the sternly reserved de Gaulle just barely cracking a smile as he acknowledged the vast, cheering crowd.

The mood of exhilaration was suddenly shattered in the Place de l'Hôtel de Ville when sniper fire from the top of several buildings opened up on the procession. Ignoring the danger to himself, Capa photographed as some five thousand panic-stricken people took shelter behind or under the dozens of cars, trucks, and jeeps—or else simply dropped to the pavement, curling up to make themselves as small as possible and piling themselves two or three deep in some places—while those who had guns (and hundreds had) fired up at the snipers. By that night scattered incidents of sniping, mostly by diehard collaborationists, were breaking out all over, but the battle for Paris was in reality over.

Even before then the Allied correspondents had settled down to life in the liberated city. Within hours of their arrival, Capa and Wertenbaker set up a temporary Time Inc. office in a huge, grandly furnished room of the Hôtel Scribe, which had been designated as the Allied press headquarters. By evening the room was crowded with Time Inc. correspondents who had accompanied the various forces converging on Paris. William Walton, Jack Belden, Robert Landry, Frank Scherschel, David Scherman, Ralph Morse, and George Rodger all showed up on the day of the liberation, and until they could find more comfortable quarters, their bedrolls covered the floor. Mary Welsh arrived from London that day but moved into the Ritz, where Hemingway had established himself with his "irregulars." John Morris came over from London a few days later to take charge of the *Life* operations, and Wertenbaker's wife, Lael Tucker, also came over to work. *March of Time* producer Richard de

* Forces Françaises de l'Intérieur, the collective organization of all the French Resistance forces.

Rochemont soon turned up, as did Will Lang. George Stevens, Irwin Shaw, and William Saroyan had the room next door to the Time Inc. crowd. And Hemingway, though not resident in the Scribe, was very much a presence in the hotel's basement bar, where virtually the entire press corps gathered in the evening to compare notes and to enjoy an apparently inexhaustible supply of champagne, an especially great luxury since most cafés could then offer little but "vin blanc and vile beer."

Because the Scribe was so crowded, noisy, and scruffy, Wertenbaker suggested after a few days that Capa, Walton, and Collingwood move with him and Tucker to the Lancaster, an elegant hotel just off the Champs-Elysées that had once been a private house, keeping the room at the Scribe as the Time Inc. office. Monsieur Wolf, the owner, put the Lancaster at the disposal of the Americans, who made themselves right at home—to the point of turning this usually quiet and reserved hotel into such a lively gambling center that the police eventually investigated. But M. Wolf was very indulgent, and when the correspondents started playing craps on the carpet in the lobby, he graciously set aside a parlor for them. Capa liked the feel of the place so much that, with only a few interruptions, the Lancaster remained his base of operations for the rest of his life.

Now that Paris was liberated, Capa was home. This was his city, and he knew his way around. He immediately got himself a girlfriend—a very attractive and spirited young woman named Marlene who ran a café. Soon he was introducing correspondents and officers alike to the best black-market restaurants and taking them out to the races at Longchamps or the casino at Enghien-les-Bains. (In return he was invited to join the American officers' tennis club at St.-Cloud.) He also served as an unofficial liaison between the Americans and his many old friends who were still in Paris or had recently returned. When John Morris arrived, Capa put him in touch with Cartier-Bresson, who had photographed the rising of the Parisian Resistance before the Allies arrived. Capa got his friend Taci Czigany a job as the Time Inc. darkroom man. And when Wertenbaker, now the Paris bureau chief, decided to solve the formidable problem of transportation by buying the bureau four old cars on the black market, it was Capa who spent hours and hours dickering for the cars and getting them running. "You don't just buy a car in Paris," explained Wertenbaker to the New York office. "You practically buy it part by part."

Capa spent much of his first few days back in Paris looking up old friends. Some who had been involved with *Vu* turned up at a party given by Michel de Brunhoff, Lucien Vogel's brother-in-law, in the *Vogue* offices; Chim came in toward the end wearing his helmet and gun, a rather improbable soldier.

In the former offices of *Paris-soir*, which had moved south to the Vichy area early in the Occupation, Capa found Louis Aragon editing the revived *Ce Soir*. And in the bars and cafés that had been his haunts before the war, he was welcomed with embraces and champagne.

But not everyone had gotten through the war so well. Capa found his relatives Béla and Szeren Fischer ill and almost penniless, while their daughter Susie, though "a clever big girl and a real little Parisienne," was not quite old enough to work. Capa advised her to study English and typing, and he gave her parents money as well as black-market cigarettes, coffee, and chocolates. (For four years most Parisians had had only "café nationale," made from barley. Real coffee was practically worth its weight in gold, and cigarettes cost about five dollars a pack.) In a letter to his mother, Capa asked her to send him as much of these commodities as she could, "because everybody is hungry for those things, and I am the great white brother." Not long after his arrival in Paris, when word got around that he was in town and well supplied, Capa complained, "My telephone is ringing from seven in the morning, and I am going straight crazy."

Through his old Arab girlfriend Capa met a lively group of young writers, actors, and painters (among them was Françoise Gilot, who had been having a secret affair with Picasso for a year) all of whom were making ambitious plans in the heady atmosphere of post-liberation Paris, where young artists and intellectuals were intoxicated by a sense of release and freedom. With these friends Capa went out many evenings, talking and laughing until the small hours of the morning at the Café de Flore, Les Deux Magots, or the Dôme.

At the beginning of September the New York office of *Life* assigned Capa to remain in Paris; Wertenbaker cabled in reply, "I am delighted that Capa is to remain in Paris, and so is Capa." For the time being Capa had had his fill of war. Paris was free, and it appeared that Germany was about to collapse. He was quite content to let others cover what everyone hoped would be the final battles of the war in Europe. As he wrote in *Slightly Out of Focus*, "going back to the front would be a dull prospect." He felt that there were no new pictures left for him to take; if he returned to the front, he would end up just repeating himself. He much preferred to remain in town and cover stories like Picasso's daily eleven o'clock open house, where, when he showed up on September 2, he found the artist (whom he had never before met) chatting with Nusch Eluard (the beautiful wife of poet Paul Eluard) and a group of Spanish Loyalists.

When Bill Graffis, a public-relations officer of the 82nd Airborne and a close friend of Capa's, asked him to go on a small troop-carrier supply mission to the Resistance (the "Maquis") in the south of France, Capa replied, "To your pilots and the Maquis the mission is important. To my editor it means only one or two pictures at most. To Capa, it is not worth the trouble of such a small affair to get his beautiful head blown off without benefit, at least, of a four-page spread. I refuse, mon vieux." But Capa and Graffis did go off on a brief pleasure jaunt to the south, for which they persuaded Chuck Romine to let them borrow his commanding general's C-47, equipped with a ramp for loading a jeep. When the general discovered that his plane was missing, he was furious—until he learned that it was Capa who had taken it. Any other correspondent would have been court-martialed for such a prank, but Capa had more or less been adopted by Romine's IX Troop Carrier Command.

Capa was not, however, entirely able to avoid going to the front. Early in October, when all the other *Life* photographers were busy, Wertenbaker had to send him with *Time* correspondent Noel Busch to the front near Aachen, where the U.S. 1st Infantry Division had just crossed the German border and broken through the Siegfried Line. But even there he avoided the fighting and instead photographed Archbishop Francis J. Spellman saying Mass for the troops (an altar was set up on the cloth-shrouded hood of a jeep) and did a story on German civilians in the captured town of Breinich registering with the Allied military government.

On the morning of October 11, just after he got back from the Aachen front, Capa set out for central and southern France with Wertenbaker and Lael Tucker in one of the bureau's black market cars. (Wertenbaker had wanted him to come along not only as a photographer but also because of his "unique ability to pick up all manner of Frenchmen.") Starting off with their most pleasurable assignment—a story on the French wine situation—they drove first through Burgundy, where they found, as elsewhere, plenty of good wine but a great shortage of food and fuel. Since the inns had no heat or hot water and the weather had turned too cold for bathing in cold water, they soon had to resort to dousing themselves with eau de cologne.

Proceeding by way of the Vercors region and Lyons to Toulouse for a three-day meeting of the Unión Nacional Española, they arrived—despite Capa's immediately landing the car in a ditch on the one occasion when Wertenbaker let him drive—on November 3. Toulouse, which had become the center of Spanish Loyalist activities in France, was filled with Spaniards who believed that since they had helped to liberate France, the Allies now had a responsibility to help them liberate Spain. During October, in fact, several groups of Spanish exiles had tried to take matters into their own hands. On the twenty-second, a group of about 150 of them (Spanish government reports of thousands were wildly exaggerated) crossed the border southeast of Bagnères-de-Luchon and briefly gained control of a few frontier villages in the Aran valley. Government troops moved in quickly, killing, wounding, or capturing many and sending the rest fleeing back across the mountains. From Toulouse, Capa went up into the mountains to see where they crossed the border, and then he went to a hospital to visit some of the survivors, most of whom had light wounds and frostbitten feet. His photographs of their faces reveal that even after years of exile and struggle these men retained the courage, determination, and warm humor that had appealed to him so greatly during the Spanish Civil War.*

When he returned to Paris in the second week of November, Capa was pleased to discover that Martha Gellhorn had arrived and was staying at the Lancaster. She had just told Hemingway that she wanted a divorce, and, despite his romance with Mary Welsh (about which Gellhorn as yet knew little), he had flown into a rage, declaring that Martha was destroying his life and would cause him to die in battle and leave his children orphans. Furious at being rejected by his wife (he preferred to do the rejecting himself), he even threatened to shoot her rather than give her a divorce. When Capa went to her room at about four in the morning, he found her in tears. He had just won at poker and, squatting down like a Gypsy to count his winnings, he told her to call the Ritz and ask for Mary Welsh; as he had predicted, Hemingway answered. Capa then said to Gellhorn, "Tell him you want a divorce." Trembling, she did so, and Hemingway let out a stream of obscenities. Then Capa said, "Tell him that you know all about him and Mary Welsh and that he *must* give you a divorce." Hemingway let out another stream of obscenities, but he was forced to yield to her demands.

It must have been about this time, when Hemingway began to talk about marrying Mary Welsh, that Capa remarked, "You know, Papa, you don't have to *marry* Mary." Hemingway, who never fully forgave Capa for what he took to be a slur on his future wife's morals, was so indignant that he threw a champagne bottle across the room at him; it missed and crashed against a door. But Capa may not have meant to be insulting at all; he was probably just passing on a bit of advice based on his own way of dealing with women and the issue of marriage. Indeed, the subject was very much on his mind, for in her letters Pinky (who had finally gotten a divorce) had been nagging him to propose, and when he went to England for a few days at the end of November to celebrate her twenty-seventh birthday, she really put the pressure on, trying to force his hand by threatening to marry the first rich man who

---

* Capa's account of this episode in *Slightly Out of Focus* is completely fictionalized. For his unembroidered account, see *Life*, December 25, 1944, p. 4.

came along. (Reporting all this in a letter to his family, he added that the rich men in the wings were "many and willing.") Capa had no intention of marrying Pinky, but he didn't want to lose her—even if she was beginning to take their romance too seriously (which he must have found both awkward and flattering). So he came up with a compromise; she would move to Paris and they would take an apartment together, although first, to her great annoyance, she would have to undergo more treatments for the after-effects of her appendicitis.

After all these petty squabbles, as well as the boredom of being "unofficial office manager in Paris," Capa told his family the first week of December that he was relieved to be going back to the front. But even there he met with frustration. Arriving at the U.S. 95th Infantry Division's bridgehead in Saarlautern (now Saarlouis)* as German artillery was trying to knock out American pontoon bridges, he found a battalion of black troops blanketing the entire area with chemical smoke to provide cover. He made his way across the river and located the headquarters of one battalion in the cellar of a small building, but since the smoke made it impossible for him to take pictures, there wasn't much he could do for the next five days but sit in that cellar reading *War and Peace*. "As for the sound effects," he wrote, "they seemed made to order." At last, when it became apparent that the situation was not about to improve, he left. If he was going to have to be bored one way or the other, he preferred to take his chances in Paris.

31

After returning to Paris, he didn't have long to wait for something interesting to develop. On December 16, 1944, by which time the Allies were confident that they had the enemy entirely on the defensive, the Germans

---

* Although he states in *Slightly Out of Focus* that he joined the 80th Infantry Division at the Saar River, it was the 95th that was crossing the river around Saarlautern at the time. The 80th, just south of the 95th, had not yet reached the river.

launched a powerful counteroffensive in the Ardennes. Taking the Allies almost totally by surprise, and aided by foggy weather that protected them from Allied planes, the Germans swiftly penetrated deep into Belgium, bulging into the Allied lines (thus the popular name of the campaign, "Battle of the Bulge") and threatening to break through to Antwerp, the Allies' main supply port in the area.

On December 18, just as three German divisions were rapidly approaching the important road junction of Bastogne in southeastern Belgium, the U.S. 101st Airborne Division entered the town and secured it. Over the next several days the division resisted so fiercely that the German vanguard had to bypass Bastogne, although a sizable force was left behind to encircle the town and cut the Americans off from their reserves and supplies. To relieve the 101st, Patton ordered the newly created III Corps to withdraw from the Saar front and to "drive like hell" to the Ardennes. The attack, spearheaded by the 4th Armored Division, was to jump off from Arlon, twenty miles south of Bastogne, on December 22.

Capa, Charles Collingwood, and Will Lang left Paris for Arlon on December 21. One problem with their sudden departure was that Capa and Collingwood had invited Connie and Doris Dowling, two beautiful sisters who were in a USO show touring Italy, to come to Paris for Christmas, and they were due to arrive that day.* Unable to reach them to notify them of the change in plans, Capa left word at the Lancaster that they were to stay in his suite, and he arranged for a bouquet of flowers and a magnum of champagne to be delivered to them every day until he and Collingwood returned.

As the three journalists approached Arlon, they were repeatedly stopped by GIs who, ordered to search for English-speaking German infiltrators, quizzed the occupants of every vehicle near the front with questions to which only Americans were likely to know the answers. Capa, whose accent certainly didn't help matters, of course had no idea what city was the capital of Nebraska, nor, when the GIs sprang their favorite question, did he know who had won or lost the World Series that fall. Furthermore, he made no secret of his annoyance with the constant delays. Fortunately, Collingwood knew that the St. Louis Cardinals had won the Series (and that the St. Louis Browns had lost it). Reassured, the GIs agreed not to arrest Capa, and they let the jeep pass.

Following the recommendation of a public-relations officer they had met

---

* Connie Dowling had played supporting roles in two Hollywood films released that year: *Knickerbocker Holiday* and *Up in Arms*.

along the way, the journalists attached themselves to the 4th Armored Division, which was advancing up a corridor centered on the main Arlon–Bastogne road. The going was very slow, for the troops of the German 5th Parachute Division were resisting bitterly in every town, hamlet, and wood along the way (prompting Capa to remark, "These do-or-die boys are good. They stay and hold"). Perhaps they were afraid to surrender to the 4th Armored, for German propaganda claimed that to qualify for the division a man had to be both a bastard and a matricide; from such men prisoners could expect no quarter.

On December 23, the weather finally cleared, permitting Allied planes to attack the Germans and to drop supplies into Bastogne. With the clearing came a fall in temperature to below zero, freezing the mud solid enough so that tanks could cross the rolling fields of the region to take shortcuts and bypass German roadblocks. Will Lang observed that when Capa ran around to photograph the tanks lumbering across the fields he looked "incongruous, a puny ringmaster in a herd of trumpeting (and oblivious) elephants."

The threat of infiltrators continued to keep the Americans jittery, and, as Capa told the story, when he began to photograph some infantrymen crossing a snow-covered field beside the road,

> suddenly a GI from the infantry battalion, about 150 yards away, yelled something to me and raised his tommy gun at the same time. I yelled back "Take it easy!" but as he heard my accent he began to shoot. For a fraction of a second I didn't know what to do. If I threw myself flat on the snow he could still hit me. If I ran down the embankment, he would run after me. I threw my hands high in the air, yelled "Kamerad!" and surrendered. Three of them came at me with raised rifles. When they were close enough to make out the three German cameras around my neck, they became very happy GI's. Two Contax cameras and a Rolleiflex—I was the jackpot! I still kept my hands as high as I could, but when they were a rifle's length away from me, I asked one of them to search my breast pocket. He took out my identification and the special photographer pass signed by Eisenhower himself. "I should have shot the bastard before!" he groaned.

Capa remarked after this incident, "The war gets serious when I get shot at by GIs too."

For the final push toward Bastogne, Capa and his friends decided to stick with Lt. Col. Creighton W. Abrams, commander of the 4th Armored Division's 37th Tank Battalion. Abrams, whom Capa described as looking like "a cigar-smoking Jewish king," vowed that his men would be the first to reach Bastogne and relieve the besieged 101st Airborne.

On the twenty-fourth, American reconnaissance discovered that the German defenses were relatively weak west of the Arlon–Bastogne road. Accordingly, the 37th Tank Battalion was rushed that night from the division's eastern flank, where the unit had just taken the Luxembourg village of Bigonville after a day and a half of hard fighting, to the western flank. Having taken the village of Remichampagne by noon on the twenty-sixth, the tanks and infantry surged cross-country until they reached a hilltop from which they could see Bastogne, which lay, as Capa put it, "only 3,000 yards and 2,000 Germans away." Abrams then lined up his tanks and announced, "We are going in to join those people *now!*" Although his tankers were running short on ammunition, he told them, according to Capa, "to keep on going and keep on shooting, without stopping to aim, until they had reached the town below."

Jumping off at 3:15, the tanks and infantry forged ahead through extremely heavy fire from German artillery, anti-tank guns, and machine guns. Some Germans even hurled mines onto the road, while bazooka teams closed in. Nevertheless, an hour and a half later the lead tanks, churning past burning houses and barns, made contact with the outer defenses of the 101st Airborne. Shortly after five o'clock, Capa, Collingwood, and Lang accompanied Abrams into Bastogne, where General McAuliffe, the division's acting commander, dryly remarked, "It's good to see you, Colonel," and broke out a bottle of bourbon he had been saving for the occasion.

Although fighting continued around Bastogne well into January 1945, as the Germans tried unsuccessfully to encircle the town again, Capa had to return to Paris on December 27 to send his story to New York in time for the next *Life* deadline. When he got back to the Lancaster, he found in his suite seven bouquets, some of them rather wilted, and seven silver wine coolers, each containing a magnum of champagne. The Dowling sisters had never arrived.

That was just the beginning of his problems with plans falling through and people failing to show up. He had planned to go to New York in January to visit his family, but when he learned that Toni Sorel—having met a man she wanted to marry in earnest—had filed for divorce, he canceled his trip, for he feared that if he went home he would become involved in the proceedings and be unable to return to Europe when he wanted to. Then, with his usual enterprise, he arranged with Chuck Romine for Pinky to travel to Paris aboard one of the IX Troop Carrier Command's daily flights from London. Unfortunately, the plan involved her wearing a war correspondent's uniform (which she borrowed from one of the women in the Time Inc. office) and resulted in her being arrested. Worse, British intelligence decided that she was a spy and subjected her to questioning that went on for days. Even after she was finally released, she was forced to stay on in London, where, she realized, she was kept under observation. Afraid that if she made contact with Capa directly she might implicate him, she asked the Time Inc. office to get word to him that she had been unavoidably delayed, that she didn't know when she would be able to get to Paris, and that he should under no circumstances come to London.

While waiting for Pinky to show up, Capa did a few routine stories for *Life*. Paris was freezing (the winter was so harsh, and fuel shortages so severe, that everyone had to keep an overcoat on indoors), and at the beginning of February he came down with "a very bad grippe and sinusitis." He was, he told his family, "run down" and "sick and tired of waiting for Pinky." Winning $3,000 from Saroyan at poker made him feel a little better—although, given his superstitious ideas about poker and considering Pinky's inexplicable delay, he must have begun to wonder about her faithfulness.* Ill, bored, and puzzled, he decided that what he really needed was several weeks of sun and skiing in Megève.

Just before leaving, he received a request from the U.S. Army radio station in Paris to make a broadcast to Budapest asking the inhabitants not to resist the liberating Russians but to fight the pockets of Germans who were still holding out. The casting seemed splendid, but in the event, Capa's by now very rusty Hungarian failed him, leading his friends to tease him unmercifully about being a "fake Hungarian" and prompting Hemingway to jibe, "Capa speaks seven languages, all of them badly."

Capa went off to Megève knowing that he had been chosen to jump into Germany with the newly organized First Allied Airborne Army, commanded by Lt. Gen. Lewis H. Brereton. It was rumored at the time that the target might be Berlin, but it would obviously be a while before such a mission could be launched. Capa could go off to ski in the meantime; Elmer Lower, the new head of *Life*'s Paris bureau, would notify him when it was time to report.

Around the middle of March—after four weeks of sun, skiing, and gin rummy, as well as a bit of romance with a "very pretty French girl" at Megève— he received Lower's cable. Tanned, healthy, and rested, he reported to the U.S. 17th Airborne Division in northern France, where the entire division was loaded into freight cars. Emerging from his boxcar after forty-eight hours of being "shuffled all over France" in an attempt to confuse enemy spies,

---

* In a September 1943 letter to Crocky he had written: "I've started winning at poker. Has Pinky gone wild?"

Capa found himself at an airbase near Arras, about sixty miles from where he started out.

The day before the jump, the paratroopers shaved their heads Mohawk-style, leaving only a strip of hair extending from their napes to their foreheads. They did so for luck and esprit de corps, but although he might well have wanted an extra bit of luck for his first combat jump, Capa declined the offer of a haircut.

Then the men were briefed on their mission, which was not to be a drop on Berlin after all. Instead, they were to participate in General Montgomery's massive crossing of the Rhine near the German town of Wesel, not far from the Dutch border. That night (March 23), after thousands of Allied planes and heavy guns had battered the five German divisions in the area, Mont-gomery's twenty-five divisions were to begin to cross the river. The next morn-ing (unlike most other airborne invasions of the war, this was to be a daylight operation), the planes carrying the American paratroopers would rendezvous over Belgium with the British, forming an air armada consisting altogether of more than 3,000 transports carrying paratroopers or towing gliders and some 2,000 escorting fighters. The men would then jump in behind the enemy line of defense and push westward, squeezing the Germans toward the ad-vancing infantry and blocking any attempt to retreat.

Taking off shortly after eight o'clock on the clear, bright morning of Saturday, March 24, the planes flew so low over France, Belgium, and the Netherlands that they cast large shadows on the ground, and the paratroopers could see people below waving to them. The flight was smooth, the men were quite confident and relaxed, and, as Capa put it, nobody puked. When the get-ready signal flashed on, Capa made sure that his cameras were well-strapped to his legs and that his flask of Scotch was in his breast pocket, over his heart. "Fifteen minutes before I had to jump," he wrote, "I started thinking over my life. I went over everything I ever ate and did and I finished up in twelve minutes."

Despite the intense Allied pounding of the area the previous night, the column encountered a good deal of fire from light anti-aircraft guns as the transports came down to 600 feet for the drop, but, as Capa observed, "com-pared to the Normandy defenses, the defenses of the Rhine were definitely nonexisting." At 10:25 he jumped. Forty seconds later he landed in a large open field that was under enemy fire.

"The most amazing thing I ever saw," wrote Capa, "is the way everybody just lies on the ground when they get down. It seemed like two minutes, and everybody was just lying there. The first thing is a certain relief. You are down, you are not hurt. You are reluctant to start the next phase." As soon as they had unfastened their chutes and collected their wits, the men ran for cover behind a hedgerow, where they organized their platoons for the advance toward their first objective: a farmhouse and its outbuildings filled with German troops and civilians.

On his caption sheets Capa described the surrounding landscape as surreal, for chutes were everywhere—covering the fields, draped over high wires, and hanging from trees. (Many of the men who landed in trees were shot by the Germans as they dangled helplessly.) For two hours, parachutes and gliders kept coming into the area, and the men on the ground had to keep a sharp lookout to evade not only German fire but also landing gliders. But the paratroopers soon flushed the Germans out of the burning farm buildings and took their first prisoners of the day. The Germans fought hard until they knew they were beaten, and then, wrote Capa, "afterwards they all have cousins in Philadelphia. That is what I like about the French. They do not have cousins in Philadelphia."

Capa photographed the action until about 6:30 p.m. and then went to look for the 17th Airborne Division's command post, hoping that he might be able to get transportation back to Paris; he knew he had gotten a great story and wanted to send it through as quickly as possible. He found the post, but, learning that he would be unable to cross over to the west bank of the river that night, he could do nothing but roll himself up in a silk parachute and go to sleep. The next day he made his way across the river and then hitchhiked all the way to Paris. "Bone-weary, unshaven, still clad in a dirty paratroop uniform," Capa turned up late that night at Wertenbaker's apartment, where he "consented to eat some ham and eggs and beefsteak and bread and butter and cheese and cake, and to drink some coffee and burgundy and champagne and cognac." That was only the beginning of the champagne, for *Life* gave Capa's story eleven pages.

During the first two weeks of April, as the Allies swept across Germany, Capa remained in Paris. "From the Rhine to the Oder," he wrote, "the shooting war quickly changed into a looting war," and he had no interest in photographing it. Nor did he have any interest in photographing the liberated concentration camps, for they "were swarming with photographers, and every new picture of horror served only to diminish the total effect." But as the U.S. First Army approached Leipzig, Capa rushed to catch up with it; Leipzig had been Gerda's home. On April 18 he joined the 2nd Infantry Division (misidentified as the 5th in *Slightly Out of Focus*) as it fought its way across the Zeppelin Bridge over the Weisse Elster Canal into the center of the city.

The first platoons were already crossing it [wrote Capa], and we were very afraid it was going to be blown up at any minute by the Germans. A fashionable four-story apartment building stood on the corner overlooking the bridge, and I climbed to the fourth floor to see if the last picture of crouching and advancing infantrymen could be the last picture of the war for my camera.

He entered an open apartment and photographed a young corporal who was covering the advance across the bridge with a machine gun set up on the balcony outside. Just after Capa had snapped a shot of him reloading his gun, a sniper in the street below hit the soldier—apparently in the neck—killing him almost instantly. Standing inside the apartment and aiming his camera toward the open doorway in which the young man's body had collapsed, Capa shot a horrifying series of pictures showing his blood as it formed an ever-spreading puddle on the floor. The photographs closed the decade of war for him as the Falling Soldier in Spain had opened it.

While one of the dead man's comrades took over the gun on the balcony, Capa accompanied the others as they went down to find the sniper, who had hidden with several other German soldiers in a group of abandoned streetcars. After the Americans had stealthily surrounded the cars and fired a few warning shots, the Germans came out with their hands up. The Americans were almost angry enough to shoot their prisoners on the spot. One of Capa's pictures shows an American soldier giving a swift kick in the rear to one of the Germans being led away, and another shows an American about to strike a German a hard blow across his face.

That night the correspondents in Leipzig learned that Ernie Pyle had been killed on Ie Shima. Capa was very shaken by the news, for he had liked him and felt that Pyle was somehow "charmed" and thus immune to danger—the way Capa had always felt himself to be. The next day Capa received further shocking news. A correspondent arriving from London told him that Chuck Romine had just gotten engaged to an English girl. Capa, who had known for some time that Romine was in love with Pinky, put two and two together and left at once for Paris—though not in such a great hurry that he couldn't stop briefly in Nuremberg, which fell to the U.S. Seventh Army on April 20. There he encountered Hubert Strickland, who had driven him and Wertenbaker into Paris on the day of the liberation; *Life* used Capa's photograph of Strickland mockingly giving a Nazi salute in front of a huge swastika at Hitler's mammoth stadium on the cover of its May 14 issue.

As soon as he got his travel papers, Capa flew to London, where he and Pinky argued for a week. It wasn't so much that he was trying to talk her out of marrying Romine; it was simply that he feared (with some justification, as it turned out, for Pinky left Romine two years later and tried to win back Capa) that she had gotten engaged for the wrong reasons. He was afraid that she was trying to bluff him into proposing or to spite him for having kept her waiting so long. But Pinky insisted that she was marrying Romine because she loved him.

When Romine finally worked up enough courage to speak of his engagement, Capa told him, "It's easier for me to hear than for you to tell." Although Capa had been distressed by the news at first, he was also relieved by it, for the pressure to marry Pinky had been making him increasingly uncomfortable. He had always assured Pinky that she had no reason to be jealous of a woman who had been dead for years; but the truth of the matter, as he told Romine, was that Gerda was the only woman he had ever really loved.

During the first week of May, while Capa was still in London, the coordinator of the photographic pool telephoned Elmer Lower and told him that he needed a *Life* photographer to cover an event, although the Public Relations Office of Allied headquarters wouldn't say what or where it was to be. Reluctantly, Lower sent Ralph Morse, the only one of his photographers then in Paris. The event turned out to be the German surrender at Reims early on the morning of May 7. When Capa—who returned to Paris just before V-E Day—learned that he had missed the surrender, he was furious. That was the assignment he had been waiting for. *

On V-E Day Capa went out onto the roof of a building overlooking the Place de l'Opéra to photograph the enormous crowd that had gathered in the square below to celebrate. Capa, too, celebrated the end of the war; but his feelings must have been somewhat ambivalent. He had complained toward the end that the war was "like an aging actress, less and less photogenic and more and more dangerous." But he had become famous as a war photographer, and now there was no more war for him to photograph. There was, of course, still the war in the Pacific, but he had bad memories of China and didn't want to go to Asia. Furthermore, he had been "spooked" by Ernie Pyle's death in the Pacific. For Capa, World War II was a European war, and that war

---

* In "The Man Who Invented Himself," John Hersey gives a very different account of this incident based on what Capa had told him:

> One night Capa was playing poker at SHAEF headquarters while waiting for the Armistice assignment. A P.R.O. [Public Relations Officer] came in and said cryptically, "I've got a little job for you, Capa." "*Little* job?" said Capa. "Don't bother Capa. Capa is playing cards." The P.R.O. gave the "little job" to another photographer, and Capa missed the Armistice.

As believable as that version is (and it is perfectly in keeping with Capa's general behavior), Elmer Lower told the present author that it is apocryphal.

was over. Only half jokingly, he talked about having business cards printed up to read:

ROBERT CAPA
War Photographer
Unemployed.

32

The Allies had won the war in Europe, but now that it was over, Capa—out of work and out of love—was almost as exhausted, confused, and depressed as he had been at the end of the Spanish Civil War. He had spent most of the last three years at the front and his pictures had made him famous, but what good would his reputation do him now? He had no money, having squandered all his earnings on Pinky, their penthouse, champagne, whisky, and gambling. He had had an amusing romance, but now it too was over, ended by his fear of attachment. He had his freedom, but for what? He still, of course, had his contract with *Life*, and there were always attractive young women around; but neither the assignments nor the women seemed to mean much to him. He was on the loose and puzzled about what to do next. He was only thirty-one, an age at which most people have barely begun a serious career, but his coverage of the war would be a tough act to follow, and the range of possibilities open to him—photojournalism, documentary filmmaking, directing commercial movies, writing his memoirs and screenplays—only made his decision all the more difficult. He would try them all and more, and, not finding any single endeavor that engaged his talents or satisfied his craving for excitement the way war photography did, he would remain caught in a perpetual crisis of identity. Outwardly, however, he seemed more charming and exuberant than ever, for only by emphasizing those qualities could he find some relief from the unhappiness and the sense of being lost that tormented him.

But something was about to happen that would give his life a new focus and excitement, at least for a while. Back in Paris after a trip to the Netherlands to do a story on the severe food shortages and unemployment that were ravaging the country in the wake of war, Capa was talking with Irwin Shaw in the lobby of the Ritz when Ingrid Bergman, on her way to entertain American troops in Germany, checked into the hotel. That afternoon the two men sent her a note:

Subject:	Dinner. 6.6.45. Paris, France.
To:	Miss Ingrid Bergman
Part 1.	This is a community effort. The community consists of Bob Capa and Irwin Shaw.
2.	We were planning on sending you flowers with this note inviting you to dinner this evening—but after consultation we discovered it was possible to pay for the flowers or the dinner, or the dinner or the flowers, not both. We took a vote and dinner won by a close margin.
3.	It was suggested that if you did not care for dinner, flowers might be sent. No decision has been reached on this so far.
4.	Besides flowers we have lots of doubtful qualities.
5.	If we write much more we will have no conversation left, as our supply of charm is limited.
6.	We will call you at 6:15.
7.	We do not sleep.
	Signed:
	Worried.

Bergman was charmed, and, when the call came, she accepted the invitation, even though she had never heard of either Capa or Shaw.* "It was a great evening," Bergman wrote many years later. "We had a wonderful time. We ate at a little restaurant. I met their friends. We all laughed, we all danced. From that very first evening I liked Bob Capa very much." And Capa, from that first evening, was quite understandably taken with Bergman. But she was leaving for Germany the next day, and, marvelous as it was, the evening gave no promise of leading to anything more. Besides, so everyone assumed, she was happily married and a model of virtue.

The two months following the end of the war in Europe were a terrible

---

* Although Bergman had probably heard Capa's name in connection with *For Whom the Bell Tolls*, in which she starred, she didn't remember it; she wrote in her autobiography that she had never heard of him.

anticlimax for Capa, and the tantalizing encounter with Bergman only made things worse; he was paralyzed with inertia. Early in July 1945, just before Elmer Lower left Paris for a week, he assigned Capa to do a story on the Nazi "baby farm" in Hohenhorst, in northern Germany, but when Lower returned, he found Capa still sitting at the bar in the Scribe. Asked for an explanation, Capa blithely remarked that there had been some nice girls around and, shrugging his shoulders, said, "I just couldn't move." At the end of the month, however, he did go to Hohenhorst, where he photographed the fat, blond babies who, in accordance with a Nazi policy encouraging Aryans to have illegitimate children to keep up the birth rate, had been conceived by SS men and their chosen "reproductrices." It was clear that he would soon have to break with *Life*; he just couldn't face this kind of story much longer.

But for the moment, since he didn't have anything better lined up and needed to make a living, he duly went on to Berlin to photograph the appalling ruins of the city he had left twelve years earlier. He had intended to visit only briefly, but when he discovered, much to his pleasure, that Bergman was there—and that she seemed as happy to see him as he was to see her—he immediately decided to extend his stay.

Bergman—two years younger than Capa and, having just won an Academy Award for her performance in *Gaslight*, well on her way to becoming the number one actress in Hollywood—had been married for eight years to Petter Lindstrom, a dentist-turned-neurosurgeon. By the mid-1940s, according to Bergman's autobiography, Lindstrom had begun to nag her almost constantly—about her weight, about her posture, about getting wrinkles, about drinking at parties, and about his suspicions of what went on between her and her leading men. He was, she wrote, also increasingly dictatorial, insisting on making even the smallest decisions for her, and he was extremely tight with money. By the time she met Capa, she had already raised—and, for the time being, dismissed—the question of divorce. But she was only waiting for the right man to come along.

Not long after she met Capa, she began to wonder whether he might be the man she was looking for. He was certainly the polar opposite of Petter Lindstrom; in fact, he must have reminded her of her father, whom she had loved intensely. A studio photographer who had loved life and had a wonderful sense of humor, Justus Bergman was something of a bohemian and a free spirit. Like Capa, he was easy with money, believing that it existed to be enjoyed. Until his death when she was thirteen (her mother had died ten years earlier), he had been Ingrid's closest friend, encouraging her to do what she really loved to do in life and delightedly photographing her in silly costumes and poses, as Capa also did. (One day when Capa and Bergman were walking together in Berlin, he spotted a broken bathtub in the middle of a street of ruins and announced that he was about to get one of the greatest scoops of his career: the first photograph ever of Ingrid Bergman in a bathtub. Bergman laughed and climbed into the-tub—fully clothed, of course.*) Beyond her obvious beauty, warmth, glamour, and success, it was Bergman's sense of humor that particularly appealed to Capa. "It was, it is, your merry mind that I love," he wrote her toward the end of their affair, "and there are very few merry minds in a man's life." After her years of Lindstrom's repression and criticism, she undoubtedly found Capa, so similar to her father, not only wonderfully refreshing but almost a dream come true.

For Capa, too, his involvement with Bergman had a certain dream-come-true improbability and headiness. Who, ten years earlier, could have imagined that the impoverished André Friedmann would so totally live up to the reputation of his invented alter ego that he would have an affair with a great movie star? In its utter absurdity and unpredictability, perhaps life could, after all, be generous as well as cruel. And perhaps, now that the war was over, the world might even be safe for love.

In Berlin the friendship blossomed, but there was no talk yet of anything more serious. Nor could Capa spend all his time with Bergman; they both had work to do. For *Life* he photographed the thriving black market in the wooded Tiergarten in the center of the city, where hard-up Berliners offered their household goods and valuables in exchange for food, cigarettes, and foreign currency, while gullible Red Army soldiers, lugging suitcases filled with the back pay they had just received, bought up consumer goods of every kind. They were especially crazy about watches, which, *Life* reported, "went for as much as $1,000 [and] were the best legal tender in Berlin. Mickey Mouse watches, originally $3.95, were being bought by wide-eyed Russians for $500 apiece."

When he and Bergman got back to Paris in mid-August, Capa told Charles Collingwood about the black market and how much money was to be made in it. Since the two men had gotten quite heavily into debt from gambling, Capa suggested that they pool their cash and buy as many cheap watches as they could; Collingwood, who was about to go to Berlin anyway, could sell them and clear a huge profit. They put the plan into effect, but when Collingwood arrived, he found that the bloom was off the rose. Many of the

---

* Bergman wrote in her autobiography that Capa developed his film in such a hurry that he ruined the negative. However, Capa's friend Carl Goodwin was along and also snapped a picture of Bergman in the tub. (See illustrations following page 216.)

Russians were already wearing two or three watches on each arm, and they were now paying only about $100 per watch. After a couple of afternoons of hard bargaining, he netted about $2,000, which was just enough to pay off most of their debts.

It was in Paris toward the end of August that Bergman really fell in love with Capa and began to talk of leaving her husband for him. But, as much as he loved her in return, Capa wasn't ready for such talk; still wary of attachments and uncertain of the direction he wanted to take, he discouraged her from making a hasty move that they might both come to regret. Her life then seemed firmly rooted in Hollywood; since there was no changing that fact, Capa would have to make a career there himself if they were to think of marriage; and he knew from his 1941 visit that the place was "no paradise." Nevertheless, he was willing to give it a try. He was ready for a big change; after the atomic bomb was dropped on Hiroshima, he told his friends, "The profession of war photographer is finished forever." And he certainly wasn't willing to continue the sort of work he had been doing for *Life* over the summer—essentially the same sort of boring stories he had done for the magazine after the Spanish Civil War. Capa, the unemployed war photographer, found himself in a situation rather like that which had prompted him ten years earlier to say, "I must get into the movies, for with photography I have no hope." Before Bergman left for the States, they made plans for him to follow her to Hollywood as soon as he could.

Fulfilling what was to be his final obligation to *Life* as a staff photographer (though he didn't actually resign until January), he made a trip to Berlin early in September 1945 to photograph the first Rosh Hashanah services to be held in any of the city's synagogues since 1938. Arriving in New York at the beginning of October, he remained there for over two months, visiting his family (whom he hadn't seen in three and a half years), spending time with friends, and taking care of business, rather than rushing out to California to be with Bergman. There was, in fact, an air of schoolboy mischief about Capa's side of the romance at this point, as he boasted to practically everyone he knew about his liaison with the great star, telling them it was supposed to be a big secret. He was skeptical about things working out for him and Bergman, and, anyway, he didn't really know *what* he wanted—so he wasn't letting himself take it all too seriously.

When he finally arrived in Hollywood in December and moved into the Garden of Allah, he was hardly a stranger in town. In Sun Valley, before the war, he had become friendly with Gary Cooper, Margaret Sullavan, agent

Leland Hayward, and Howard Hawks and his wife, Slim. During the war, he had gotten to know directors John Huston, George Stevens, Irving Reis, Anatole Litvak, and Billy Wilder, as well as writers William Saroyan, Irwin Shaw, John Lardner, Peter Viertel, and writer-cartoonist Bill Mauldin, all of whom were then working on screenplays. Director Luis Buñuel, whom he knew from Spain, was then in Hollywood. Charles Collingwood was around, courting his future wife; Bill Graffis was doing public-relations work for one of the studios; and Connie and Doris Dowling (the Bastogne no-shows) were both getting supporting roles. And then there was Hollywood's large Hungarian community; before long, Capa was seeing a good deal of director Zoltan Korda as well as of his old friend Geza Korvin, who had changed his first name to Charles and signed an acting contract with International Pictures. All in all, it's no wonder that Litvak jokingly complained, "After only two weeks here, Capa is getting invited to parties it took me ten years to get invited to."

In January, William Goetz, head of International Pictures, hired Capa as a writer and apprentice director-producer for the ample but hardly extravagant salary of $400 a week. He was to write his war memoirs as the basis for a screenplay (he had begun writing autobiographical short stories in Sun Valley, in 1941, at which time Hemingway had helped him polish up the first few), and he was to spend time at screenings of classic films, on the sets, and in the cutting room. But he found he couldn't concentrate on his writing, and he was thoroughly bored by his other responsibilities, complaining that when he went to his office at the studio there was nothing for him to do. "Moviemaking is very, very slow," he told Cornell. "Considering the time, patience, and talent used to make shit, it is very painful."

Soon, instead of going to the screening and cutting rooms, Capa was having long lunches at Mike Romanoff's and spending many afternoons at the races with Collingwood. He spent so much time around the pool at Howard Hawks's house that Slim Hawks had to assure her husband she wasn't having an affair. He played lots of tennis and went to lots of parties, but he often found them boring and hated having to call up the host or hostess the next day to say what a great time he'd had. Because he was so bored, he began to drink heavily—and then he complained that the bright sunshine made California a bad place to have a hangover. Most frustrating of all, he was able to see very little of Bergman, for not only her jealous husband but also the ubiquitous columnists watched her closely. The lovers saw each other at parties and had an occasional tryst at Irwin Shaw's house on the beach in Malibu, but it wasn't until Hitchcock began filming *Notorious*, starring Bergman and Cary Grant, that Capa had any excuse for hanging around her: he announced that he was covering the filming for *Life*. In fact, he was beginning to regret his resignation from the magazine.* Early in April he wrote to Cornell, "I wish I were a newspaperman again."

After the filming of *Notorious* was finished around the middle of May 1946, Bergman went to New York for a vacation, without her husband. As was usual on such trips, Joe Steele, producer David Selznick's publicity director, went along to screen her incoming phone calls, to accompany her when she needed an escort, and generally to act as her guardian. But this time Bergman asked the hotel switchboard to ring her directly, and she often went out without telling Steele where she was going. He soon learned the reason: Capa was in town, and Bergman was going out with him almost every night. A friend told Steele that he had seen them "very chummy in a dark corner of some Village hot spot" at about four o'clock one morning. If any mention of such a rendezvous had appeared in the gossip columns, not only Lindstrom but also Ingrid's fans would have raised an uproar—as they eventually did when she began her affair with Italian director Roberto Rossellini—for they revered her as a symbol of purity and fidelity and felt betrayed when she turned out to be human.

Bergman herself was very uncomfortable with the situation, for she still earnestly believed that when two people loved each other they should get married, not carry on an illicit affair. "I was so moral," she wrote in her autobiography, "so prudish you might say." But, as fond as he had grown of Bergman, Capa was still not prepared to marry her. Realizing that Hollywood was not for him and that he would have to get back into photojournalism, he told her that he couldn't tie himself down; if they were married and had children, he wouldn't feel free to accept the dangerous assignments in which he was again beginning to see his future. "I'm not the marrying kind," he told her. But neither did he want to lose her. He did everything he could to encourage her to be more independent, insisting that she mustn't let her husband or Joe Steele or anyone else treat her like an adolescent schoolgirl. He even confronted Steele, telling him, "For a grown woman, she's so naïve it hurts. . . . She's afraid to let go. . . . Scared to bust out of that goddam built-in conformity. . . . Safeness and security—that's what motivates her. She hasn't the vaguest notion of what the world's about. It's a stinking shame." To Bergman herself he said that she was letting her husband and the movie companies drive her too hard. "It's just work, work, work," he told her. "You don't take the things you should out of life, because you've got no time for living. You're like a cart running on three wheels; you don't realize you've lost the fourth wheel, but at any moment now you're going to topple sideways."

---

* He did eventually sell the story to *Life*, but it was never published.

Bergman took Capa's advice to heart, but she simply couldn't change herself overnight, even to keep the man she had come to love so much. Without realizing it, Capa was preparing the ground for Bergman to leave her husband and Hollywood for Rossellini three years later. (He was also among those who encouraged Bergman to see Rossellini's film *Open City*; until then she had never heard of the director. The film moved her so greatly that she immediately wrote to Rossellini to say that she would like to work with him.)

Capa wasn't in New York just to be with Bergman. Early on the morning of May 27, he reported to the Immigration and Naturalization Service for his oral quiz, the final step before being sworn in as a citizen.* Not only was he obviously very sleepy, for he'd been out late the night before, he was also nervous, since to prepare himself he had done little more than glance at the text of the Constitution in the *World Almanac* while sitting at the bar of "21." When it was finally his turn to be examined, the official asked him (as Charles Collingwood, one of his sponsors, recalls the dialogue), "Mr. Capa, you are, of course, familiar with the Constitution of the United States?"

"Yes, sir," replied Capa.

"Let me ask you a few questions. What are the first ten amendments called?"

"The Bill of Rights."

"And what freedoms are guaranteed by the Bill of Rights?"

"Freedom of assembly."

"Yes . . ."

"Ummm . . . freedom of religion."

"Yes. That's right. What else, Mr. Capa?"

Capa scratched his head and finally said, "Freedom to bear arms."

"Yes. What else?"

Capa looked around helplessly.

"What is first? Freedom of what?"

Capa still looked blank.

The examiner, who was quite charmed by Capa and ready to help him, bent forward and said, "Mr. Capa, you were a war correspondent. Now what other freedom does that bring to mind?"

Capa still couldn't come up with the answer.

---

* The time Capa had spent as a correspondent accredited to the U.S. Army was counted as the equivalent of residence in the United States.

Finally the examiner asked, "Mr. Capa, what about freedom of the press?"
"Sir," replied Capa cryptically, "I was a photographer."
The examiner laughed and approved Capa for swearing in.

For the first time in fifteen years Capa was a man with a country. But even that was something of a fiction, for he remained at heart very much a European and continued to spend far more time in Europe than in the country of which he was now—legally, but really only as a matter of convenience—a citizen. Less of a fiction, paradoxically, was his assumed identity. Legally changing his name to Robert Capa at the time of his naturalization, he was only confirming the truth: he had, for all practical purposes, *become* Robert Capa.

Although he was growing increasingly pessimistic about things working out with Bergman, Capa resolved to make one more attempt. After all, one didn't just walk away from Ingrid Bergman. So, having signed a contract with publisher Henry Holt for his war memoirs (which were beginning to come along, although the stipulated delivery date of August 15, 1946, was totally unrealistic), he followed her back to Hollywood in June. No longer working for International Pictures, Capa was supposed to devote himself to writing. Instead, he became a daily visitor on the set of Bergman's new film, *Arch of Triumph*. After spending the entire day photographing the action that was being filmed, he would join Bergman and a lively group of friends for a party in director Lewis Milestone's office almost every evening.

Despite all his friends, however, Capa was out of his element in Los Angeles. For one thing, unable to hail a taxi whenever he wanted to go somewhere, he was forced to confront his old nemesis, driving. One of the first things he had done on arriving in California in December was to obtain a temporary driver's license, but he used it as little as possible, instead depending on friends to drive him around and commandeering studio limousines as high-handedly as he had commandeered jeeps at the front. But when he returned from New York in June, he decided it was time to get a car and bought a black 1941 Lincoln convertible. At the end of July he hit another car and smashed into a lamppost. No one was hurt, but for years the city's Bureau of Street Lighting hounded him for the cost of repairs—$101.18.

The *Arch of Triumph* set wasn't the only one on which Capa spent time that summer. After watching his friend Charles Korvin rehearse for his role in *Temptation*—a melodrama about an Egyptologist (George Brent) and his murderous wife (Merle Oberon)—Capa told him that he could play his Egyptian servant Hamza better than the Egyptian who had been hired for the part.

In any case, Capa wanted to know what it was like to be in front of the camera. The part was a small one; the character, his face largely hidden by the hood of his burnoose, spent most of his brief appearances on camera bowing and backing out of the set, and he spoke a few lines of gibberish. Irving Pichel, the director, decided that Capa's accent sounded right with those of Korvin and Arnold Moss and fired the real Egyptian.

All went well until one day early in October when they were shooting on a set that reproduced the platform of the Cairo railway station, complete with piles of baggage and an old locomotive belching steam. At the end of the day's shooting Capa went to Korvin's dressing room and announced that he was leaving at once for New York. He claimed that seeing all those bags had fired his wanderlust, but a more plausible explanation is that Ingrid Bergman had just left for New York to begin rehearsals for Maxwell Anderson's play *Joan of Lorraine*. It wasn't so much that he couldn't bear to be away from her, it was simply that he had stayed in Hollywood as long as he had for her sake; once she left, there was nothing to keep him there a moment longer.

They were still close enough for him to send her a single white rose when the play opened in Washington at the end of the month (he went down to see it a few nights later), and for her to cable him saying, "My white rose is very near me," but they were beginning to drift apart. For one thing, Capa had to get back to doing work that excited him, and that meant traveling. Although he had finally given up on a Hollywood career (he summed up his feelings when he told a friend, "Hollywood is the biggest mess of shit I ever stepped in"), he still hadn't given up the idea of making films. Since August he had been in touch with Richard de Rochemont about making a *March of Time* film on Vienna as a center of psychiatric research, but that project had been postponed, and Capa was instead to direct a documentary about Turkey.

Stopping in London to make a deal with *Illustrated* for the still photographs he was also planning to take in Turkey, he found that he missed Bergman but was glad to be away from the United States. "London is so quiet and empty," he wrote her, "but still Europe and so much more real and refreshing after the States. Every time I go to a bar, to a play, for a walk in the foggy streets, I want to see you there next to me." They wanted each other, but each unyieldingly demanded terms the other couldn't accept.

Although Capa was eager for challenging and engrossing work, he went to Turkey somewhat reluctantly, for he feared that, never before having directed a film, he was getting in over his head. "I disliked the subject," he later wrote, "and did not fancy to make a film about which New York had only a very vague idea and not even an outline, and I had no time to prepare and arrived the same day as the cameraman." The New York office's concept was indeed vague. Since 1945 the Soviet Union had been trying to wrest joint control of the Bosporus and the Dardanelles from Turkey; resisting the Soviet demands, the nation turned to the United States for help, but the American government felt it couldn't grant large amounts of aid to a country with a system of state capitalism and a ban on opposition parties. In 1946, largely in order to win American aid, the Turks moved toward a system of free enterprise and established an opposition party. The producers of *The March of Time* now wanted to portray Turkey as a rapidly Westernizing nation deserving of American support.

Capa's experience there was not a happy one. "From the very first day in Turkey till the last," he wrote to de Rochemont, "I was up against most everything. At the same time I had to make my research, get the permissions from an extremely bureaucratic and fascistic government, coordinate between a scared government spy and a very excitable cameraman and very camera-shy subjects. All this in winter, which was every bit as severe as in New York." The government spy to whom Capa refers was a representative of the Turkish cinematographic service whose principal task was to make sure that Capa and his French cameraman, Paul Martellière, didn't get shots of anything that might be unflattering to the national image. It was the same situation that had caused so much frustration in China—only now Capa, as the director, had to deal with it himself. Nevertheless Capa, who was shooting stills while Martellière filmed, could write to Bergman: "I am a newspaperman again, and it is all right. I sleep in strange hotels, read during the nights and try to grasp the problems of a country in a short time. It is good to work, to think, and to be lonely."

Despite all the difficulties, Capa and Martellière covered Turkey with remarkable thoroughness, from the palaces and mosques of Istanbul to the modern buildings of Ankara, from a garrison guarding the Dardanelles to an airbase for border patrols, from fishermen in the Bosporus to tobacco-growers in primitive villages, and from Turkish president Ismet Inönü in his office to a meeting of the opposition Democratic Party. As Capa summed up, "We got as much and as good film as you could get in two months in Turkey with no scenario, no preparation, and a green director—in between six snow storms. . . . The lack of excitement and human feeling in our movie are due to severe supervision, and it is very hard to steal scenes in a country immobilized in winter." Martellière recalls that "working with Capa was at once difficult and pleasant: many ideas, but working hours that were rather upsetting in view of the constraints of the light at that time of the year. . . . Capa was a very agreeable man but rather eccentric in his hours, though always ready to take responsibility for the welfare of the team."

If Capa got up late in the mornings, it was at least partly because he was working hard at night to finish his book. The manuscript was already four months late, and the publisher was furious. In Ankara, through the U.S. Information Service, Capa hired an English-speaking graduate student named Rosette Avigdor to type as he dictated—a procedure that explains some of the book's direct, conversational quality. He sent the last chapter off to Holt just before Christmas 1946. Working together, Capa and Avigdor became such good friends that when she told him she would be leaving for New York in January to study at Columbia University, he suggested that she move in with his mother, who would soon be living alone now that Cornell and his wife, Edie, were going to Texas on extended assignment from *Life*. Julia liked the idea, and Avigdor became Capa's "Turkish sister."

Capa had told Bergman that he was hoping to return to New York late in January for two weeks, and toward the end of the month he arbitrarily declared the film project completed and left (he was fed up with Turkey). But instead of going to New York, he went to Paris and then on to Megève to ski for several weeks, postponing his trip to New York until the middle of March, by which time Bergman was back in Hollywood. However, they arranged to meet shortly before Easter in Sun Valley, where Bergman was going skiing with her husband. There, realizing for the first time that Ingrid was in love with Capa, Lindstrom confronted her, and she admitted that there was something between them, although she also decided that their affair couldn't go on any longer. If they weren't going to get married, they would have to make a clean break.

> I know the Hungarian influence [she wrote to a friend]; I'll always be grateful for it. I don't know but I feel sure it has changed much in me. . . . But he knows we are closing the chapter. It is a bad thing when all other things around him are bad too. But then you can't choose your time. We are drinking our last bottles of champagne. I am tearing a very dear piece away from my life, but we are both learning and also making a clean operation so that both patients will live happily ever after.

They parted without bitterness. They had helped each other to laugh while each was going through a difficult time—Bergman with Lindstrom, Capa with his career. But they had different and irreconcilable ideas about how they wanted to live their lives, and so they would have to part. Nevertheless, they remained friends, occasionally corresponding after they broke up (she sent Capa a snapshot of herself beside an oversized dummy champagne bottle when she visited Reims in 1948, on a tour of the Joan of Arc country), and later running into each other in Europe from time to time (one friend recalls having dinner with Capa, Bergman, and Rossellini in Paris in the early 1950s).

Although Bergman's full reaction to Capa's influence was delayed until she met Rossellini, who was probably the greatest love of her life, she realized early on that Capa had changed her, and she was grateful. But Capa himself never changed; there would be one more important woman in his life, and the pattern of their romance would be essentially the same as the one with Bergman.

33

When Bergman said that their break-up was hard for Capa because "all other things around him are bad too," she was, of course, referring to his work, which was actually beginning to go better just about the time they parted. One night at Sun Valley, Capa remained at the gambling tables until he had lost two thousand dollars, his entire savings. "What difference does it make?" he said to Bergman the next morning. "It's very good for me. Now I have to work harder." And at last he had a couple of things he could work hard at and get excited about. He was, in fact, on the verge of fulfilling two longstanding ambitions—a trip to the Soviet Union and the formation of a photographers' agency.

In March 1947, Capa had run into John Steinbeck in the bar of the Hotel Bedford, and before long their wartime acquaintance had begun to burgeon into a real friendship. It was almost as difficult a time for Steinbeck as it was for Capa. His novel The Wayward Bus had been published in February to generally unenthusiastic reviews, and he was casting around for a new idea. He had been working since January on a play about a modern Joan of Arc, but it wasn't going well. His marriage was in serious trouble. And he was drinking heavily. Capa's undauntable sense of humor and love of fun were just what he needed. (Some years later Steinbeck would delightedly say of Capa, "He is so funny, so full of life.") And so these two lost, unhappy men, understanding each other very well, began drinking together, reminiscing about the war, telling funny stories, making each other laugh, and cooking up plans.

One day Steinbeck told Capa he was thinking of getting away for a while, perhaps going to the Soviet Union to see how things had changed since his last visit in 1936. It was just the sort of opportunity Capa had been looking for; when he suggested that they go together and collaborate on a book of text and photographs, Steinbeck agreed at once. They resolved that they would compile as objective a report as possible on the lives and opinions and hopes of ordinary Russians. "We would avoid politics and the larger issues," wrote Steinbeck. "We would stay away from the Kremlin, from military men and from military plans. We wanted to get to the Russian people if we could."

Capa was thrilled, not only because a trip with Steinbeck would automatically command far more attention than any trip he took alone ever could, but also because Steinbeck's influence in the Soviet Union, where his works were greatly admired, could perhaps sway the authorities at last to grant the visa they had always withheld in the past. Things were, however, not to be quite so simple. The New York *Herald Tribune* bought the idea immediately, but the Russian government was less enthusiastic. Steinbeck's visa came through without difficulty, but Capa's application was rejected until the writer made it clear to the Russian consul in New York that he wouldn't go without the photographer. Then, in mid-May, just as they were about ready to set off, Steinbeck had a bad fall and broke a kneecap. Their departure would be delayed at least six weeks.

While waiting for his visa, Capa had devoted himself to organizing the agency he had been talking about since 1938. If he was going to have to remain a photographer, he was determined to do so on his own terms. He certainly had no intention of going back to work for *Life*, as he wanted to choose his own assignments from now on—and he resented *Life's* retention of all negatives and rights to pictures taken by its staff photographers. He wanted to be able to sell his stories to magazines all over the world, and he wanted control over how they were used. The only way to achieve that kind of independence and control, he felt, was to form a group of like-minded and congenial photographers so talented that they could get whatever terms they demanded. They could command high fees, and even after having a percentage taken out to cover the agency's expenses, they would come out ahead.

Before Cartier-Bresson set off on a trip across America, Capa discussed the idea of the agency with him, and (like Chim, then in Europe, and George Rodger, in the Middle East) he had said he wanted to be counted in if the thing ever got started. Bill Vandivert, who was then based in New York, was less eager to join, for he was well established and had plenty of work, but, out of a sense of loyalty and friendship, he said he would go along.* Len Spooner, in New York on a visit, thought the agency had tremendous potential and agreed with Capa that a special arrangement with *Illustrated*—the kind of deal Capa had wanted to make with *Life* in 1941—would be mutually beneficial. Capa promised that Spooner would be the first editor to see all stories and proposals by the group's photographers; in return, Spooner promised to give the stories special preference, to pay higher than usual rates, and to pay as much as possible in advance to cover the photographers' expenses. After a year, Spooner as an individual or *Illustrated* as a corporation would have the option of buying stock and becoming a partner in the agency.

The final discussion took place over lunch in the members' penthouse restaurant of the Museum of Modern Art. Rita Vandivert, who had been handling her husband's contracts and knew the business very well, was appointed president of the agency and head of the New York office, which was to move into the office and darkroom the Vandiverts had set up for themselves in a small apartment on West Eighth Street. Also in New York for a visit and present at the meeting was Maria Eisner, for whom Capa and Gerda had worked in the mid-1930s. Eisner was appointed secretary-treasurer and head of the Paris office. Each of the seven original shareholders (the five photographers plus Rita Vandivert and Maria Eisner) put up four hundred dollars and agreed that the agency would take forty percent of the photographers' fees for assignments it had arranged.† This money was to be used primarily to pay rent, salaries of office staff, and other agency expenses, but the photographers would also be able to borrow from the pot when necessary. The agency was conceived not as a profit-making concern in itself so much as a way to give its members freedom to do the stories that interested them.

The thoroughly international group of photographers—a Hungarian, a Pole, a Frenchman, an Englishman, and an American—had agreed to spread themselves out around the world, taking territories that especially interested them. Chim took Europe, Cartier-Bresson took India and the Far East, Rodger took Africa and the Middle East, and Vandivert took the United States. Capa was to roam at large. Such a division had advantages both for the photographers

---

* Cornell, satisfied with his position as a *Life* staff photographer, decided not to join at that time; he didn't join the agency until 1954, after his brother's death.

† The agency took thirty percent from assignments the photographers had gotten on their own and fifty percent of reprint fees.

and for the agency: the photographers could remain in their territories as long as they needed or wanted to, confident that the agency would sell their photographs, send them money, and get them new assignments, while the agency could save itself and magazines a great deal of money in travel expenses by assigning stories to the photographer who was already in a given area.

There is some disagreement as to whether it was Capa or Rita Vandivert who came up with the name "Magnum." In any case, it was perfect for such an international group. Like "Capa," it was punchy and easy for anyone of any nationality to remember. With the connotation of a two-quart bottle of champagne, it suggested glamour, high spirits, and success—and gave the members a good excuse to down a magnum of champagne at every board meeting. Its association with the name of a gun implied a certain toughness, and the Latin meaning announced—accurately if not modestly—greatness.

The postponement of Capa's departure for the Soviet Union gave him and John Morris, who had recently left *Life* to become picture editor of *The Ladies' Home Journal*, time to cook up the first project to take advantage of Magnum's ability to produce coordinated international stories. A few months earlier, Morris had taken great interest in a story in *The New York Times* for which the paper's correspondents in eighteen countries had reported on the economic problems of locomotive drivers. The concept fascinated him, and he felt that such an international survey could be even more effective if done with pictures. The *Journal* editors liked the idea and worked with him and Capa to develop it into a project to show that "people are people the world over." Settling on farming as a truly universal occupation, they decided to photograph the daily life of a farming family in each of twelve nations. Each installment of the story would juxtapose photographs of all the families engaged in a particular activity—working in the fields one month, doing housework the next, then worshiping, and so on.

But before the *Journal* editors would commit themselves, they wanted to see a sample set of photographs and suggested that Capa and Morris go out to Iowa and find a family. Accordingly, the two men flew to Des Moines. (On the plane, Capa, who had a terrible hangover when they left New York, soon called for oxygen, telling Morris that it was the best cure.) The morning after they arrived, they drove north to Ames and then west, keeping a lookout for a classic farm. After about four hours, they spotted one just outside the little town of Glidden. The family that lived there—Don Pratt, his wife, and their three children—turned out to be perfect for the story and gladly agreed to be photographed. The *Journal* was pleased with the pictures and gave the go-ahead for the project.* The series, published in monthly installments from May to December 1948, was a great success and established the formula Capa would draw on for many future Magnum projects. The most important outgrowth of "People Are People," however, wasn't undertaken by Magnum itself, although the agency contributed greatly to it. Edward Steichen was much impressed by the series; in fact, it was one of the sources of inspiration for his 1955 Museum of Modern Art exhibition "The Family of Man," which grouped together photographs of people in different parts of the world doing essentially the same things. This exhibition was seen by more people than any other photographic exhibition in history.

By the end of June 1947, Steinbeck was sufficiently recovered to hobble around with a cane, but since he wouldn't be up to extensive traveling for a while yet, he and Capa decided to spend a few weeks in Paris before going on to the Soviet Union. Finally, at the end of July, with stopovers in Stockholm and Helsinki, they flew from Paris to Moscow, arriving there (unmet, since the *Herald Tribune* correspondent, out of town for a week, hadn't received their cable) on the thirty-first. They had no Russian money and spoke no Russian; it was raining; there were no taxis; and the buses were far too crowded for the two stranded travelers and all their luggage. They were rescued at last by a French diplomatic courier who offered them a ride into town, but when they arrived at the Metropole Hotel, they were told that they had no reservations and that there were no rooms available either there or at the Savoy, the only other hotel reserved for foreigners. They finally got permission to stay in the absent *Herald Tribune* correspondent's room, and other Americans stationed in Moscow fed them and showed them the ropes, but it was an inauspicious beginning.

Things soon improved, however. VOKS, the cultural-relations organization that was sponsoring their visit, got them a large room with a private bath (a great luxury) in the Savoy and assigned an interpreter to show them around Moscow. Nevertheless, Capa had to wait five or six days for his photography permits, and even after they came through he was frequently stopped by policemen who insisted on checking and double-checking his papers.

---

* In addition to the Pratts, the plan called for Capa to photograph a Czech family, which he would do on his way back from the Soviet Union. Chim was to do a French family and a German one, and George Rodger was to photograph families in Egypt, French Equatorial Africa, and Pakistan. Magnum arranged for Phil Schultz to do a family in Mexico, for Horace Bristol to do Japan and China, for Larry Burrows to do England, and for Marie Hansen to do Italy.

At length, when their travel permits arrived, Capa and Steinbeck flew to the Ukraine (most Russian airliners at the time were overcrowded, unventilated, lend-lease U.S. Army transport planes so rickety that they were safe to fly only during the day and then only at extremely low altitudes), and about ten days later they went on to Stalingrad. No accounts of the siege or photographs of the ruined city had fully prepared them for what they saw. Hardly a building in the center of the city was habitable, and many of the former residents who had not yet been relocated lived under the rubble, in the cellars of their old buildings. The area for miles around the city was still heavily littered with the debris of war.

Capa had particularly wanted to photograph the city's famous tractor factory, which had been converted to the production of tanks during the war and heroically defended by its workers. The factory was now once again producing tractors, melting down German tanks and guns for raw material—a transformation that was cited, even by atheistic Soviet officials, as an illustration of the Biblical prophecy that "they shall beat their swords into plowshares." Arriving at the factory, however, Capa was terribly disappointed to learn that there was an inflexible rule prohibiting photography. Even though he was more interested in pictures of the workers than of the machines, there could be no exception to the rule.

After a ten-day trip to Georgia that left them suffering from "overeating, overdrinking, and overseeing," they returned to Moscow just in time for the beginning of the celebration of the city's eight-hundredth anniversary. A week later, two nights before they were to leave, Capa was informed that despite earlier promises to the contrary, his negatives would have to be examined before he could take them out of the country. Fortunately, as he had never believed that he would be allowed to take his hundreds of rolls of film home undeveloped and uncensored, he had regularly sent his latest batches out to be developed in Moscow, although he was very unhappy about the quality of the processing. Early the next morning a messenger came for the negatives, and Capa spent that day and that night in agony. "He paced about," wrote Steinbeck, "clucking like a mother hen who has lost her babies. He made plans, he would not leave the country without his films. . . . Half the time [he] plotted counterrevolution if anything happened to his films, and half the time he considered simple suicide."

The box of negatives was returned to him at the airport just before he boarded the plane, but he was told not to break the seals until after the plane had taken off from Kiev, the last stop in the Soviet Union. On the four-hour flight to Kiev he tried to estimate from the weight of the box how many negatives had been confiscated, but when at last he was permitted to look inside, he was relieved to discover that nothing he considered important had been taken. (In retrospect, it seems that there was little of any real importance to take; most of the pictures now seem very dull indeed, although at the time they were of interest simply because so few pictures of life in post-war Russia had been published.)

After a pleasant few days together in Prague, Capa left Steinbeck and went off alone to the little Slovakian village of Furolac, high in the Carpathian Mountains, where he spent a week photographing a family for the "People Are People" series. Then, at the end of September, he proceeded to Budapest to see his brother László's widow, Angela, and her thirteen-year-old daughter, Eva, who had experienced terribly hard times during the war and were still struggling. (Julia was helping them out as much as she could by providing frequent packages of food and clothing.) He spent the evening of his arrival with them, saw the American consul the next day about getting them out of Hungary, and then, having been told that the application would take quite some time to process and that there was nothing further he could do for the moment, he left at once for New York.

It was his first visit to Budapest since 1933, but it was so brief—he stayed only twenty-four hours—that he didn't really have time to get sentimental. Indeed, that was precisely the idea. The fate of the Hungarian Jews was simply too horrible to think about. (He, his immediate family, and most of his close relatives had escaped the Holocaust, but his uncle Adolf, his wife, and one of their two children had died in forced labor camps, and many of his friends and schoolmates had also died.) And he could hardly bear to see either the suffering of his surviving relatives or the devastation of Budapest. (All the Danube bridges had been destroyed, the once-elegant Corso was in ruins, and some seventy percent of the buildings in Buda had been heavily damaged. The city, wrote Capa, "appeared like a beautiful woman with her teeth knocked out.") It was only the following year that he could bring himself to pay an extended visit, and by then the Communist takeover was changing things so drastically that he was fascinated and amused. More seriously, he was still trying to get Angela and Eva out of the country, but with no success. (They didn't get out until 1956.) Meanwhile, during that second visit, he took his niece out to fancy restaurants and showered her with presents—although when it came time to buy the desperately needed winter coat he had promised her, he had to admit that he had lost the money for it at the racetrack. But it was all right; the memories she had of her worldly and charming uncle ultimately meant far more to Eva than any coat ever could have.

By the time Capa returned to New York in October 1947, *Slightly Out of Focus* had been published to reviews that can best be summed up by the *Time* critic who expressed great admiration for the photographs and remarked that "at worst, the text can hardly spoil the pictures." Scarcely more gratifying was the news that he was one of twenty correspondents to whom the U.S. Army had awarded the Medal of Freedom "for exceptionally meritorious achievement which aided the United States in the prosecution of the war against the enemy in Continental Europe." Capa's forced smile in a photograph of Eisenhower pinning the medal on him calls to mind his reaction to Wilson Hicks's praise in 1943—"all that fight and struggle for this . . ."

On the whole, the next several months were a miserable period for Capa. The trip to the Soviet Union and the publication of A Russian Journal, both in book form and in a nationally syndicated newspaper serialization, attracted a lot of attention—but that attention wasn't nearly as positive as Capa and Steinbeck had hoped, for the Cold War had recently heated up with the House Un-American Activities Committee beginning its investigation of Communist influence in the movie industry. (Addressing the Herald Tribune Forum in October, Capa said that when the Russians had asked about the persecution of liberals in America, he and Steinbeck had told them that to the best of their knowledge there were as yet no political prisoners in the United States. To the Forum audience he added, "I am holding my fingers crossed.") Although the Russian press denounced A Russian Journal, in which Steinbeck criticized the inefficiency of the Soviet bureaucracy and emphasized the primitiveness of Soviet technology, the FBI regarded the trip and the book as suspicious and entered a report on them into the dossier it had been keeping on Capa since the early 1940s, when an unidentified informant accused him of having joined the Communist Party during the Spanish Civil War.

Even Capa's poker turned sour that fall. As usual, he was staying at the Bedford, and every Friday night he would play there for fairly high stakes. By the time he realized that a couple of the men were professional cardsharps, he had been cleaned out.

On top of that, Pinky—who had found life in Chicago unendurably dull—showed up in New York proposing to divorce Chuck Romine and marry Capa. He did all he could to help her through her crisis, but, fond of her as he was, he had no intention of marrying her. Finally, she returned to her husband for a few more years, although her letters to Capa continued to make clear her yearnings.

And then there were troubles with Steinbeck. The two men had gotten along very well while traveling together (Steinbeck had written in a letter toward the end of the collaboration, "Capa is an ideal man to work with. He gets along with people and seems effortless, yet gets a tremendous amount done . . ."), but several episodes in the aftermath of their trip severely strained their friendship. Just before they left Moscow, both men had given away a lot of clothes, and Capa had also given away a great deal of extra camera equipment and unused film. But even this didn't satisfy his obligations, because he had promised prints to a number of people and a camera to the Tass photographer who had helped him cover Moscow's eight-hundredth anniversary. After they had been back in New York for some time and Capa still hadn't kept his promises, Steinbeck grew angry. Capa finally did send the camera, but not until the *Herald Tribune* correspondent wrote frantically from Moscow that the Tass man was hounding him.

Steinbeck became even more upset when he learned that *The Ladies' Home Journal* had offered Capa $12,500 for the second serial rights to his Russian pictures, more than four times as much as the $3,000 they offered Steinbeck for a brief text and captions. The writer agreed to the deal very reluctantly and—as he reminded Capa repeatedly over the following months—did so at all only for the sake of friendship. But Capa felt it was fair, since Steinbeck had been paid four times as much as he for the newspaper syndication rights.

Far more serious were the disagreements that arose between them over World Video, the company they founded with former United Artists radio director Henry S. White to produce television shows for sale to the networks. Believing that television might soon render obsolete not only radio but also movies, magazines, and even books—and realizing that there was a great deal of money to be made—the three men decided to invest their time and money in producing high-quality programming. White, the firm's president, was to handle the business end of things; Steinbeck, the vice-president, was to be "counsellor-guide, script supervisor, idea creator and integrity-reminder"; and Capa, the assistant vice-president, was to direct and produce films in Paris, where costs were lower than in the United States. He made an initial investment of $2,000 and came up with the idea of doing a series on the great fashion houses of Paris, a suggestion he came to regret once he realized that he—who, despite having grown up in a dressmaking salon, knew hardly anything about fashion except that he enjoyed seeing beautiful women in elegant clothes—would be almost entirely responsible not only for directing and producing the series but also for developing the idea into a workable shooting script. Remembering what had happened when he plunged in over his head in Turkey, he told White and Steinbeck that he wanted to take things slowly at first, but they insisted that he deliver eight programs in six weeks, a demand made all the more unrealistic by low production budgets.

In mid-January 1948 and "in very bad shape," Capa sailed from New York on the *Queen Elizabeth*. During the voyage he picked up some pointers for the task ahead from twenty-three-year-old Richard Avedon, who was on his way to Paris with *Harper's Bazaar* editor Carmel Snow to photograph his second round of collections, but not even Avedon's advice could rescue Capa's project from the mediocrity to which it was clearly doomed.

Nonetheless, Capa was determined to make the best of a bad situation. Because Paul Martellière had done such a good job under extremely difficult conditions in Turkey, he now turned to him again and hired him as the cameraman for the fashion series. For six weeks Martellière shot footage behind the scenes and during showings at Dior, Balmain, Schiaparelli, and other houses of haute couture while Capa directed and shot stills. Their approach had to be simple, for there was neither time nor money to develop any interesting ideas. The programs, adequate but uninspired, were broadcast on NBC later in the year.

Capa felt he had worked hard and done quite well under impossible conditions, but White and Steinbeck took a different view of the matter. They considered their schedule and budget reasonable; moreover, believing that everyone involved had to make sacrifices if the venture was to succeed, they were angered not only by the poor quality of the programs but also by Capa's expense account, which included numerous lunches (one for Avedon and Snow, another for Pamela Churchill and Doris Dowling, and others for models and publicity directors from various houses), as well as "entertainment for seven mannequins from Lelong after a special show," a $170 difference between his travel allowance and the fare on the *Queen Elizabeth*, and a $300-a-week living allowance. They were so angry, in fact, that they vowed never to let Capa direct or produce anything else for World Video and even asked him to sell back his stock. When he refused to do so, they decided to withhold reimbursement for his expenses. In a letter written in the pidgin English his friends referred to as "Capanese," Capa complained to his family, "I done my best and finally they ruined the whole thing in New York, so I worked for six weeks on my own expenses and without pay besides the $2,000 which I had put in the company. So the plaisir of being a capitalist did cost around $3,500 altogether." On top of that, because of the Red Scare, *The Ladies' Home Journal* decided not to publish his story on a Slovakian wedding (they had already published his Russian story), and *Holiday* and *This Week* dropped their projected layouts of his Russian pictures, depriving him of another $4,000 he had been counting on. Capa was flat broke.

The pressure on him to sell back his stock mounted, and late in the summer he gave in, although he remained on the board of directors until December, when he and Steinbeck—who had also grown sick of the whole business—resigned and, making up with each other, resumed their friendship.

Steinbeck's biographer Jackson J. Benson has observed that "once he loved you, he tended to love you regardless of your faults and offenses." After he had cooled down, he came to see whatever had angered him as "an accidental rather than essential quality of the person involved," and he would say, "Oh, you know how Capa is"; and Capa was equally forgiving. So, despite the serious disagreements they had had, whenever Capa and Steinbeck found themselves in New York or Paris at the same time (usually not more than two or three weeks a year), they would spend as much time as they could together, drinking, telling stories, and laughing, as they always had. In May 1954, while Capa was in Indochina, Steinbeck was in Paris and, as the woman who was then his secretary recalls, he was talking about Capa constantly and counting the days until his return. When he learned of Capa's death, he was so shaken that he went out and walked the city for fourteen straight hours. Later he wrote of him, "He may have had closer friends, but he had none who loved him more."

34

Soon after it was announced that the British would leave Palestine in May 1948, Capa asked *Life* for an assignment to cover the birth of the state of Israel, but was told that three photographers had already been assigned. *Life* wanted Capa to go instead to northern Greece to do a story on the Communist guerrillas, and he seriously considered accepting this assignment, but in the end Israel meant so much to him personally that he decided to go there even though he could get an advance commitment only from *Illustrated*.

On May 8 he flew to Tel Aviv and moved into the beachfront Armon Hotel, where he shared a room with Jack Winocour, assistant editor of *Illustrated*, and with Frank Scherschel of *Life*. Capa was in his element in Tel Aviv, a cosmopolitan city highly charged with the excitement of the founding of the Jewish state and frantic with preparations for war. Once hostilities broke out, the city was reminiscent of Madrid during the siege or London during the Blitz; for Capa the similarity with London was reinforced by the presence of Quentin Reynolds, who was covering the story for *Collier's*. Much of the international press had gathered in Tel Aviv, and there was an exhilarating atmosphere of camaraderie, with poker games under fire and impassioned political arguments. Food shortages were severe, but Tel Aviv had a large Hungarian population, and before long it seemed as though Capa knew every Hungarian in the city; through them he kept himself and his fellow journalists well supplied with black-market food and liquor. He worked the system the way he did everywhere, and he was, as always, immensely generous to his friends. As Winocour recalled, "Capa was moneyless and yet a giver."

Soon after he had covered the official declaration of the founding of the state of Israel that took place in the Tel Aviv Museum on May 14, Capa went with Scherschel and Hungarian-born photographer Paul Goldman to the northern Negev desert to cover what he later called "the bitterest and most romantic fight of the whole war." Of their visit to the kibbutz of Negba, whose heroic resistance was effectively halting the Egyptian advance from the south, Goldman later reminisced:

> Negba was then almost completely surrounded by the Egyptians. Because of the continuous shelling, you literally had to crawl into the settlement. We had to lie flat for about two hours, and during that period we counted about three hundred shells. Suddenly—and characteristically—Capa said, "Who the hell can lie still when a fight is going on?" Jumping up, he ran for the settlement. Scherschel, frightened to death, shouted after him, "Bob, keep low! You'll get hit!" So Capa shouted back, "My address isn't on those ———— shells," and he kept running [followed by Goldman]. We reached the settlement safely and were shown to the shelters where the settlers took cover. Capa jumped down and greeted everyone with his spicy Hungarian-accented Shalom. . . . He cheered them up and kept them in high spirits all afternoon. Naturally, there was soon a circle of girls and women around him, and so he got his story seemingly almost without effort. The people gave freely and happily.

The most urgent and crucial task facing the new government—and Capa's biggest story of the war—was the relief of Jerusalem, whose only lifeline, the road to Tel Aviv, had been cut by the Arabs, stranding the city without food or other supplies. Several times during the last two weeks of May, Capa accompanied troops from Tel Aviv to the Ramle front, only about twelve miles to the southeast, going one day to the village of Yasur, which had just been captured by the Haganah. Although the next village, two miles away, was still held by the Arabs, there was little action to photograph, as the fighting consisted mostly of night skirmishes. During the day, the long hours of observation were only occasionally punctuated by a few bursts of machine-gun fire from the no-man's-land between the villages.

The troops went from Tel Aviv out to the Ramle front in buses, reminding

PALESTINE WAR : FIRST FRONTLINE PICTURES

Photographed by
ROBERT CAPA

Rooftop Outpost has been set up in captured Arab village. Jewish troops are hurrying into position as enemy movements are spotted at two thousand yards. The next village, two miles away, is occupied by Arab Legion. Fighting in this area is mostly confined to night skirmishes: during day there is sporadic machine-gunning and rifle fire

Once again the violence of war has caught up with Robert Capa. Spain, North Africa, France, Germany, and then his words: "I hope to stay unemployed as a war photographer till the end of my life." He must have remembered this as he crouched in a hurriedly dug slit-trench on the Central Front in Palestine when the battle got a little too near, or stood, unprotected, in No-Man's-Land to get the first frontline pictures to come out of this stricken country. These pictures tell the story of the Jewish settlements—Kibbutzim—dotted between the Arab villages and under constant rifle and machine-gun fire from the ground and bombs from

the air. It was to these battlegrounds that "new soldiers" of Tel Aviv took buses and trucks. The new soldiers varied from born Palestinians (Sabras—Sons of the Cactus) to immigrants who, after years in Europe's concentration camps at last reached Israel and enlisted in the ranks of Haganah. They mingled well with the old defenders of the Kibbutzim, teaching them what they themselves had learned, and learning much about this strange warfare. Capa and his cameras have captured the atmosphere of the Holy Land War, the misery of death, the peril that comes from a sniper's bullet. Robert Capa had found another war

Capa of the streetcars to the front in Madrid. Indeed, Israel brought back many memories of Spain. "This is the beginning of the Jewish Army and reminds one strongly of the Republican [i.e., Loyalist] Army of Spain at the beginning of the Civil War," wrote Capa. "The same enthusiasm, the same differences in politics, professions, and age." Even much of the terrain was the same: small villages, dusty roads, and olive groves. And as there had been in Spain, there was much argument about whether there should be a democratic and egalitarian militia or a traditionally disciplined and hierarchical army. In the Haganah there was a good deal of the informality that had characterized the POUM and CNT militias. And, as in Spain, the lack of military discipline, compounded by lack of training, led to many costly defeats. On May 23, Capa witnessed one of the worst—at Latrun, where, as an oppressively hot, parching wind blew steadily, a battalion of Hungarian immigrants, off the boat less than a week, was thrown into an attack without training, without water bottles, and without officers who spoke Hungarian. Such a rout could not but make Capa fear that Israel was destined to suffer the same fate as the Spanish Republic.

Although some of the similarities between Israel and Spain were most discouraging, Capa found others—notably the prominent role of women in the army—quite pleasant. He photographed many women soldiers, but his interest in at least one of them was not professional. Once when fighting suddenly broke out at night, the light from signal flares revealed Capa and a beautiful Sabra making love on a hillside. The affair continued intermittently throughout Capa's stay in Israel, and the young woman eventually followed him back to Paris, but to no avail.

Capa was also pleased to encounter something of the spirit of the International Brigades. He found it especially in David Michael Marcus—an extroverted, robust, and disarmingly informal West Point graduate and former New York City Commissioner of Corrections who had been appointed commander of the forces between Tel Aviv and Jerusalem. It was Marcus's job to find an alternative way of getting supplies into Jerusalem in a hurry, for a cease-fire was to go into effect on June 11, and if the city wasn't relieved by then, nothing further could be done. Late in May, when he arrived on the scene, he learned of a footpath through the mountains that could possibly (with a great deal of work) be widened and smoothed into a usable detour. The government approved the plan at once and sent hundreds of laborers, along with as many engineers and bulldozers as could be rounded up, to aid the troops in the construction of the "Burma Road." Work continued twenty-four hours a day, often under Arab artillery and sniper fire. Capa, whose most dramatic picture shows a man leaping from a bulldozer as shooting broke out, covered the construction from beginning to end.

> Whenever Marcus told Capa not to go to a certain area [recalled David Eldans, head of the Government Press Office Photo Department], you could take it for granted that he would go. So then began a game, Marcus claiming that one place was dangerous in order to keep Capa away from the real danger elsewhere. But in the end, Capa always found him out—so Marcus had to turn to other methods. There were very strict security regulations, and the commandos and patrols had orders to turn the photographer back from places that were too hot. But Marcus failed to take Capa's cleverness and personal charm into account. He simply made friends with all the soldiers—with fascinating stories and with the brandy flask he always carried in his hip pocket—and so he went everywhere.

So much for military discipline. But Marcus wasn't really angry, for he had come to like and admire Capa very much. On the evening of June 8, only a week after construction had begun, they drove together over the new road, which was passable but extremely dangerous. Capa slept most of the way, even though the road was so bumpy that he was nearly jolted out of the jeep many times. When they arrived safely at the military headquarters in Abu Ghosh, seven miles west of Jerusalem, he seemed as well rested as any man who had just had a good night's sleep.

The next morning Capa went into Jerusalem, where he photographed Haganah troops in the ruined buildings surrounding the Arab-held Old City. (His pictures look very much like those he had taken in Madrid's University City; appropriately, they were published in *Regards*, as the earlier ones had been.) On the following day, June 10, he went back out to Abu Ghosh and, when he found Marcus at the Monastère de la Nouvelle Alliance, told him that the Eden Hotel in Jerusalem "was preparing its highest honor for an American commander: a hot bath." It would, Capa predicted, be "a delirious experience." Late that night, returning from a walk outside the monastery compound, Marcus failed to give the password when challenged and was shot dead by one of his own sentries. Devastated, Capa accompanied Marcus's body into Jerusalem in the morning, and then, that afternoon, left with the convoy carrying it back to Tel Aviv, where an even more serious—and more personally shaking—incident was about to occur.

On the morning of June 22, while the cease-fire was still in effect, a group of extreme right-wing Irgunists anchored the *Altalena*, a ship carrying five hundred men and women of military age, several thousand guns, and millions of rounds of ammunition, off the main beach of Tel Aviv and announced over a loudspeaker their intention of unloading the ship at once. Because bringing arms into the country would violate the terms of the cease-fire agreement, thus giving the Arabs an excuse to resume hostilities before Israel had time to recover from the first round, the government had warned the Irgun that it would, if necessary, use force to stop any attempt to unload the *Altalena*. Calculating that the government wouldn't dare order its troops to fire on Jews while the international press was looking on, the Irgun deliberately anchored the ship in full view of the Public Information Office and the United Nations headquarters.

While the first wave of Irgunists landed on the beach and set up machine-gun nests to cover subsequent waves, Haganah troops stood by, waiting for orders from the government, which was meeting in emergency session. By the time the second wave of Irgunists landed, orders had arrived and the Haganah, having taken up positions in the rubble of houses destroyed in earlier fighting, opened fire. Soon a full-scale battle was raging on the beach, while Haganah artillery shelled the *Altalena*.

As Capa moved forward on the beach to photograph people jumping off the blazing ship and swimming ashore, bullets were whizzing around him from all directions. (New York *Herald Tribune* correspondent Kenneth Bilby later recalled having seen a man killed not five feet away from the photographer.) When Capa was close enough to get his pictures, he assumed a half-crouching stance with his legs well apart. All of a sudden a bullet grazed the inside of his thigh. For one sickening moment of blind panic, before he could locate the area of pain precisely, he feared that the bullet had unsexed him. When he told the story later, he claimed that, despite the danger around him and the encumbrance of the cameras hanging from his neck, he undid his belt on the spot and pulled down his pants, all the while spinning like a dervish from fear and pain. Everything was intact; the bullet had only grazed his thigh, leaving a bad bruise but not even breaking the skin. He told his friends that, taking this terrifyingly close call as a warning, he ran back to his hotel, packed his bags, and left Israel on the next plane for Paris.

He took that warning very seriously and swore that he would never again photograph on the field of battle. "They went too far—or rather got too close—this time," he said to his friends in Paris. "I am not going to continue to photograph for posterity the men who play this little game." Then he muttered, "That would be the final insult—to be killed by the Jews."

Nonetheless, once the armistice had been signed the following January, Capa was eager to return to Israel. When he learned that Irwin Shaw, with whom he had maintained his wartime friendship, was going to Israel in May to do a series of three articles for *The New Yorker* about conditions at the end of the nation's first year of independence, Capa talked him into a collaboration. Combining text and photographs, he argued, Shaw could turn his articles into a book.* The collaboration was, however, to be much looser than that with Steinbeck, for only in Tel Aviv and Jerusalem did the two men work together; the rest of the time they went their separate ways.

Capa spent much of his second trip to Israel revisiting places he had been the previous year, and one of the first things he photographed in Tel Aviv was the rusting hulk of the *Altalena*, still aground just offshore. The beach where he had had his close call was now covered with sunbathers, and the water was filled with people cooling off. The year before, passengers and crew had jumped overboard in panic as the burning ship threatened to explode; now the adventurous climbed up a ladder and jumped off in sport.

Capa and Shaw observed at length the burgeoning middle-class life of Tel Aviv, paid a visit to President Chaim Weizmann at the research institute he had founded, and attended the new symphony orchestra, the new theaters, and a session of the Knesset. Then they made their way over the "Burma Road" to Jerusalem, where Capa's charm enabled him to photograph Orthodox Jews (whose religious beliefs usually make them hostile to photographers) and the preparation of a Bokharan Jewish bride, usually forbidden to any man's eyes. But charm was not enough when it came to getting permission to photograph in the Old City, still held by the Arabs. As Shaw later wrote:

> We were halted by no less a personage than Major Tal, the military commander of the place, who spoke knowledgeably and approvingly of Capa's work, even though he regretted that he could not let us enter his territory, since, he said, as Jews we would be torn apart by the frenzied inhabitants. I was ready to take him at his word, but Capa appealed to our vice-consul, a man of traitorous disposition, and did everything but smuggle himself in as a Bedouin camel driver to get the shots he wanted. Happily, he failed, and the films we took back of the Great Mosque were made by an Arab photographer.

Capa went next to Negba, where he photographed men eating in a room whose walls were still pocked from the fighting he had covered the previous year. He then headed north to Haifa to photograph the immigrants who were

---

* The collaboration was complicated somewhat by the fact that *The New Yorker* publishes no photographs. Capa and Shaw did a story together on Jerusalem for *Holiday* and *Illustrated*, but Capa published other pictures in *Look* and *Illustrated* with his own text. Shaw's articles and Capa's photographs were collected in *Report on Israel* (New York, 1950).

arriving by ship at the rate of a thousand a day from Tunisia, from Turkey, and from all over eastern Europe. But on arrival these people, so many of whom had endured the horrors of Nazi concentration camps and post-war displaced-person camps, and who had now at last reached the land of their fathers, were loaded into trucks and driven to internment camps surrounded by barbed wire, where they would remain until work and housing—usually in a remote settlement—could be found for them. "Great experts in this kind of life," wrote Capa, "they settle down in no time to the camp routine."

Himself essentially a stateless person and perpetual refugee by temperament and profession, Capa was dismayed by the plight of these reluctant internees, but he was also fascinated by the whole process of assimilating the immigrants into the life of the new nation, in whose overcrowded cities there were neither jobs nor apartments for them. The situation was made even worse the following year by the passage of the Law of the Return, which decreed that any Jew from anywhere in the world would be welcomed in Israel and made a citizen. Therefore, when the United Jewish Appeal asked him to make a fund-raising film for them in Israel in the fall of 1950—and, despite the Turkey and Paris fashion fiascos, he accepted—he knew that he wanted the film to focus on the arrival, internment, and eventual settlement of immigrants.

When Capa returned to Paris from an assignment in Germany on September 30, he had only four days to get ready. He was the only member of the film team who had ever been to Israel, and he seemed full of enthusiasm for the project, but when he sat down to discuss it with John Fernhout, the producer, and Millard Lampell, the writer, all he talked about was how to get good food and liquor on the black market. He didn't seem to be at all worried about the lack of concrete preparation. Lampell recalls that during those few days in Paris, he and Capa drank and prowled the city, one night "careening around in the pre-dawn dark with three actresses from the Comédie Française, pasting up posters [reading] 'Contre l'Armament Allemand!' while Capa made time with a slim blonde by off-handedly, laughingly describing how he had landed with the American troops in the invasion of France."

As soon as the film team arrived in Israel, they began having problems. The UJA coordinator wanted a sentimental film, while they wanted to make a strong, tough one. In addition, Capa's "lordly way of throwing money around" created friction with the organization. And there were other problems. It was only once they started shooting that Lampell discovered that Capa really didn't know what he was doing. "He wasn't much of a director," Lampell recalls. "He shouted, he was excitable, and the air around him was always electric with confusion." When he yelled, everyone being filmed would turn around and look at him, ruining the shot. While they were filming former

U.S. Treasury Secretary Henry Morgenthau, Jr., on a visit to a settlement he had sponsored in the Judaean Hills, "a stiff, courteously correct Morgenthau was somewhat unnerved by Capa's wild, unintelligible orders and his curses about the light." And whenever Capa, who was also working on a *Life* assignment, began to click away with the cameras that were always slung around his neck, filming would be abruptly interrupted. "Strangely," Lampell observes, "for a man so used to being in the middle of action, capturing it as it happened, Capa never really seemed to get the hang of working out a movie sequence."

In and around Haifa, while cameraman Jacques Letellier filmed, Capa re-photographed the scenes of arrival and internment he had shot the previous year, although this time he focused on the immigrants' faces; and in the camp of Rosh Hay'n in Shaar Aliyah he caught some of the quirks of camp life, such as women breaking out through holes in the barbed wire to visit friends and relatives. When Capa and Lampell discovered that at night a truck—which was actually a rolling brothel—backed up to those same holes, they found the situation wonderfully funny.

Much time was wasted as the concept of the film was changed repeatedly, but finally they found a boy who was willing to be sent anywhere and do anything; they decided to build the film around the contrast between him and a boy who wanted to study to become a doctor and was bitterly disappointed at being told that he would have to go to a kibbutz to learn Hebrew before he could attend a university. In a re-enactment of the scene in which the arrogant boy learns his fate, Capa's current girlfriend, Pita Wolff, beautiful and obviously very intelligent and serious, played the part of the interviewer with just the right air of no-nonsense toughness.

Despite the demands of his work and the presence of Pita Wolff, Capa was bored; he had already seen it all. He did his best to carry out his assignments, but when he was bored, he had a very short attention span. As Lampell remembers, "Capa alternated between filming and going off on mysterious errands, returning with a jerry-made can of precious petrol for our wreck of a car, or with a bottle of Polish vodka, which was, for some reason, our favored booze." Indeed, as their discussions in Paris had suggested, what Capa liked best about Israel was dealing with the challenge of living well in a country plagued by shortages—a challenge made all the more interesting by the government's recent intensive crackdown on the black market. He had brought along a great deal of extra film and camera equipment to trade for food and alcohol, and he always had elaborate ration-coupon deals going. In Haifa, he had lots of Hungarian friends and connections. And along the way to the kibbutz just south of the Sea of Galilee to which the two boys being filmed were sent, Israeli and Arab photographers with whom Capa traded would, as Lampell recalls, "appear mysteriously and lead us to cramped rooms in back alleys where we ate chicken pilaf and drank French burgundy." But he was still bored, and so when they went out to film on a hillside along the border, he ostentatiously lit one cigarette after another, as though he were deliberately trying to attract the attention of the Syrian artillery observers across the valley— just to see whether something interesting might develop.

When shooting was completed in mid-November, Capa wrote to Maria Eisner that he thought the finished film would be "more than quite good." Indeed, despite all the problems in making it, the film conveys a remarkably strong sense of what it must have been like to arrive in the new nation and be sent out to a remote settlement.

Settling in Israel himself was increasingly on Capa's mind. He felt that the nation was already showing signs of becoming just one more bureaucratic state, but nevertheless, in his brief moods of longing for some sort of permanent home, he began to entertain the idea of eventually finding a place in Tel Aviv and encouraged his mother to think about doing the same. However, like all his ideas of permanence, it was to dissipate quickly.

35

Early in February 1949, back in New York at a party given by Barney Josephson, owner of the Greenwich Village nightclub Café Society, Capa met the very beautiful Jemison McBride Hammond, recently divorced from jazz record producer John Hammond. He was immediately taken with Jemy, who was thirty-two, warm, charming, and intelligent, and asked her out to dinner after the party. They had a wonderful time, but Capa was leaving for Paris the next day. When he called her from the airport to say goodbye, she thought that would be the end of it, and the months of silence that followed seemed to confirm her judgment. But as soon as he returned in September, he called her, and she was thrilled to hear from him. He found it quite touching that she seemed so genuinely pleased to see him again.

By the time Capa left New York at the end of December, he and Jemy had grown very fond of each other. The problem was that he was more ambivalent than ever about settling down. On the one hand, he found himself increasingly desiring some sort of permanence—a family, even—for it was exhausting to be always on the go, always living in hotels, always fleeing attachments. On the other hand, he feared that if he tried to settle down, he would soon grow bored and restless. Furthermore, despite his vow against doing any more war photography, the argument he had given Ingrid Bergman about marriage still more or less applied: if he had a wife and children, he wouldn't feel free to accept an extended or dangerous assignment if an interesting one came along. There was no simple solution to the dilemma, which was complicated by the fact that Jemy had two young sons from her previous marriage to take care of. Her life was in New York, and, by the terms of her divorce settlement, she wasn't free to move with her sons to Paris, where Capa wanted to continue to live. Only in the summer, when her former husband took the boys, was she free to travel. So she and Capa saw relatively little of each other. He spent a month or two in New York every winter, and she spent a month or two with him in Europe every summer, but the rest of the time they were apart. During those times, Jemy would receive an occasional letter from him, but mostly there were just laconic cables informing her of his whereabouts and plans ("Leaving Tuesday for London, then directly to Klosters. Love, Capa").

Capa did sometimes seriously consider marrying Jemy, but he would always come up with a reason not to—such as that she would be crazy to marry him, for she was receiving generous alimony payments from her former husband, whose mother was a Vanderbilt. Ironically, before the war Capa had wanted to do a story for *Life* about an American divorcée who couldn't afford to remarry because she would lose her alimony. He had then found the situation fascinating and hilarious, but now it wasn't so funny, for Jemy loved Capa deeply and wanted to marry him, and in his own way he loved her in return. So Jemy waited—sometimes patiently, sometimes less so—while he ran around the world working, chasing other women, and trying to figure out what to do with the rest of his life.

The intense ambivalence that seemed to pervade every aspect of Capa's life in the late '40s and early '50s was nowhere more evident than in his career, for he found himself becoming more of a businessman than a photographer, and he wasn't particularly happy about it. When the Vandiverts, feeling they could do better on their own, dropped out of Magnum in July 1948, Maria Eisner became the agency's president, but it was Capa who made most of the big deals and arranged the major projects. In 1948, for instance, it was he who tapped the lucrative potential of the Marshall Plan, negotiating a contract to sell work by Magnum photographers for exceptionally high rates to the magazines published under the Plan's auspices throughout Europe. "Capa was the boss," Inge Morath has written, "because, for one thing, he kept on the lookout for stories for all Magnum photographers. But equally vital were his experience, generosity, connections, aggressiveness, and the vision he had for Magnum, which kept us going."

Capa was also the agency's idea man, very much as Guttmann had been at Dephot, coming up with ideas not only for group projects but also for stories to be done by individual members. When someone told Capa that he could make millions with all his ideas, he replied, "I'll never make millions. It's the man with one good idea who makes millions. If you have twenty ideas a day, you have to give them away." The corollary to this was his dictum that "coming up with ideas is not difficult—the hard part is making those who can carry them out believe that they came up with them in the first place."

One of the most ambitious projects Capa dreamt up, inspired by the success of the "People Are People" series, was a survey of the generation that was turning twenty in 1950. For this inquiry into the attitudes, endeavors, and aspirations of post-war youth, Magnum photographers were to find a representative boy and girl in each of fourteen countries. Advances would enable everyone to travel widely—all the while, of course, working on other stories, which, since expenses were already covered, could be sold for one hundred percent profit.

Capa was a very shrewd businessman, enjoying, as always, the challenge of beating the system. (He was proud of the shrewdness that he considered part of his Hungarian birthright, and he used to joke, reversing the old Hollywood maxim, that "it's not enough to have talent, you also have to be Hungarian.") Typical of his deals were elaborate schemes to take full advantage of Europe's constantly fluctuating rates of exchange, insisting on payment of an advance in one currency, for instance, and then converting it to a more favorable one with which to buy a plane ticket. He was also a very tough bargainer who looked out for the best interests of all the agency's photographers, wangling substantial advances for them whenever he could.

Despite all this business to attend to, Capa spent as little time as possible in the Magnum office, which, after Maria Eisner married and moved to New York in 1949, took over her large, fourth-floor apartment at 125 Rue du Faubourg St.-Honoré, only a few blocks from the Lancaster, where Capa was living. (Eisner remained the agency's president and headed its New York office.) He would drop in several times a day to make phone calls, to dictate texts and captions for his stories, and to pinch and slap the bottoms of the attractive young women (including the indispensable Crocky, whom he had hired away from *Life*) with whom he kept the office staffed. But he preferred to conduct business in the café downstairs, where, while discussing even the most serious matters, he played pinball with great energy and enthusiasm, squinting as smoke from the inevitable Chesterfield dangling from his lower lip got in his eyes.* He didn't like to talk for more than five or ten minutes on any subject and grew very impatient if anyone tried to go on and on. Day-to-day details bored him, but, given a quick summary of a problem, he usually came right up with a solution—albeit perhaps an unorthodox one.

Indeed, Capa's way of doing business was often highly unorthodox, hinging on his gambler's approach to life and his view of Magnum less in terms of cooperative capitalism than of outright anarchism. Since Cartier-Bresson had an independent income and was away in the Far East, Capa felt free to borrow all the money coming in from his friend's sales—not just the agreed-upon forty percent—for himself or for other photographers who needed it for expenses. Maria Eisner worried about what would happen if Cartier-Bresson suddenly demanded his money, but Capa didn't worry about such things. If the situation had arisen, he would undoubtedly have solved it the way he solved the cash-flow crisis that arose when Pierre Gassmann, whose firm did all of Magnum's photographic processing in Paris, told him that he urgently needed the four hundred dollars the agency owed him in order to pay his staff. Magnum was broke, but Capa had an idea. Discovering that Gassmann had about seventy dollars in cash, Capa suggested putting all the money on a horse he had a hot tip on; the winnings would take care of the payroll. Gassmann declined, but Capa placed a bet anyway, winning enough to pay Gassmann everything Magnum owed him. Capa's winnings—and those of the other Magnum members and staffers who acted on his tips—got the agency through more than one crisis.

Gambling might solve a short-term crisis, but in longer-range terms the most urgent problem facing Magnum after Bill Vandivert's resignation was the recruitment of new talent to ensure a steady income. In order to continue getting fat fees for group projects, however, the agency had to remain an elite and exclusive club. Furthermore, the original members had agreed not to take on anyone who wouldn't fit in personally as well as professionally. As an immediate solution, Capa came up with the notion of "associates," free-

---

* According to columnist Leonard Lyons, Sam Wanamaker based his characterization of a liberal *Life* photographer in the Broadway comedy *Goodbye, My Fancy* on Capa. After seeing the play in December 1948, Capa offered a criticism: "I always have a cigarette dangling from the corner of my mouth." That touch, replied Wanamaker, was too theatrical for him to use.

lancers whose work Magnum would handle for a percentage. They could use the prestigious name "Magnum" in their credit lines and they would benefit from the agency's distribution operations, but they would own no shares and have no say in the running of the organization. Among the first in this category were Gisèle Freund, Fenno Jacobs, Herbert List, Homer Page, and Carl Perutz, but the list eventually grew long, for Capa was very free about inviting photographers he met and liked to become associates.

Ever since he had begun talking about a photographers' organization, Capa had envisioned it not only as an agency for accomplished and successful photographers but also as a training ground for younger ones. But it wasn't to be any mere school or apprenticeship program. Taking on a young photographer was to be like adopting him or her as a member of the family, and the decision to adopt was to be treated with appropriate seriousness. To maintain Magnum's high standards, any young candidate for full membership would have to have already demonstrated exceptional talent.

In July 1948, at the time of Vandivert's resignation, the only candidate on whom a majority could agree was Werner Bischof, a thirty-two-year-old Swiss who in 1944 had turned from abstract still-life photography to photojournalism. In 1945 the distinguished Swiss magazine *Du* had devoted a special issue to his photographs of European refugees, and his work had continued to attract attention. In September, Bischof finally received the letter inviting him to become a shareholder. A cautious perfectionist, not one to rush into such a big decision, he waited until early the following year to accept. ("What is important to me," he wrote to his wife, "is that they are all sound people and socialist-inspired.") By 1950 not only was Capa taking an intense personal interest in the development of Bischof's career, but they were becoming like father and son—an unusual relationship for two men whose ages differed by only three years. Due to Bischof's relative lack of experience, Capa regarded him as much younger than himself.

The other "second generation" Magnum member with whom Capa developed a very close relationship was Ernst Haas, who, like Bischof, had abandoned abstraction for photojournalism. Born in Vienna in 1921, Haas had begun working for the Munich-based, American-sponsored magazine *Heute* in 1946, traveling around Europe with researcher Inge Morath (who eventually turned to photography herself and became a Magnum photographer). In 1947, while in Vienna on a fashion assignment, Haas heard that the trains bringing Austrian prisoners of war home from Russia had begun to arrive. Dropping everything else, he covered the story; the resulting pictures were featured in magazines all over Europe and brought him to Capa's attention. By the time Haas arrived in Paris in July 1948—accompanied by

Morath, who then became a Magnum researcher—he had accumulated a $1,200 credit with the agency as an associate. The day after his arrival, Capa took him out to lunch and congratulated him on becoming a shareholder.

"What does that mean?" asked Haas.

"It means," replied Capa, "that your money is in Magnum, that Magnum is a non-profit company, and that you will never see your money again."

But one way or another Capa would always see to it that Haas had money; he did everything he could to get assignments for the young photographer, and even when Haas's work began to take a direction of which he didn't really approve, he stood by him. When Capa was in London in 1953, he looked at the semi-abstract color photographs Haas had been taking there and said they were fabulous, even though he was actually worried that Haas was becoming too "artistic" and that he might influence the younger photographers in Magnum to move away from photojournalism. Nevertheless, when Haas announced that he was running out of money and would soon be forced to accept a journalistic assignment elsewhere, Capa told him he would see what he could do. Very late that night, having had a winning streak at poker, he burst into Haas's hotel room, woke him up, and threw a giant wad of pound sterling notes into the air. "All right," he said as the bills floated down all over the floor. "Now you can stay."

Between 1949 and 1953, Magnum took in eight more shareholding members—Eve Arnold, Elliott Erwitt, Burt Glinn, Erich Hartmann, Erich Lessing, Inge Morath, Marc Riboud, and Dennis Stock—most of whom were in their middle-to-late twenties when they joined. Robert Frank, then a very successful free-lancer who would have brought a good deal of money into Magnum's treasury, was considered for membership, but Capa said he thought Frank was too complicated and had no sense of humor. "He wouldn't work well with the group," observed Capa. "He will make his way very well alone."

Some people felt that the younger photographers in Magnum were Capa's surrogate children, others that they were his stable of racehorses. Both views were certainly true to some extent. Capa encouraged Magnum's younger members, guided them, did his best to get them assignments and advances, joked with them, gave them tips on horses, took them to parties or out to dinner in Paris or London or New York, and cared about them as human beings. Most of them still regard him as having been one of the greatest influences on their lives and work.

As demanding as Magnum business was on Capa's time, he was still struggling to maintain his career as a photographer. (Out on an assignment in the summer of 1950, he quipped in a letter to Maria Eisner, "I'm having so much fun being a photographer again that I think I'll try to make a habit of it.") But, although he wasn't ready to give up photography altogether for business, he couldn't settle on any single direction for his work.

Besides his three trips to Israel, Capa did very little serious political photojournalism from 1948 on. In March of that year he and Charles Wertenbaker worked together covering the Italian elections, in which the Communists appeared to have a chance of scoring a major victory ("The only excitement," wrote Capa, "is in the hysterical New York press"), and that fall he traveled with Theodore H. White, then chief correspondent of the Overseas News Agency, through eastern Europe to investigate the ways in which the new order was changing life. (The Communists had seized complete control of the Hungarian and Czech governments early in 1948, and the Sovietization of Poland was well under way.) But Capa's pictures of Hungary and Poland were as dull as those he had taken in Russia, and in Czechoslovakia he was able to take hardly any pictures at all, for his cameras were confiscated soon after his arrival. Later that year and in 1949, stories on Harry S Truman's daily constitutional (during which he talked informally with reporters) and on Morocco's political and economic problems proved equally unexciting. Early in 1951 Capa wrote to Ed Thompson at *Life* saying, "This will be election year all over Europe, and I would like to get back to my old specialty of political reporting again"; but Thompson was annoyed at Capa's irresponsible handling of his recent story on Israel (the captions arrived inexcusably late) and gave him no assignments.

As for the biggest story of the period—the Korean War—Capa seems to have made no attempt whatsoever to get an assignment to cover it. True, he had vowed after his close call in Israel that he would never again photograph war, but such a vow, however seriously he may have meant it at the time, seems insufficient to explain why a man whose career might have been rescued from the doldrums by Korea chose not to go. (This was, after all, the kind of assignment for which he was supposedly guarding his freedom from marital attachments.) Perhaps the answer lies in a statement that Capa had once made to Martha Gellhorn: "In a war you must hate somebody or love somebody, you must have a position or you cannot stand what goes on." Although Capa's sympathies certainly didn't lie with the Communists, American involvement in the war was tainted by overtones of McCarthyism and the Red Scare. Moving in a strongly anti-McCarthy circle, Capa probably regarded the war as a morally ambiguous one, and thus one to be avoided. (John Morris, one of his closest friends, was particularly opposed to the war.) An added factor may have been that Capa was no longer on good terms with *Life*, the only publication that could have made his going to Korea financially worthwhile. (In any case, *Life* already had plenty of photographers covering the war.) Whatever his reasons, even after his old friend Gen. Matthew Ridgway was appointed commander in Korea, an appointment that would have ensured Capa a warm welcome, he stayed away. We can only speculate about his reasons, for no one seems to remember any discussion of them. As Jemy Hammond recalls, "Discussions of such matters simply didn't come up. It would have been out of character for Capa to make a pronouncement about why he wasn't going."

Opting not to go to war, he had to make do with the boredom of peace— although if he had to be bored, he wanted at least to be well paid. So he turned once again to the movies, this time making profitable deals to take publicity stills for films being shot on location in Europe and North Africa. He had begun this line of work in 1948, when he covered the filming of Giuseppe de Santis's *Bitter Rice* in Italy. (Capa was then finally having his long-postponed romance with the film's supporting actress, Doris Dowling.) But it was only after 1950 that he fully recognized the money-making potential of this work; he began not only to do more of it himself but also to make deals with such directors as John Huston and Howard Hawks giving Magnum exclusive coverage of their productions.

Far more interesting, both for Capa and for the viewer, are his pictures of Pablo Picasso and Henri Matisse. Every morning for a week in August 1948, while he was vacationing on the Riviera, Capa went with Picasso, Françoise Gilot, and their one-year-old son Claude to the beach at Golfe-Juan, where he took some wonderful, playful pictures of the family. The following August he returned to Picasso's unpretentious villa in Vallauris, near Antibes, with Gjon Mili, who wanted to photograph the artist drawing in the air with a flashlight. Working in a darkened room, Mili would be able to capture the ephemeral drawings on time exposures. Picasso was intrigued by the idea—and delighted with the results. Meanwhile, Capa went to Cimiez, a suburb of Nice, to photograph the seventy-nine-year-old Matisse in his apartment in the grand Victorian Hôtel Régina, where he was working on decorations for the chapel of the Dominican convent in Vence. Capa photographed the artist as he worked sitting up in bed, surrounded by art, books, and cats. But Matisse was far from bedridden; Capa's most memorable picture shows him grasping one end of a seven-foot-long bamboo pole tipped with charcoal to draw on a huge sheet of paper tacked to the wall, a working method that must have demanded considerable strength and extraordinary control.

While they were on the Riviera, Capa and Mili stayed at the house in Antibes that Irwin Shaw and his wife had rented for the summer, but they were hardly ideal houseguests. The Shaws never knew when the photographers were going to show up for meals or whom they might bring home, for they often picked up girls on the beach and brought them back to the house to spend the night. In the morning Shaw would have to steal clothes from his wife's closet for these girls to wear so that they could leave without creating a local scandal. When objections about any of this behavior were raised, Capa would apply his Hungarian charm—and, Shaw later wrote, you would not only forgive him but also "lend him the two hundred dollars he needed to replace the two hundred dollars you had lent him the night before and which he had promptly lost at the casino in Cannes." Finally, Marion Shaw gave her husband an ultimatum: as much as she liked Capa, he and Mili had to go.

During the late 1940s, no single American magazine had published Capa's work as regularly as *Illustrated* did in Britain. *Life* only rarely bought a story from him (it published his pictures of Moscow's eight-hundredth anniversary in 1947 and his coverage of the *Altalena* incident in 1948, but nothing further until his 1950 Israeli story ran in 1951*), so he turned increasingly to *Look*, *Collier's*, and *This Week* (the Sunday supplement to the New York *Herald Tribune*). But by 1950 *Holiday*, devoted to travel and rich living, was giving him nearly all the pleasurable and lucrative—if not terribly challenging or stimulating—assignments he wanted, and before long Magnum had an arrangement with the magazine much like that with *Illustrated*.†

Founded in 1946, *Holiday* was cashing in on the post-war boom in tourism and proffering snob-appeal to the American upper middle class eager to acquire at least a veneer of sophistication and cosmopolitanism. Capa, the seasoned man of the world, at home in glamorous circles everywhere, was the magazine's ideal contributor—so much so that the editors commissioned him not only to take photographs but also to write articles. Indeed, whatever charm or interest Capa's stories for *Holiday* may have lies in his amusing anecdotes and eccentric prose; most of the photographs can make no claim to being anything

---

* In the fall of 1949 *Life* sent him to Danbury, Connecticut, to do a story on artist Ludwig Bemelmans and his White Turkey Inn. The idea was apparently that the Parisian Capa would have especially good rapport with the painter of Parisian scenes, but the story was a disaster and mercifully remained unpublished.

† He had begun working for the magazine in 1948–49 in collaboration with Theodore White and Irwin Shaw; it was only in November 1949, with the publication of his own article on Budapest, that the pattern of Capa's contributions was set.

more than mere illustrations. (Capa, who was now beginning yet again to see his future more in writing than in photography, delighted in the by-line "By Robert Capa, with photographs by the author.")

The situation could hardly have been more comfortable for Capa; the magazine virtually paid him to go on vacation—to the Alps in the winter, to Deauville and Biarritz in the summer; to Rome, Norway, or the Netherlands in between. True, he had to take some pictures,* but mainly he had to have as many of his usual picaresque adventures as possible so that, when he returned to Paris or New York, he could dictate an entertaining account to one of the Magnum secretaries. For all this trouble he was not only paid, but paid well; and, of course, he could resell the stories to *Illustrated* and other European magazines for additional handsome fees.

Capa even tried to convince himself, through a somewhat comically contorted line of reasoning, that all this had some real significance and was a logical extension of his earlier career. "The most professional American tourists call themselves foreign correspondents," he wrote in one of his *Holiday* articles. "For years I have been talking with and taking pictures of kings, peasants and commissars, and I have ended up believing that curiosity, plus freedom to travel and low fares, is the closest thing to democracy in our time—so maybe democracy is tourism."

But of all Capa's projects for *Holiday* during the early 1950s, only one, the global survey of post-war youth ("Generation X"), made any real attempt to contribute to international understanding—and that project wasn't originally intended for the magazine. Capa talked the editors into buying it only after *McCall's* tried to impose "soppy" directives that he feared would render the survey worthless. "We intended to present the problem of a generation which has as its main problem 'going to war or not,' " Capa complained, "and we have not one soldier or even one militant person representing the trends of today: Communists, existentialists, Catholics, nationalists, imperialists, etc." For personal reasons, Capa decided to tackle the prototype story on a German boy himself. "I spent my twentieth year in Germany in 1933," he wrote, "when the twenty-year-old Germans were marching in shining boots and fighting in the streets under swastikas. The next time I saw young Germans was at the surrender of the Afrika Korps in Tunisia, and their boots were worn and dusty and their faces sullen. I didn't look forward with any pleasure to my third meeting, but my curiosity was greater than my dislike." The boy he

---

* Whenever possible, he would also have lined up additional stories to work on for other publications wherever he was.

chose, an Essen coal miner, was a thoroughly disillusioned former Nazi Youth member and soldier. "Will he continue to believe in the folly of Nazism and in 'no politics for me'?" asked the *Holiday* text based on Capa's observations. "Or is his deadly grim life, his defeat and his frustrated romanticism the perfect breeding place for another eruption of violent nationalism . . . ?"

Like nearly everything else about Capa at this time, his contribution to the project was characterized by profound ambivalence. Of his four stories, the two brief Norwegian ones were full of happiness and optimism almost too good to be true, while the longer studies of the German boy and a French girl were dark, troubled, and pessimistic. It was perhaps inevitable that a survey of the experiences and hopes of a "generation which has as its main problem 'going to war or not' " would lead him to a serious consideration of where he himself had come from, what he had become, and where he was going. The answers would help to lay the groundwork for a climactic year of personal crisis in 1953.

36

During his six-week stay in Budapest in the fall of 1948, Capa, highly amused by the irony of the situation, boasted to his friends that he was having a romance with an impoverished countess. But perhaps the irony had less to do with the countess's having come down in the world than with the young revolutionary's having adopted over the years so many traits of the old aristocracy. A few years later, Ernst Haas's wife, also a Hungarian countess, began to tease Capa that, like him, her father had five interests in life: women, cards, horses, eating, and drinking. "Why were you fighting us?" she would ask. "You should have joined us sooner instead of taking such a long way around."

Outwardly, at least, the boy of Pest had become a man of Buda. But, just as he had insisted in 1935 that he was really a "false petit bourgeois," so was he now something of a false aristocrat. His friends included movie stars and directors, famous writers and successful businessmen; he consorted with glamorous women, ate at the best restaurants and drank the best champagne, stayed in the best hotels, wore custom-made clothes, and bet heavily at cards and at the track, but he couldn't really afford such a life at all. He had a decent income, but he was living like a millionaire and, as a result, he was practically always broke. Of course, he made a great show of nonchalance about money, implying that it was good for nothing except bringing pleasure to himself and others. Extraordinarily generous, as always, he threw money around as though he had an endless supply. And yet, some of his closest friends recall that he used to spend a good deal of time rather nervously calculating his cash flow.

Capa could live as well as he did on his income partly because his friend Monsieur Wolf charged him much less than the Lancaster's usual rates; when the hotel became crowded, Capa would move into a room usually reserved for the staff. At the Lancaster, he wasn't a client, he was a member of the family. Whenever he returned from a trip, he would have presents for all the chambermaids, who, in turn, fussed over him and got his suits cleaned and his laundry done. With the *chasseurs* he joked and laughed, traded tips on the horses, went to the racetrack, drank, and played pinball. And they would run all sorts of errands for him, from placing bets to taking care of the green 1948 Ford roadster he inherited when Yale Joel left Paris. (Capa persisted in occasionally trying to drive and, inevitably, in having minor disasters when he did so. Once when he was driving back from the races, his car broke down, and he abandoned it on the side of the road. Having hitched a ride back to the Lancaster, he asked one of the *chasseurs* to retrieve the car and have it repaired; it turned out that it had simply run out of gas.) One of the *chasseurs*, whom Capa hired to work in the Magnum office, later recalled, "He was not a *patron* to me, but a friend." Indeed, Cartier-Bresson has remarked that Capa was a true anarchist, for he treated all people exactly the same way, no matter what their station in life.

Paris was Capa's home, and when he was in town he enjoyed a comfortable routine. He began each day with a long soak in the tub, during which he would read five or six newspapers before turning to a serious study of the day's racing papers. During and after his bath, he received a steady stream of visitors, many of them Hungarian and many of them petitioning for favors. To one he might give a pair of trousers, to another a jacket, and to still another money. In return, they ran bets for him; when they showed up at the Magnum office later in the day, everyone could tell whether Capa had won or lost simply by looking at their faces.

Often, especially during the summer when Jemy was around, Capa would go out to the races with her and such friends as John Huston, Howard Hawks, Anatole Litvak, John Steinbeck, Irwin Shaw, Gene Kelly, and Aly Khan. Through jockey Billy Pearson, who was racing in France in the early 1950s,

Capa got to know a lot of the jockeys and picked up inside tips. Even so, he lost much of the time anyway, for he would frequently change his bets on a whim at the last moment. Sometimes, unable to decide on one horse, he would buy tickets for several and stick them in different pockets. At the end of the race he would triumphantly reach into the appropriate pocket and pull out a winning ticket.

Many days there were lunches with friends at Fouquet's or Au Vert Bocage, late afternoon drinks at the Crillon with the journalists who congregated there or else a gin-rummy game in the photographers' locker room at the Time Inc. office, and dinners at Chez Anna, Maxim's, or some little restaurant that Chim, a great gourmet, had discovered. If Jemy wasn't in town, Capa would often have a date—always with a beautiful woman, like Hedy Lamarr or Ala, an Oriental model who worked at Dior. Then there were poker games with Huston at the Lancaster or evenings on the town with stops at such nightclub-bars as Monseigneur, Jimmy's, Novy, and Alexandre's. But Capa's favorite place was Chez Carrère, a nightclub on the Champs-Elysées, where he could count on meeting Sydney Chaplin, Charlie's son and himself an aspiring actor, and Noel Howard, a former Free French night-fighter pilot who worked on the production of films for Howard Hawks and Gene Kelly. When they first met, at a Parisian dinner party, Capa asked for a light and Howard obliged, extending his arm toward Capa and exposing a cufflink that his former wife had had custom-made for him at Cartier's; Capa, reaching for the light, exposed an identical cufflink. He had had a brief affair with the woman in New York early in the war. It was an amazing coincidence and marvelously funny; on the basis of their long-past, unwitting triangle, the two men became close friends and were soon spending a great deal of time together (along with Syd Chaplin, whom Capa met through Howard) in cafés, bars, nightclubs, and at the track, joking, teasing (Capa habitually called Howard "l'idiot"), and talking endlessly about women.

Every year around the first of December, Capa would go off to New York to see Jemy, to take care of Magnum and personal business, and to visit family and friends. After his return to Paris, he would usually spend a couple of weeks in the then little-known Swiss ski resort of Klosters. (Before the town's ski lift opened in 1949, people stayed very inexpensively in Klosters and went to Davos, half an hour away by train, to ski.) The crowd—which usually included such friends as Howard, Chaplin, Litvak, Peter Viertel, and Irwin Shaw—was mostly young and fun-loving, partying until three or four in the morning in the cozy and atmospheric cellar bar of the Chesa Grischuna (where a comfortable room and full board cost six dollars a day), sleeping late, then skiing the rest of the day.

On the surface, it seemed a glamorous and enjoyable life, and—troubled though he may have been about his career, romance, and the future—Capa generally gave the impression of being quite a happy and self-confident man in the late 1940s and early 1950s. Eve Arnold, for instance, recalls, "He had a charm and a grace and a lightness and a sense of self I've never seen in anybody else. There would be energy in a room as soon as he walked into it, the light would suddenly go on. You wanted to be near him, you wanted part of that effervescence, part of that zest." But there was also something quiet and understated about him. His funny stories were droll, never uproarious. At parties, according to dancer Sono Osato (who, with her husband, businessman Victor Elmaleh, saw a lot of Capa in New York and Paris), he never held court; he would usually be off to the side somewhere, slightly aloof, chatting with a few friends. Even his laughter was quiet. Noel Howard has written that "Bob had a very particular way of manifesting his amusement: his eyes half closed, his mouth split from ear to ear and clamped on his cigarette, he chuckled, very softly, with little gasps. You waited for him to burst into laughter, but he never did. From this purring one discerned an immense interior joy. Bob didn't miss much."

Very few glimpsed beyond that impression of joy. One who did was Irwin Shaw, who, as early as the fall of 1947, wrote:

Only in the morning, as he staggers out of bed, does Capa show that the tragedy and sorrow through which he has passed have left their marks on him. His face is gray, his eyes are dull and haunted by the dark dreams of the night; here, at last, is the man whose camera has peered at so much death and so much evil, here is a man despairing and in pain, regretful, not stylish, undebonair. Then Capa drinks down a strong, bubbling draught, shakes himself, experimentally tries on his afternoon smile, discovers that it works, knows once more that he has the strength to climb the glittering hill of the day, dresses, sets out, nonchalant, carefully light-hearted, to the bar of "21," or the Scribe, or the Dorchester, all places where this homeless man can be at home, where he can find his friends and amuse them and where his friends can help him forget the bitter, lonely, friendless hours of the night behind him and the night ahead.

By early in 1951, even the debonair and nonchalant public façade was beginning to show a few cracks under the pressure of Magnum's problems. "I am sorry that the New York situation is black, black, black," Capa wrote to Maria Eisner in February, "and considering that the outfit is fully bankrupt and you are expecting [a child] makes some radical thinking and acting very necessary." It's hardly surprising that Capa developed a painful stomach ulcer at this time. Among other things, his doctor prescribed a vacation and told him that he would have to drink milk and stay away from alcohol for a while. To carry out the first order, he went skiing in Klosters for a month with Gene Kelly and Noel Howard. As for the second, he jokingly told his friends that he was simply heeding Pierre Mendès-France's perennial call to all Frenchmen to drink less wine and more milk.

Maria Eisner left in May to have her baby. When Capa arrived in New York that fall, he asked Elmer Lower, who had just resigned from *Life*, to take over as president of Magnum, but Lower had other plans, and Capa ended up taking the job himself. He had been president in all but name for some time; now it was official. Ostensibly to announce his new responsibilities—but actually in a desperate attempt to create the impression that the collapsing agency was more successful than ever—Capa threw a big cocktail party at the Algonquin Hotel, near Magnum's new office in the Fawcett Building. The $900 tab was a great burden, but Capa still figured that nothing succeeds like the illusion of success—and he was right; his strategy turned the agency around. There would be plenty of further crises, but things would never again get quite so bad for Magnum.

Worried as he was about money—his own and Magnum's—that fall, Capa could at least still joke about the situation. At a party one night, he announced that he was planning to establish a new country for himself and his friends. Leaning against a mantel, a cigarette dangling from his mouth, his Italian silk shirt rumpled, he declared, "In my state of Cashpoor, of which I will be the treasurer, there will be no money."

Beneath the humor, there was a distinct note of weariness, for Capa was rapidly tiring of having constantly to maintain the illusion of success. Unable or unwilling to express his dissatisfaction directly, he expressed it obliquely in a story he did in the spring of 1952 for the "Generation X" project. Colette Laurent, a very pretty twenty-two-year-old French girl who worked as a model in haute couture salons and occasionally as an actress, was living in a hotel on the Rue du Faubourg St.-Honoré; Capa first met her in the café below the Magnum office. Although she projected an image of elegance, happiness, and wealth, was much in demand at fashionable parties, and was pursued by a never-ending succession of men who took her out to expensive restaurants and nightclubs, Colette was lonely, bored, pessimistic, desperately unhappy, and far from wealthy. She had long since lost touch with her family, had few close friends, no real home, and no regular job. She was very intelligent, well read, and cultured, but, wrote Capa, "Her life is superficial, artificial on the surface, and holds none of the good things except the material ones."

Like Colette Laurent, Capa himself had an irregular and far from large income on which he lived what appeared to others a very glamorous life. Like her, he lived in a succession of hotel rooms and owned very little besides beautiful clothes. And like her, he usually hid his loneliness and boredom behind a façade of gaiety and elegance. Surely he intended her story as both a vicarious confession and a cautionary tale.

Along the same lines, Ernst Haas remembers Capa telling a story (probably apocryphal and certainly metaphorical) that clearly reflects his jaundiced view of the pursuit of success. During the war, said Capa, Pinky had told him that the first thing she would like from Paris once the city was liberated was a bottle of Arpège; so when he entered the city, he was pleased to see a huge bottle of Arpège behind a broken shop window. The perfume was there for the taking, and he took it. Throughout the rest of the day, while he was trying to photograph the liberation and stay clear of snipers, he was encumbered by the bottle, but he managed to keep it safe. The next time he got to London, he gave the perfume to Pinky, who was absolutely thrilled. It was the most extravagant present she had ever received, she said, and she wanted to do with it the most extravagant thing she could imagine: she wanted to stand in the bathtub and have Capa pour the perfume over her from head to toe. She undressed and got into the tub, and Capa started to pour the perfume—but there was no scent! The bottle had been filled with water for the window display.

By the end of 1952, Capa had had enough of being Magnum's president and of having to deal constantly with everyone's problems. He wanted to get on with his own work, for which the agency's business left him far too little time; he had conceived Magnum as a convenience, but it had become an enormous burden. In January 1953 he persuaded John Morris to leave *The Ladies' Home Journal* and take over as president. At a big party, Capa got up on a chair to announce the new appointment. "Well, boys," he said with a sigh of relief only slightly exaggerated for comic effect, "from now on, take your problems to *him!*"

Soon it was Capa who was taking urgent problems to Morris. Upon his return to Paris on January 24, he found waiting for him a letter from the American embassy asking him to come in with his passport. Fearing the worst, he waited until February 2 to comply, at which time he was informed that instructions to confiscate his passport had been received from the State Department. When he demanded an explanation, he was told that it had been alleged he was a Communist and that a new regulation made the passports of suspected Communist Party members and sympathizers subject to revocation.

Capa never did learn who had accused him or what evidence had been brought against him. Noel Howard recalls that society columnist Cholly Knickerbocker had mentioned Capa in an article denouncing members of the expatriate crowd in Paris as "un-American"—apparently just because they lived outside the United States—but when Capa applied for a renewal of his passport in October 1952, he had executed an affidavit explaining in detail the reasons for his protracted residence abroad. After the FBI had checked up on his past and present affiliations with *The March of Time, The Ladies' Home Journal,* World Video, Magnum, and *Holiday*—for all of which he had worked or was working in Europe—the renewal was approved.

Although the joint FBI-State Department dossier on Capa runs to well over one hundred pages (much of which is devoted to routine bureaucratic paperwork), an examination of it—heavily censored—provides not a single clue to what actually triggered the revocation of his passport. Beyond the false accusation that had prompted the FBI to open the dossier, all the evidence in the file as of March 1948 was trivial and circumstantial: he had sold photographs to *Regards* during the Spanish Civil War; some of his pictures had appeared in a magazine published by the Friends of the Abraham Lincoln Brigade; he had been either a member or an honorary member of the "radical anti-fascist" Photo League; he had gone to the Soviet Union with Steinbeck; the *Daily Worker* had reported his *Herald Tribune* Forum speech with approval. In 1950 it was added that he had spoken out against jailing the Hollywood Ten. Nevertheless, although the Passport Office under Mrs. Ruth Shipley high-handedly denied passports to suspected Communists from the late 1940s on, Capa's was renewed in 1950 and again in 1952.

In regard to what has been blacked out from the dossier (the copies of some pages were almost entirely obliterated before being released), we can only speculate that Capa was mentioned as a member of two groups—the Hankow "Last Ditchers" and the so-called Jack Goodman Group—that came under government scrutiny during the period 1950–52. Freda Utley, who had herself been one of the "Last Ditchers," turned informer for Sen. Joseph McCarthy in 1950 and testified, during that and the following year, in various investigations into American support for the Chinese Communists. She was, however, primarily concerned with exposing writers and editors—such as Jack Belden, Joseph Barnes, Edgar Snow, and Theodore H. White, all of whom were friends of Capa's—whom she felt were misleading the American public about China. In her 1951 best-seller, *The China Story*, in which she attacked those men as well as the late Brig. Gen. Evans Carlson, the late Agnes Smedley, and other "Last Ditchers," Utley didn't even mention Capa. Whatever charges, if any, she may have made secretly against him seem to have carried little weight, for although a brief intensification of the investigation of

Capa in August 1951 may possibly have been sparked by them, they were not substantial enough to prevent the renewal of his passport in 1952.*

As it happened, a number of the China experts denounced by Utley also belonged to the Jack Goodman Group, which, during the spring and summer of 1952, was investigated by the Senate's Internal Security subcommittee as part of its inquiry into "subversive infiltration of the radio, television, and entertainment industries." During his two-month stay in New York in the winter of 1951–52, Capa had been involved with the informal group of writers, journalists, and editors who met once a week at the Greenwich Village house of Simon and Schuster editor-in-chief Jack Goodman to discuss what could be done to oppose the blacklisting to which anti-Communist hysteria had given rise. He was introduced to the group by either Millard Lampell, Jack Belden, or Joseph Barnes, a former *Herald Tribune* foreign editor who was then working at Simon and Schuster. John Morris, whom Capa brought into the group, recalls that among the writers who put in appearances were John Hersey, Arthur Miller, William L. Shirer, and Edgar Snow.

Although the Senate subcommittee accused the group of being "in a position to exert a synchronized and powerful influence for Communism or pro-Communist causes throughout a large segment of the publishing field," it actually did nothing of the sort. The members put up money to investigate *Counterattack*, a witch-hunting newsletter; they contributed to a column in *The New Republic*; and they placed a full-page ad in *The New York Times* protesting the blacklist. (Capa was present when the ad was signed, but he didn't sign it himself, for he was already afraid of passport troubles.) But most of the time the group just sat around drinking Jack Goodman's whisky and talking, getting down to politics only occasionally. Lampell recalls that Capa didn't attend many meetings, but when he was present he often spoke passionately. "One found oneself nodding agreement with Capa as he prowled the room and shouted—and then, afterward, wondering what the hell he had actually said." Indeed, Capa was such a marginal figure in the group that he wasn't even mentioned in any of the published hearings, and, once again, any evidence brought against him secretly was not serious enough to prevent the renewal of his passport in 1952.

As soon as John Morris received Capa's cable telling him what had happened at the embassy, he hired Morris Ernst, co-counsel of the American Civil Liberties Union and a senior partner of a prestigious New York law firm,

---

* Capa's FBI dossier provides evidence that such an investigation took place but doesn't indicate what prompted it.

to appeal the revocation.* Following Ernst's advice, Capa proceeded to answer all possible charges that he could imagine. Furthermore, he not only denied past or present membership in the Communist Party (the Board of Passport Appeals reviewed only the cases of those who made such a declaration) but also stressed his coverage of World War II for such unimpeachably American magazines as *Life, Collier's,* and *The Saturday Evening Post,* as well as his friendships with such highly respected American generals as Matthew Ridgway, James Gavin, and Manton Eddy. He then went on to mention that the Voice of America and the pamphlet division of the State Department had just approached Magnum about reproducing and distributing the "Generation X" project, which *Holiday* was then publishing in three installments.

At the end of his affidavit Capa wrote, "At this very moment, when I should proceed to Italy to do a story for *Holiday* magazine on the skiing resort of Cortina d'Ampezzo, and right after that a story on an American movie which will be shot in Amalfi in southern Italy, my professional existence and livelihood is gravely compromised." Unable to do anything but wait, and unable to leave France, Capa went off to ski in Val d'Isère. Two weeks later, early in March, he wrote to John Morris, "I am back, indeed I am back in circulation." The American embassy in Paris had given him a "patchwork document" that would enable him to go to Italy while waiting for the final decision on his appeal. In the middle of the month he left for Amalfi and Ravello (only a few miles from Maiori and the Chiunzi Pass), where he spent three weeks on assignment from *Picture Post* photographing the production of John Huston's film *Beat the Devil,* based on a novel that Claud Cockburn had written under the pseudonym James Helvick. Although Huston and Truman Capote were writing the script under great pressure as the filming proceeded (and although Capa must still have been nervous about his passport), the atmosphere on and off camera was generally characterized by jovial camaraderie—with alfresco meals, lots of clowning around, and all-night poker games. Huston and Humphrey Bogart, who was starring in the film, won most of the time; Capa and Capote were the big losers. "Their services on the picture came pretty cheap," Huston has written, "because we regularly won back whatever salaries we paid them."

It wasn't until mid-May—when he was shocked to receive a bill for $5,400 from Morris Ernst—that Capa fully realized how little he could afford such losses. He had gotten his passport back at the beginning of the month, but

---

* Ernst had successfully represented Margaret Bourke-White in 1951 when she had been accused of being a Communist.

he'd had no idea that it would cost him so much. John Morris recalls that Ernst was "very cold and secretive" in his handling of Capa's case, but he remembers hearing that Ernst had hinted that "someone in Denmark—or was it a Dutch woman?—had put the finger on Capa." According to his recollection, moreover, the crisis was resolved when it turned out to be a case of mistaken identity.*

The loss of his passport was the catalyst that finally brought to a head Capa's increasing dissatisfaction with his life—the kind of dissatisfaction that he had begun to express indirectly in his story about Colette Laurent a year earlier. Sick of a superficial life holding "none of the good things except the material ones," bored with his insubstantial and meaningless work, frustrated in his relationship with Jemy, heavily in debt, and rapidly approaching his fortieth birthday, he said in the first letter he had written to Jemy in months,

> The last four months' passport crisis has become a general crisis, and now that the passport is there the user doesn't know what to do or where to go. My writing stank and the pictures are no good and Magnum is an office and I must do something again not only to make a living but to live again. And all this is cruel and not writing is even more cruel and lying and fooling ourselves would be also cruel and there is no solution anywhere. I do love you, but the routine of the past years has become impossible and to change it and settle down is even more impossible from every angle and I don't know what to say or propose.

Confused as he felt about Jemy, Capa had at last reached one firm decision about his career. To John Morris he wrote, "I have now definitely decided to get back to real work, and soon. What and where I do not know, but the Deauville and Biarritz and motley movie period is over." He knew what he didn't want to do, but he still couldn't quite make up his mind about what he *did* want to do. On the one hand, he wrote, he was playing with the idea of traveling around the world for *Holiday* to do an updated version of Jules Verne's famous story. (He had already discussed the project with the editors, and they were enthusiastic.) On the other hand, however, he was seriously

---

* Peter Viertel recalls that Ernst was able to do very little for Capa. Finally Capa asked Viertel to help, and Viertel asked his friend Henry B. Hyde, a lawyer and a Republican with important connections in Washington, to intercede. Viertel claims that Hyde spoke to Mrs. Shipley at the Passport Office and cleared things up, but Hyde says he doesn't remember talking to Mrs. Shipley about Capa. He was called in on the case, but he doesn't recall what action he took or how the matter was finally settled.

thinking about trying to get an assignment to cover the French Indochina War "or any other proposition which would get me back to reporting on my own type of territory." He still didn't mention the Korean War (which continued until the armistice was signed at the end of July), even though—at least in retrospect—that war appears to have been far less ambiguous from a moral standpoint than that in Indochina. But evidently Capa—or part of him, anyway—was so desperate to get back to the kind of work he did best that he was in no mood for splitting hairs. Indeed, he was impatient to be off, "in any direction," by the first of June if possible.

But, at the end of May, before he could put any of his big plans into action, a slipped spinal disk pressing against his sciatic nerve began to cause him intense pain. "I need an express note," he wrote to John Morris, "explaining what is the most favorable way to fill out my insurance documents. Should it be sickness, or should it be accident? Should the accident have come from skiing or handling cameras? . . . While it cannot be determined on which exact date or [in which] accident the disk slipped out, it happened this spring and could have been due to any rash movement, and it could have been and must have been on its way out for some time." Because his insurance covered only work-related accidents, he ended up claiming that the pain had begun on May 26 when a heavy camera bag on his shoulder suddenly slipped— and then he joked in a letter to the New York office of Magnum, "I'm now convinced that paying insurance is considered an American activity, and that the different committees and investigators will indict me of perjury instead of injury."

A few days after the pain began, he went to London to see a specialist and, despite his discomfort, to help Bischof and Haas cover the coronation of Queen Elizabeth II. (He took a few shots of the wet and chilly crowd lining the route and then watched the procession with Huston and Bogart from the balcony of Les Ambassadeurs.) Ordered to take two weeks of complete rest in sunshine, he went off to the Lido in Venice, but, since the pain got worse rather than better, he left early and returned to Paris for orthopedic treatments. After the first one, the pain got so bad that codeine no longer helped. Capa was in such agony that he just lay on the floor of the Magnum office and wept. At the end of the month he wrote to John Morris, "This is definitely my black year—which is promising, because after these disasters of mine everything will be such a relief and so easy to do."

Since daily X-ray treatments failed to alleviate the pain, Capa flew to London on July 7 and entered the Harley Street Nursing Home, where he was put into traction and given "faradic and galvanic treatments." After a week of this he felt somewhat better. He felt well enough, in fact, that although he was still in traction during the day, he was taking one of the nurses out dancing at night—which is probably why he had a relapse.

When he was discharged early in August, still practically crippled with sciatica, he was ordered to wear a corset-like brace day and night. In physical and emotional misery, he went with Jemy down to St.-Jean-de-Luz, near Biarritz, to stay with John Huston's wife Ricki. Syd Chaplin, screenwriter Harry Kurnitz, and lyricist Adolph Green were also staying at the house, and Peter Viertel and Irwin Shaw had rented houses nearby, but, even surrounded by friends, Capa was miserable. He didn't see how he could work if the pain continued, and, if he couldn't work, how was he ever going to get out of debt? (He still hadn't paid Morris Ernst, and, on top of that, he now had enormous medical bills. His insurance eventually paid most of them, but it didn't cover loss of income incurred through disability, and he had to borrow several thousand dollars from Magnum and from friends.) He was overweight, his complexion looked pasty, and he was drinking heavily, even though alcohol did little to help the pain. In desperation he would lie face down on the ground and have Ricki Huston walk on his back to massage it, and he even tried acupuncture, but for a while nothing really seemed to do much good.

Finally, at the beginning of September, though still far from fully recovered, he felt well enough to try to begin functioning again. The first order of business was the Magnum shareholders' meeting, where there was much talk of shaky finances and of saleable group projects—"Trains of the World" was one, "The Seventh Day" another. But Capa, despite his bad experience with World Video, was most excited about getting Magnum involved in television projects. "I myself," he wrote to John Morris, "as undecided as I am for my future, find one of my main temptations in this sphere." He was particularly eager to get Magnum photographers to carry movie cameras as well as still cameras wherever they went on assignment. "You cannot do both at the same time," he wrote, "but you can at one place exhaust yourself photographically and then use the still job as research and do the whole subject differently in movies."

Capa's interest in movies, however, wasn't so great that he was willing to get involved with directing a Hollywood production; his 1946 experiences had cured him of that desire forever. During September, Howard Hawks offered him "a nice sum of money" to co-direct his film *Land of the Pharaohs*, to be shot in Egypt in the spring of 1954. Desperately broke and heavily in debt as he was, Capa turned the offer down, gracefully pointing out that his passport was so full of Israeli stamps that he would never be able to get an Egyptian visa.

His back somewhat improved, Capa spent much of the fall shuttling back and forth between London and Paris. Staying at the Pastoria Hotel, where he had taken a room briefly in 1941 and where his room now became known as "The Racing Room," he was involved in all sorts of secret and not-so-secret negotiations to get Len Spooner hired as picture editor of *Picture Post*, to get himself hired as a consultant on retainer, to enlarge the magazine, and to have it replace *Illustrated* as Magnum's British outlet and patron. All these negotiations proved successful.

In the middle of December, before going to Klosters for a two-and-a-half-month recuperative vacation, Capa went to Cannes to try to photograph the Aga Khan for *Holiday*. Knowing that it would be difficult to get the old man to cooperate, he had asked Aly Khan to intercede with his father—to which Aly replied, "Ask me for a horse, ask me for a girl, but not for this." The Aga Khan did, indeed, prove to be a reluctant subject and kept Capa waiting for ten days before giving in.

Early in February 1954, while he was still in Klosters, Capa received an offer that was exactly what he needed to get himself back on his feet. The Mainichi Press, for which he had free-lanced in Paris in 1935–36, was planning to launch a new magazine, *Camera Mainichi*, in April and invited him to visit Japan for six weeks to help promote it. He could photograph whatever interested him, and Mainichi—besides paying all his expenses—would pay generously for any pictures it published. The only stipulation was that he use Japanese-made cameras, lenses, and film, all of which Mainichi would supply free of charge; at the end of his stay they would become his to keep. He would also be free to work on assignments from American and European magazines, although Mainichi reserved the right to publish the stories in Japan.

Excited by the prospect of the trip, Capa remained in Klosters until mid-March, doing a lot of skiing to strengthen his back (he was still wearing his brace) and to work off some of the weight he had gained during the previous year. In his enthusiasm, however, he nearly went too far. One afternoon, coming down the mountainside very fast, he approached a narrow ridge above a high, jagged cliff and suddenly found that he couldn't turn; his skis were out of control, and he was heading right for the precipice. All he could do was collapse and hope that he wouldn't skid over the edge. He came so close that a skiing instructor, Flury Clavadetcher, who was with him, had to inch over, grab his feet, and pull him back out of danger.

Superstitious though he was, Capa chose to ignore this "warning" and went back to work full speed ahead. From Klosters he went to Rome, where he spent a week shooting stills of Joseph L. Mankiewicz's film *The Barefoot Contessa*, starring Bogart and Ava Gardner. Next he made a quick trip to London to arrange some Magnum projects, taking time out only to visit Pinky, who had gotten a divorce from Chuck Romine and was living at the Mileses' house near Reading. And from London he went on to Ireland to see John Huston and discuss his film *Moby Dick*, for which he was to shoot stills upon his return from Japan. He was also eager to work out a deal giving Magnum exclusive coverage of all movies made by a group of independent filmmakers (Capa called it "a big Magnum") that Huston was trying to organize.

Although it had been almost two years since *Life* last gave Capa an assignment, as soon as he returned to Paris he received an urgent request from the magazine to do a story on Schweinfurt, a city in northern Bavaria whose ball-bearing and gelatin-explosive factories had made it a primary target for Allied bombers during the war. The editors were working on a special issue about the rebirth of Germany and had just learned that Schweinfurt, one of the few cities where extensive ruins could still be seen, offered dramatic contrasts of devastation and reconstruction; Capa, who had taken such memorable photographs of Germans amidst ruins at the end of the war, seemed the perfect man for the story. Having two weeks free before he was to leave for Japan, he accepted.

With Time Inc. correspondent Simon Bourgin, Capa spent several days just walking around Schweinfurt, talking to people, getting acquainted with possible subjects, enjoying life, but taking very few pictures. When Bourgin began to worry, Capa explained that he was doing his research—and besides, he said, Henry Luce owed them a good time.

Once he finally began to work, he photographed the reconstructed ball-bearing factory and the still ruined explosives plant, as the *Life* editors had particularly requested, but most of his story focused on people. He was especially delighted to discover that the U.S. 16th Infantry Regiment (the outfit he had photographed at El Guettar, at Troina, and on D-Day) was stationed in Schweinfurt, although there was only one officer left who had seen action in all those battles. Adding a postscript to one of his biggest stories of the war, Capa photographed him with a German former officer who had fought at Troina; the two were now good friends.

By the time Capa returned to Paris, he had only four or five days to get ready to leave for Japan. He was quite excited about going, but—becoming, if anything, progressively less able to figure out what he wanted to do with the rest of his life—he couldn't decide whether to regard the trip as a new beginning or as an ending for his picture-taking career. He was at last getting back to work after his "black year." (He wrote to his mother that he had "a year to catch up with.") And he had already lined up some work for after his return from Japan. But for the past nine years photography had brought him more frustration than satisfaction, and now that he was forty perhaps it was really time to move on to something else. In March he had said to Pinky, "It's not a job for a grown man to click a camera." And just before he left for Japan he told his old Arab girlfriend that he was tired of photography and reporting; he would come back, he said, and give a party to celebrate the end of his career. "I will find a beautiful apartment in Paris," he told her, "and you will decorate it for me. I cannot be bothered. Perhaps I'll even marry." The day of his departure for Japan, April 11, Capa told Bourgin that he thought photography was for kids. He was sick of it, but he was a prisoner of his own legend. He said that what he really wanted to do was either to write a novel or to become involved in a major business venture—something really big and exciting and challenging.

37

For three weeks Capa had a marvelous time in Japan, where his work was so highly esteemed that he received a hero's welcome. He wrote to Werner Bischof, "I am very happy with the Orient," and to his friend Hiroshi Kawazoe, whom he hadn't seen since before the war, he jubilantly remarked that Japan was "a photographer's paradise." He traveled to Kyoto, Nara, Osaka, Kobe, Amagasaki, and everywhere he went he focused especially on children. He was also fascinated by the contrast of East and West in Japanese cities and took many pictures of Western-style amusement districts, where American movies were being shown and one could play the slot machines—as, of course, he proceeded to do.

At the end of April 1954, Howard Sochurek, the *Life* photographer who had been covering the French Indochina War for the past several months, learned that his mother had had a heart attack and might live only another few days. When he cabled the New York office for permission to go home immediately for thirty days, the editors asked him to give them one day to find a replacement. That day Ray Mackland, *Life*'s assignment editor, had lunch with John Morris in New York and, knowing that Capa was in Japan, asked whether he might be interested. Morris said he didn't think Capa could possibly take the assignment, but he saw no harm in asking him. *Life* then cabled Capa an offer of $2,000 for the thirty-day period, plus expenses from Tokyo and a $25,000 Lloyds of London insurance policy. Without waiting for an answer, the editors authorized Sochurek to start for home but asked him to make a stopover in Tokyo to talk to Capa.

They arranged to meet at 6:30 p.m. on April 29 in the bar of the Tokyo Press Club. When Capa finally showed up at eight o'clock, he didn't apologize for being an hour and a half late but was so charming that Sochurek couldn't stay angry for long. At dinner Sochurek briefed him, telling him what *Life* had already covered and explaining the magazine's position on the war. David Douglas Duncan had spent two months on assignment in Indochina in 1953 and had filed a story in which he claimed that the French were fighting very badly and that it was just a matter of time before they would be driven out. Since Ed Thompson was away on vacation when the story was filed, and Henry Luce, who believed that it was in America's best interest to back the French in Indochina at any cost, was also away, the story was published, creating something of an international diplomatic incident. Luce, of course, was furious and insisted that *Life* send another photographer to Indochina to do a story that would counteract the effect of Duncan's piece. Thompson sent Sochurek, instructing him to try to find places where the French were fighting well but telling him that if what he saw only confirmed Duncan's view, he should report that.

Duncan had been in Indochina during a relatively slow period, but when Sochurek got there, all hell was breaking loose. He arrived just in time to cover the first French parachute drop on the military base at Dienbienphu in November 1953, and then went on to cover fighting in the Red River delta. By March 1954 some 50,000 Vietminh troops had encircled Dienbienphu, and by the end of April the situation of the trapped 13,000-man French garrison was desperate; but no journalists could get anywhere near the place.

Sochurek recalls that since he felt rather competitive toward Capa and didn't particularly want this famous photographer on his turf, he emphasized the constant, omnipresent danger of guerrilla attacks and booby traps in Indochina and stressed that it wasn't possible to protect oneself rationally; it was a crazy war. They talked until after midnight, but Capa seemed very remote, as though lost in his private thoughts, and Sochurek felt he wasn't really reaching him. Several times Capa questioned the value of his going to Indochina and expressed great reluctance about taking the assignment. When they parted, he said he still hadn't made up his mind.

Perhaps, however, he was simply playing hard to get; he had, after all, been thinking for at least a year about going to Indochina. And although he talked about giving up photography altogether, he was enjoying his work in Japan so much that he was having second thoughts. If he was going to remain a photographer, he would, as he had resolved during his passport crisis, have to "get back to reporting on [his] own type of territory"—in other words, he would have to cover politics and war. Photographer Evelyn Hofer remembers seeing Capa in Paris shortly before he left for Japan and getting the impression that he felt rather threatened by David Douglas Duncan, who seemed to be eclipsing his reputation as the greatest living war photographer. Indochina, he must have reasoned, would give him an opportunity to re-establish himself.

Furthermore, Capa needed the money. The *Life* offer was hardly over-generous,* but it would certainly help to pay off the debts he had accumulated the previous year, and the $2,000 was just basic guarantee money. For this Capa was expected to do no more than "sit on his ass in Hanoi." If the situation flared up and he had to cover combat, he would get paid more,† and he would be paid for whatever photographs *Life* ended up publishing. Finally, his contract with Mainichi expressly provided that he was free to leave at any time if an assignment came up outside Japan, as long as he eventually returned to complete his six weeks' obligation.

Capa decided to accept the assignment, and on April 30 he cabled Morris to tell him. That night, when Morris called to say, "Don't think you *have* to go," Capa replied that he was going only because he wanted to. Following up the next day, he wrote,

> I much appreciate your calling, but be assured that I didn't take the job from a sense of duty but with real great pleasure. Shooting for me at this moment is much fun and possibly shooting on a very complicated subject but down my own alley [will be] even more so. I know that Indochina might be only sheer frustration, but somehow it should be one story anyway.

Perhaps he was too enthusiastic for his own good. Several years earlier Ernst Haas had volunteered to cover the Korean War for Magnum, but Capa had sent him off to do a story in Greece instead. Later, when Haas asked him for an explanation, he replied, "Ernst, you were so enthusiastic to go into war. One gets very easily killed that way."

---

* It was exactly double the $1,000 per month that the magazine was then paying Sochurek.
† John Morris cable to Capa, April 30, 1954: "Price subject considerable upraising if becomes hazardous."

Since he had promised Mainichi that he would cover the big demonstrations in Tokyo on May Day, Capa postponed his departure until the following day. Then, on Sunday, May 2, he flew to Bangkok, where he waited several days for his visas. He finally reached Hanoi on about May 9, just after Dienbienphu had fallen to the Vietminh. "Here I am in Hanoi," he wrote to Magnum's Paris office, "and the story is over before I could have touched my cameras." He hadn't, however, entirely missed the story of Dienbienphu, for the Vietminh announced that they would allow the French to evacuate some 750 wounded soldiers from among the thousands who had been taken prisoner. Capa and *Life* reporter Don Wilson left at once for Luang Prabang, in northern Laos, to cover the operation.

Capa duly photographed the seriously wounded being transferred from helicopters to the planes that would rush them to Hanoi for treatment, but he seems to have been more interested in the tent city where soldiers who had made a long march in retreat from positions around Dienbienphu endured boredom while waiting for transport. He focused particularly on one barefoot French soldier sitting in a tent, his eyes still glazed from his ordeal. This exhausted, unshaven, and swollen-footed soldier must have seemed to Capa a symbol of the French plight in Indochina.

From Luang Prabang, where he also photographed the life of the city extensively, Capa returned to Hanoi on about May 17. On Friday, May 21, he went for the day to Namdinh, forty-five miles to the southeast, to do some preliminary reconnaissance for a story on the military situation in the Red River delta. When he got back to Hanoi that night, he told Wilson that his best pictures of the day were of a young, grief-stricken Vietnamese woman weeping over her husband's grave in a military cemetery.

Over the weekend, Capa roamed Hanoi and photographed an eclectic cross-section of its sights, from a Catholic children's procession to people swimming at the swank Cercle Sportif. Then, on Monday, he and *Time* correspondent John Mecklin flew to Namdinh with Gen. René Cogny, the strapping commander of French ground forces in northern Vietnam, who was making the trip to inspect Foreign Legion troops and award decorations in an effort to raise morale badly hurt by the fall of Dienbienphu. During lunch, Capa and Mecklin accepted sector commander Lt. Col. Jean Lacapelle's invitation to go along on the next day's mission to evacuate and raze two small forts, Doaithan and Thanhne, along the road from Namdinh to Thaibinh, twenty miles to the east. With the rice harvest under way in the delta, the French feared that the Vietminh—already stepping up its activity in the area— might soon launch an all-out battle to capture as much as possible of the nation's food supply, and they wanted to preclude any further Dienbienphu-style disasters. They would withdraw from the countryside and instead concentrate their strength in such major centers as Namdinh.

That afternoon, the two journalists drove out to take a look at the critical town of Phuly, a few miles to the west, where the Vietminh had leveled every vestige of French influence except a large church and the Foreign Legion fort. Back in Namdinh that night, in a seedy and bug-ridden establishment that called itself (incongruously and in English) the Modern Hotel, they ran into Scripps-Howard correspondent Jim Lucas, whom Capa had met in Hanoi. As the three men sat around talking, Capa, sipping cognac mixed with warm soda water, remarked, "This is the last good war. The trouble with all you guys who complain so much about French public relations is that you don't appreciate that this is a reporter's war. Nobody knows anything and nobody tells you anything, and that means a good reporter is free to go out and get a beat every day."

At seven o'clock the next morning, Tuesday, May 25, a jeep stopped by the Modern Hotel to pick up Capa, Mecklin, and Lucas, whom the other two had invited to join them. While waiting on the outskirts of Namdinh for the task force of 2,000 men and 200 vehicles to be ferried across the river, Capa—who had equipped himself for the day not only with a Contax camera loaded with black-and-white film and a Nikon with color film but also with a flask of cognac and a thermos filled with iced tea—assured his companions that this was "going to be a beautiful story" and promised them, "I will be on my good behavior today. I will not insult my colleagues, and I will not once mention the excellence of my work."

Having gotten across the river, the column began to proceed toward Doaithan, the day's first objective, but it hadn't gone far when, at 8:40, snipers attacked the lead trucks. The convoy halted and French tanks opened fire, but the peasants working in rice fields beside the road or walking along it, carrying baskets of rice or driving flocks of ducks to the market in Namdinh, kept right on as though nothing were happening. Admiring their sangfroid, which accorded with his own sense of the necessity of retaining one's dignity under fire, Capa refused to stay under cover and instead waded out into a rice paddy to get good shots of the peasants juxtaposed with the French convoy. (When a French motorcyclist deliberately rode so close to the roadside that he forced some peasants to jump out of the way, Capa scornfully remarked to Mecklin, "Look at that s.o.b. making new Viet Minh.") He was so pleased with his shots that he decided to make this juxtaposition the theme of his Red River delta story, which he planned to call "Bitter Rice," taking the name from the Giuseppe de Santis film for which he had shot stills in Italy in 1948.

The column started up again after a few minutes but soon halted once more when a truck drove over a mine, killing four men and wounding six.

Viet Minh mortars gouged at our column [wrote Lucas], Viet Minh snipers picked off an occasional straggler, and our own artillery roared back. Villages along the road caught fire as tanks sent shells crashing through them. An abandoned church that concealed snipers was destroyed. The Viet Minh dead lay where they fell. Our own we carried back.

Capa was everywhere. Once under mortar fire he loaded a wounded Vietnamese soldier into the jeep and drove him back to an outpost.

By mid-morning the column reached the fort at Dongquithon, where word came through that there would be a delay of several hours while the road ahead was repaired. Using a favorite tactic, guerrillas had cut the road with several wide, deep trenches and had completely destroyed the approaches to two bridges. Capa walked to the head of the column to photograph the bull-dozers and the work crew of two hundred captured Vietminh who had been brought along in anticipation of such damage.

An officer had invited the three journalists to lunch at the fort, but Capa didn't show up. Instead, he went on working for a while and then, to get out of the intense midday sun, he stretched out for a snooze in the shade under a truck, where Mecklin and Lucas found him shortly after two o'clock. A few minutes later, when they heard that advance units had reached Doaithan, they jumped into their jeep, maneuvered around the other vehicles in the column, and, at about 2:25, arrived at the small, crumbling fort surrounded by barbed wire and creeping vegetation. The French and Vietnamese flags had already been lowered, and Capa was able to get only a few good shots of the garrison—carrying its furniture and its pots and pans—evacuating the fort. Demolition experts were planting explosives around the crenellated Beau Geste–style structure, and as soon as the convoy was safely past, they would blow it up. Capa very much wanted a good shot of the explosion.

A couple of hundred yards beyond Doai Than [wrote Mecklin] the column was stalled again by a Viet Minh ambush. We turned into the field and talked to the sector commander, Lt. Col. Jean Lacapelle. Capa asked, "What's new?" The colonel's reply was a familiar one: "*Viets partout*" ("Viet Minh everywhere").

As the column began moving again Capa climbed on the jeep hood for a shot. A truck loaded with infantry behind us tooted vigorously but Capa took his time. "That was a good picture," he said as he climbed down.

But the column halted again almost immediately. This was at a point one kilometer beyond Doai Than and three kilometers short of the final objective, Thanh Ne. The road was three or four feet above the paddies and here served as a dike for a little stream which ran along the right side. . . .

The sun beat down fiercely. There was firing in every direction: French artillery, tanks and mortars behind us, the clatter of small arms from woods surrounding a village 500 yards to our left, heavy small arms fire mixed with exploding French shells in another village 500 yards ahead and to our right, the sporadic ping of slugs passing overhead, the harrowing curr-rump of mines and enemy mortars.

A young Vietnamese lieutenant approached us and began practicing his English, which was limited to a labored "How are you, sir? I am good." Capa was exquisitely bored and climbed up on the road, saying, "I'm going up the road a little bit. Look for me when you get started again." This was about 2:50.

Mecklin and Lucas judged the situation too dangerous for wandering around, but Capa refused to let the danger stop him; he was, after all, a gambler. "For a long, indecisive minute," wrote Lucas, "he crouched behind the protective bulk of our jeep—ready to leap back or spring ahead—as if testing the temper of the Viet Minh fire. He decided he would risk it." Mecklin had noted earlier in the day that Capa always showed "an expertness in calculated risk that only a man in his fifth war could know. He was cautious about crossing exposed areas, but if he saw a good picture which could only be made with risk he took the risk."

When he left Mecklin and Lucas, Capa walked up the road to where it curved to the left, and then he went down into the protected, V-shaped area between the road and the dike of the stream that flowed off to the right. After photographing a platoon advancing through the tall grass, he went back up onto the road and took a few pictures of bored soldiers passing the time beside their jeeps and trucks. Then he went back down into the field and caught up with the advancing men, of whom he shot one more picture in black and white and one in color. The latter was the last photograph Capa ever took, for as he reached the gentle, grassy slope of the dike and began to walk up it—perhaps to photograph the men from another angle or to catch the explosion at Doaithan, which took place at 2:55—he stepped on a Vietminh anti-personnel mine.

As soon as Mecklin and Lucas heard that Capa had been killed—or at least gravely injured—they rushed to find him. When they reached him, just before 3:10, he was on his back and still breathing—although his left leg had been blown off almost completely and he had a gaping chest wound. His Contax was clutched in his left hand, but his Nikon had been blown several feet away by the blast.* Mecklin called Capa's name softly several times, and the second or third time he did so Capa moved his lips slightly, as though he had been disturbed in his sleep, but no sound came. When the explosion of several other mines nearby brought Colonel Lacapelle to where Capa was lying, he quickly flagged down an ambulance and had him taken back to Dongquithon, five kilometers away. There a Vietnamese doctor pronounced Capa dead.

Word of Capa's death reached Paris and New York within hours. Many who received the news thought at first that there must be some horrible mistake, some crossed wires confusing the identities of two Magnum photographers, for earlier in the day they had learned that Werner Bischof had been killed in Peru on May 16, when his car plunged off a road high in the Andes. But there was no mistake.

Capa's remains were buried in Hanoi until arrangements could be made for transport to New York. (At the request of Julia Friedmann, whose grief and rage were unassuageable, John Morris, a Quaker, arranged for burial in the cemetery of his meeting house in Amawalk, thirty miles north of the city. Julia had turned down the U.S. Army's offer of a plot in the Arlington National Cemetery, saying that her son was not a soldier, but a man of peace.) At the ceremony in Hanoi, General Cogny provided an honor guard and pinned one of France's highest honors, the Croix de Guerre with Palm, Order of the Army, to the American flag draped over Capa's casket. Capa had, however, never cared much for military decorations. A much more appropriate and touching tribute was a wreath from the staff of La Bonne Casserole, a Hanoi restaurant where, wrote Mecklin, Capa had "terrified the waiters, charmed the hostess and taught the bartender to mix American martinis." The ribbon on the wreath was inscribed simply, "A notre ami."

---

* He had switched back to the black-and-white Contax but stepped on the mine before he had a chance to use it. The Nikon was then presumably hanging by a strap.

38

When Capa died, he left behind a few unpaid hotel bills, some cameras, a closetful of beautiful clothes (he had never owned a stick of furniture and had few material possessions of any kind), a devastated family, a woman who had hoped to marry him, and a couple of hundred people who considered him a friend (although in many cases the degree of affection they felt was out of all normal proportion to the amount of time they had spent with him). But, above all, he left behind an extraordinary body of work that showed not only the nature of war as it had never been shown before but also a tremendous sympathy for individuals in all kinds of circumstances, and a legend that would long continue to inspire other photographers and to delight and sadden his friends.

His mother was implacable; she never really recovered from his death, and herself died seven years later. As for Cornell, his brother's death changed his life radically. Beyond his grief, he was haunted by the question of what would become of Capa's work. Photojournalism, for all its immediate impact, seemed highly ephemeral; few museums were then collecting or exhibiting such work, there was almost no market for original prints, and the handful of photographic monographs being published reached a small audience (although the potential audience was greatly enlarged by the success of the "Family of Man" exhibition and book in 1955).

During much of the period from 1956 to 1967, Cornell Capa had three concurrent jobs: his own photojournalism, his work as president of Magnum, and his efforts to fulfill the obligation he felt to his brother and his deceased colleagues. (The responsibility grew in 1956, when Chim was killed by an Egyptian machine-gunner four days after the Suez armistice.) With Bischof's widow and Chim's sister, he established a fund in memory of the three photographers and edited monographs of their work, but he gradually realized that it was counterproductive to separate them from all the other humanitarian photojournalists whose work would sooner or later be in the same predicament. In 1966 the original fund was expanded into the International Fund for Concerned Photography, which sponsored, among other exhibitions, two very successful shows of work by "concerned photographers," including Robert Capa, Bischof, and Chim. From 1967 on, while continuing his own photojournalism, Cornell Capa devoted more and more of his time to the fund and its activities; in 1974 he founded and became the director of the International Center of Photography, which occupies a small mansion at Fifth Avenue and Ninety-fourth Street in New York City and maintains a full schedule of exhibitions and educational programs, many of them devoted to photojournalism.

Nor is ICP Robert Capa's only memorial. In 1955 *Life* and the Overseas Press Club of America established the annual Robert Capa Award "for superlative photography requiring exceptional courage and enterprise abroad." Among the recipients have been Howard Sochurek, Larry Burrows, David Douglas Duncan, Horst Faas, Henri Huet, W. Eugene Smith, and Susan Meiselas.

Capa set a standard of bravery and compassion for all war photographers who have followed him, and he died, as his posthumous citation from the American Society of Magazine Photographers stated, working "in the tradition which he invented, for which there is no other word but his name."

A Note on Sources

Nearly all of Robert Capa's personal papers are collected in the files of his estate, of which Cornell Capa is the executor. Those files contain originals or photocopies of his letters to his family, as well as to Jemison McBride Hammond, John Morris, and Magnum. They also contain copies of Time Inc. and Magnum correspondence pertaining to Capa. In addition, the estate preserves all of Capa's original caption sheets, a complete set of his contact sheets, and many vintage prints bearing original captions. Along with Capa's published stories, those resources have been the most valuable in piecing together the chronology of his life.

The estate's papers are supplemented by transcripts of all the interviews conducted by Jozefa Stuart in the early 1960s for her never-completed biography of Capa. To those, the present author has added transcripts of all his interviews and copies of all relevant correspondence. Interviews and/or correspondence with the following are now in the estate files (the initials "JS" in parentheses after a name indicate that the interview was conducted by Jozefa Stuart):

Dr. Erwin H. Ackerknecht
Lucien Aigner
Ted Allan (JS & RW)
Eve Arnold
William Attwood
Dr. Eugene Bard
José Bartoli
Nathaniel Benchley (JS)
Ruth Cerf Berg
Ingrid Bergman
Gladys Berkowitz (JS & RW)
Eva Besnyö
Connie Bessey
Kenneth Bilby (JS)
Ilse Bing
Hug Block (JS & RW)
Inge Bondi
Simon Bourgin
Allen Brown
Luis Buñuel (JS)
Rossellina Bischof Burri (JS & RW)
Cornell Capa (JS & RW)

Henri Cartier-Bresson (JS & RW)
Dr. William Chardack
Flury Clavadetcher
Charles Collingwood (JS & RW)
Rosette Avigdor Coryell
Larry Craig
George Cserna
Taci Czigany (JS)
Leon Daniel (JS)
Myron Davis
Prof. Istvan Deak
Paul Deutschman
John Donovan (JS)
Bill Downs (JS)
Victor Elmaleh
Eva Escobedo (JS & RW)
Jay Eyerman
John Fernhout
Geraldine Fitzgerald
Monica Flaherty
Judith Freed
Gisèle Freund

Julia Friedmann (JS)
Franz Furst
Mary Stuart Gardner (JS)
Pierre Gassmann (JS & RW)
Gen. James M. Gavin
Martha Gellhorn
Tim Gidal
Françoise Gilot
Paul Goldman (JS)
Carl Goodwin
Fritz Goro
Ruthi Guler
Chaja Gusten
Theo Gusten (JS)
Simon Guttmann
Ernst Haas (JS & RW)
Gabriel Hackett
Jemison McBride Hammond (JS & RW)
Erich Hartmann
Lillian Hellman
John Hersey
Evelyn Hofer
Eric Holt
Kati Deutsch Horna (JS & RW)
John Huston
Henry B. Hyde
Seiichi Inouye
Christopher Isherwood
Joris Ivens (JS & RW)
Yale Joel
Col. Bert Kalish (JS)
Ata Kando
Nancy, Lady Keith
György Kepes (JS & RW)
Prof. Diethart Kerbs
André Kertész (JS & RW)
Dmitri Kessel
Khadeija (JS)
Alexander King (JS)
Herbert Kline
Bernard Knox
Arthur Koestler
Geza Korvin (JS & RW)
Stephen Laird (JS)
Millard Lampell (JS & RW)
Will Lang
Dr. Henry Lax

Harald Lechenperg
Maria Eisner Lehfeldt
Dr. Rosa Lenz
Alexander Liberman (JS & RW)
Jack Lieb (JS)
A. J. Liebling (JS)
Stefan Lorant
Elmer Lower (JS & RW)
Holland McCombs
Felix H. Man
Susie Fischer Marquis
Paul Martellière
Romeo Martinez (JS & RW)
Jerry Mason
Herbert Matthews (JS)
Bill Mauldin
Ernest Mayer
John Mecklin (JS)
Hansel Mieth
Helen Kirkpatrick Milbank
Blossom Miles
Jaume Miravitlles (JS)
Jessica Mitford
John Morris (JS & RW)
Ralph Morse
Carl Mydans
Hans Namuth
Dr. José Negrin (JS)
Tom Orchard
Ruth Orkin
Sono Osato
Colin Osman
Gabor Peterdi
Pete Petersen
John Phillips
Edouard Pignon
Dorothy Dennis Prebicevic
Marcel Rebière
Elizabeth Crockett Reeve
Edward K. Regan
Gustav Regler (JS)
Richard de Rochemont
George Rodger (JS & RW)
Chuck Romine (JS & RW)
Elaine Fisher Romine (JS)
Imre Rona (JS)
Prof. Ivan Sanders

David E. Scherman
Rosemarie Scherman
Alexander Schneider
June Herman Shaplen
Irwin Shaw
Diana Forbes-Robertson Sheean (JS & RW)
Eileen Shneiderman
S. L. Shneiderman (JS & RW)
Edith Laufer Sinaiberger
Howard Sochurek
Toni Sorel
Len Spooner
John Stais (JS)
Judith Thorne Stanton
Fred Stein (JS)
Hans Steinitz
Kurt Steinitz (JS & RW)
William H. Stoneman

Rozsi Strasser
Suzanne Szasz
Edward K. Thompson (JS & RW)
Alexander Trauner (JS)
M. C. Vaillant-Couturier
William & Rita Vandivert
Peter Viertel
William Walton (JS & RW)
Imre (Csiki) Weisz (JS & RW)
Lael Tucker Wertenbaker (JS & RW)
Theodore H. White
Laszlo Willinger
Jack Winocour (JS)
M. Wolf (JS)
Katherine Wolfe (JS)
Lothar Wolff
Milton Wolff

Robert Capa's Published Photo-Stories

In addition to the stories on which Capa and Gerda Taro collaborated, Taro's solo stories are also included in this listing.

Ce Soir was published in the late afternoon and carried the following day's date. It published many single photographs by Capa that are not listed here.

For post–World War II stories, only major English-language publications are listed.

The following abbreviations have been used:

BIZ	*Berliner Illustrirte Zeitung*
ILN	*Illustrated London News*
SEP	*Saturday Evening Post*
SIZ	*Schweizer Illustrierte Zeitung*
WI	*Weekly Illustrated* (London)
WS	*Der Welt Spiegel*
ZI	*Zürcher Illustrierte*

An asterisk following a page number indicates that not all photographs of the subject specified are by Capa.

1932

December 11 — WS, p. 3: Trotsky.

1933

March 12 — WS, p. 3: Berlin exhibition.

1934

November 7 — *Vu*, pp. 1411–14: Saarland. (Text & photos credited to Gorta, but most photos are by Capa.)

November 21 — *Vu*, pp. 1502–3: Saarland.

1935

June 5 — *Vu*, pp. 755–7: Spanish balloonist.

June 20 — BIZ, pp. 897 (cover)–8: Spanish balloonist; p. 937: Paolino Uzcudun, boxer.

1936

April 14 — WI, pp. 18–19: Holy Week in Seville. (Photos taken in 1935.)

April 25 — WI, p. 3*: French elections.

May 27 — *Vu*, p. 604: Herriot.

June 13 — WI, p. 13: Sit-in strikes.

July 8   Vu, p. 787: League of Nations.
July 15   Vu, cover & p. 826*: Bastille Day.
July 24   ZI, p. 943: Verdun peace rally.
August 29   Vu (special issue on the Spanish Civil War), pp. 22–3, 26*, 28*, 30*–
                1*, 34–5, 42, 43*, 46*, & 48: Barcelona & Aragón front. (Some photos
                are by Gerda Taro.)
September 3   BIZ, pp. 1396–7: Barcelona (Capa/Taro).
September 10   Regards, cover, pp. 11 & 21: Barcelona & Aragón front.
September 23   Vu, pp. 1106–7: Falling Soldier & Cerro Muriano refugees.
September 24   Regards, cover & pp. 6–7: Córdoba front.
October 14   Vu, cover & p. 1206: Strasbourg rally.
October 21   Vu, pp. 1242–3: Paris air-raid drill.
October 22   Regards, cover & pp. 8–9: Paris air-raid drill.
October 24   ILN, p. 717: Paris air-raid drill; pp. 726*, 727, 731*: Spain.
October 28   Vu, p. 1271: Radical-Socialist Party congress.
October 29   Regards, pp. 2–3: Radical-Socialist Party congress.
December 10   Regards, cover & pp. 11–14: Madrid.
December 17   Regards, cover & pp. 6–17: Madrid.
December 19   ILN, pp. 1141–3: Madrid.
December 24   Regards, cover & pp. 8–11: Madrid.
December 28   Life, pp. 58–9: Madrid.
December 31   Regards, pp. 12–13: Madrid.

1937
January 2   WI, pp. 4–5: Madrid.
January 9   WI, p. 8: International Brigades.
January 13   Vu, pp. 42–5: Madrid.
January 16   WI, p. 7: Madrid.
January 18   Life, p. 46*: Madrid.
January 20   SIZ, pp. 94*–5*: Spain.
January 21   Regards, cover & pp. 4–5: Madrid.
February 10   Vu, cover: Refugees.
March 3   Ce Soir, p. 10: Spain (Capa/Taro).
March 5   Ce Soir, p. 1: Laurel & Hardy fan club, Paris.
March 6   Ce Soir, p. 3: Salon des Artistes Indépendants.
March 8   Ce Soir, p. 8: Artists' gala.
March 9   Ce Soir, p. 10: Clinical Hospital, Madrid. (Like other Capa photos of
                Spain published in Ce Soir during March, taken January–February.)
March 10   Ce Soir, p. 8: Madrid.
March 11   Ce Soir, pp. 1 & 10*: Madrid.
March 12   Ce Soir, pp. 1 & 10: Madrid.
March 13   Ce Soir, p. 10: Málaga refugees (Capa/Taro).
March 17   Ce Soir, p. 1: Jarama front.
March 18   Ce Soir, p. 10: Agricultural show, Paris.
March 18   Regards, cover & pp. 6–7: Málaga refugees (Capa/Taro).
March 22   Ce Soir, pp. 1 & 3: Clichy funeral (Capa/Taro); p. 10: Military training,
                Valencia (Capa Taro).
March 22   Life, p. 34 (bottom): Parachutist.

March 26	*Ce Soir*, p. 8: French–Spanish border.
March 27	*Ce Soir*, p. 8: Andorra; p. 10: Refugee children, Perpignan.
March 29	*Ce Soir*, p. 1: Almadén (Capa/Taro, August–September 1936).
March 31	*Ce Soir*, p. 10: Madrid.
March 31	*SIZ*, p. 468: Madrid.
April 1	*Regards*, pp. 6–7: Madrid (not Guadalajara, despite accompanying text; photos Capa/Taro, February 1937).
April 8	*Ce Soir*, p. 12: Brussels election.
April 8	*Regards*, p. 5: Guadalajara (Taro).
April 12	*Ce Soir*, pp. 1 & 10: Brussels election.
April 15	*Regards*, cover & pp. 6–7: Military training, Spain (Taro).
April 26	*Ce Soir*, p. 10: Bois de Vincennes rally.
April 26	*Life*, pp. 68–9: Madrid (Capa/Taro, February 1937).
May 14	*Ce Soir*, p. 1: Mt. Solluve.
May 15	*Ce Soir*, p. 1: Mt. Solluve; p. 12: Bilbao gasoline dump fire.
May 17	*Ce Soir*, p. 1: Bilbao air raid.
May 20	*Regards*, p. 9: Basque front.
May 20	*Ce Soir*, p. 12: Valencia air-raid victims (Taro).
May 21	*Ce Soir*, p. 1: Bilbao air raid; p. 10: Asturian *dinamiteros*.
May 27	*Regards*, pp. 6–7: Bilbao.
May 29	*WI*, p. 11: Bilbao gasoline dump fire.
June 2	*SIZ*, pp. 754*–5: Bilbao.
June 10	*Regards*, cover & pp. 4–5: Valencia air-raid victims (Taro).
June 18	*Ce Soir*, p. 10: Carabanchel (Capa/Taro).
June 18	*ZI*, pp. 778–9: Bilbao.
June 20	*Ce Soir*, p. 10: General Lukacz's funeral.
June 23	*SIZ*, pp. 858*–9*: Bilbao.
June 24	*Regards*, cover & pp. 4–5: Bilbao.
July 9	*Ce Soir*, p. 10: Writers' Congress (Taro).
July 10	*Ce Soir*, p. 8: Writers' Congress (Taro).
July 12	*Life*, p. 19: Falling Soldier.
July 14	*Ce Soir*, p. 1: Writers' Congress (Taro); p. 10: La Granjuela (Capa/Taro).
July 14	*Regards*, pp. 11 & 23: Spain (Taro/Chim).
July 16	*Ce Soir*, p. 8: Brunete.
July 18	*Ce Soir*, p. 8: Spain (Capa/Taro).
July 22	*Regards*, pp. 12–13 & back cover: Brunete (Taro).
August 5	*Regards*, pp. 8–9: Homage to Gerda Taro.
August 10	*Ce Soir*, p. 8: Brunete (Taro).
August 16	*Life*, pp. 62–3: Gerda Taro.
September 30	*Ce Soir*, pp. 1 & 8: American Legion, New York.
December 30	*Ce Soir*, p. 8: Teruel.

1938

January 1	*Ce Soir*, p. 10: Teruel.
January 6	*Regards*, pp. 11–13 & back cover: Teruel.
January 8	*Ce Soir*, pp. 1, 5 (text by Capa), & 10: Teruel.
January 8	*WI*, pp. 2–3: Teruel.
January 12	*SIZ*, pp. 54–5: Teruel.

January 13   *Regards*, pp. 8–9: Teruel.
January 24   *Life*, pp. 9–13: Teruel.
March 24   *Regards*, cover & pp. 11–13: Belgian coal miners (Chim & Fried, i.e. Capa).
April 28   *Regards*, pp. 12–13: Miners at cockfight.
May 5   *Regards*, cover & pp. 4–7: China.
May 7   WI, p. 13: Hankow demonstrations.
May 9   *Life*, pp. 56–7: Propaganda play.
May 13   *Ce Soir*, p. 8: Taierhchwang.
May 14   WI, pp. 8–9: Propaganda play.
May 16   *Life*, cover & pp. 12, 13, 15: China.
May 23   *Life*, pp. 18–21: Taierhchwang.
May 23   *Ce Soir*, p. 8: Chinese transport.
May 25   *Ce Soir*, p. 8: Air battle over Hankow, April 29. (Caption erroneously says photos were taken May 2.)
June 9   *Regards*, p. 3: Taierhchwang.
June 11   WI, cover & pp. 2–7: China.
June 23   *Regards*, cover & pp. 12–13: China.
July 7   *Regards*, cover & pp. 4, 6–7, 9–10: China.
July 19   *Ce Soir*, p. 8: Chinese floods.
August 1   *Life*, p. 18: German advisers leave; p. 19: Chiang Kai-shek's war council.
August 4   *Regards*, pp. 12–13 & back cover: Chinese floods.
August 13   *Ce Soir*, p. 6: Hankow.
August 19   *Ce Soir*, pp. 1 & 6: Hankow (text & photos by Capa).
August 31   SIZ, pp. 1088–97: China.
September 1   *Regards*, pp. 12–14 & back cover: Hankow.
October 14   *Ce Soir*, p. 1: Canton front.
October 15   *Ce Soir*, p. 8: Canton front.
October 15   *Picture Post*, p. 53: Hankow.
October 17   *Life*, pp. 27*, 29–30 (color), 32*, 33*: Hankow.
October 26   *Ce Soir*, pp. 1 & 8: Hankow.
October 27   *Regards*, pp. 6–7 & back cover: International Brigades.
October 29   *Ce Soir*, p. 8: International Brigades (Capa/Chim).
November 3   *Regards*, pp. 11–13: Hankow.
November 5   *Picture Post*, pp. 26–8: Chiang Kai-shek & Mme. Chiang.
November 10   *Regards*, pp. 12–13: International Brigades.
November 12   *Picture Post*, pp. 34–7: International Brigades.
November 15   *Ce Soir*, p. 8: Segre River battle.
November 17   *Regards*, p. 9: International Brigades.
November 24   *Regards*, pp. 11–15 & back cover: Segre River battle.
December 3   *Picture Post*, pp. 13–24: Segre River battle.
December 8   *Regards*, pp. 12–13: Chinese children.
December 12   *Life*, pp. 28–9: Segre River battle.

1939
January 16   *Ce Soir*, pp. 1 & 8: Barcelona mobilization.
January 19   *Regards*, pp. 11–12: Catalonian front.

January 22	*Ce Soir*, p. 8: Tarragona refugees.
January 26	*Regards*, pp. 3–7: Barcelona.
January 29	*Ce Soir*, pp. 1 & 8: Barcelona refugees.
January 30	*Ce Soir*, pp. 1* & 8*: Refugees at French border.
January 31	*Ce Soir*, p. 8*: Refugees.
February 2	*Regards*, pp. 9–13: Barcelona air raids & refugees.
February 2	*Match*, pp. 9–14: Barcelona.
February 4	*Collier's*, pp. 12–13: Barcelona.
February 4	*Picture Post*, pp. 13–19: Tarragona refugees.
February 9	*Regards*, p. 9: Refugee children.
February 16	*Regards*, pp. 16–17: Roller derby to benefit refugees.
February 26	*Ce Soir*, p. 8: Roller derby to benefit refugees.
March 23	*Match*, pp. 37–43: Parachute school, Pujaut.
April 15	*Picture Post*, pp. 13–20: Spanish Loyalist soldiers in French internment camps.
April 20	*Regards*, pp. 8–11: Military air school, Provence.
May 5	*Ce Soir*, pp. 1 & 8: Orphanages for Spanish refugee children, Biarritz.
June 8	*Match*, pp. 27–33: Military air school.
June 22	*Match*, pp. 15–20: China (photos taken in 1938).
July 20	*Match:* Tour de France.
July 27	*Match*, pp. 26–9: Tour de France.
August 17	*Match*, p. 20: Duke & Duchess of Windsor at boxing match.
November 20	*Life*, p. 17: Seamen.
December 11	*Life*, pp. 41–2: Dorothy Maynor.
December 25	*Life*, pp. 56–8: Elk hunt.

1940

February 19	*Life*, pp. 17–21: Taft campaign.
March 25	*Life*, pp. 19–21: Boss Crump; p. 100: Hemingway in Madrid.
June 10	*Life*, pp. 51 & 56*–7*: Nazis & Communists in Mexico.
July 1	*Life*, pp. 19–23: Mexican presidential campaign.
July 22	*Life*, pp. 20–21: Election day violence, Mexico.
September 9	*Time*, p. 32: Trotsky's cremation (text only).
November 4	*Life*, p. 26: Roosevelt Club dinner; p. 30: Wendell Willkie speech.
December 2	*Life*, pp. 96*, 97–8, 99*, 100–1: Avila Camacho.

1941

January 6	*Life*, pp. 49–51: Hemingway & Gellhorn, Sun Valley; pp. 52–7: *For Whom the Bell Tolls*.
January 20	*Life*, pp. 74–7: Calumet City.
January 27	*Life*, p. 35: Jinx Falkenburg.
June 28	*Illustrated*, pp. 3–7: Atlantic convoy (text & photos).
July 19	*Illustrated*, cover & pp. 14–15: Lord Beaverbrook; pp. 8–10: Fourth of July party.
July 26	*Illustrated*, pp. 3–7: RAF bombing raid (text & photos).
August 9	*SEP*, pp. 20–21ff.: Atlantic convoy (text & photos, two in color).
August 11	*Life*, p. 63: American food for England.
August 23	*SEP*, pp. 9–11ff.: English factory workers.

August 30	*SEP*, pp. 34–5: RAF bombing raid (text & photos).
August 30	*Illustrated*, pp. 18–19: Sir Walter Citrine.
September 6	*Illustrated*, pp. 3–9: Battle of Waterloo Road.
September 13	*Illustrated*, pp. 16–19: ibid., pt. 2.
October 4	*Illustrated*, pp. 14–15: ibid., pt. 3.
October 11	*SEP*, pp. 34–5: Battle of Waterloo Road.
November 24	*Life*, pp. 116–19: Sun Valley.
December 6	*Illustrated*, pp. 17–19: Battle of Waterloo Road, pt. 4.

1942

March 23	*Life*, p. 45: Gertrude Lawrence, Stage Door Canteen.
June 13	*Illustrated*, pp. 3–7: Atlantic convoy.
July 18	*Illustrated*, pp. 10–13: Welsh miners.
August 1	*Collier's*, pp. 16–19: Atlantic convoy.
August 22	*Collier's*, pp. 18–19: RAF Eagle Squadron.
August 22	*Illustrated*, pp. 14–16: Parachute training.
September 26	*Illustrated*, pp. 7–9: U.S. Army in Northern Ireland.
October 10	*Collier's*, pp. 12–13: U.S. Army in Northern Ireland.
October 17	*Collier's*, pp. 22–3: U.S. Navy in Northern Ireland.
October 17	*Illustrated*, pp. 18–19ff.: U.S. Navy in Northern Ireland.
October 24	*Collier's*, pp. 20–21: Reconstructive surgery.
November 7	*Collier's*, pp. 22–4: Welsh miners.
November 14	*Collier's*, pp. 22–3: Parachute training.
December 5	*Illustrated*, pp. 9–13: Bombing raid on France (text & photos).

1943

February 6	*Collier's*, p. 22: "Short snorting."
February 27	*Collier's*, pp. 52 & 55: Grease monkeys for Flying Fortresses.
February 27	*Illustrated*, pp. 9–11: Bristol by-election.
March 27	*Collier's*, p. 54: GI & British war orphans.
April 3	*Collier's*, pp. 64–5: London pubs.
June 19	*Collier's*, pp. 12–14: El Guettar.
June 26	*Collier's*, pp. 18–19: Bristol by-election.
July 17	*Collier's*, pp. 14–15: Camel Corps (text & photos, all color).
July 24	*Illustrated*, pp. 14–16: Camel Corps.
July 31	*Illustrated*, pp. 5–9: Troopship to Africa.
August 7	*Illustrated*, pp. 14–16: Port of Casablanca.
August 14	*Illustrated*, pp. 20–22: Axis prisoners, N. Africa.
August 21	*Collier's*, p. 13: Destroyed German planes, El Aouina.
August 23	*Life*, pp. 25–31: Palermo.
August 30	*Life*, pp. 26–33: Troina & POWs.
September 18	*Collier's*, pp. 18–19: Sicily invasion.
October 9	*Illustrated*, pp. 5–11: U.S. Air Force, N. Africa.
October 18	*Life*, pp. 28*–9*: Naples; pp. 30–35: Chiunzi Pass.
November 1	*Life*, pp. 32*–3*: Naples Post Office explosion.
November 8	*Life*, pp. 28*–9*, 30–31: Naples.
November 22	*Life*, pp. 126–9: Benedetto Croce (text incorrectly says photos were taken by George Rodger).

1944
January 8   *Illustrated*, pp. 12–13: Benedetto Croce.
January 15   *Illustrated*, pp. 5–8: Sicily invasion.
January 31   *Life*, pp. 17–23: Liri Valley.
February 14   *Life*, pp. 28–31: Liri Valley.
February 21   *Life*, pp. 29–33: Anzio.
March 18   *Illustrated*, pp. 5–9, 25: Liri Valley (text & photos).
March 25   *Illustrated*, pp. 5–9: Liri Valley (text & photos).
April 1   *Illustrated*, cover & pp. 11–17: Anzio (text & photos).
April 29   *Illustrated*, pp. 5–10, 26: Moroccan troops in Italy.
May 13   *Illustrated*, pp. 5–11: Sicily campaign.
June 19   *Life*, pp. 25–31: D-Day.
June 26   *Life*, p. 37: Hemingway in London hospital.
July 3   *Life*, pp. 13*, 15*, 19*, 21*: Normandy.
July 10   *Life*, pp. 30*, 31*, 32*: Cherbourg.
August 14   *Life*, pp. 22–3: St.-Lô breakthrough.
September 4   *Life*, pp. 21*–2*: Chartres.
September 11   *Life*, pp. 28*–9*, 34–6: Liberation of Paris.
November 13   *Life*, p. 73: Picasso.
December 11   *Life*, p. 4: Spanish Loyalists.

1945
January 15   *Life*, pp. 15–19: Bastogne.
January 20   *Illustrated*, pp. 5–11: Bastogne.
April 2   *Time*, p. 28: Rhine jump (text only).
April 9   *Life*, pp. 27–37: Rhine jump.
April 14   *Illustrated*, pp. 5–10: Rhine jump.
May 14   *Life*, cover & pp. 40b–c: Nuremberg & Leipzig.
August 13   *Life*, pp. 37–40: Nazi baby farm.
September 10   *Life*, pp. 51, 52*, 54*: Berlin black market.
October 6   *Illustrated*, pp. 11–13: Rosh Hashanah in Berlin.
October 8   *Life*, pp. 49–50, 52*: Rosh Hashanah in Berlin.

1947
July 13   *This Week*, pp. 16–17: *Arch of Triumph*.
September 6   *Illustrated*, pp. 20–21: *Arch of Triumph*.
October 6   *Life*, pp. 31–5: Moscow's 800th anniversary.
October 23   New York *Herald Tribune*: USSR (text only).
December 20   *Illustrated*, pp. 5–8: Ukraine.

1948
January 14–31 New York *Herald Tribune*, usually p. 3 of daily edition; Section II, p. 1 of Sunday edition: USSR.
February   *Ladies' Home Journal*, pp. 44–59: USSR.
March 27   *Illustrated*, pp. 9–11: Turkey.
April 3   *Illustrated*, pp. 21–6: Paris fashion.
May–December   *Ladies' Home Journal*: "People Are People."
May 1   *Illustrated*, special issue: USSR (Capa/Steinbeck).
May 11   *Look*, pp. 86–90: Paris fashion.

May 30	*This Week*, cover & pp. 4–5: American model in Paris.
June 19	*Illustrated*, pp. 5–9: Israeli War for Independence.
June 20	*PM*, pp. 16–17: Col. Mike Marcus.
June 26	*Collier's*, pp. 14–15: Italian elections.
July 3	*Illustrated*, pp. 5–10: Jerusalem & "Burma Road."
July 12	*Life*, pp. 38–9: *Altalena* incident.
July 17	*Illustrated*, pp. 16–19: *Altalena* incident.
November 13	*Illustrated*, pp. 10–13: Picasso.
November 27	*Illustrated*, pp. 20–21: *Bitter Rice.*

1949

January 4	*Look*, pp. 42–7: Picasso.
March 19	*Illustrated*, pp. 11–13: Jacques Fath.
March 20	*This Week*, pp. 10–11: *Bitter Rice.*
March 26	*Illustrated*, pp. 28–31: Budapest.
June	*Holiday*, pp. 80–88: Poland.
July 23	*Illustrated*, pp. 31–3: Morocco.
August 20	*Illustrated*, pp. 26–9: Poland.
August 27	*Illustrated*, pp. 9–17: Israel (text & photos).
November	*Holiday*, pp. 64–70, 120: Hungary (text & photos).
November 8	*Look*, pp. 25–33: Israel (text & photos).

1950

January 17	*Look*, pp. 68–71: Matisse.
February 18	*Illustrated*, pp. 26–7: St. Anton.
March 4	*Illustrated*, pp. 39–40: Matisse.
April	*Holiday*, pp. 114–27: Jerusalem.
June 17	*Illustrated*: Jerusalem.
August	*Holiday*, pp. 38–41: Indianapolis.
August 12	*Illustrated*: Israel.
October 21	*Illustrated*, pp. 28–30: Oktoberfest (text & photos).

1951

January	*Holiday*, pp. 90–103: Skiing in the Alps (text & photos).
January 6	*Illustrated*: Skiing in the Alps.
January 13	*Illustrated*, pp. 20–22: Carnival in Zürs.
May 14	*Life*, pp. 116–26: Israel.
June 2	*Illustrated*: Israel.
July 14	*Collier's*, p. 17: Anthony Biddle.
October	*Holiday*, pp. 16–22: Oktoberfest in Munich (text & photos).
November	*Holiday*, pp. 52–5ff.: Dutch royal family (text & photos).

1952

April	*Holiday*, pp. 34–57: Rome (with architectural photographs by Ewing Krainin).
May 12	*Life*, pp. 32–5: Eisenhower (photos by Robert & Cornell Capa).
August 2	*Illustrated*, pp. 22–5: Dutch royal family.

| September | *Holiday*, pp. 90–97: Norway (text & photos). |
| October 7 | *Look*, pp. 57–63: *Moulin Rouge*. |

1953

January 10	*Picture Post*, pp. 3–27: "Generation X."
February	*Holiday*, pp. 57–9: French girl; pp. 61–3: German boy.
March	*Holiday*, pp. 46–7: Norwegian boy & girl.
March 7	*Illustrated*, pp. 18–21: *Moulin Rouge*.
March 24	*Look*, pp. 88–94: *Invitation to the Dance*.
April	*Holiday*, cover & pp. 58, 114–15, 144, & 147: Paris.
August 1	*Picture Post*, pp. 27–9, 46: *Beat the Devil* (text by Capa, photos by Ernst Haas).
August 8	*Picture Post*, cover & pp. 18–21: *Beat the Devil*, pt. 1 (photos by Capa).
August 15	*Picture Post*, pp. 26–9: ibid., pt. 2.
August 22	*Picture Post*, pp. 10–13: ibid., pt. 3.
September	*Holiday*, pp. 89–97ff.: Deauville & Biarritz (text & photos).
September 22	*Look*, pp. 128–33: *Beat the Devil*.

1954

April	*Holiday*, p. 61: Aga Khan.
May	*Holiday*, p. 57: Aga Khan.
May 31	*Life*, pp. 22–3: Luang Prabang.
June 7	*Life*, pp. 27–33: Red River delta.
June 7	*Time*, pp. 24–5: Red River delta.
July 23	*Collier's*, pp. 28–9: *The Barefoot Contessa*.

Books by Capa

Death in the Making. Photographs by Robert Capa and Gerda Taro [and Chim]. Captions by Robert Capa, translated by Jay Allen. Preface by Jay Allen. Arrangement [i.e., layout] by André Kertész. New York: Covici, Friede, 1938.

The Battle of Waterloo Road, by Diana Forbes-Robertson [text] and Robert Capa [photographs]. New York: Random House, 1941.

Slightly Out of Focus, by Robert Capa [text and photographs]. New York: Henry Holt, 1947.

A Russian Journal, by John Steinbeck, with pictures by Robert Capa. New York: Viking, 1948.

Report on Israel, by Irwin Shaw [text] and Robert Capa [photographs]. New York: Simon and Schuster, 1950.

Monographs and Catalogues
of One-Man Exhibitions

Images of War. Photographs by Robert Capa, with text from his own writings. New York: Grossman, 1964.

Robert Capa. Edited by Anna Farova. New York: Grossman, 1969.

Robert Capa. Edited by Cornell Capa and Bhupendra Karia. (ICP Library of Photographers.) New York: Grossman, 1974.

Robert Capa. Edited by Romeo Martinez. Milan: Mondadori, 1979.

Robert Capa. [Catalogue of an exhibition curated by Cornell Capa.] Tokyo: Pacific Press Service, 1980.

Robert Capa. [Catalogue of an exhibition curated by Cornell Capa, Hiroji Kubota, and Richard Whelan.] Tokyo: Pacific Press Service, 1984.

Bibliography

Works preceded by an asterisk reproduce photographs by Capa.

Air Historical Group, United States Air Force. *The Army Air Forces in World War II.* Prepared under the editorship of Wesley Frank Craven and James Lea Cate. Chicago: University of Chicago Press, 1948–58.

Allan, Ted. *This Time a Better Earth.* New York: Morrow, 1939.

Aragon, Louis. "Adieu Capa," in *Les Lettres Françaises*, May 27–June 3, 1954.

Arnold, Eve. *The Unretouched Woman.* New York: Alfred A. Knopf, 1976.

"At Chartres." *Time*, September 11, 1944.

Baker, Carlos. *Ernest Hemingway: A Life Story.* New York: Charles Scribner's Sons, 1969.

Barea, Arturo. *The Forging of a Rebel.* New York: Reynal & Hitchcock, 1946.

Barnouw, Erik. *Documentary: A History of the Non-Fiction Film.* New York: Oxford University Press, 1974.

* Barr, Alfred H., Jr. *Matisse: His Art and His Public.* New York: Museum of Modern Art, 1951.

* ———. *Picasso: Fifty Years of His Art.* New York: Museum of Modern Art, 1946.

Baumgartner, Lt. John W., et al. *The 16th Infantry, 1798–1946.* N.p., n.d.

* Beaton, Cecil, and Gail Buckland. *The Magic Image.* Boston: Little, Brown, 1975.

Belden, Jack. "The Fall of Troina." *Time*, August 23, 1943.

Benson, Jackson J. *The True Adventures of John Steinbeck, Writer.* New York: Viking, 1984.

Bergman, Ingrid, and Alan Burgess. *My Story.* New York: Delacorte, 1980.

Berkman, Ted. *Cast a Giant Shadow: The Story of Mickey Marcus.* New York: Doubleday, 1962.

Besnyö, Eva. *'N Halve Eeuw Werk.* Amsterdam: Feministische Uitgeverij Sara, 1982.

Bilby, Kenneth. *New Star in the East.* Garden City, New York: Doubleday, 1950.

Blumenson, Martin. *The Duel for France, 1944.* Boston: Houghton Mifflin, 1963.

———. *Salerno to Cassino.* (The U.S. Army in World War II. The Mediterranean Theater of Operations.) Washington, D.C.: Office of the Chief of Military History, 1969.

* ———, and the editors of Time-Life Books. *Liberation.* Alexandria, Virginia: Time-Life Books, 1978.

* "Bob Capa Inedito." *Fotografia Italiana*, June 1972.

Borkenau, Franz. *The Spanish Cockpit.* London: Faber and Faber, 1937.

* Botting, Douglas, and the editors of Time-Life Books. *The Second Front.* Alexandria, Virginia: Time-Life Books, 1978.

Bradley, Gen. Omar N., and Clay Blair. *A General's Life.* New York: Simon and Schuster, 1983.

Braham, Randolph L. *The Politics of Genocide: The Holocaust in Hungary.* New York: Columbia University Press, 1981.

Brinnin, John Malcolm. *Sextet.* New York: Delacorte, 1981.

Brook-Shepherd, Gordon. *Dollfuss.* London: Macmillan; New York: St. Martin's Press, 1961.

Burhans, Robert D. *The First Special Service Force.* Washington, D.C.: Infantry Journal Press, 1947.

————. *History and Heraldry of the 80th Division.* Richmond, Virginia: 80th Division Headquarters, 1960.

Burri, Rossellina Bischof, and René Burri, eds. *Werner Bischof, 1916–1954.* (ICP Library of Photographers.) New York: Grossman, 1974.

* Capa, Cornell, ed. *The Concerned Photographer.* New York: Grossman, 1968.

————, and Bhupendra Karia, eds. *David Seymour—"Chim."* (ICP Library of Photographers.) New York: Grossman, 1974.

* "Capa's Camera." *Time,* February 28, 1938.

Carlson, Evans Fordyce. *Twin Stars of China.* New York: Dodd, Mead, 1940.

* "Coal Mine Characters by Capa." *U.S. Camera,* June 1943.

Coke, Van Deren. *Avant-Garde Photography in Germany, 1919–1939.* San Francisco: Museum of Modern Art, 1980.

Cole, Hugh M. *The Ardennes: Battle of the Bulge.* (The U.S. Army in World War II. The Mediterranean Theater of Operations.) Washington, D.C.: Office of the Chief of Military History, 1965.

Colodny, Robert. *The Struggle for Madrid.* New York: Paine-Whitman, 1958.

Cox, Geoffrey. *Defence of Madrid.* London: Victor Gollancz, 1937.

* Davis, Franklin M., Jr., and the editors of Time-Life Books. *Across the Rhine.* Alexandria, Virginia: Time-Life Books, 1980.

Deak, Istvan. *Weimar Germany's Left-Wing Intellectuals.* Berkeley: University of California Press, 1968.

* "Death Stops the Shutter." *Time,* June 7, 1954.

D'Este, Carlo. *Decision in Normandy.* New York: E. P. Dutton, 1983.

Deutscher, Isaac. *The Prophet Outcast, Trotsky: 1929–1940.* London and New York: Oxford University Press, 1963.

Devillers, Philippe, and Jean Lacouture. *End of a War: Indochina, 1954.* New York: Praeger, 1969.

Dos Passos, John. *1919.* New York: Harcourt, Brace, 1932.

* "Eloquent Album." *Time*, September 22, 1947.

Elson, Robert T. *Time Inc.: The Intimate History of a Publishing Enterprise, 1923–1941.* New York: Atheneum, 1968.

———. *The World of Time Inc.: The Intimate History of a Publishing Enterprise, 1941–1960.* New York: Atheneum, 1973.

Eyck, Erich. *A History of the Weimar Republic.* Vol. 2: *From the Locarno Conference to Hitler's Seizure of Power.* Cambridge, Massachusetts: Harvard University Press, 1963.

Fielding, Raymond. *The March of Time, 1935–1951.* New York: Oxford University Press, 1978.

* Fondiller, Harvey V. "Magnum: Image and Reality." *35-mm Photography*, Winter 1976.

Fraser, Ronald. *Blood of Spain: An Oral History of the Spanish Civil War.* New York: Pantheon, 1979.

Freund, Gisèle. *Photography and Society.* Boston: David R. Godine, 1980.

———. *The World in My Camera.* New York: Dial, 1974.

* *Front Populaire.* Photos by Robert Capa and David Seymour ("Chim"). Text by Georgette Elgey. Paris: Chêne-Magnum, 1976.

Gavin, Gen. James M. Letter to the editor. *"47": The Magazine of the Year*, October 1947.

———. *On to Berlin.* New York: Viking, 1978.

Gay, Peter. *Weimar Culture: The Outsider as Insider.* New York: Harper & Row, 1968.

Gellhorn, Martha. *Two By Two.* ("Till Death Us Do Part.") New York: Simon and Schuster, 1958.

George Rodger. Introduction by Inge Bondi. London: Gordon Fraser, 1975.

Gidal, Tim N. *Modern Photojournalism: Origin and Evolution, 1910–1933.* New York: Macmillan, 1973.

* Goldsmith, Arthur. "Moment of Truth." *Camera Arts*, March/April 1981.

* Goolrick, William K., Ogden Tanner, and the editors of Time-Life Books. *The Battle of the Bulge.* Alexandria, Virginia: Time-Life Books, 1979.

Graffis, Bill. Letter to the editor. *"47": The Magazine of the Year*, October 1947.

* *Les Grandes Photos de la Guerre d'Espagne.* Photographs by Robert Capa and David Seymour ("Chim"). Text by Georges Soria. Paris: Jannink, 1980.

György Kepes: The MIT Years, 1945–1977 [exhibition catalogue with biographical essay]. Cambridge, Massachusetts: MIT Press, 1978.

Hall, James Baker. "The Last Happy Band of Brothers." *Esquire*, April 1974.

Hammond, John, with Irving Townsend. *On Record.* New York: Ridge Press/Summit, 1977.

Haulisch, Lenke. "Kassák és a foto." *Fotoművészet* (Budapest), no. 3, 1967.

Hegedus, Adam de. *Hungarian Background.* London: Hamish Hamilton, 1937.

Hemingway, Ernest. *For Whom the Bell Tolls.* New York: Charles Scribner's Sons, 1940.

———. *Selected Letters, 1917–1961*. Edited by Carlos Baker. New York: Charles Scribner's Sons, 1981.

Hemingway, Mary Welsh. *How It Was*. New York: Alfred A. Knopf, 1976.

* Hersey, John. "The Man Who Invented Himself." *"47": The Magazine of the Year*, September 1947.

Herzog, Chaim. *The Arab-Israeli Wars*. New York: Arms & Armour Press, 1982.

Hill, Paul, and Thomas Cooper. *Dialogue with Photography*. New York: Farrar, Straus & Giroux, 1979.

Hofmann, George F. *The Super Sixth*. Louisville, Kentucky: 6th Armored Division, 1975.

Hood, Robert E. *Twelve at War*. New York: G. P. Putnam's Sons, 1967.

Howard, Noel. *Hollywood sur Nil*. Paris: Fayard, 1978.

Howe, George F. *Northwest Africa: Seizing the Initiative in the West*. (The U.S. Army in World War II. The Mediterranean Theater of Operations.) Washington, D.C.: Office of the Chief of Military History, 1957.

Huston, John. *An Open Book*. New York: Alfred A. Knopf, 1980.

Ignotus, Paul. *Hungary*. London: Benn, 1972.

Isherwood, Christopher. *Christopher and His Kind, 1929–1939*. New York: Farrar, Straus & Giroux, 1976.

———. *Journey to a War*. With poems and photographs by W. H. Auden. London: Faber and Faber; New York: Random House, 1939; New York: Octagon, 1972.

* *Israel/The Reality*. Edited by Cornell Capa. New York and Cleveland: World Publishing, 1969.

Ivens, Joris. *The Camera and I*. New York: International, 1969.

Jäckh, Ernst, ed. *Politik als Wissenschaft: Zehn Jahre Deutsche Hochschule für Politik*. Berlin: Hermann Reckendorf, 1931.

Jackson, Gabriel. *A Concise History of the Spanish Civil War*. London: Thames & Hudson, 1974.

Janos, Andrew C. *The Politics of Backwardness in Hungary, 1825–1945*. Princeton, New Jersey: Princeton University Press, 1982.

Kantorowicz, Alfred. *Politik und Literatur im Exil*. Hamburg: Christians, 1978.

———. *Spanisches Tagebuch*. Berlin: Aufbau-Verlag, 1949.

———. *Tschapaiew, das Bataillon der 21 Nationen*. Madrid: Torrent, 1938.

Keegan, John. *Six Armies in Normandy: From D-Day to the Liberation of Paris*. London: Jonathan Cape; New York: Viking, 1982.

Kellner, Douglas. *Karl Korsch: Revolutionary Theory*. Austin: University of Texas Press, 1977.

Kerbs, Diethart, Walter Uka, and Brigitte Walz-Richter, eds. *Die Gleichschaltung der Bilder: Zur Geschichte der Pressefotografie, 1930–1936*. Berlin: Frölich & Kaufmann, 1983.

Knightley, Phillip. *The First Casualty*. New York: Harcourt, Brace, 1975.

3 2 5

Knox, Bernard. "Remembering Madrid." *The New York Review of Books*, November 6, 1980.

Koestler, Arthur. *Arrow in the Blue*. London: Collins, 1952.

———. *The Invisible Writing*. New York: Macmillan, 1954.

Kovrig, Bennett. *Communism in Hungary from Kun to Kadar*. Stanford, California: Hoover Press, 1979.

Koyen, Kenneth A. *The 4th Armored Division; From the Beach to Bavaria*. Munich: 4th Armored Division, 1946.

Lang, Will. "Doughboys' Beachhead." *Time*, February 7, 1944.

———. "The Story of Fort Schuster." *Life*, October 25, 1943.

Laqueur, Walter. *Weimar: A Cultural History, 1918–1933*. New York: G. P. Putnam's Sons, 1974.

Larmour, Peter J. *The French Radical Party in the 1930s*. Stanford, California: Stanford University Press, 1964.

Lechenperg, Harald. "Hochzeit beim Maharadscha." *Die Dame*, August 1932 (Sonderheft).

* Lewinski, Jorge. *The Camera at War: A History of War Photography from 1848 to the Present Day*. New York: Simon and Schuster, 1978.

Liddell Hart, B. H. *History of the Second World War*. New York: G. P. Putnam's Sons, 1970.

Liebling, A. J. *The Road Back to Paris*. Garden City, New York: Doubleday, 1944.

LIFE: The First Decade, 1936–1945. Boston: New York Graphic Society, 1979.

Lottman, Herbert R. *The Left Bank: Writers, Artists, and Politics from the Popular Front to the Cold War*. Boston: Houghton Mifflin, 1982.

Lucas, Jim. "Bob Capa Planned to Leave Indo-China by Sea." Washington *Daily News*, May 27, 1954.

Mallinson, Vernon. *Belgium*. London: Benn, 1970.

Man, Felix H. *Man with Camera: Photographs from Seven Decades*. New York: Schocken, 1984.

Markos, György. "My Friend Capa." *The New Hungarian Quarterly*, Winter 1976.

Matthews, Herbert L. *The Education of a Correspondent*. New York: Harcourt, Brace, 1946.

———. *Two Wars and More to Come*. New York: Carrick & Evans, 1938.

[Mecklin, John.] "Forward Lies the Delta." *Time*, June 7, 1954.

* ———. "He Said: 'This Is Going to Be a Beautiful Story.'" *Life*, June 7, 1954.

Miravitlles, Jaume. *Notes dels meus arxius: Episodis de la Guerra Civil Espanyola*. Barcelona: Collecio Portic, 1972.

Mora, Constancia de la. *In Place of Splendor*. New York: Harcourt, Brace, 1939.

* Morris, John. "Magnum Photos: An International Cooperative." *U.S. Camera Annual*, 1954.

* ———. "This We Remember." *Harper's*, September 1972.

Newhall, Beaumont. *The History of Photography from 1839 to the Present.* New York: Museum of Modern Art, 1982.

Orwell, George. *Down and Out in Paris and London.* New York and London: Harper & Bros., 1933.

———. *Homage to Catalonia.* London: Secker & Warburg, 1938.

* *Paris/Magnum; Photographs, 1935–1981.* Introduction by Inge Morath. Text by Irwin Shaw. Millerton, New York: Aperture, 1981.

Parks, Gordon. *A Choice of Weapons.* New York: Harper & Row, 1966.

Payne, Robert. *The Life and Death of Trotsky.* New York: McGraw-Hill, 1977.

* Penrose, Roland. *Portrait of Picasso.* New York: Museum of Modern Art, 1971.

Petofi Irodalmi Múzeum. *Kortársak Kassák Lajosrol.* Budapest, n.d.

* *Photography: Venezia '79.* Milan: Electra, 1979.

* *Photojournalism.* (The LIFE Library of Photography.) New York: Time-Life Books, 1971.

* Pollack, Peter. *The Picture History of Photography.* New York: Abrams, 1969.

Pyle, Ernie. *Brave Men.* New York: Henry Holt, 1944.

———. *Here Is Your War.* New York: Henry Holt, 1943.

Quirk, Lawrence J. *The Films of Ingrid Bergman.* New York: Citadel, 1970.

Regler, Gustav. *The Owl of Minerva.* London: R. Hart-Davis, 1959.

Renaud, Alexandre. *Utah Beach à Cherbourg.* Coutances: Editions Notre-Dame, 1968.

Renn, Ludwig. *Der Spanische Krieg.* Berlin: Aufbau-Verlag, 1955.

Reynolds, Quentin. *By Quentin Reynolds.* London and New York: McGraw-Hill, 1963.

Richter, Hans. *Dada Profile.* Zurich: Verlag Die Arche, 1961.

Rim, Carlo. "Le Grandeur et le Servitude du Reporter-Photographe." *Marianne*, February 21, 1934.

———. *Le Grenier d'Arlequin: Journal, 1916–1940.* Paris: Denoël, 1981.

* Riss, Françoise. "Robert Capa: Les Photos Retrouvées du Tour 1939." *Photo Revue* (Paris), September 1982.

* "Robert Capa." *Camera* (Lucerne), March 1961.

* "Robert Capa: 124 Photos Retrouvées." *Photo* (Paris), June 1983.

* "Robert Capa Tells You His Favorite Tricks for Shooting Striking Snow Scenes." *Holiday*, January 1952.

* [Robert Capa's photographs of the Sicilian and Italian campaigns of World War II.] *L'Europeo*, December 10, 17, & 24, 1961.

Rolfe, Edwin. *The Lincoln Battalion.* New York: Random House, 1939.

Romilly, Esmond. *Boadilla.* London: Macdonald, 1971.

Roy, Claude. *Moi Je.* Paris: Gallimard, 1969.

"Russian Journal." *Time*, January 26, 1947.

Saroyan, William. Letters to the editor. *"47": The Magazine of the Year*, October 1947.

* Scherman, David E., ed. *LIFE Goes to War: A Picture History of World War II*. Boston: Little, Brown, 1977.

Shaw, Irwin. Letter to the editor. *"47": The Magazine of the Year*, October 1947.

———. "Retreat in Indo-China." *Picture Post*, June 12, 1954.

———. *The Young Lions*. New York: Random House, 1948.

——— and Ronald Searle. *Paris! Paris!* New York: Harcourt Brace Jovanovich, 1977.

Sheean, Vincent. Letter to the editor. *"47": The Magazine of the Year*, October 1947.

———. *Not Peace But a Sword*. New York: Doubleday, Doran, 1939.

Shirer, William L. *The Collapse of the Third Republic*. New York: Simon and Schuster, 1969.

Sloan, Pat, ed. *John Cornford: A Memoir*. London: Jonathan Cape, 1938.

Smedley, Agnes. *Battle Hymn of China*. New York: Alfred A. Knopf, 1943.

Snow, Edgar. *Red Star Over China*. New York: Random House, 1938.

Sommerfield, John. *Volunteer in Spain*. London: Lawrence & Wishart, 1937.

Steele, Joseph H. *Ingrid Bergman: An Intimate Portrait*. New York: McKay, 1959.

* Steichen, Edward, ed. *The Family of Man*. New York: Museum of Modern Art, 1955.

Stein, Louis. *Beyond Death and Exile: The Spanish Republicans in France, 1939–1955*. Cambridge, Massachusetts: Harvard University Press, 1979.

Steinbeck, John. *Once There Was a War*. New York: Viking, 1958.

* ———. "Robert Capa: A Memorial Portfolio." *Popular Photography*, September 1954.

* Stone, I. F. *This Is Israel*. Photographs by Robert Capa, Jerry Cooke, and Tim Gidal. New York: Boni and Gaer, 1948.

Štraus, Tomáš. *Kassák: Ein Ungarischer Beitrag zum Konstruktivismus*. Cologne: Galerie Gmurzynska, 1975.

* Szarkowski, John. *Looking at Photographs*. New York: Museum of Modern Art, 1973.

Taggart, Donald G., ed. *History of the 3rd Infantry Division in World War II*. Washington, D.C.: Infantry Journal Press, 1947.

Thomas, Hugh. *The Spanish Civil War*. New York: Harper & Row, 1977.

Tregaskis, Richard. *Invasion Journal*. New York: Random House, 1944.

Tuchman, Barbara W. *Stilwell and the American Experience in China, 1911–45*. New York: Macmillan, 1971.

"23 Kids and Us." *Holiday*, January 1953.

Ullstein, Hermann. *The Rise and Fall of the House of Ullstein*. New York: Simon and Schuster, 1943.

U.S. Army. 1st Armored Division. *The Story of the 1st Armored Division*. N.p., 1945(?).

U.S. Army. 1st Infantry Division. *Danger Forward: The Story of the First Division in World War II*. Washington, D.C.: Society of the 1st Division, 1947.

U.S. Army. 2nd Armored Division. A *History of the 2nd U.S. Armored Division, 1940–1946*. Atlanta: Albert Love, 1946.

U.S. Army. Third Army. *After-action Report, 1 August 1944–9 May 1945*. N.p., 1945.

U.S. Army. Fifth Army. *Fifth Army History*. Florence, Italy: L'Impronta Press, 1945–47.

U.S. Army. 34th Infantry Division. *The Story of the 34th Division*. N.p., 1945.

U.S. Army. 45th Infantry Division. *The Fighting 45th*. Baton Rouge, Louisiana, 1946.

U.S. Army. 47th Infantry Regiment. *History of the 47th Infantry Regiment*. N.p., 1946.

U.S. Army. 82nd Airborne Division. *Report on Operations, 1943–45*. N.p., 1945.

U.S. Army. 83rd Infantry Division. *Thunderbolt Across Europe*. Munich, 1946.

Utley, Freda. *The China Story*. Chicago: Henry Regnery, 1951.

———. *China at War*. London: Faber and Faber, 1939.

* Wallace, Robert, and the editors of Time-Life Books. *The Italian Campaign*. Alexandria, Virginia: Time-Life Books, 1978.

Walter Bosshard: Ein Schweizer Pioneer des Photojournalismus. Photographien, 1927–1939. Zurich: Stiftung für Photographie im Kunsthaus, 1977.

Wertenbaker, Charles C. *The Death of Kings*. New York: Random House, 1954.

* ———. *Invasion!* Photographs by Robert Capa. New York: Appleton, Century, 1944.

———. "Paris Is Free!" *Time*, September 4, 1944.

Werth, Alexander. *Which Way France?* New York: Harper & Bros., 1937.

Willett, John. *The New Sobriety: Art and Politics in the Weimar Period, 1917–1933*. London: Thames & Hudson, 1978.

Wyden, Peter. *The Passionate War: The Narrative History of the Spanish Civil War, 1936–1939*. New York: Simon and Schuster, 1983.

Index

257, 284–8 *passim* (see also *Ce Soir*, Capa; *Regards*, Capa); in France, 55, 58, 61, 71, 72, 84; Kassák's influence, 15, 16–17, 18, 26, 59, 62; Korsch's influence, 26, 27; Spain and civil war, 132–3, 156, 157

skiing, fondness for, 12–13, 233, 249, 278, 281, 283, 287, 291, 314

and the U.S.: alien residency and "marriage," 165, 167, 171, 174; citizenship, 245 *n.*, 245–6; emigration, 161, 165; as enemy alien, 180; enjoys being taken for American, 82, 83; passport renewal problems, 284–8 *passim*; temporary papers, passport, and accreditation in World War II, 181–5 *passim*

women, interest in, 19, 37, 38, 58, 66, 74, 78, 127, 129, 148, 163–4, 177, 184, 225, 228, 230, 233, 238, 263, 268, 270, 276, 281; Bergman, Ingrid, 239–50 *passim*, 270; Hammond, Jemy, 269–70, 276, 280, 281, 288, 290, 301; Sorel, Toni, and "marriage," 165–7, 232; *see also* Pinky; Taro, Gerda

Capa, Robert—as photographer and writer, 307–15, 317

cameras used by: Contax, 180, 213, 214, 231, 297, 299; Eyemo, 116, 147; Leica, 39, 41, 42, 53, 63, 71, 91; Nikon, 297, 299–300; Rolleiflex, 180, 214 *n.*, 231; Speed Graphic, 180; Voigtländer, 30

career decision and early ambivalence, 30, 77; Dephot/Degephot, first photo work, 31–5, 37–42

cooperative agency, idea for, 142, 176, 178, 179, 180, 201, 250; *see also* Magnum *below*

darkroom, work in, 31, 32, 34, 45, 46, 62, 63, 64, 73

and film industry, 24, 25, 26, 30, 33, 77–82 *passim*, 157, 179–80, 238, 242–7 *passim*; bit role, 246–7; part perhaps loosely modeled on, 146–7; possible part in *For Whom the Bell*

Tolls, 172, 179–80; publicity stills for, 276, 287, 291, 292, 314, 315

film industry—documentaries, news, and television, 238, 290; on Israeli immigrants, 267–9; on Paris fashion, 258–9; Sino-Japanese War, 129, 133, 135, 136, 139, 140, 141, 143, 144; Spanish Civil War, 116, 117, 120; on Turkey, 247–9, 258, 285; World Video, 258–9, 285, 290

influence of, and help given by, 142, 163, 173, 176, 209, 274

influence on, and help given to, 15, 16, 31, 62, 77, 128, 163; *see also* Guttmann, Simon; Kepes, György

London (as base), 173–8, 181–6, 193, 206–10, 217–18, 236–7, 289–92 *passim*

Magnum, 55, 142, 251–4, 270–6 *passim*, 281–92 *passim*; *see also* Magnum

methods of working, 175–6, 261, 292

monographs and catalogues of work, 301, 319

in New York (as base), 161–7 *passim*, 172, 173, 174, 178, 180, 242, 244–5, 247, 250–3, 256–7, 269–70, 274, 278, 281, 286

in Paris (as base): Capa name and persona invented, 80–1; 1930s, 41, 47–92 *passim*, 100, 101, 108–9, 120, 124–7, 129, 133, 146, 151, 157–61, 307, 308, 309; own studio, 110–11, 141–2; World War II, 225–35; after World War II, 238–42, 265, 267, 269, 270–1, 274, 278, 280–1, 284, 288–9, 291

technical aspects of work, 128, 163, 176

writing, interest in, 16–17, 74, 278, 293, 317; and films, 179, 180, 238, 243; see also *Slightly Out of Focus*

see also *individual agencies and publications*

Capa, Robert—as war photographer and writer, 195, 143, 151, 156–7, 187, 195, 197, 200, 203, 209, 210, 211,

A Note on the Type

The text of this book was set in a digitized version of Electra, a Linotype face designed by W. A. Dwiggins (1880–1956). This face cannot be classified as either modern or old style. It is not based on any historical model; nor does it echo any particular period or style. It avoids the extreme contrasts between thick and thin elements that mark most modern faces and attempts to give a feeling of fluidity, power, and speed.

Composed by Maryland Linotype Composition Company, Baltimore, Maryland.

Printed and bound by Murray Printing Company, Westford, Massachusetts.

Designed by Iris Weinstein.